Shojo Beat

The Magic Touch

Oyayubi kara Romance

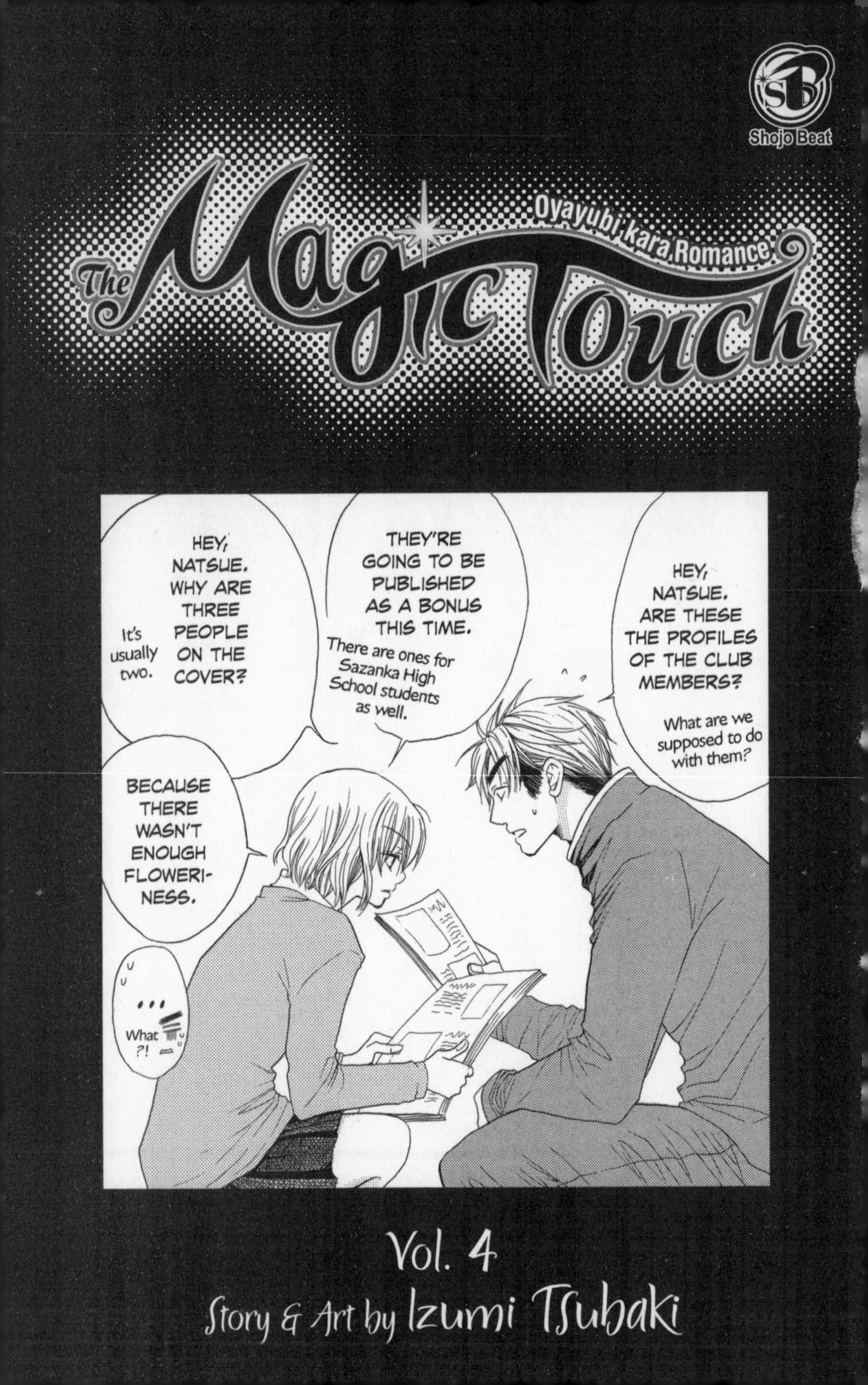
HEY, NATSUE. ARE THESE THE PROFILES OF THE CLUB MEMBERS?
What are we supposed to do with them?
THEY'RE GOING TO BE PUBLISHED AS A BONUS THIS TIME.
There are ones for Sazanka High School students as well.
HEY, NATSUE. WHY ARE THREE PEOPLE ON THE COVER?
It's usually two.
BECAUSE THERE WASN'T ENOUGH FLOWERI-NESS.
...
What?!

Vol. 4

Story & Art by Izumi Tsubaki

The Magic Touch
Oyayubi kara Romance

Story and Characters Introduction

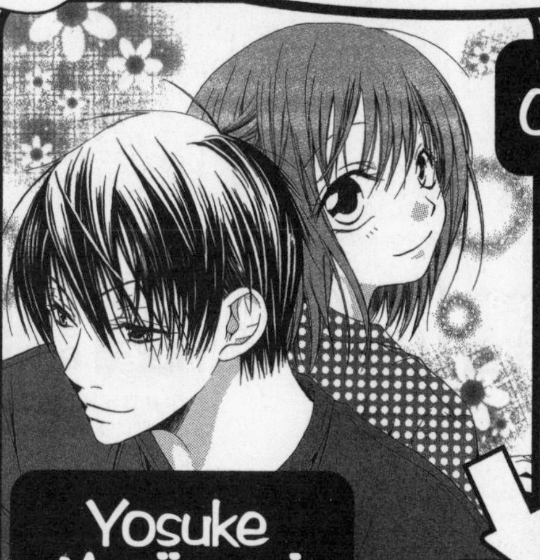

Chiaki Togu

The main character of this story. She's a first-year student in Futouka Academy's Massage Research Club and a rising star in the club.☆ She has an incredible passion and a great talent for massage! But she's normally quiet.

Yosuke Moriizumi

He has Chiaki's ideal back: He's the guy with the stiffest body at Futouka Academy. He's a popular boy with lots of experience with girls. But has Chiaki captured his heart?!

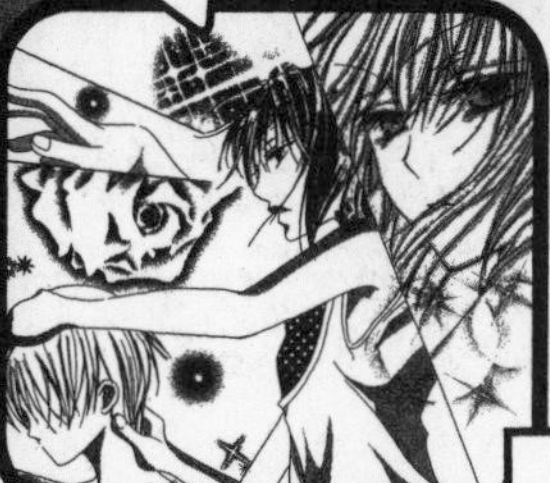

She suddenly changes when she becomes absorbed in massage!

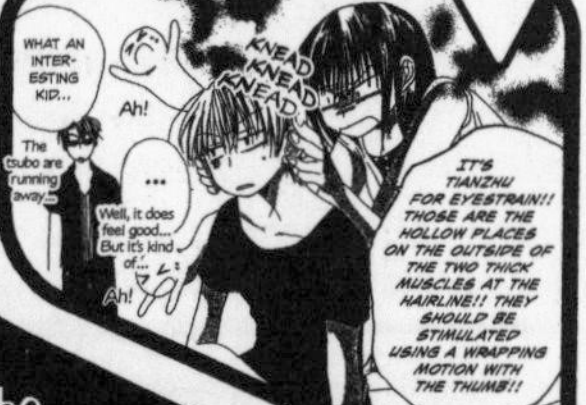
IT'S TIANZHU FOR EYESTRAIN!! THOSE ARE THE HOLLOW PLACES ON THE OUTSIDE OF THE TWO THICK MUSCLES AT THE HAIRLINE!! THEY SHOULD BE STIMULATED USING A WRAPPING MOTION WITH THE THUMB!!
KNEAD KNEAD KNEAD
...
Well, it does feel good... But it's kind of...
Ah!
Ah!
WHAT AN INTERESTING KID...
The tsubo are running away...

And further-more...

Tsuboz

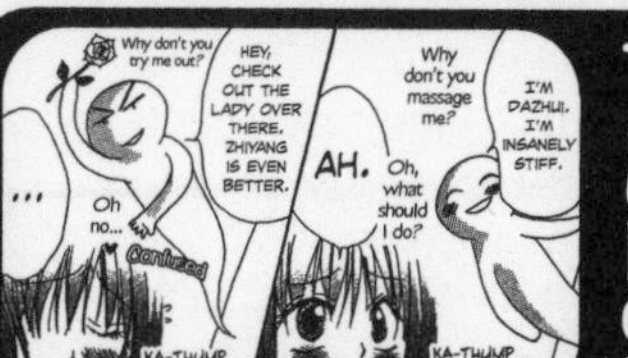
I'M DAZHUI. I'M INSANELY STIFF.
Why don't you massage me?
AH.
Oh, what should I do?
KA-THUMP KA-THUMP
HEY, CHECK OUT THE LADY OVER THERE. ZHIYANG IS EVEN BETTER.
Why don't you try me out?
...
Oh no...
Confused
KA-THUMP KA-THUMP

Creatures (?!) that can be seen (maybe) by people who love massage the most. They come out from the tsubo and complain that "it's stiff here."♥ For now, the only ones who can see them are Chiaki, Takeshi and Takeshi's mentor, Ohnuki.

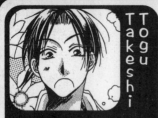

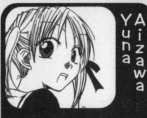

★ Futouka Academy Massage Research Club ★

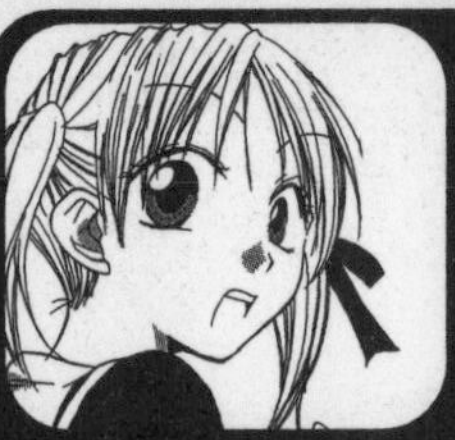

Aizawa Yuna

Chiaki's friend. She is very competent at massage. She has feelings for Togu Senpai!

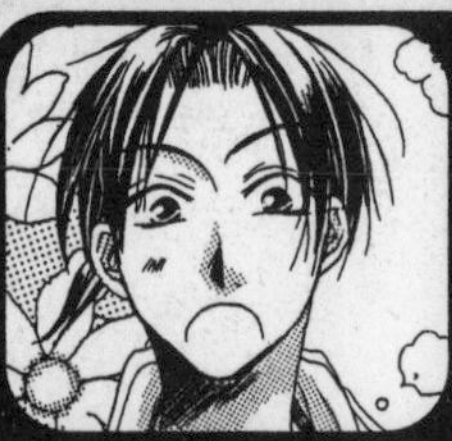

Togu Takeshi

Chiaki's brother, who's a year older. He's living with his mentor right now as an apprentice. He's a master at gal games.

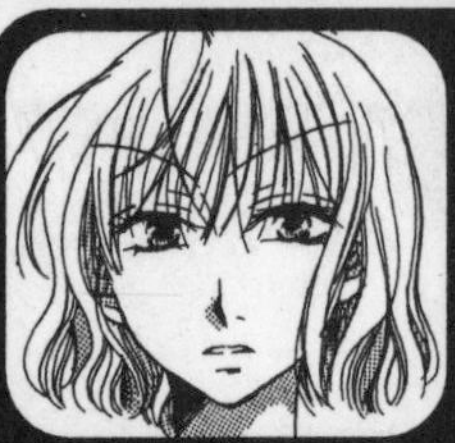

Abe Natsue

She's the treasurer for the Massage Research Club. She has a nice body, but she's ruthless when money is involved.

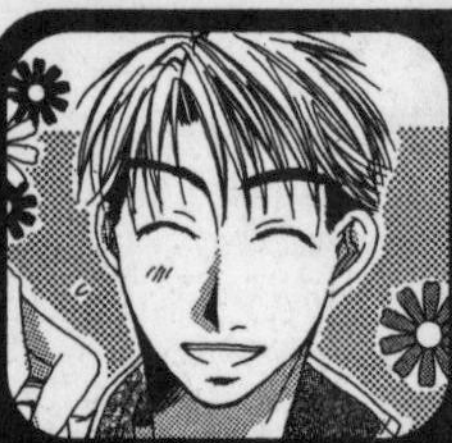

Harumi Chitose

He's the manager of the Massage Research Club. He's normally carefree. His family seems to be rich.

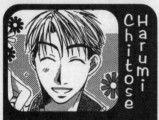

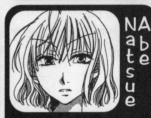

♥ The Story So Far ♥

★ Chiaki Togu is a first-year student in the Massage Research Club. One day, on her way to school, she encounters a truly "ideal" back.♥ She falls in love with it at first sight...

★ When searching for the stiffest back at her school, the person Chiaki finds is Yosuke Moriizumi, the most popular boy at school. In response to Chiaki's pleas to "let me massage your back," he sets one condition: Chiaki must make him fall in love with her!

★ Despite many events and misunderstandings, the two start going out. They make progress, but things are sometimes awkward between Yosuke, a player who has broken many hearts, and Chiaki, who is extremely shy when she's not involved in massage.

★ Chiaki and the team become friendly with Mihime, Keita and Ryo from the Sazanka High School Massage Club at the "Underground Massage Tournament." The Sazanka students start dropping by the Massage Research Club to help out...

CONTENTS

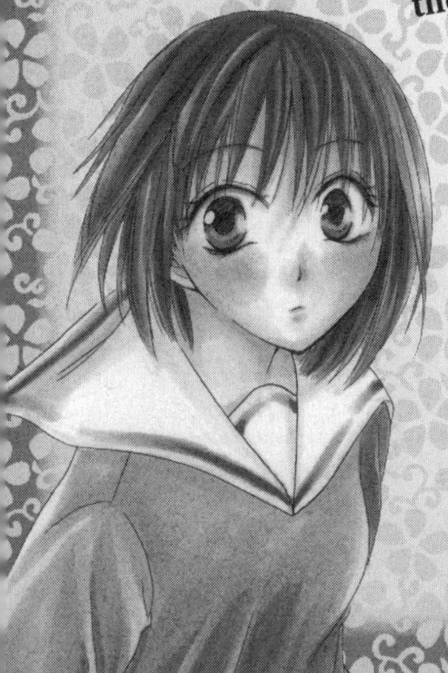

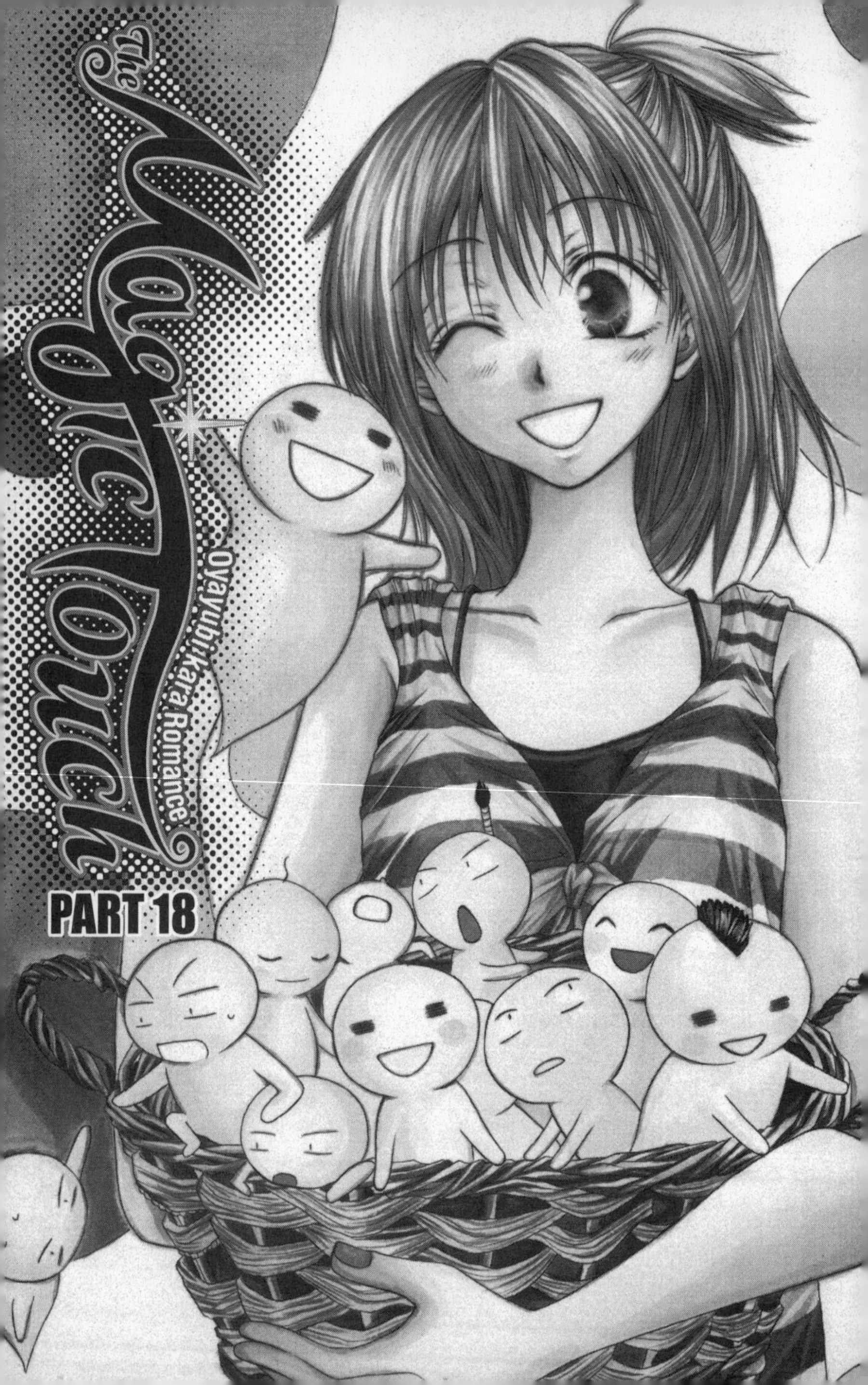
The Magic Touch
Oyayubi kara Romance
PART 18

Takeshi Togu

Birthday: May 5

Blood Type: B

Height: 176 cm (5' 9")

Hobby: Playing Games

Special Talents: Staring Contests, Cat's Cradle

What He Likes: Weird T-Shirts

What He Hates: Shiitake Mushrooms

Siblings: Two Sisters

Club Activity in Middle School: Baseball Team

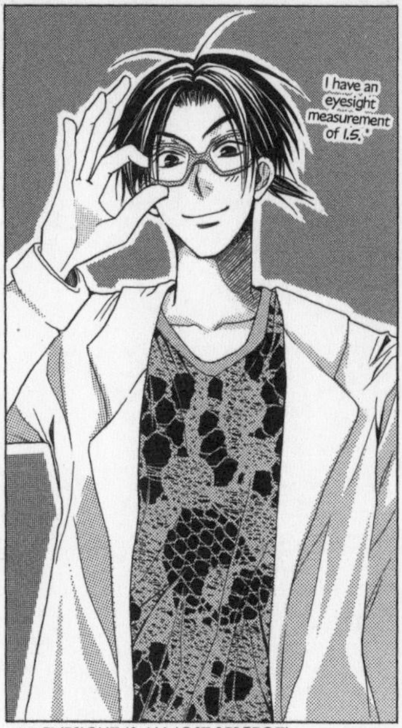
I have an eyesight measurement of 1.5.*

* 1.5 EYESIGHT IS ALMOST PERFECT!

Amane Mihime

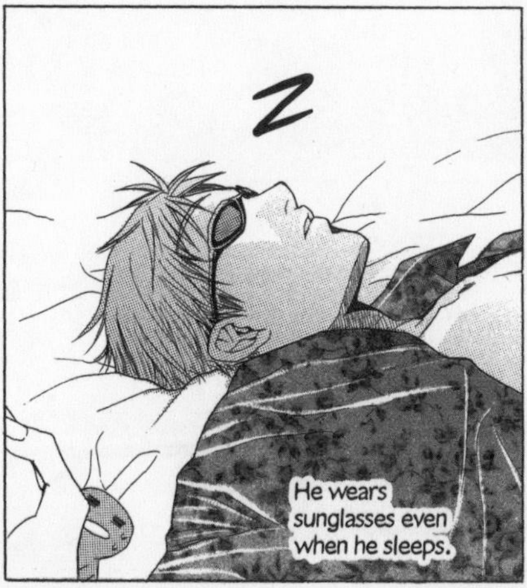
Z
He wears sunglasses even when he sleeps.

Birthday: January 1

Blood Type: A

Grade: Second-Year Student, Sazanka High School (job is to serve tea)

Height: 190 cm (6' 3")

Hobby: Making Friends

Special Talents: Fighting, Making Popcorn

What He Likes: Cute Things

What He Hates: Scary Things, Scary People

Siblings: None

Club Activity in Middle School: Calligraphy Club (but he just went straight home)

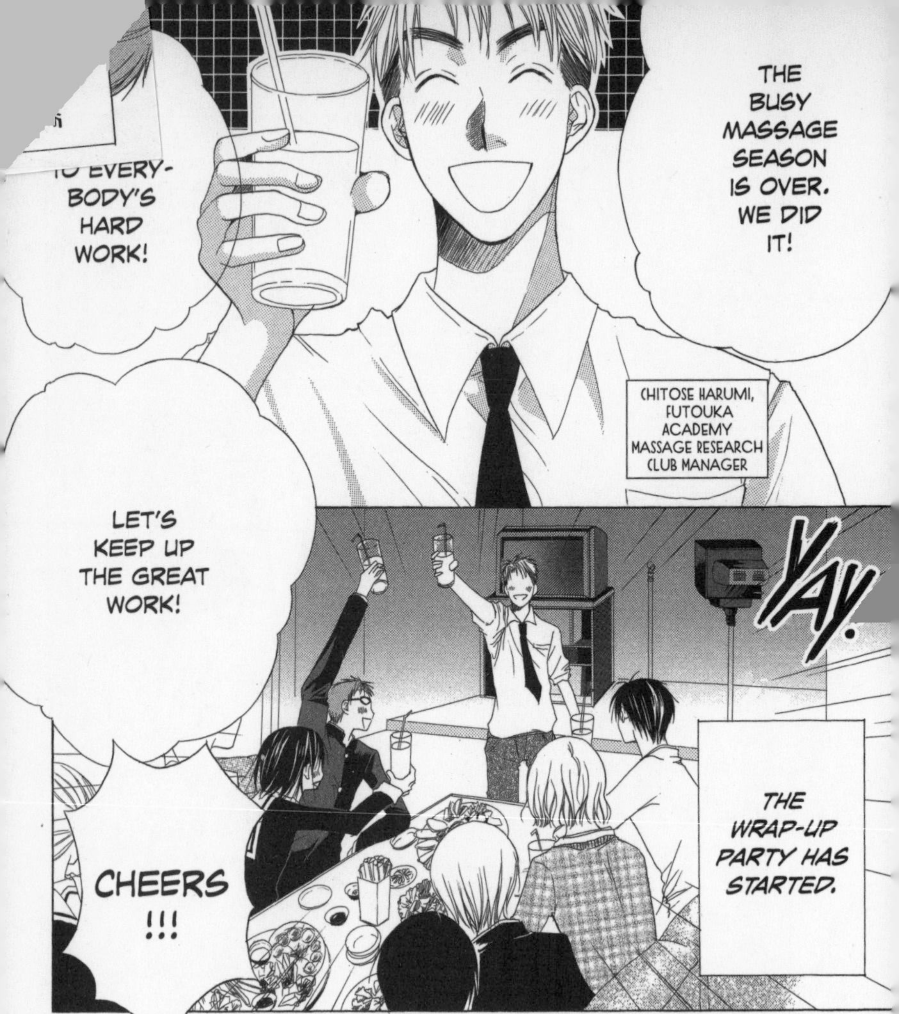
THE BUSY MASSAGE SEASON IS OVER. WE DID IT!
CHITOSE HARUMI, FUTOUKA ACADEMY MASSAGE RESEARCH CLUB MANAGER
TO EVERY-BODY'S HARD WORK!
LET'S KEEP UP THE GREAT WORK!
YAY.
THE WRAP-UP PARTY HAS STARTED.
CHEERS!!!

"Casting!"

I was able to take part in the amazing process of casting for the CD.

Because I was under the impression that I had to watch anime in order to learn about voice actors, I watched lots of anime!

I was shocked by reading some of the staff rolls, thinking, "Wow! The voice for this character also did the voice for that character?!"

Voice actors are amazing...

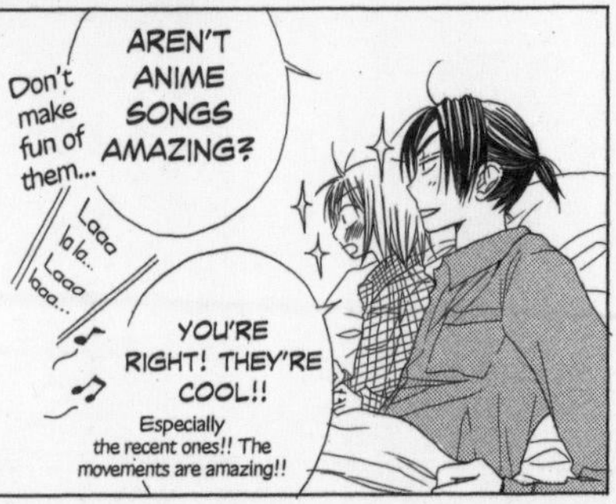
AREN'T ANIME SONGS AMAZING?
Don't make fun of them...
Laaa la la... Laaa laaa...
YOU'RE RIGHT! THEY'RE COOL!!
Especially the recent ones!! The movements are amazing!!

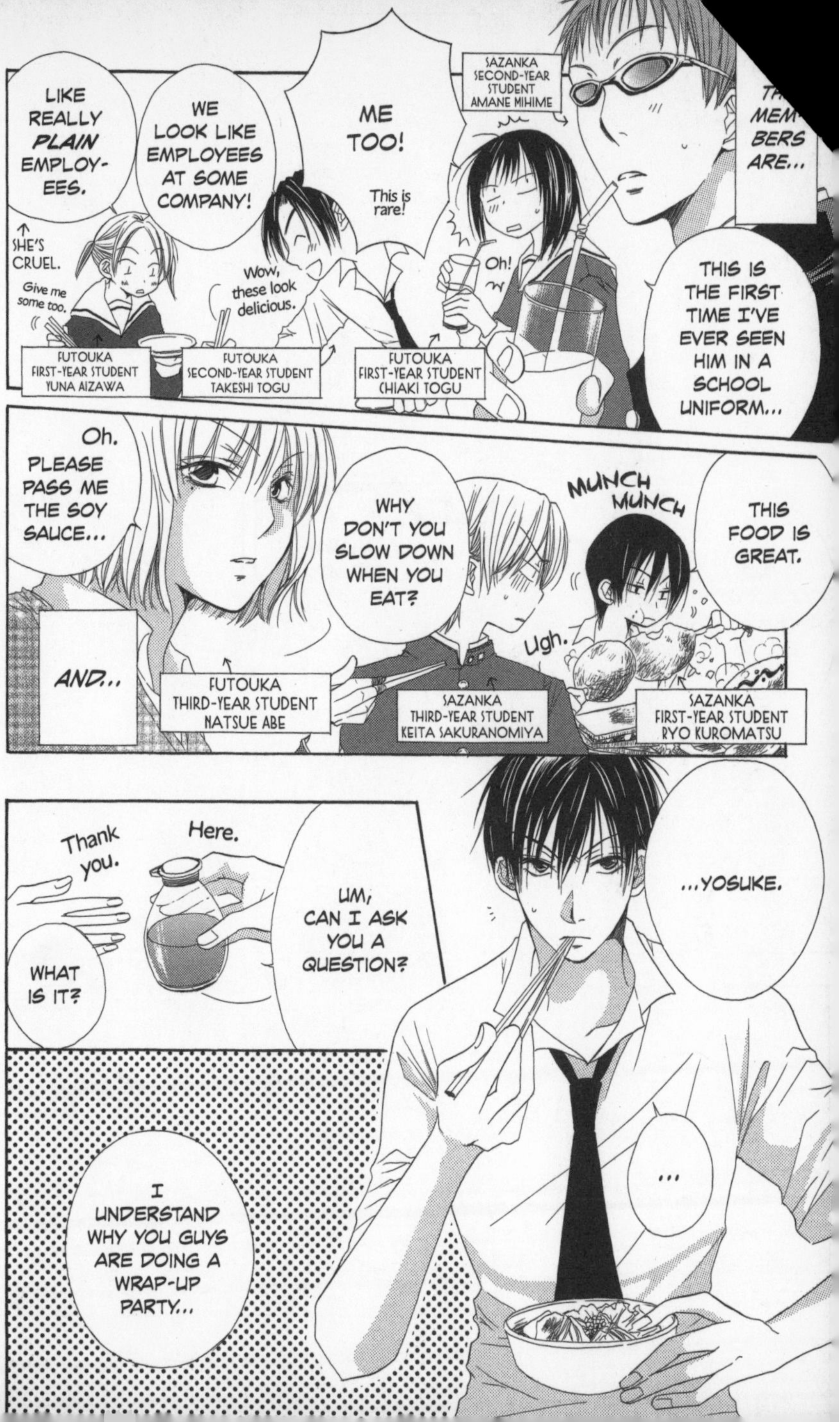
MEM-
BERS
ARE...
THIS IS THE FIRST TIME I'VE EVER SEEN HIM IN A SCHOOL UNIFORM...
SAZANKA SECOND-YEAR STUDENT AMANE MIHIME
This is rare!
Oh!
ME TOO!
FUTOUKA FIRST-YEAR STUDENT CHIAKI TOGU
WE LOOK LIKE EMPLOYEES AT SOME COMPANY!
Wow, these look delicious.
FUTOUKA SECOND-YEAR STUDENT TAKESHI TOGU
LIKE REALLY *PLAIN* EMPLOY-EES.
SHE'S CRUEL.
Give me some too.
FUTOUKA FIRST-YEAR STUDENT YUNA AIZAWA
THIS FOOD IS GREAT.
MUNCH MUNCH
SAZANKA FIRST-YEAR STUDENT RYO KUROMATSU
Ugh.
WHY DON'T YOU SLOW DOWN WHEN YOU EAT?
SAZANKA THIRD-YEAR STUDENT KEITA SAKURANOMIYA
Oh. PLEASE PASS ME THE SOY SAUCE...
FUTOUKA THIRD-YEAR STUDENT NATSUE ABE
AND...
...YOSUKE.
UM, CAN I ASK YOU A QUESTION?
Here.
Thank you.
WHAT IS IT?
...
I UNDERSTAND WHY YOU GUYS ARE DOING A WRAP-UP PARTY...

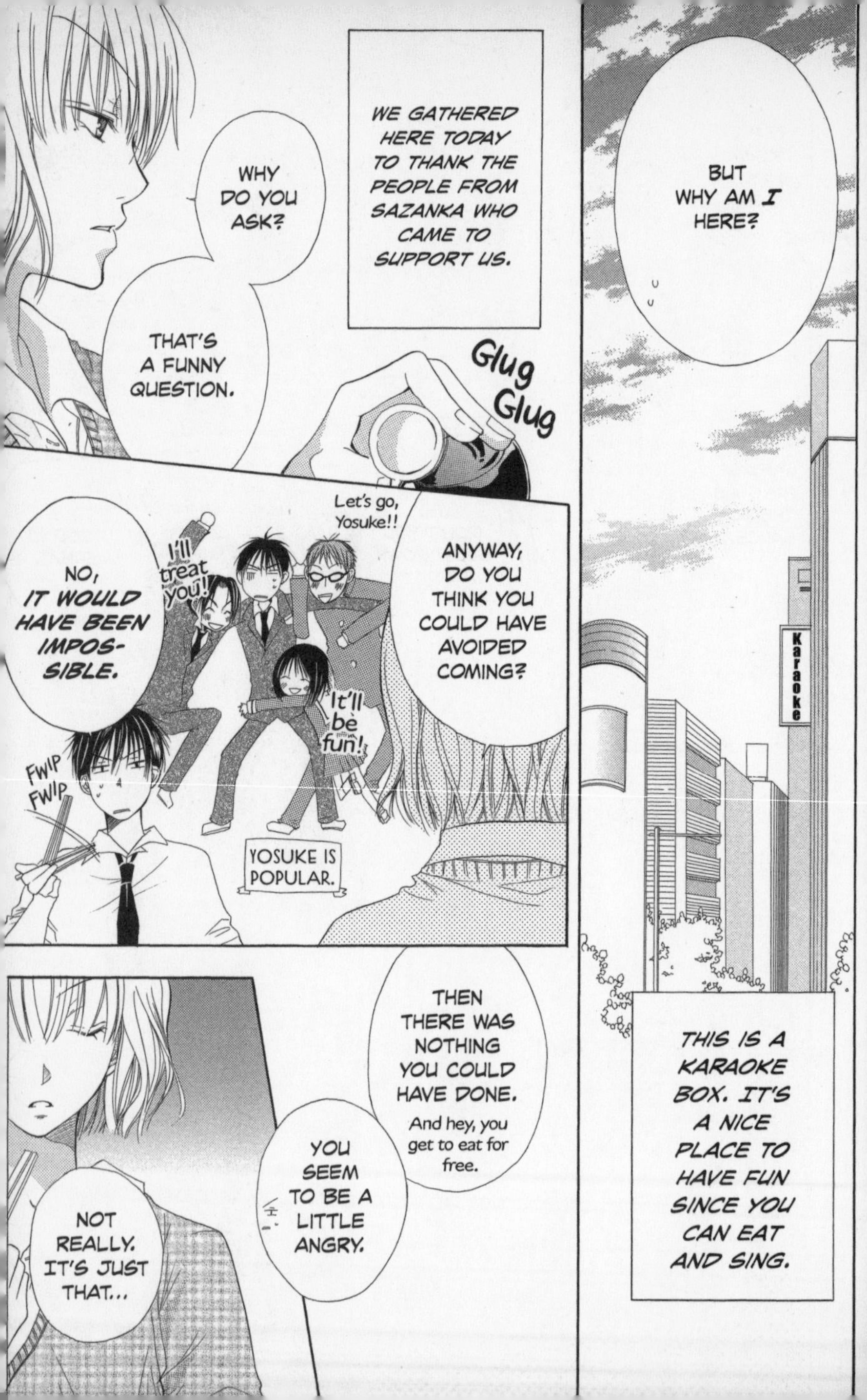
BUT WHY AM I HERE?
Karaoke
THIS IS A KARAOKE BOX. IT'S A NICE PLACE TO HAVE FUN SINCE YOU CAN EAT AND SING.
WE GATHERED HERE TODAY TO THANK THE PEOPLE FROM SAZANKA WHO CAME TO SUPPORT US.
Glug Glug
WHY DO YOU ASK?
THAT'S A FUNNY QUESTION.
ANYWAY, DO YOU THINK YOU COULD HAVE AVOIDED COMING?
Let's go, Yosuke!!
I'll treat you!
It'll be fun!
YOSUKE IS POPULAR.
NO, IT WOULD HAVE BEEN IMPOSSIBLE.
FWIP FWIP
THEN THERE WAS NOTHING YOU COULD HAVE DONE.
And hey, you get to eat for free.
YOU SEEM TO BE A LITTLE ANGRY.
NOT REALLY. IT'S JUST THAT...

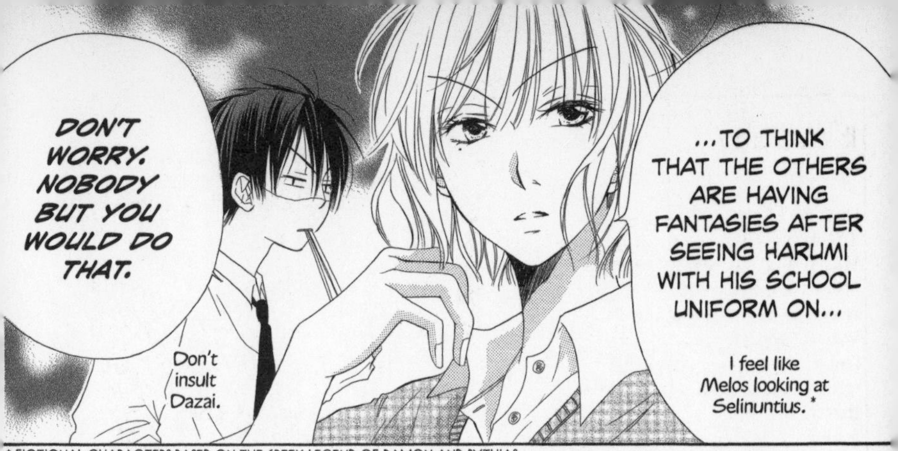
...TO THINK THAT THE OTHERS ARE HAVING FANTASIES AFTER SEEING HARUMI WITH HIS SCHOOL UNIFORM ON...
I feel like Melos looking at Selinuntius. *
DON'T WORRY. NOBODY BUT YOU WOULD DO THAT.
Don't insult Dazai.

* FICTIONAL CHARACTERS BASED ON THE GREEK LEGEND OF DAMON AND PYTHIAS.

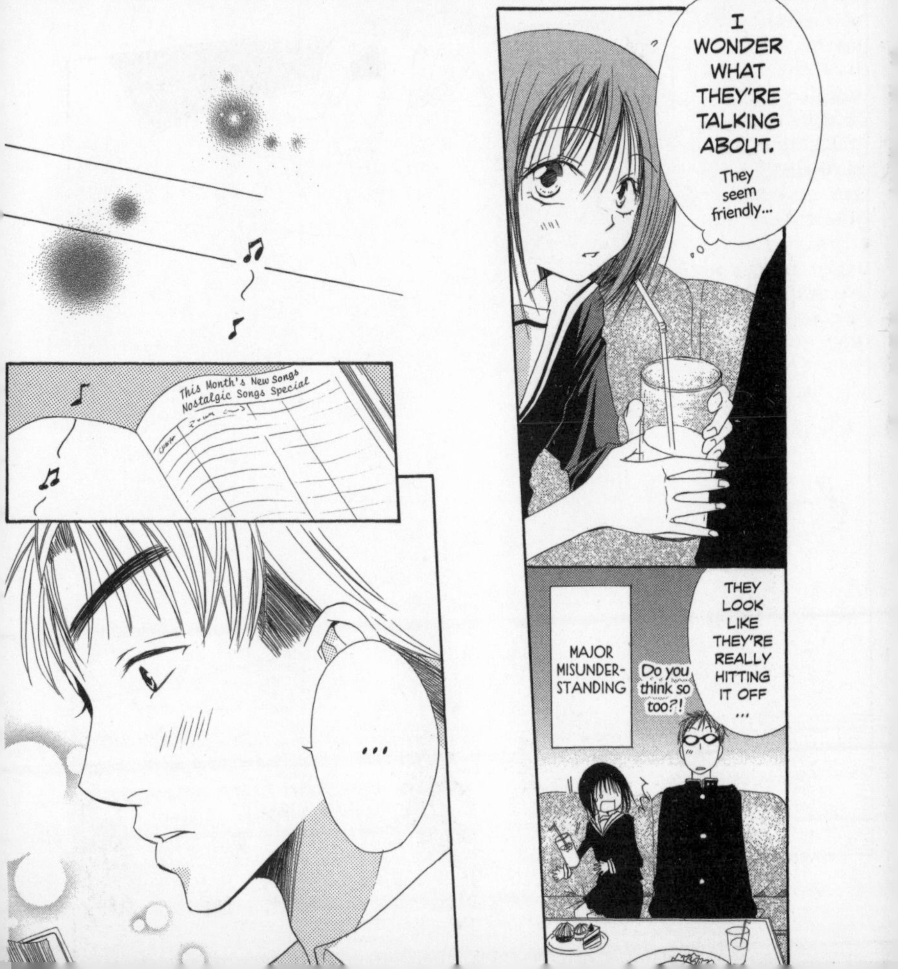
I WONDER WHAT THEY'RE TALKING ABOUT.
They seem friendly...
This Month's New Songs
Nostalgic Songs Special
...
THEY LOOK LIKE THEY'RE REALLY HITTING IT OFF...
Do you think so too?!
MAJOR MISUNDER-STANDING

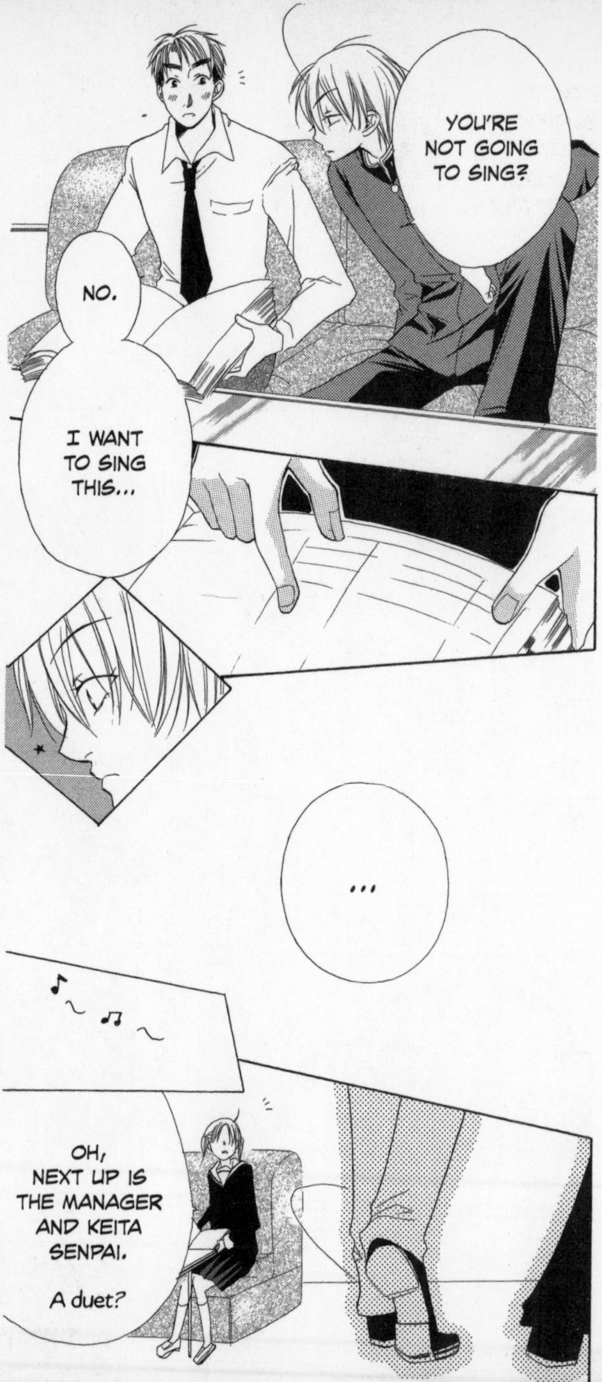

YOU'RE NOT GOING TO SING?
NO.
I WANT TO SING THIS...
...
OH, NEXT UP IS THE MANAGER AND KEITA SENPAI.
A duet?

It's Volume 4.

Hello, this is Izumi Tsubaki. It's already Volume 4 of the comics. There was a significant amount of time between Volume 3 and this one. I am still alive!! I am working hard to make the series!! (Weird assertion.) With this and that, the cover for this volume includes the manager. Also, because I received lots of suggestions to talk about the characters' profiles (thank you very much!), I would like to introduce them little by little, starting in this volume. I would be happy if you could get even a little bit of enjoyment from reading this book.

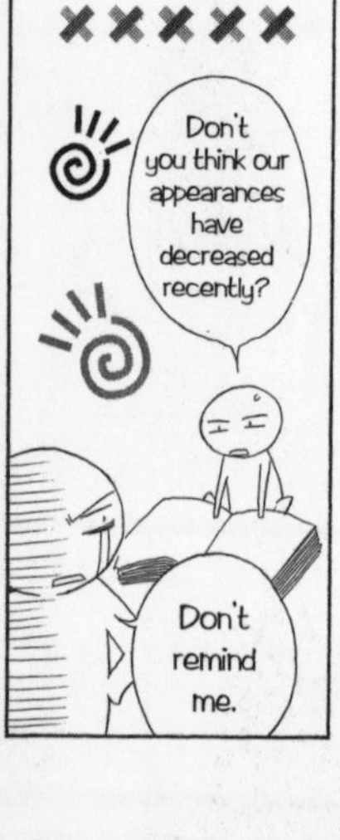

Don't you think our appearances have decreased recently?
Don't remind me.

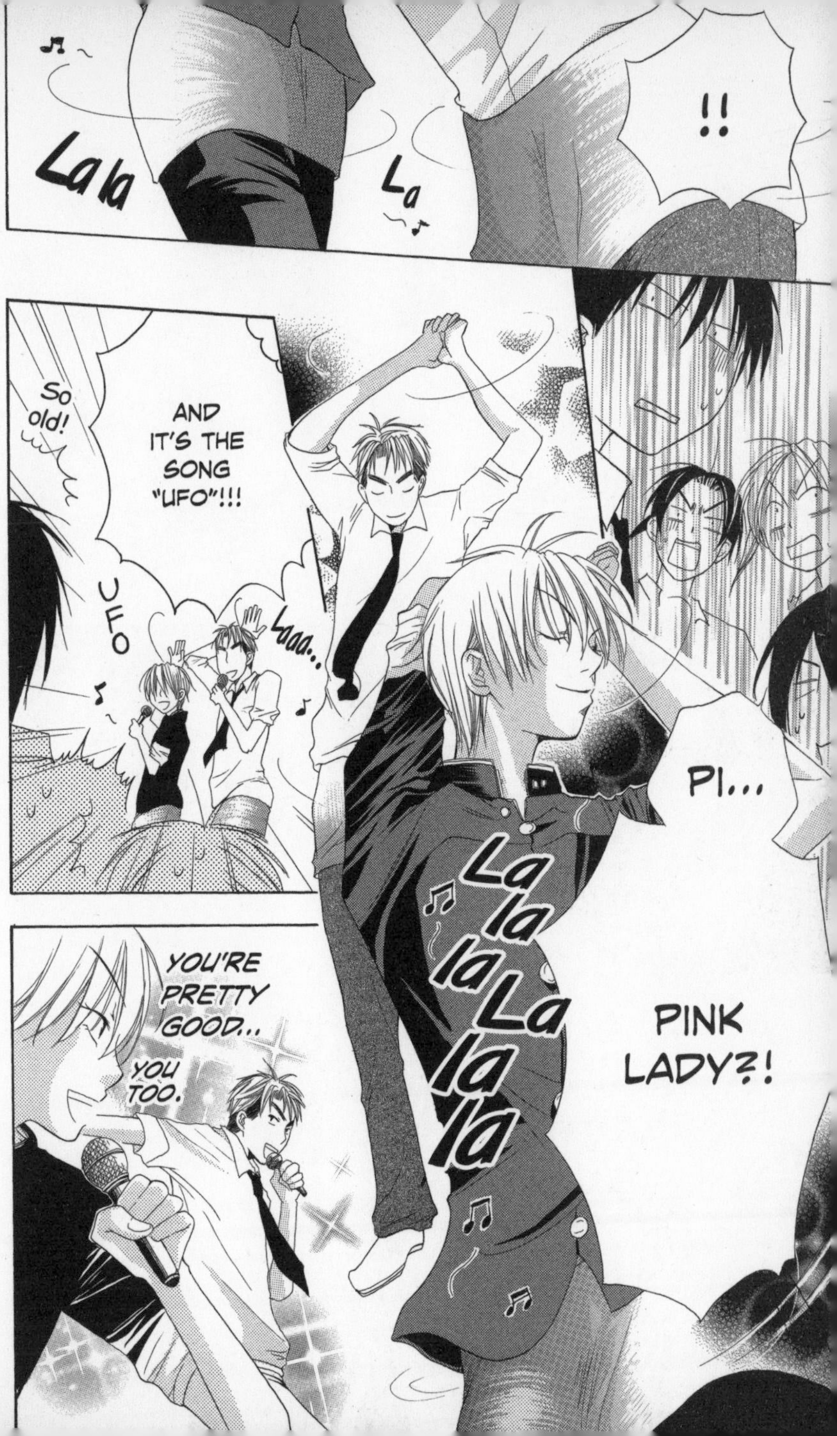
!!
La ~♪
♪~ La la
PI...
PINK LADY?!
♪~ La la la La la la ♪ ♪
AND IT'S THE SONG "UFO"!!!
So old!
Laaa...
UFO
YOU'RE PRETTY GOOD...
YOU TOO.

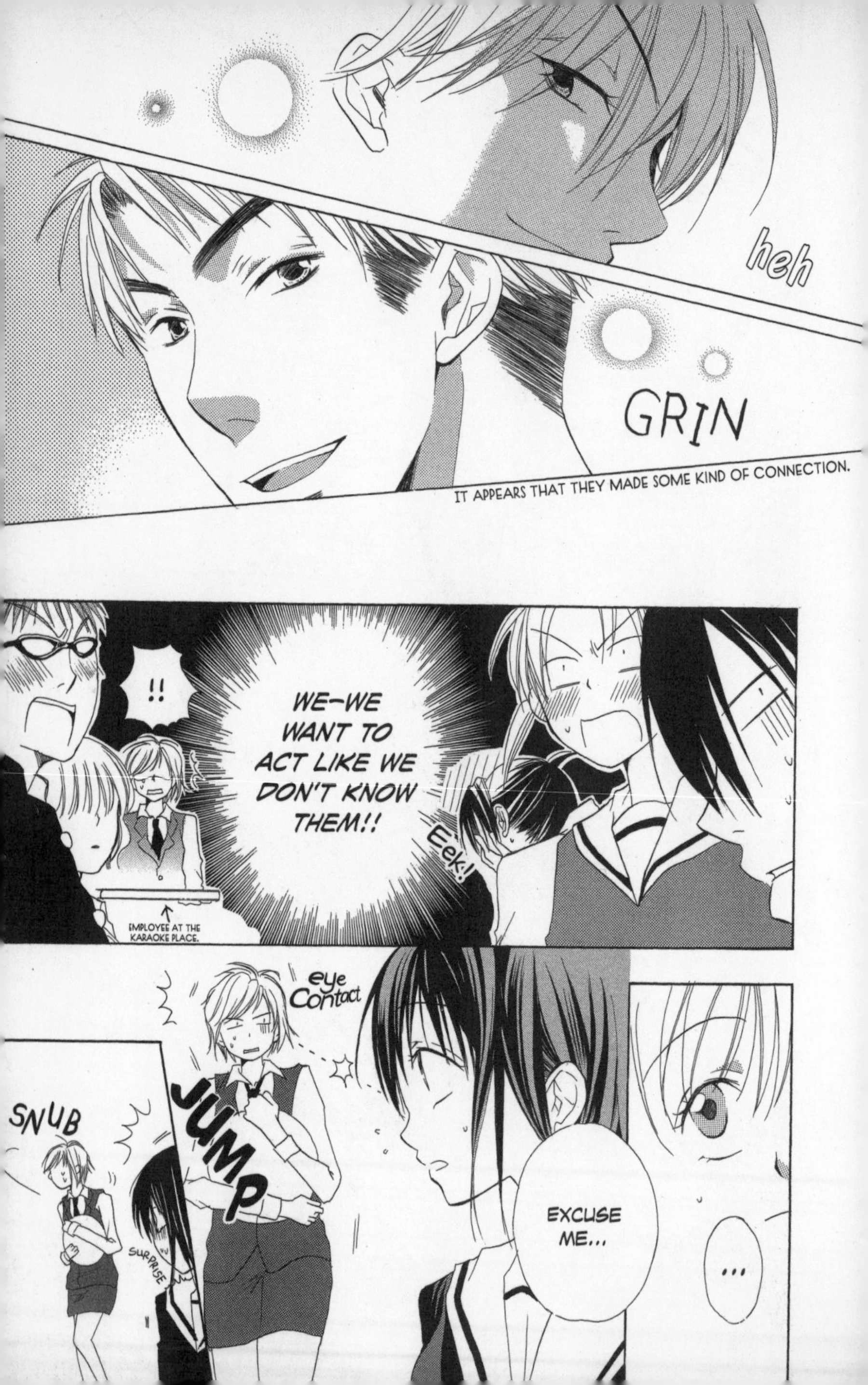
heh
GRIN
IT APPEARS THAT THEY MADE SOME KIND OF CONNECTION.
WE-WE WANT TO ACT LIKE WE DON'T KNOW THEM!!
Eek!
!!
EMPLOYEE AT THE KARAOKE PLACE.
...
EXCUSE ME...
eye Contact
JUMP
SNUB
SURPRISE

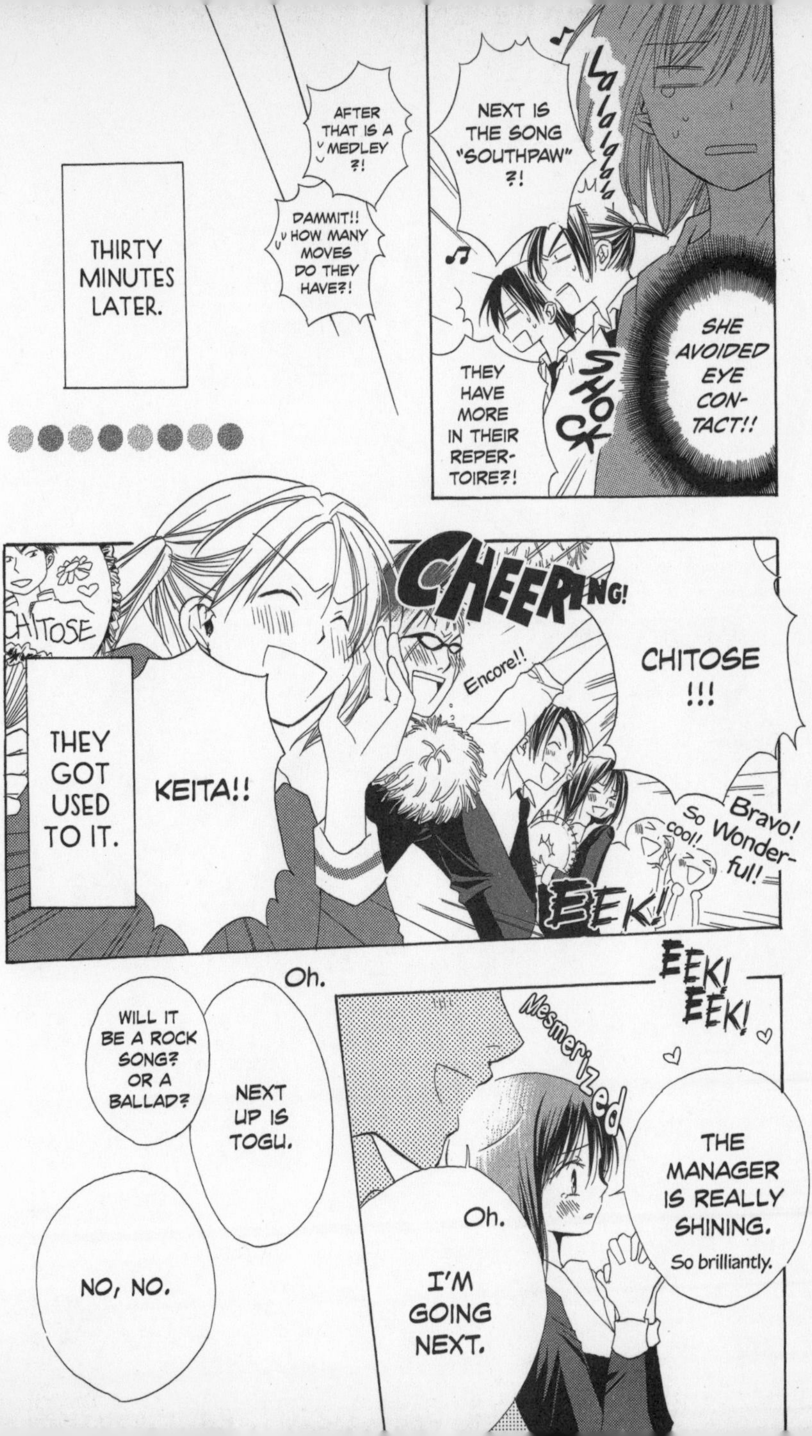
Lalalala
NEXT IS THE SONG "SOUTHPAW"?!
SHE AVOIDED EYE CONTACT!!
SHOCK
THEY HAVE MORE IN THEIR REPERTOIRE?!
AFTER THAT IS A MEDLEY?!
DAMMIT!! HOW MANY MOVES DO THEY HAVE?!
THIRTY MINUTES LATER.
CHEERING!
CHITOSE!!!
Bravo! So Wonderful!
So cool!!
EEK!
Encore!!
KEITA!!
THEY GOT USED TO IT.
CHITOSE
EEK! EEK!
Mesmerized
THE MANAGER IS REALLY SHINING.
So brilliantly.
Oh.
I'M GOING NEXT.
Oh.
NEXT UP IS TOGU.
WILL IT BE A ROCK SONG? OR A BALLAD?
NO, NO.

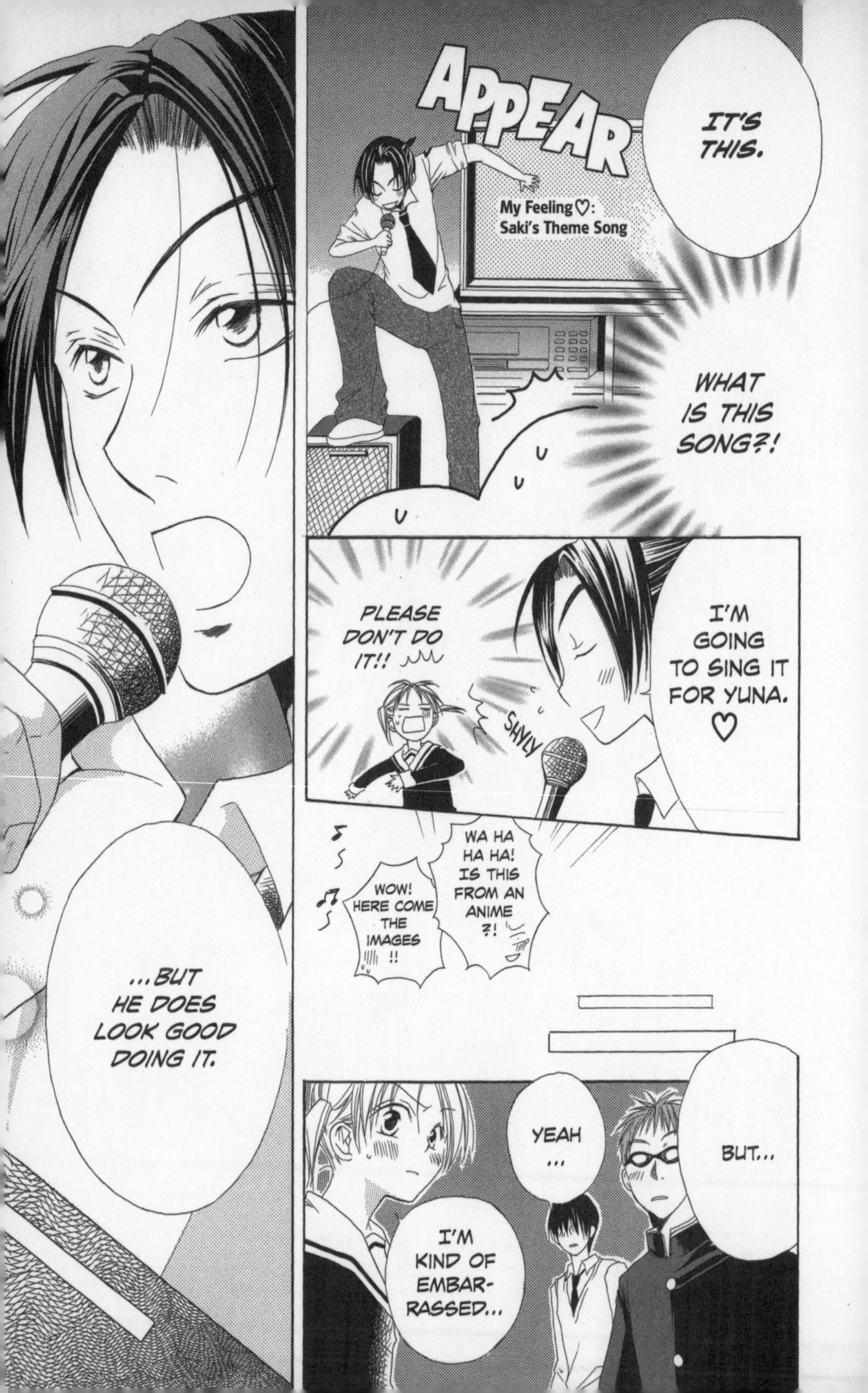
IT'S THIS.
APPEAR
My Feeling♡: Saki's Theme Song
WHAT IS THIS SONG?!
I'M GOING TO SING IT FOR YUNA. ♡
SHYLY
PLEASE DON'T DO IT!!
WA HA HA HA! IS THIS FROM AN ANIME?!
WOW! HERE COME THE IMAGES!!
BUT...
YEAH...
I'M KIND OF EMBARRASSED...
...BUT HE DOES LOOK GOOD DOING IT.

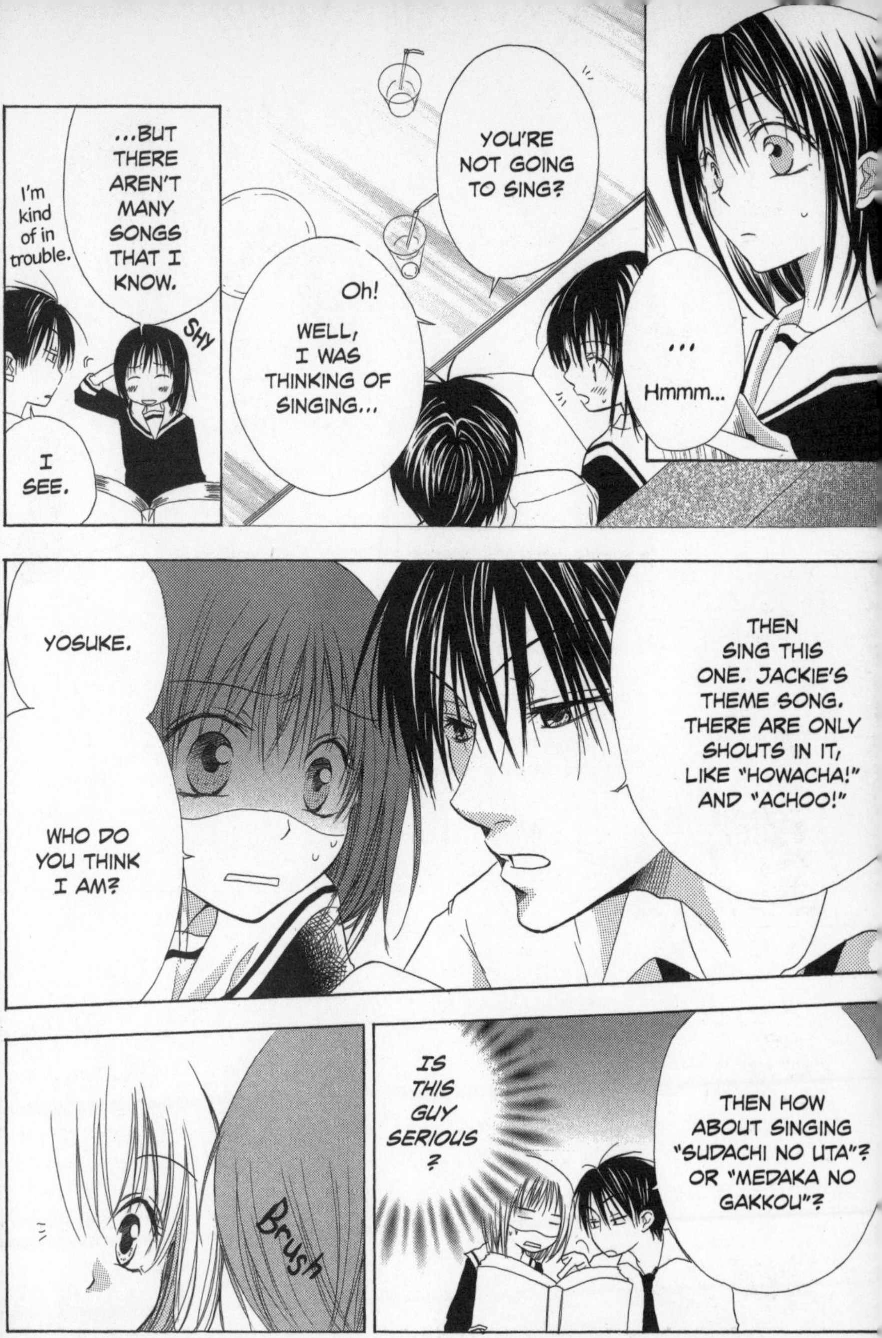
...
Hmmm...
YOU'RE NOT GOING TO SING?
Oh!
WELL, I WAS THINKING OF SINGING...
...BUT THERE AREN'T MANY SONGS THAT I KNOW.
I'm kind of in trouble.
SHY
I SEE.
THEN SING THIS ONE. JACKIE'S THEME SONG. THERE ARE ONLY SHOUTS IN IT, LIKE "HOWACHA!" AND "ACHOO!"
YOSUKE.
WHO DO YOU THINK I AM?
THEN HOW ABOUT SINGING "SUDACHI NO UTA"? OR "MEDAKA NO GAKKOU"?
IS THIS GUY SERIOUS?
Brush

* IN ORDER TO BECOME A SHIATSU MASSAGE THERAPIST, YOU HAVE TO PASS THE FINGER-PRESSURE THERAPY MASSEUR EXAM, AND THEN REGISTER WITH THE JAPANESE MINISTER OF HEALTH, LABOR AND WELFARE IN ORDER TO GET A LICENSE.

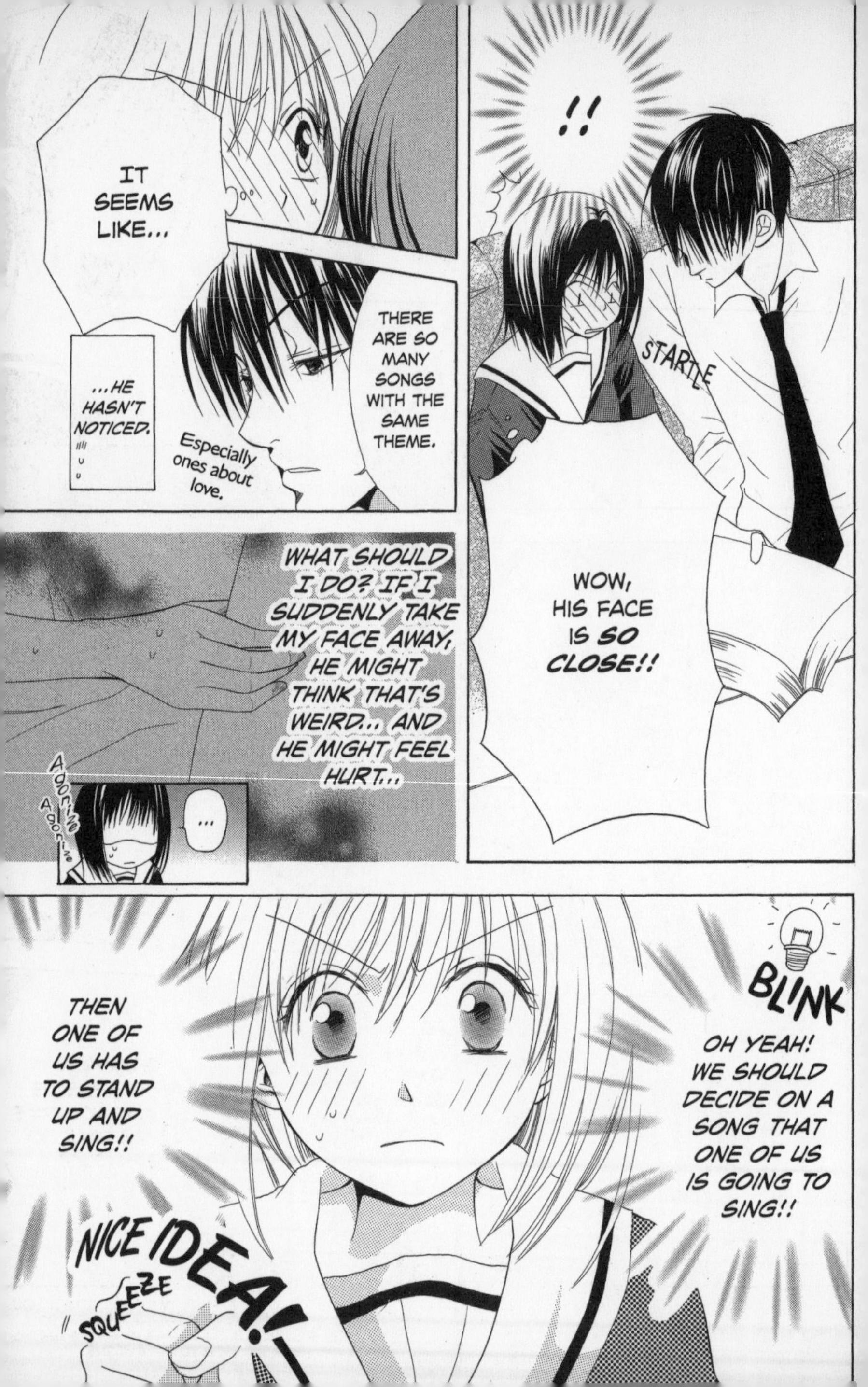
!!
STARTLE
WOW, HIS FACE IS SO CLOSE!!
IT SEEMS LIKE...
THERE ARE SO MANY SONGS WITH THE SAME THEME.
Especially ones about love.
...HE HASN'T NOTICED.
WHAT SHOULD I DO? IF I SUDDENLY TAKE MY FACE AWAY, HE MIGHT THINK THAT'S WEIRD... AND HE MIGHT FEEL HURT...
...
Agonize Agonize
BLINK
OH YEAH! WE SHOULD DECIDE ON A SONG THAT ONE OF US IS GOING TO SING!!
THEN ONE OF US HAS TO STAND UP AND SING!!
NICE IDEA!
SQUEEZE

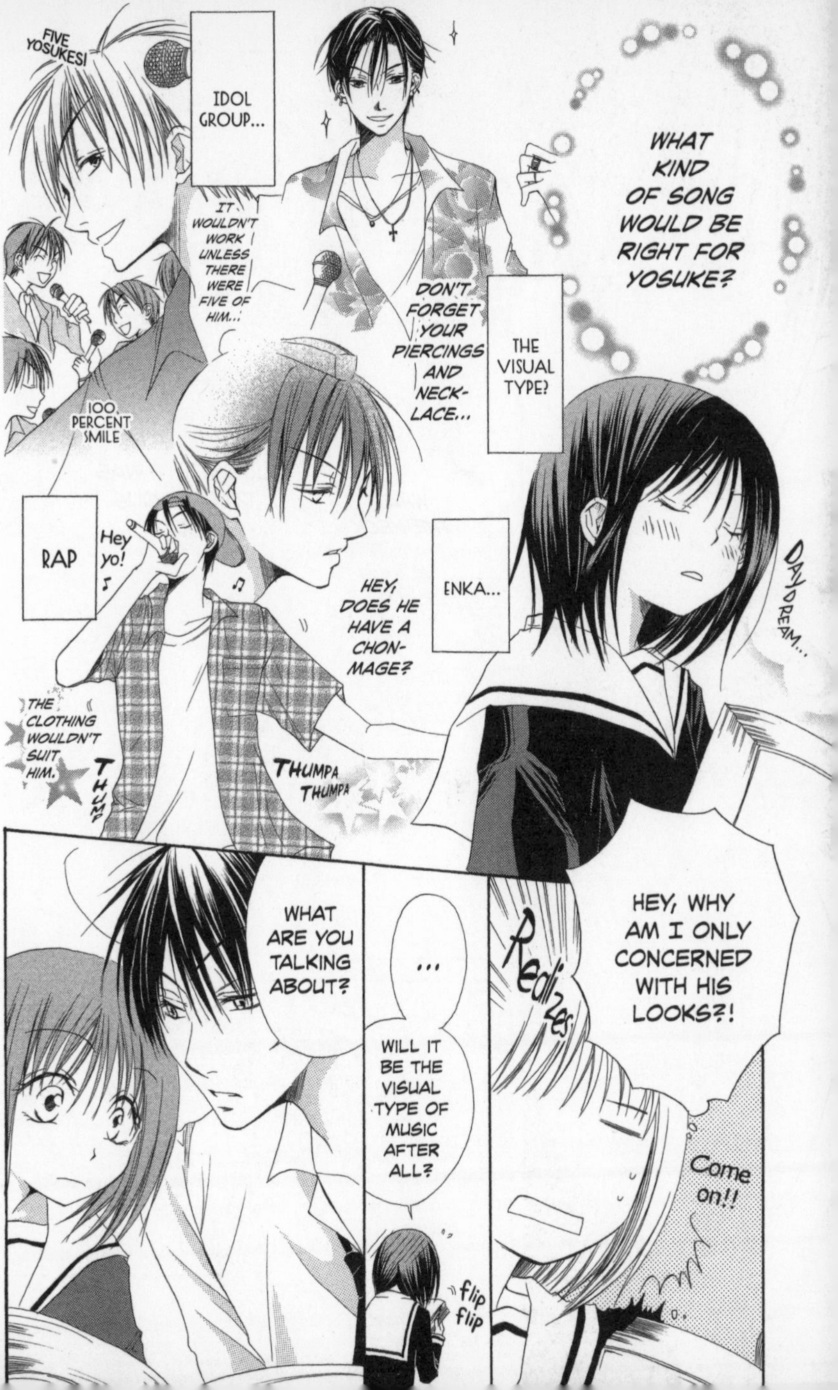
WHAT KIND OF SONG WOULD BE RIGHT FOR YOSUKE?
DAYDREAM...
THE VISUAL TYPE?
DON'T FORGET YOUR PIERCINGS AND NECKLACE...
IDOL GROUP...
IT WOULDN'T WORK UNLESS THERE WERE FIVE OF HIM...
FIVE YOSUKES!
100 PERCENT SMILE
ENKA...
HEY, DOES HE HAVE A CHONMAGE?
RAP
Hey yo!
THE CLOTHING WOULDN'T SUIT HIM.
THUMPA THUMPA
THUMP
HEY, WHY AM I ONLY CONCERNED WITH HIS LOOKS?!
Realizes
Come on!!
...
WILL IT BE THE VISUAL TYPE OF MUSIC AFTER ALL?
flip flip
WHAT ARE YOU TALKING ABOUT?

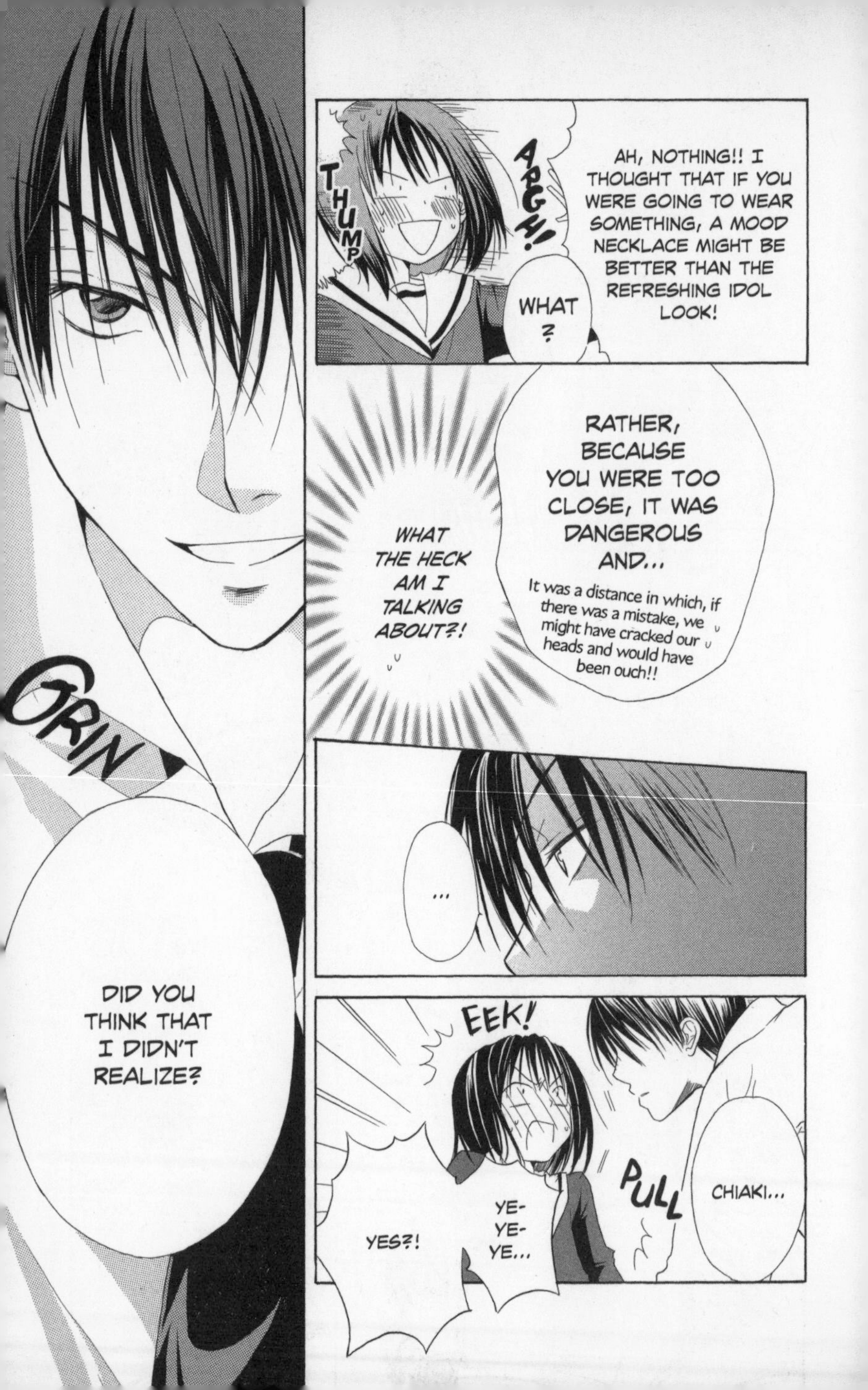
AH, NOTHING!! I THOUGHT THAT IF YOU WERE GOING TO WEAR SOMETHING, A MOOD NECKLACE MIGHT BE BETTER THAN THE REFRESHING IDOL LOOK!
ARGH!!
WHAT?
THUMP
RATHER, BECAUSE YOU WERE TOO CLOSE, IT WAS DANGEROUS AND...
It was a distance in which, if there was a mistake, we might have cracked our heads and would have been ouch!!
WHAT THE HECK AM I TALKING ABOUT?!
...
CHIAKI...
PULL
EEK!
YE-YE-YE...
YES?!
GRIN
DID YOU THINK THAT I DIDN'T REALIZE?

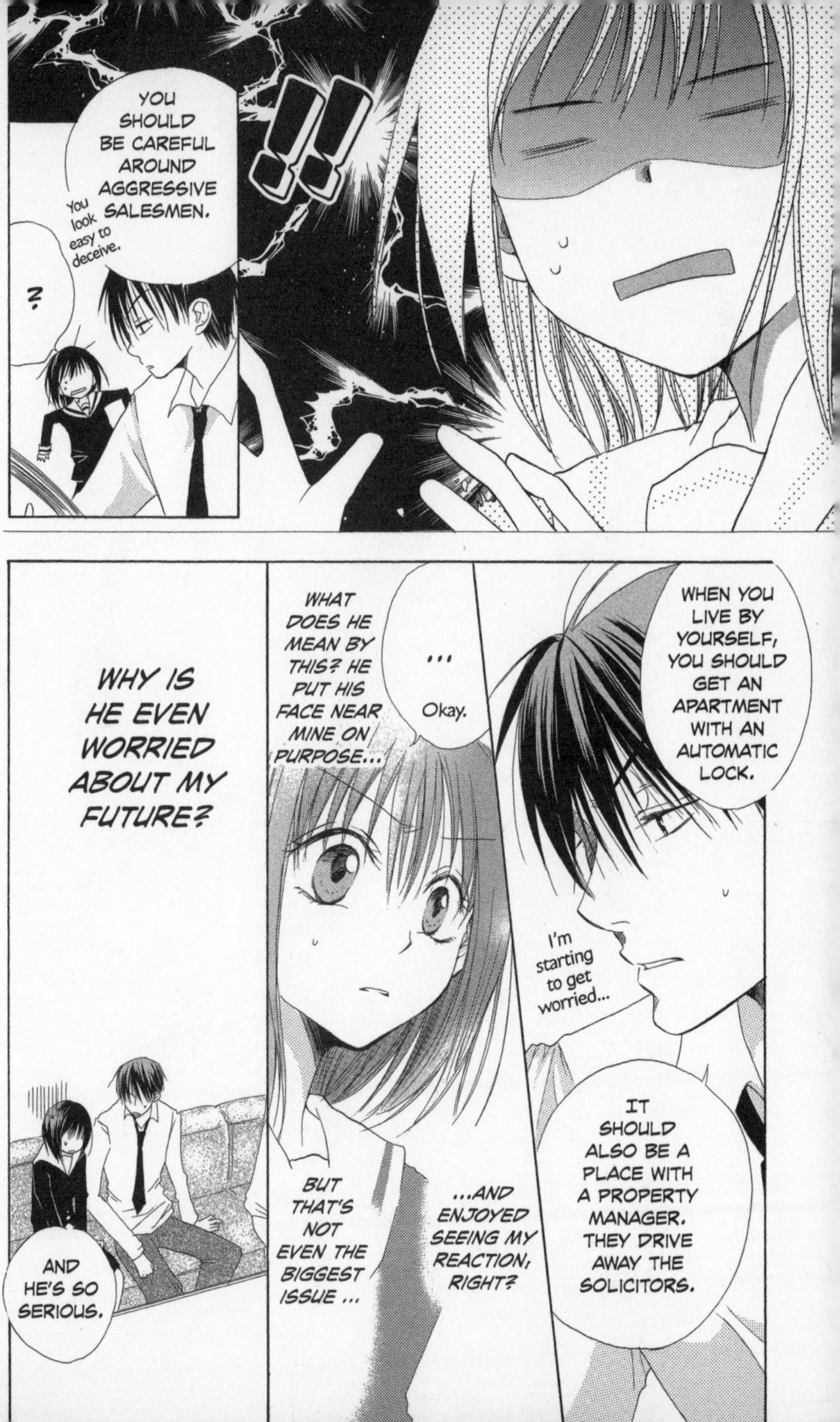
YOU SHOULD BE CAREFUL AROUND AGGRESSIVE SALESMEN.
You look easy to deceive.
?
WHEN YOU LIVE BY YOURSELF, YOU SHOULD GET AN APARTMENT WITH AN AUTOMATIC LOCK.
I'm starting to get worried...
IT SHOULD ALSO BE A PLACE WITH A PROPERTY MANAGER. THEY DRIVE AWAY THE SOLICITORS.
... Okay.
WHAT DOES HE MEAN BY THIS? HE PUT HIS FACE NEAR MINE ON PURPOSE...
...AND ENJOYED SEEING MY REACTION, RIGHT?
BUT THAT'S NOT EVEN THE BIGGEST ISSUE ...
WHY IS HE EVEN WORRIED ABOUT MY FUTURE?
AND HE'S SO SERIOUS.

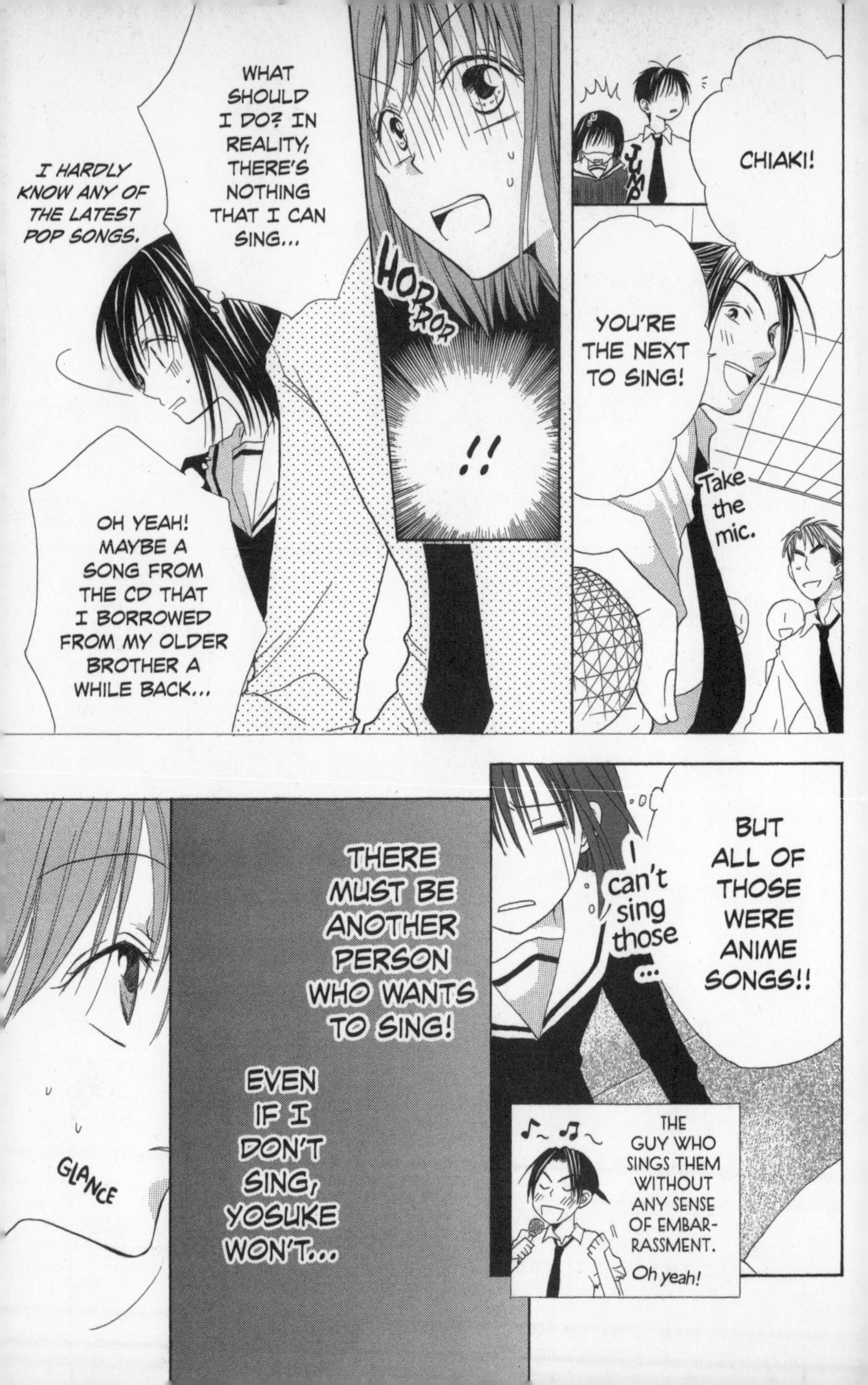
CHIAKI!
JUMP
YOU'RE THE NEXT TO SING!
Take the mic.
HORROR
!!
WHAT SHOULD I DO? IN REALITY, THERE'S NOTHING THAT I CAN SING...
I HARDLY KNOW ANY OF THE LATEST POP SONGS.
OH YEAH! MAYBE A SONG FROM THE CD THAT I BORROWED FROM MY OLDER BROTHER A WHILE BACK...
BUT ALL OF THOSE WERE ANIME SONGS!!
I can't sing those ...
THE GUY WHO SINGS THEM WITHOUT ANY SENSE OF EMBAR-RASSMENT.
Oh yeah!
THERE MUST BE ANOTHER PERSON WHO WANTS TO SING!
EVEN IF I DON'T SING, YOSUKE WON'T...
GLANCE

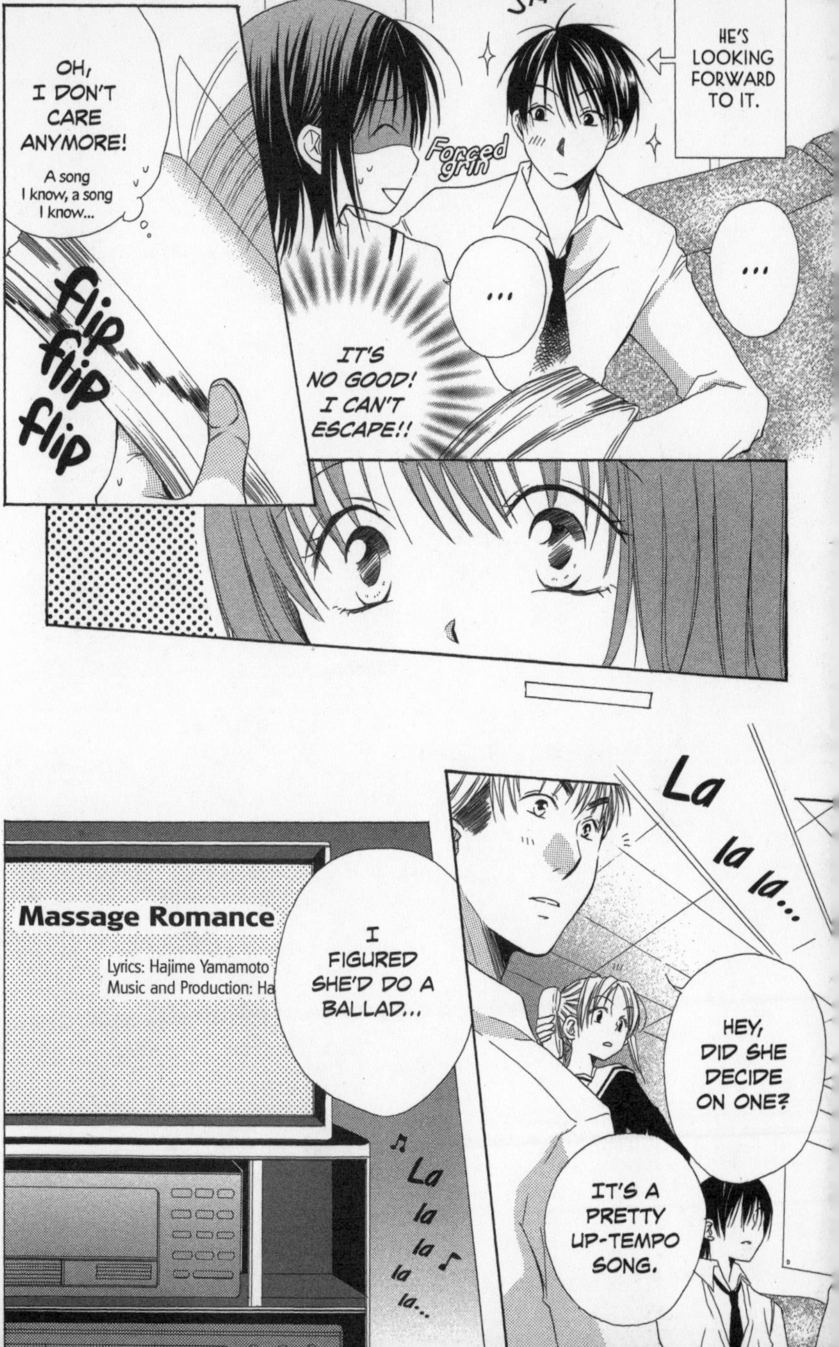
Staaaare
HE'S LOOKING FORWARD TO IT.
...
...
Forced grin
OH, I DON'T CARE ANYMORE!
A song I know, a song I know...
flip flip flip
IT'S NO GOOD! I CAN'T ESCAPE!!
La la la...
HEY, DID SHE DECIDE ON ONE?
IT'S A PRETTY UP-TEMPO SONG.
I FIGURED SHE'D DO A BALLAD...
Massage Romance
Lyrics: Hajime Yamamoto
Music and Production: Ha
La la la la la...

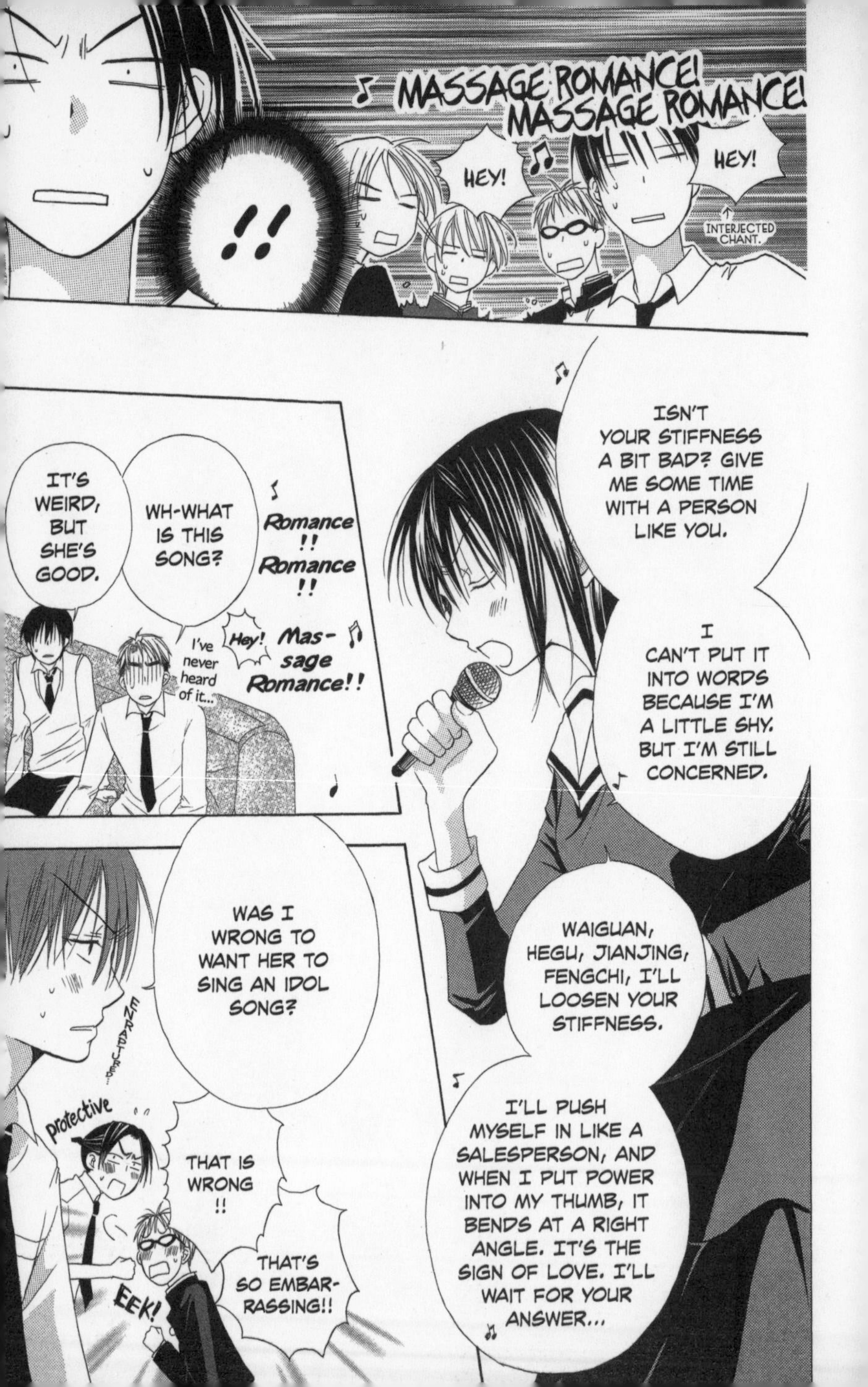
MASSAGE ROMANCE! MASSAGE ROMANCE!
HEY!
INTERJECTED CHANT.
HEY!
!!
ISN'T YOUR STIFFNESS A BIT BAD? GIVE ME SOME TIME WITH A PERSON LIKE YOU.
I CAN'T PUT IT INTO WORDS BECAUSE I'M A LITTLE SHY. BUT I'M STILL CONCERNED.
WAIGUAN, HEGU, JIANJING, FENGCHI, I'LL LOOSEN YOUR STIFFNESS.
I'LL PUSH MYSELF IN LIKE A SALESPERSON, AND WHEN I PUT POWER INTO MY THUMB, IT BENDS AT A RIGHT ANGLE. IT'S THE SIGN OF LOVE. I'LL WAIT FOR YOUR ANSWER...
Romance!! Romance!! Massage Romance!!
Hey!
WH-WHAT IS THIS SONG?
I've never heard of it...
IT'S WEIRD, BUT SHE'S GOOD.
WAS I WRONG TO WANT HER TO SING AN IDOL SONG?
ENRAPTURE...
THAT IS WRONG!!
protective
THAT'S SO EMBARRASSING!!
EEK!

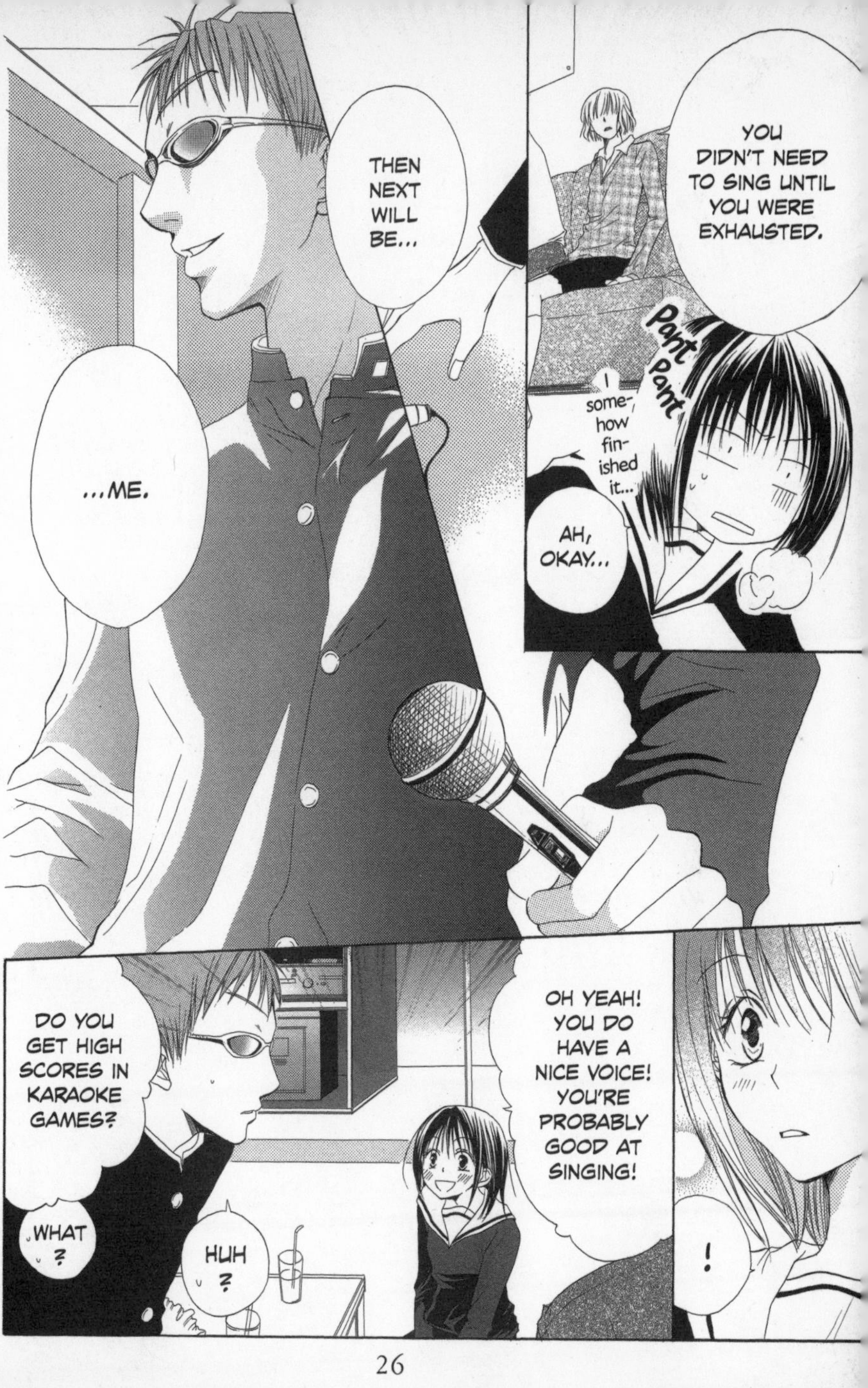

YOU DIDN'T NEED TO SING UNTIL YOU WERE EXHAUSTED.
Pant Pant
I somehow finished it...
AH, OKAY...
THEN NEXT WILL BE...
...ME.
!
OH YEAH! YOU DO HAVE A NICE VOICE! YOU'RE PROBABLY GOOD AT SINGING!
DO YOU GET HIGH SCORES IN KARAOKE GAMES?
HUH?
WHAT?

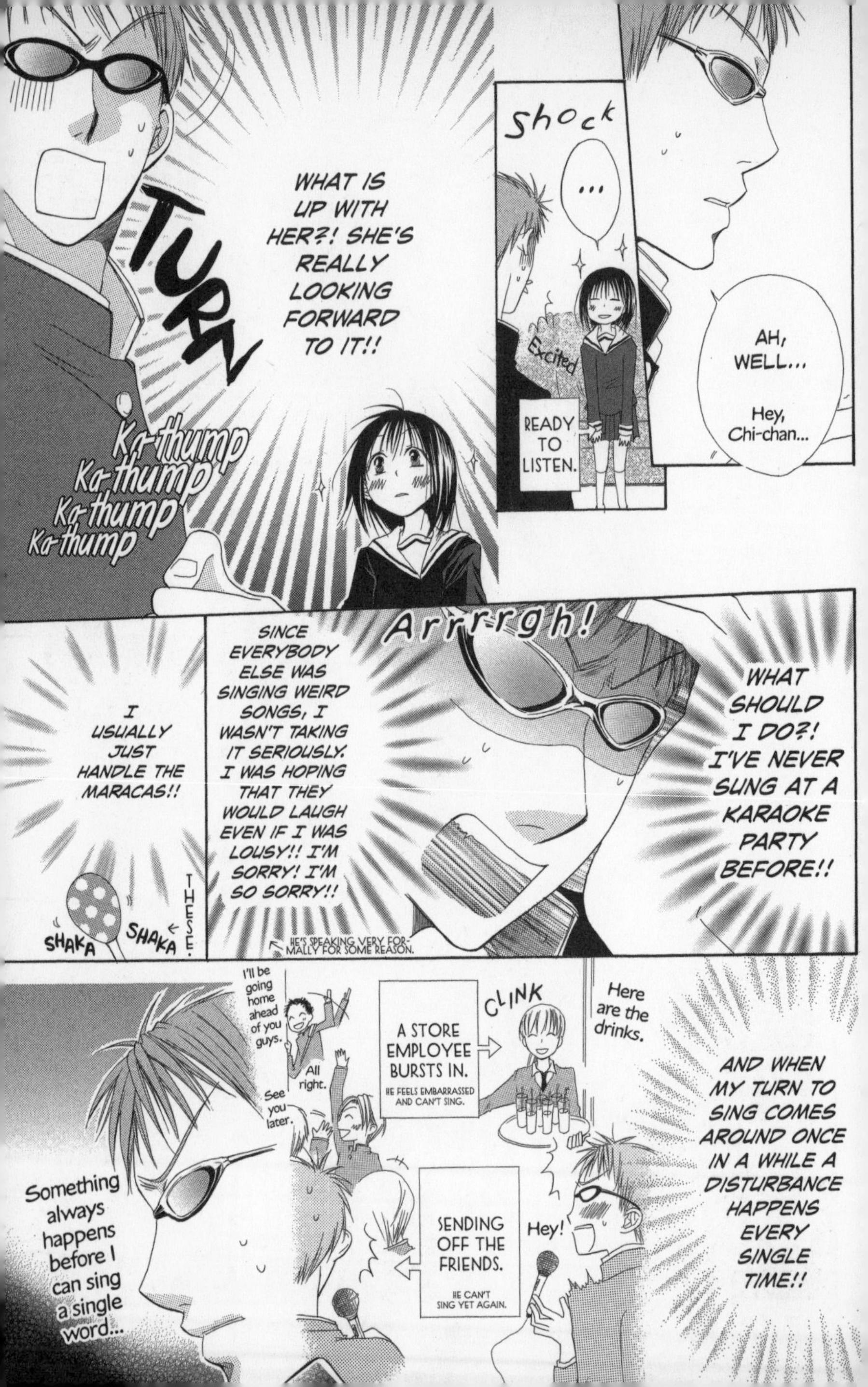
AH, WELL...
Hey, Chi-chan...
Shock
...
Excited
READY TO LISTEN.
WHAT IS UP WITH HER?! SHE'S REALLY LOOKING FORWARD TO IT!!
TURN
Ka-thump Ka-thump Ka-thump Ka-thump
Arrrrgh!
WHAT SHOULD I DO?! I'VE NEVER SUNG AT A KARAOKE PARTY BEFORE!!
SINCE EVERYBODY ELSE WAS SINGING WEIRD SONGS, I WASN'T TAKING IT SERIOUSLY. I WAS HOPING THAT THEY WOULD LAUGH EVEN IF I WAS LOUSY!! I'M SORRY! I'M SO SORRY!!
HE'S SPEAKING VERY FORMALLY FOR SOME REASON.
I USUALLY JUST HANDLE THE MARACAS!!
THESE.
SHAKA
SHAKA
AND WHEN MY TURN TO SING COMES AROUND ONCE IN A WHILE A DISTURBANCE HAPPENS EVERY SINGLE TIME!!
Here are the drinks.
CLINK
A STORE EMPLOYEE BURSTS IN.
HE FEELS EMBARRASSED AND CAN'T SING.
I'll be going home ahead of you guys.
All right.
See you later.
Hey!
SENDING OFF THE FRIENDS.
HE CAN'T SING YET AGAIN.
Something always happens before I can sing a single word...

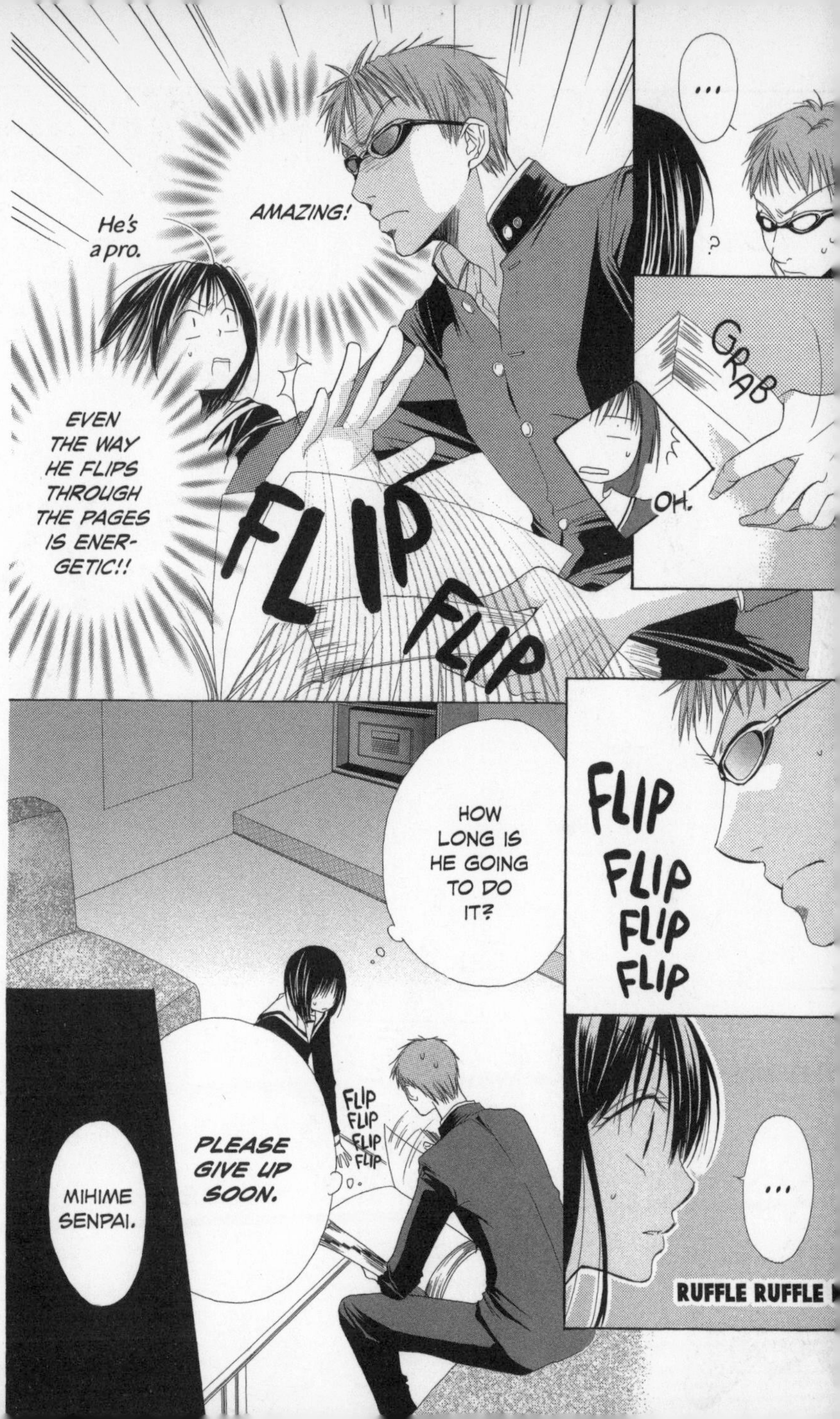
...
?
GRAB
OH.
AMAZING!
He's a pro.
EVEN THE WAY HE FLIPS THROUGH THE PAGES IS ENERGETIC!!
FLIP
FLIP
FLIP
FLIP
FLIP
FLIP
...
RUFFLE RUFFLE
HOW LONG IS HE GOING TO DO IT?
FLIP
FLIP
FLIP
FLIP
PLEASE GIVE UP SOON.
MIHIME SENPAI.

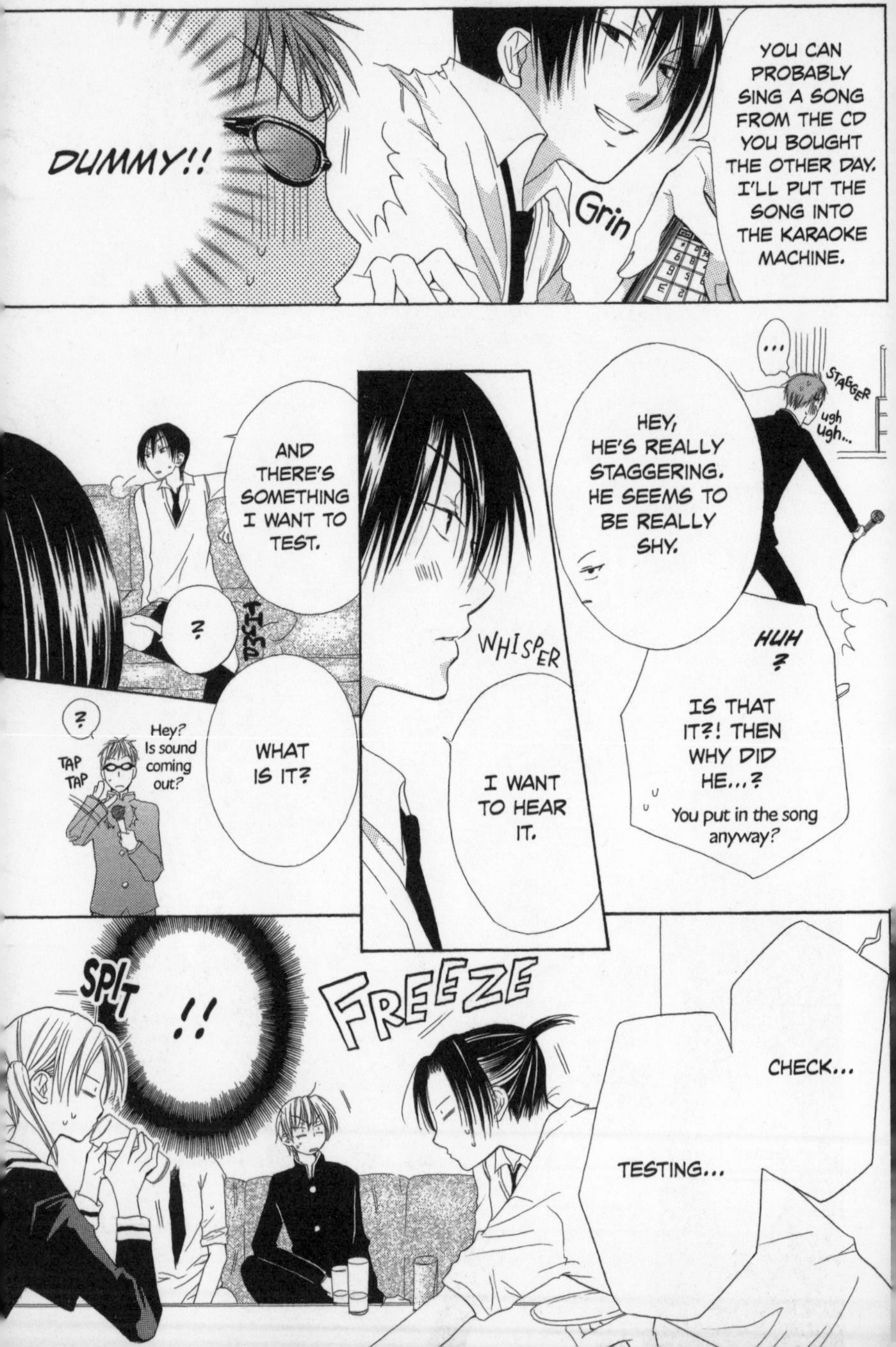
YOU CAN PROBABLY SING A SONG FROM THE CD YOU BOUGHT THE OTHER DAY. I'LL PUT THE SONG INTO THE KARAOKE MACHINE.
Grin
DUMMY!!
...
STAGGER
ugh ugh...
HEY, HE'S REALLY STAGGERING. HE SEEMS TO BE REALLY SHY.
HUH?
IS THAT IT?! THEN WHY DID HE...?
You put in the song anyway?
AND THERE'S SOMETHING I WANT TO TEST.
?
THUMP
WHAT IS IT?
?
TAP TAP
Hey? Is sound coming out?
WHISPER
I WANT TO HEAR IT.
CHECK...
TESTING...
FREEZE
!!
SPIT

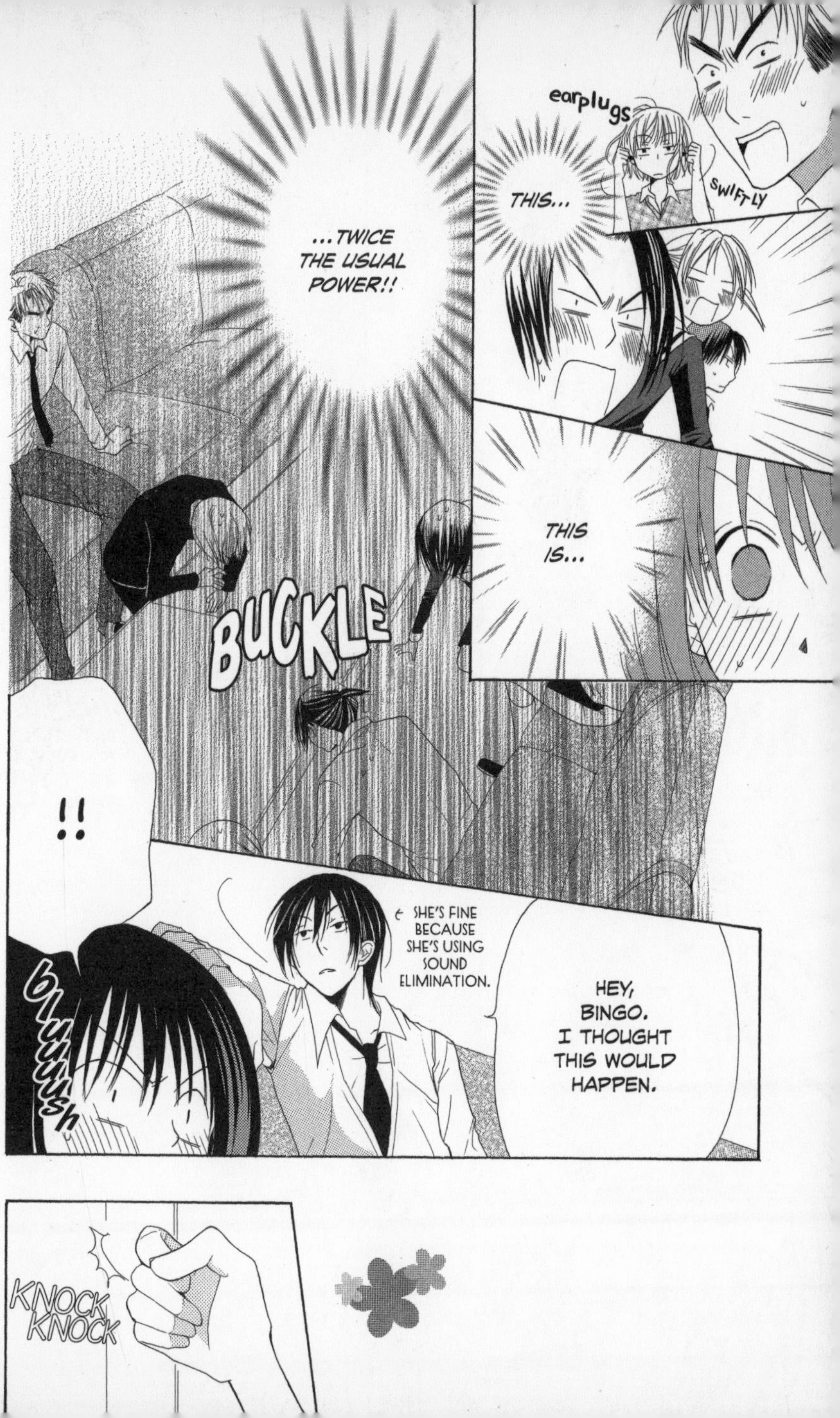
earplugs
SWIFTLY
THIS...
THIS IS...
...TWICE THE USUAL POWER!!
BUCKLE
!!
HEY, BINGO. I THOUGHT THIS WOULD HAPPEN.
SHE'S FINE BECAUSE SHE'S USING SOUND ELIMINATION.
bluuush
KNOCK KNOCK

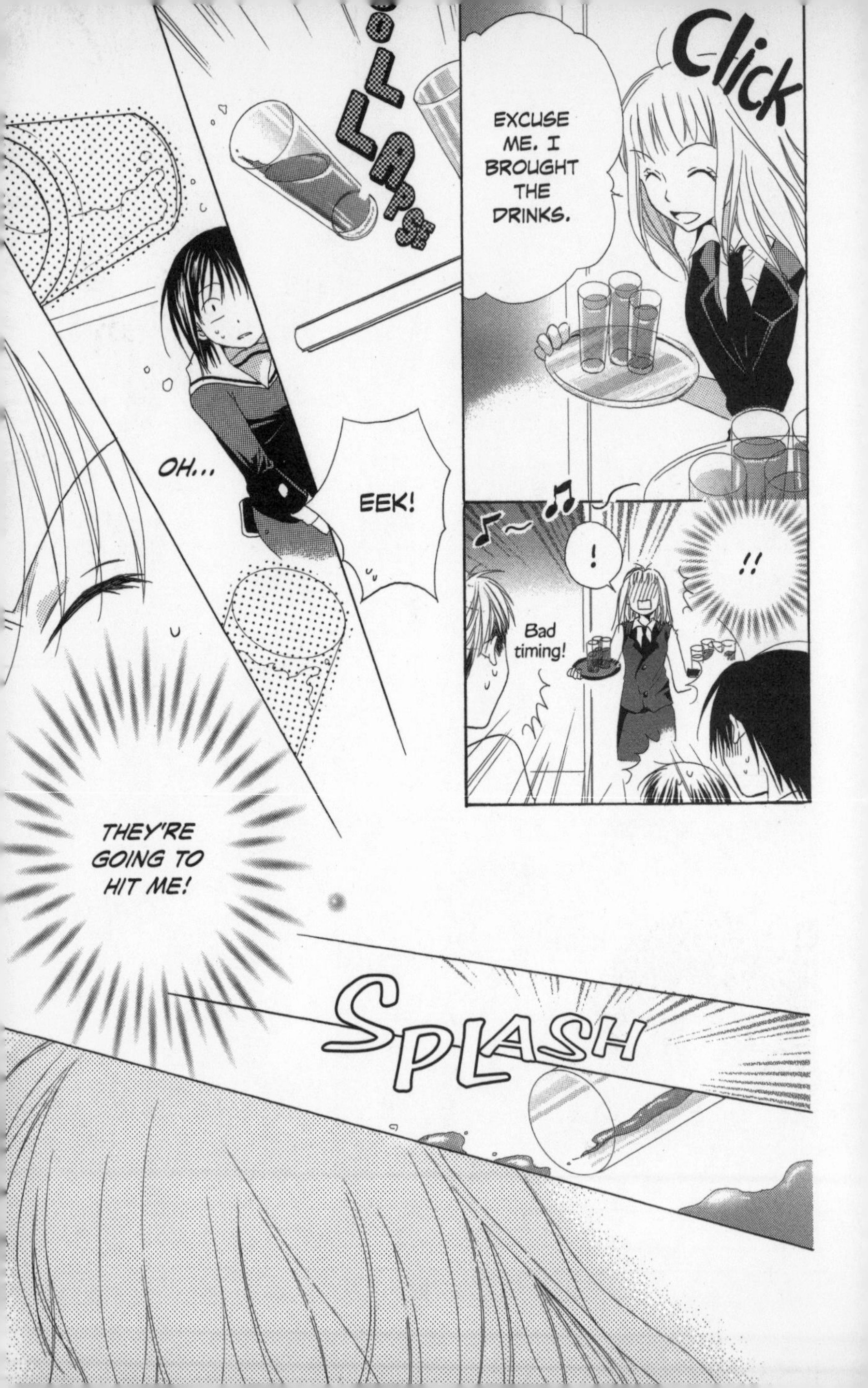
Click
EXCUSE ME. I BROUGHT THE DRINKS.
♪~♫
!
!!
Bad timing!
EEK!
OH...
THEY'RE GOING TO HIT ME!
SPLASH

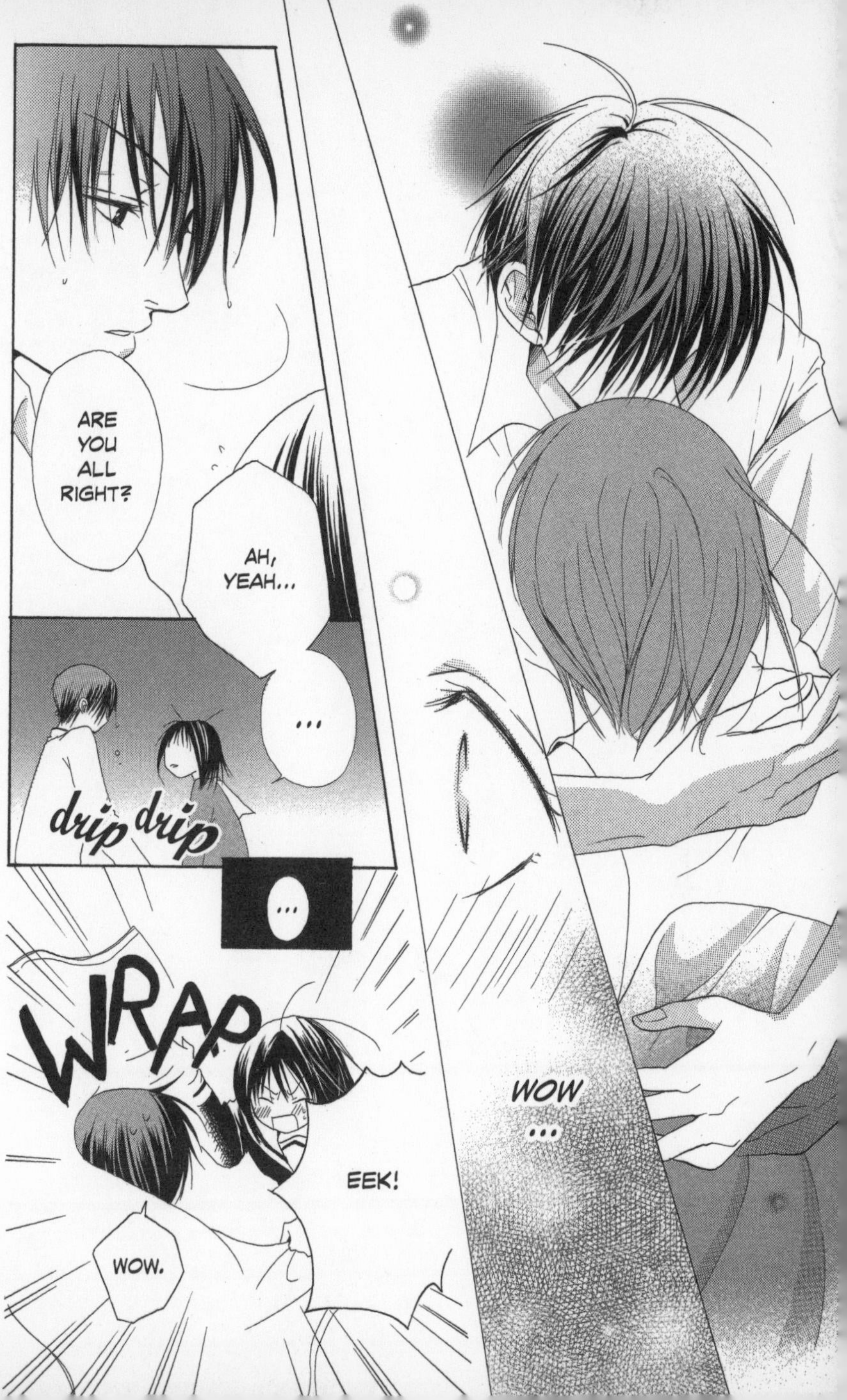
WOW ...
ARE YOU ALL RIGHT?
AH, YEAH...
...
drip drip
...
WRAP
EEK!
WOW.

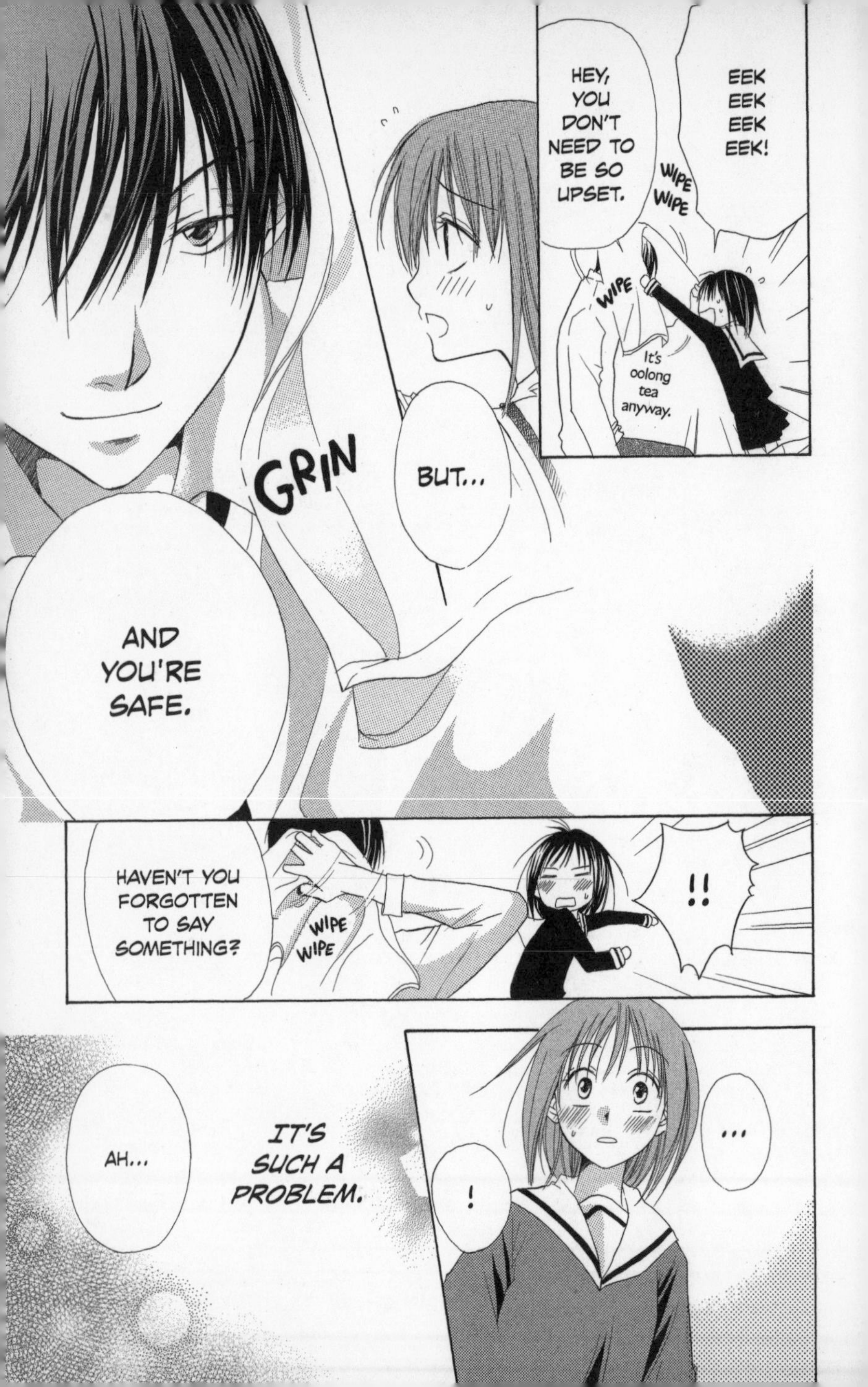
EEK EEK EEK EEK!
HEY, YOU DON'T NEED TO BE SO UPSET.
WIPE WIPE
WIPE
It's oolong tea anyway.
BUT...
GRIN
AND YOU'RE SAFE.
!!
HAVEN'T YOU FORGOTTEN TO SAY SOMETHING?
WIPE WIPE
...
!
IT'S SUCH A PROBLEM.
AH...

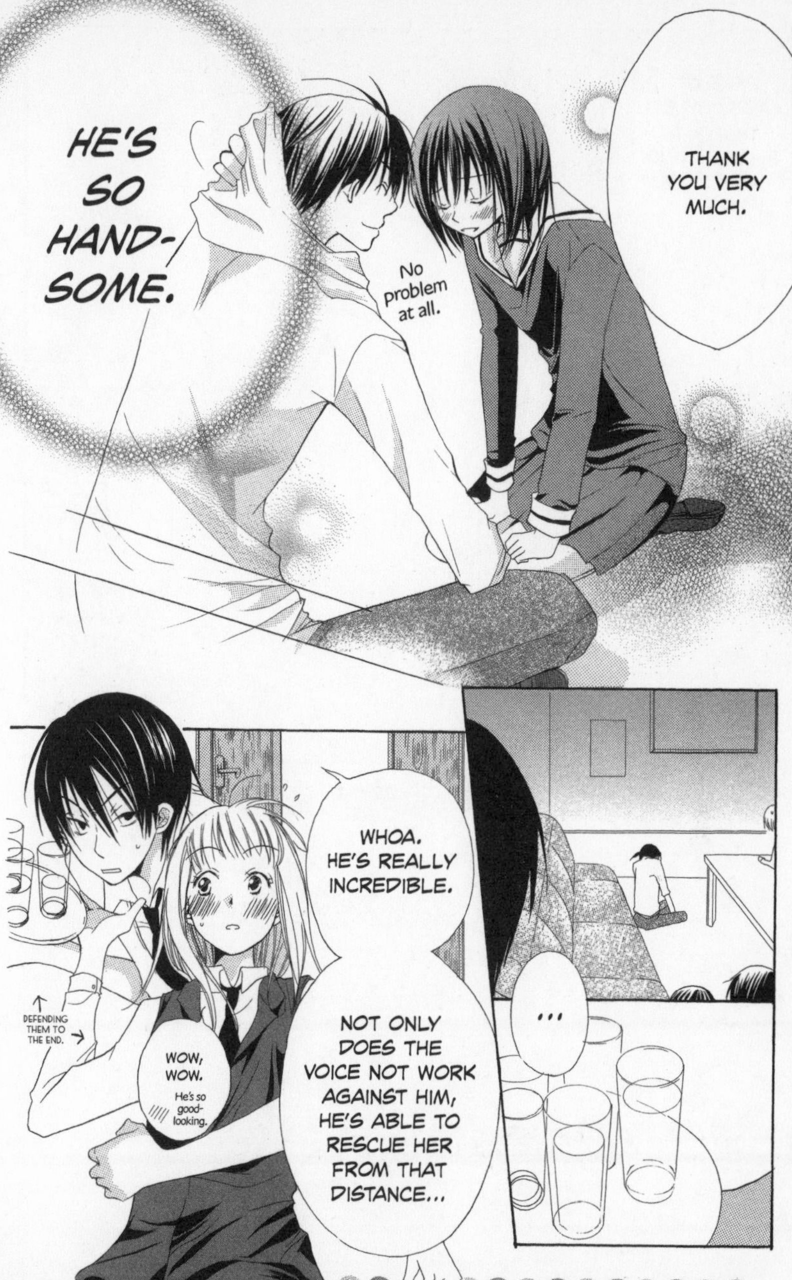
THANK YOU VERY MUCH.
No problem at all.
HE'S SO HANDSOME.
...
WHOA. HE'S REALLY INCREDIBLE.
NOT ONLY DOES THE VOICE NOT WORK AGAINST HIM, HE'S ABLE TO RESCUE HER FROM THAT DISTANCE...
WOW, WOW.
He's so good-looking.
DEFENDING THEM TO THE END.

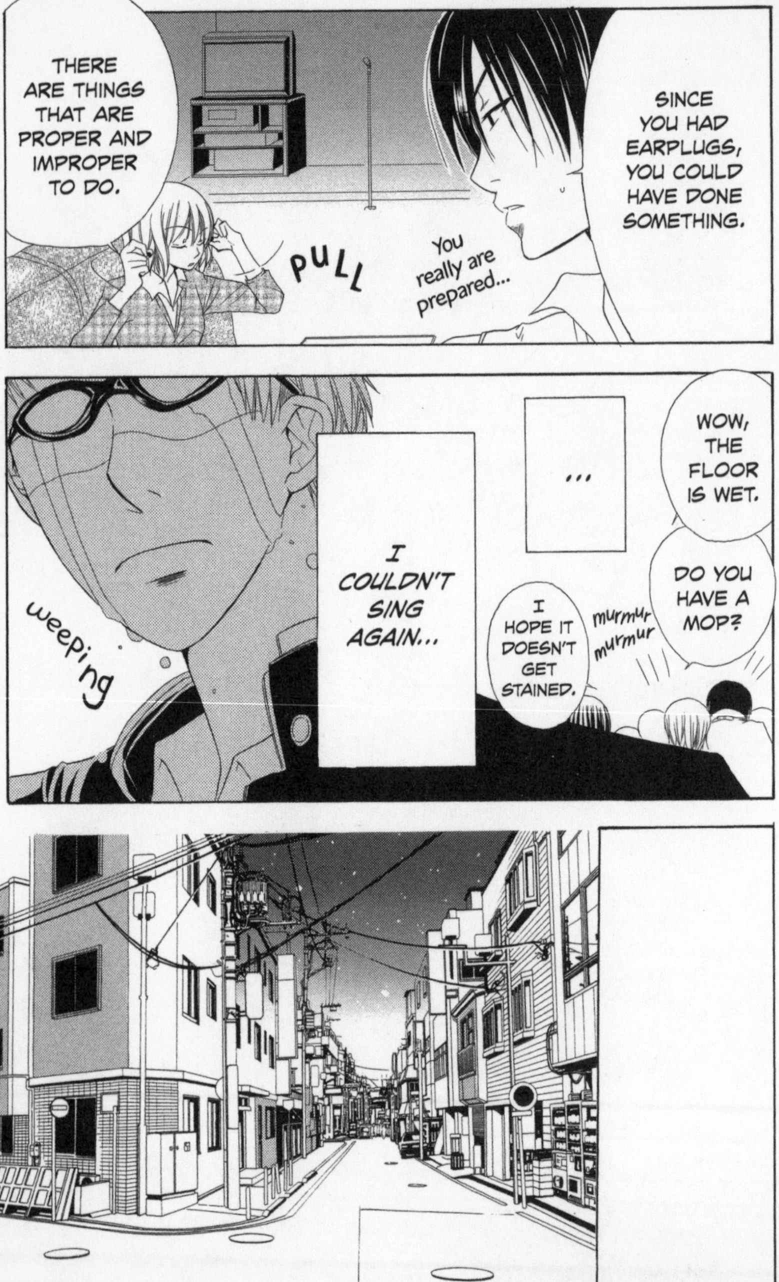
SINCE YOU HAD EARPLUGS, YOU COULD HAVE DONE SOMETHING.
You really are prepared...
PULL
THERE ARE THINGS THAT ARE PROPER AND IMPROPER TO DO.
WOW, THE FLOOR IS WET.
DO YOU HAVE A MOP?
...
murmur murmur
I HOPE IT DOESN'T GET STAINED.
I COULDN'T SING AGAIN...
weeping

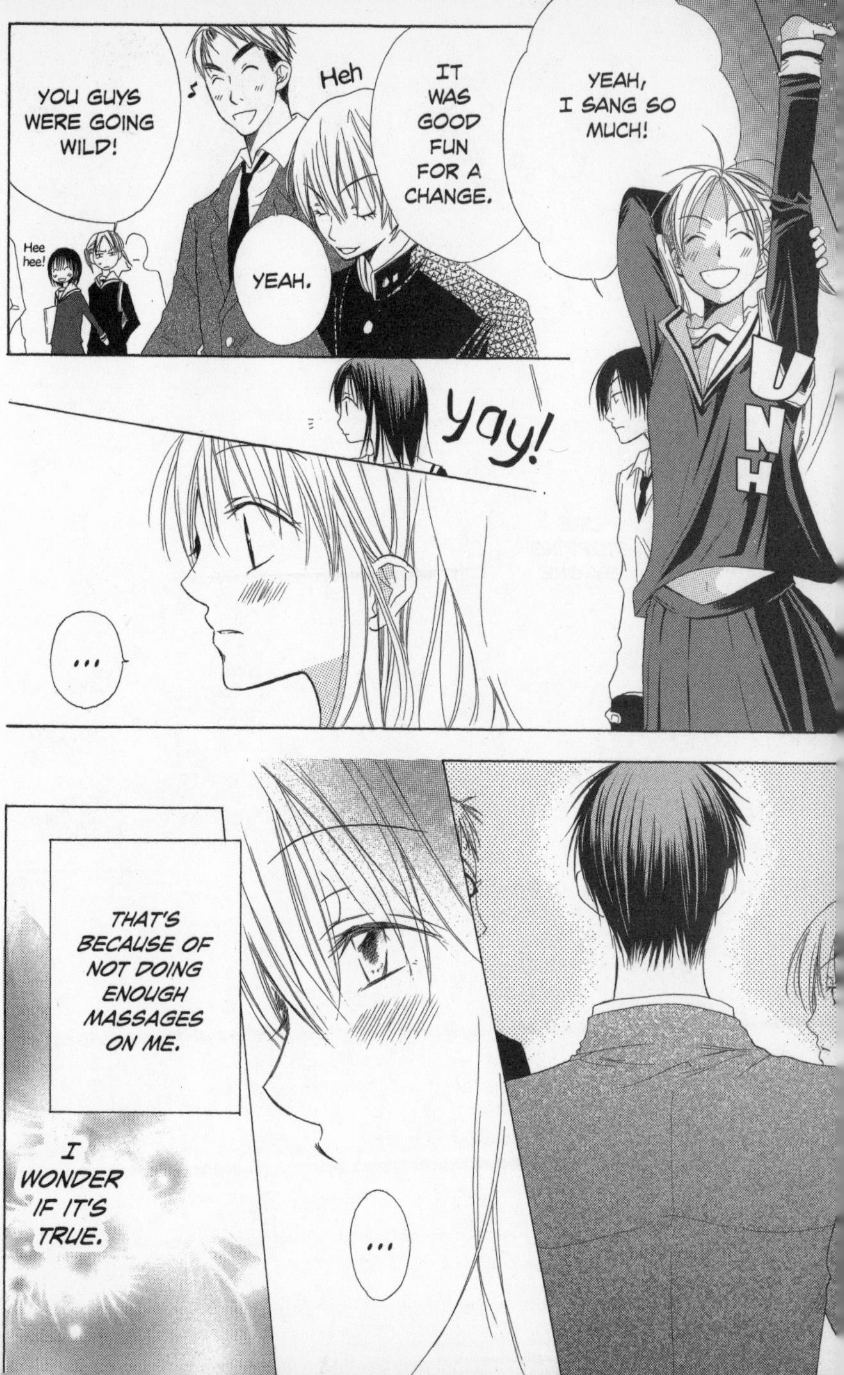
YEAH, I SANG SO MUCH!
yay!
IT WAS GOOD FUN FOR A CHANGE.
Heh
YOU GUYS WERE GOING WILD!
YEAH.
Hee hee!
...
THAT'S BECAUSE OF NOT DOING ENOUGH MASSAGES ON ME.
I WONDER IF IT'S TRUE.
...

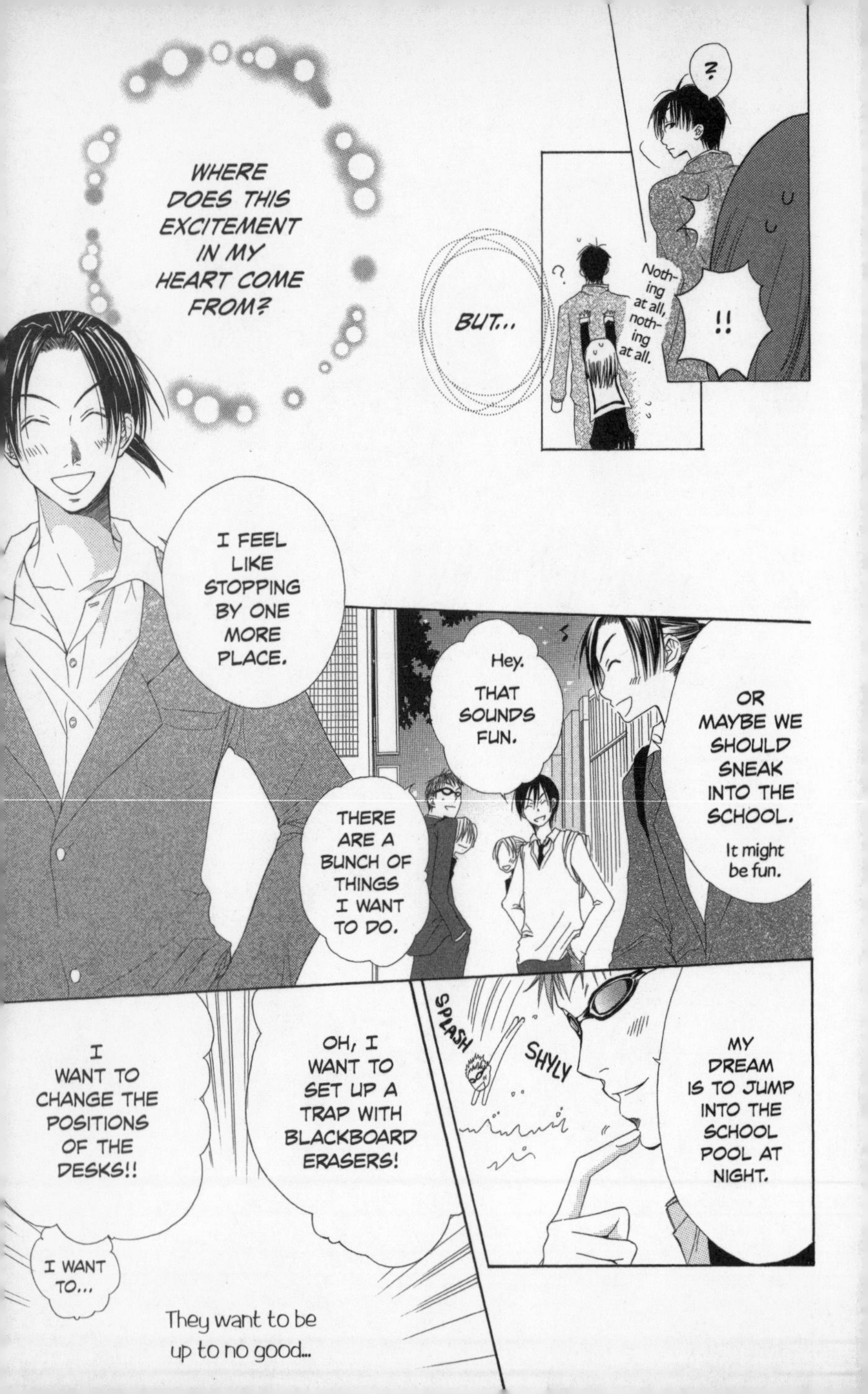
?
Nothing at all, nothing at all.
!!
?
BUT...
WHERE DOES THIS EXCITEMENT IN MY HEART COME FROM?
I FEEL LIKE STOPPING BY ONE MORE PLACE.
OR MAYBE WE SHOULD SNEAK INTO THE SCHOOL.
It might be fun.
Hey.
THAT SOUNDS FUN.
THERE ARE A BUNCH OF THINGS I WANT TO DO.
MY DREAM IS TO JUMP INTO THE SCHOOL POOL AT NIGHT.
SHYLY
SPLASH
OH, I WANT TO SET UP A TRAP WITH BLACKBOARD ERASERS!
I WANT TO CHANGE THE POSITIONS OF THE DESKS!!
I WANT TO...
They want to be up to no good...

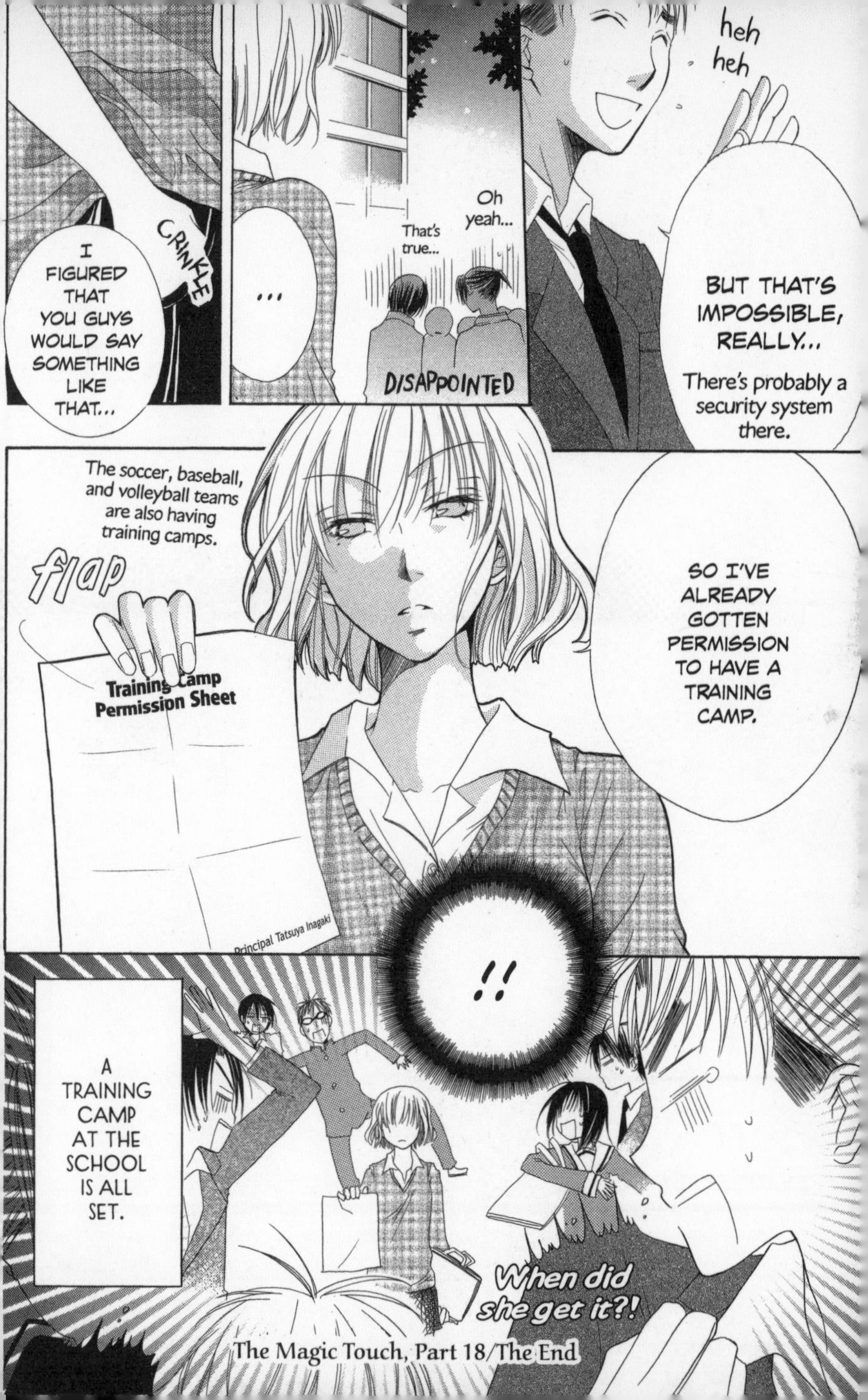
heh heh
BUT THAT'S IMPOSSIBLE, REALLY...
There's probably a security system there.
Oh yeah...
That's true...
DISAPPOINTED
...
CRINKLE
I FIGURED THAT YOU GUYS WOULD SAY SOMETHING LIKE THAT...
SO I'VE ALREADY GOTTEN PERMISSION TO HAVE A TRAINING CAMP.
The soccer, baseball, and volleyball teams are also having training camps.
flap
Training Camp Permission Sheet
Principal Tatsuya Inagaki
!!
A TRAINING CAMP AT THE SCHOOL IS ALL SET.
When did she get it?!
The Magic Touch, Part 18/The End

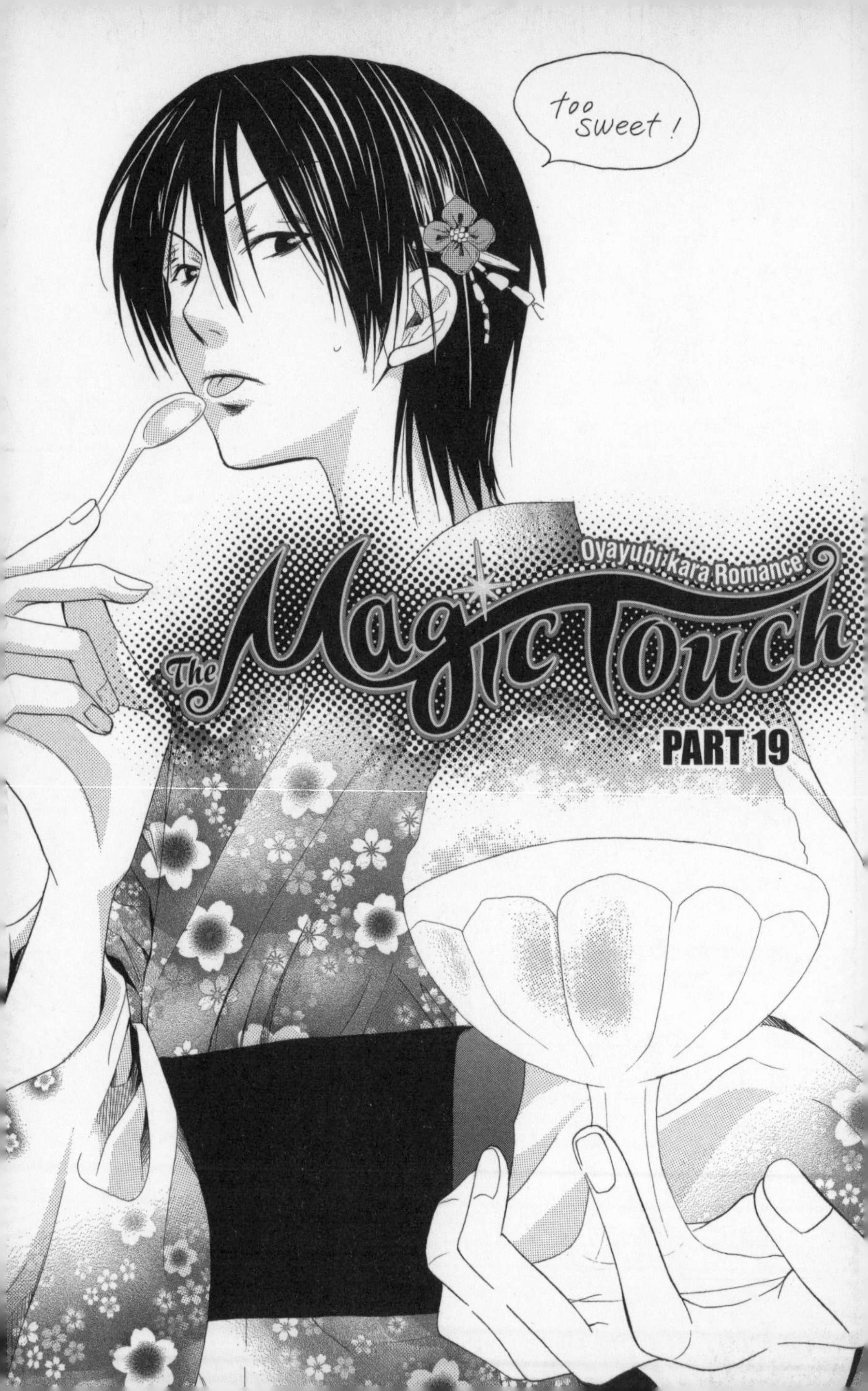
too sweet!
Oyayubi kara Romance
The Magic Touch
PART 19

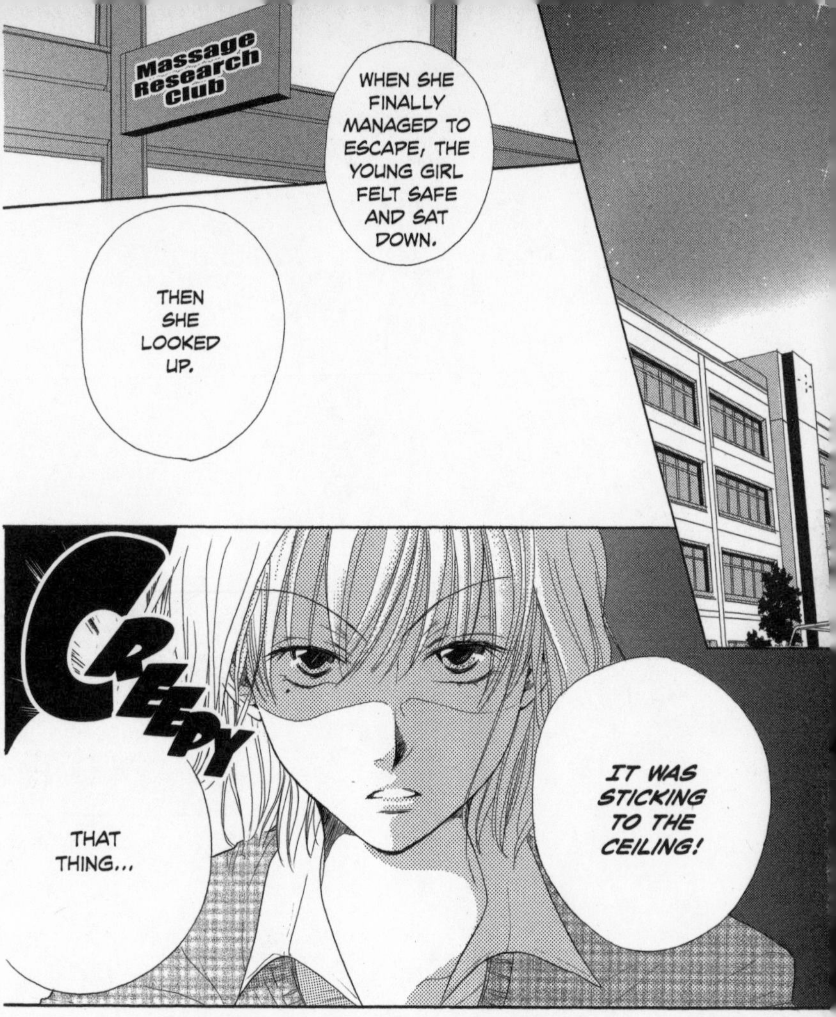
Massage Research Club
WHEN SHE FINALLY MANAGED TO ESCAPE, THE YOUNG GIRL FELT SAFE AND SAT DOWN.
THEN SHE LOOKED UP.
IT WAS STICKING TO THE CEILING!
CREEPY
THAT THING...

"I Love Radio"

I started listening to the radio after I began to draw manga. (If it's TV, I can't help but look up and watch it.) Talk radio and radio dramas are very interesting. I listen all the time, mesmerized at how the voices and conversational styles are really important because they don't use visual images. While listening to a show, I was thinking that I wished the person I heard would do the voice for my character. I was shocked that the opportunity really came up!

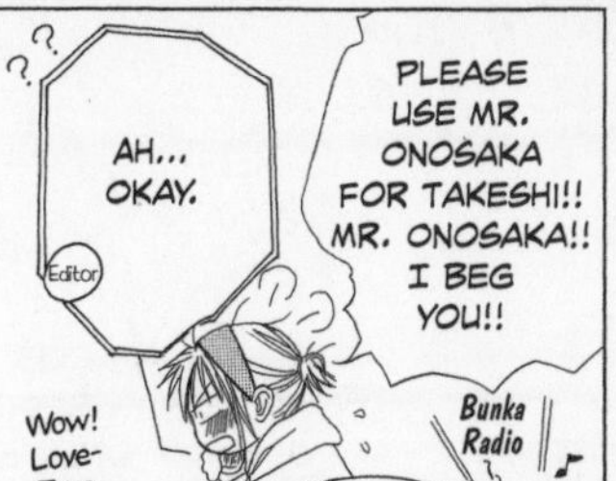
PLEASE USE MR. ONOSAKA FOR TAKESHI!! MR. ONOSAKA!! I BEG YOU!!
??
AH... OKAY.
Editor
Bunka Radio
HUGE FAN
Wow! Love-Emo, Love-Emo!

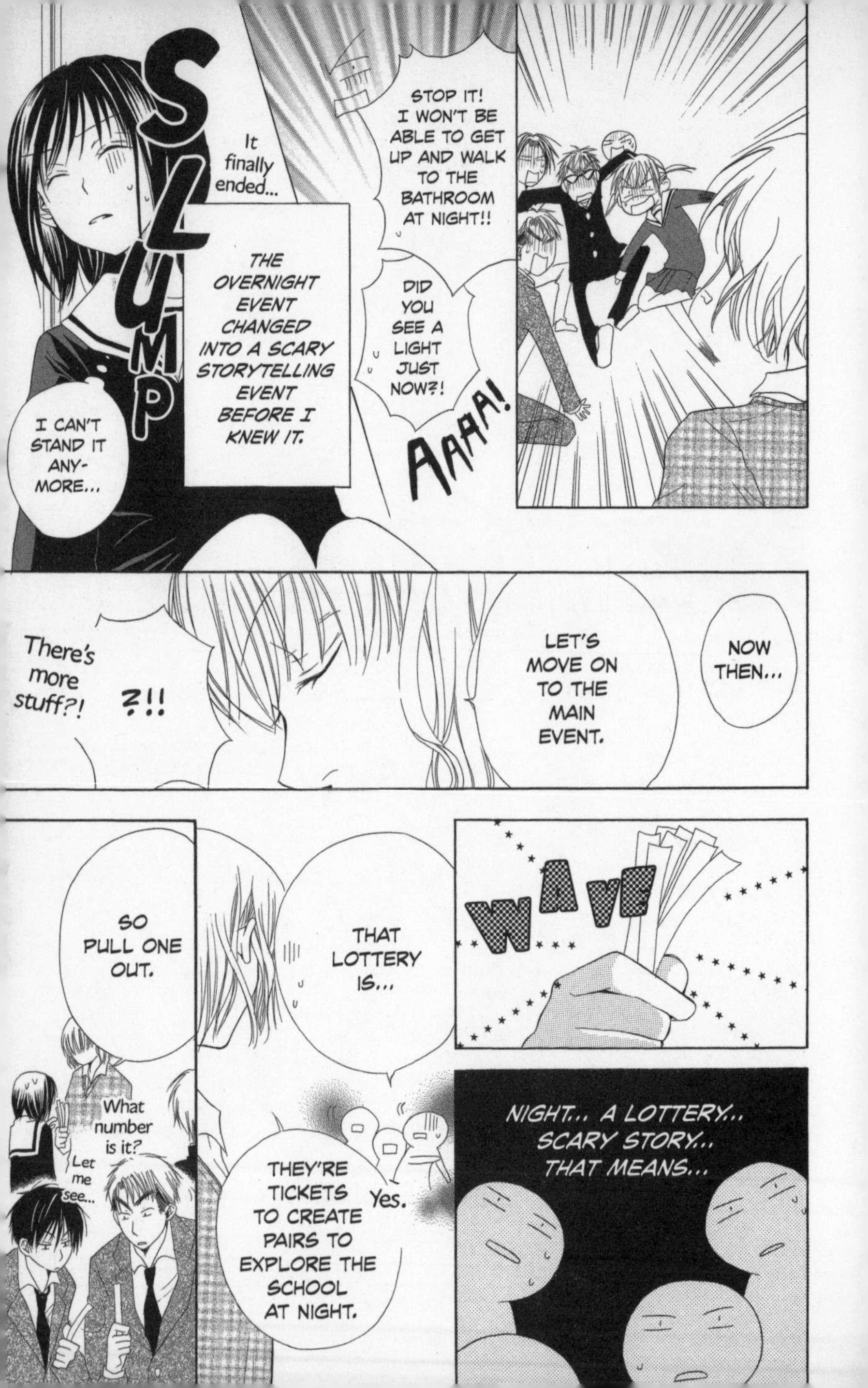
STOP IT! I WON'T BE ABLE TO GET UP AND WALK TO THE BATHROOM AT NIGHT!!
DID YOU SEE A LIGHT JUST NOW?!
AAAA!
It finally ended...
SLUMP
THE OVERNIGHT EVENT CHANGED INTO A SCARY STORYTELLING EVENT BEFORE I KNEW IT.
I CAN'T STAND IT ANY-MORE...
NOW THEN...
LET'S MOVE ON TO THE MAIN EVENT.
?!!
There's more stuff?!
WAVE
NIGHT... A LOTTERY... SCARY STORY... THAT MEANS...
THAT LOTTERY IS...
SO PULL ONE OUT.
THEY'RE TICKETS TO CREATE PAIRS TO EXPLORE THE SCHOOL AT NIGHT.
Yes.
What number is it?
Let me see...

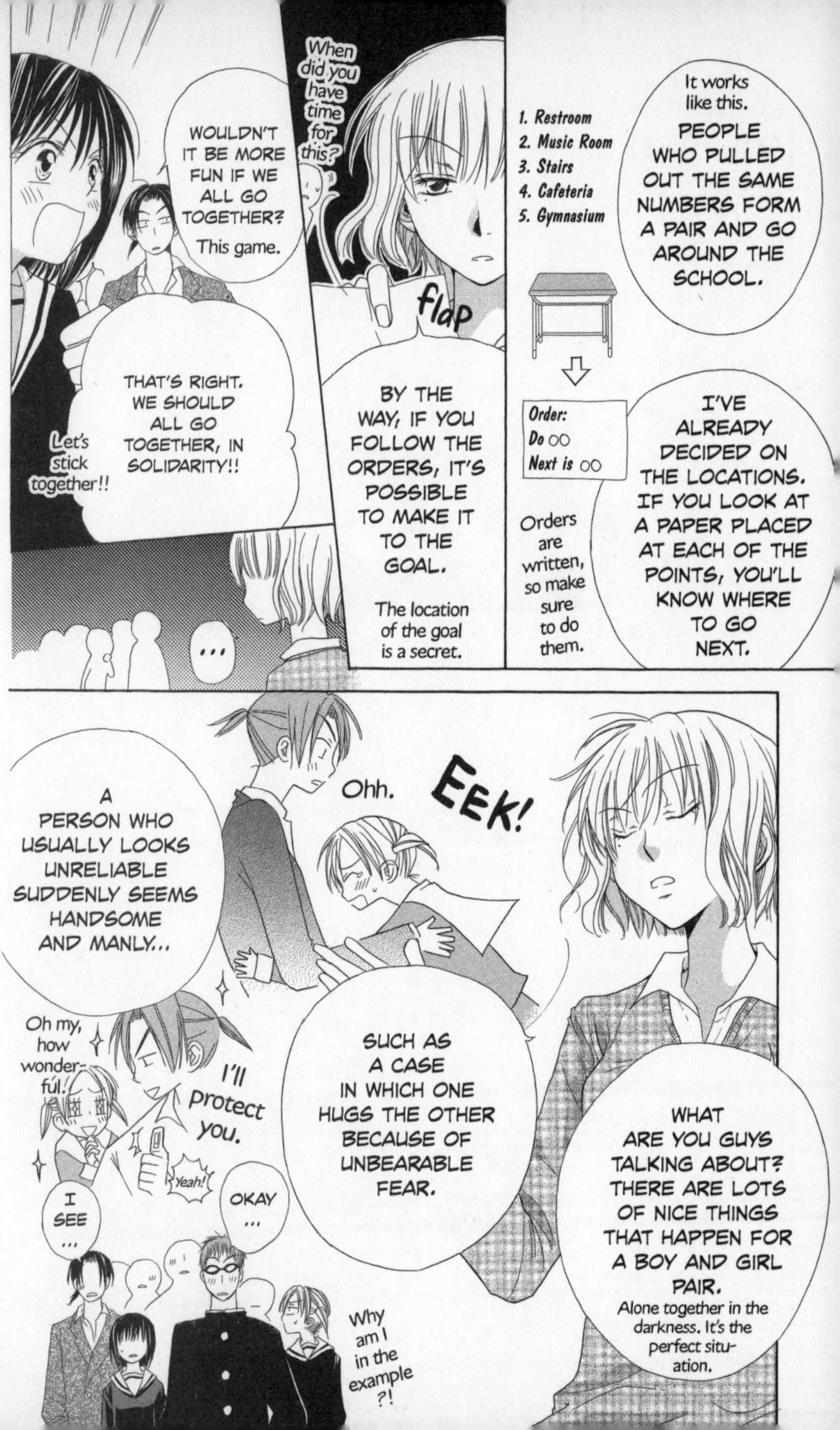
It works like this.
PEOPLE WHO PULLED OUT THE SAME NUMBERS FORM A PAIR AND GO AROUND THE SCHOOL.
1. Restroom
2. Music Room
3. Stairs
4. Cafeteria
5. Gymnasium
I'VE ALREADY DECIDED ON THE LOCATIONS. IF YOU LOOK AT A PAPER PLACED AT EACH OF THE POINTS, YOU'LL KNOW WHERE TO GO NEXT.
Order:
Do ○○
Next is ○○
Orders are written, so make sure to do them.
When did you have time for this?
flap
BY THE WAY, IF YOU FOLLOW THE ORDERS, IT'S POSSIBLE TO MAKE IT TO THE GOAL.
The location of the goal is a secret.
WOULDN'T IT BE MORE FUN IF WE ALL GO TOGETHER?
This game.
THAT'S RIGHT. WE SHOULD ALL GO TOGETHER, IN SOLIDARITY!!
Let's stick together!!
...
EEK!
Ohh.
WHAT ARE YOU GUYS TALKING ABOUT? THERE ARE LOTS OF NICE THINGS THAT HAPPEN FOR A BOY AND GIRL PAIR.
Alone together in the darkness. It's the perfect situ-ation.
SUCH AS A CASE IN WHICH ONE HUGS THE OTHER BECAUSE OF UNBEARABLE FEAR.
A PERSON WHO USUALLY LOOKS UNRELIABLE SUDDENLY SEEMS HANDSOME AND MANLY...
I'll protect you.
Oh my, how wonder-ful!
Yeah!
OKAY ...
I SEE ...
Why am I in the example ?!

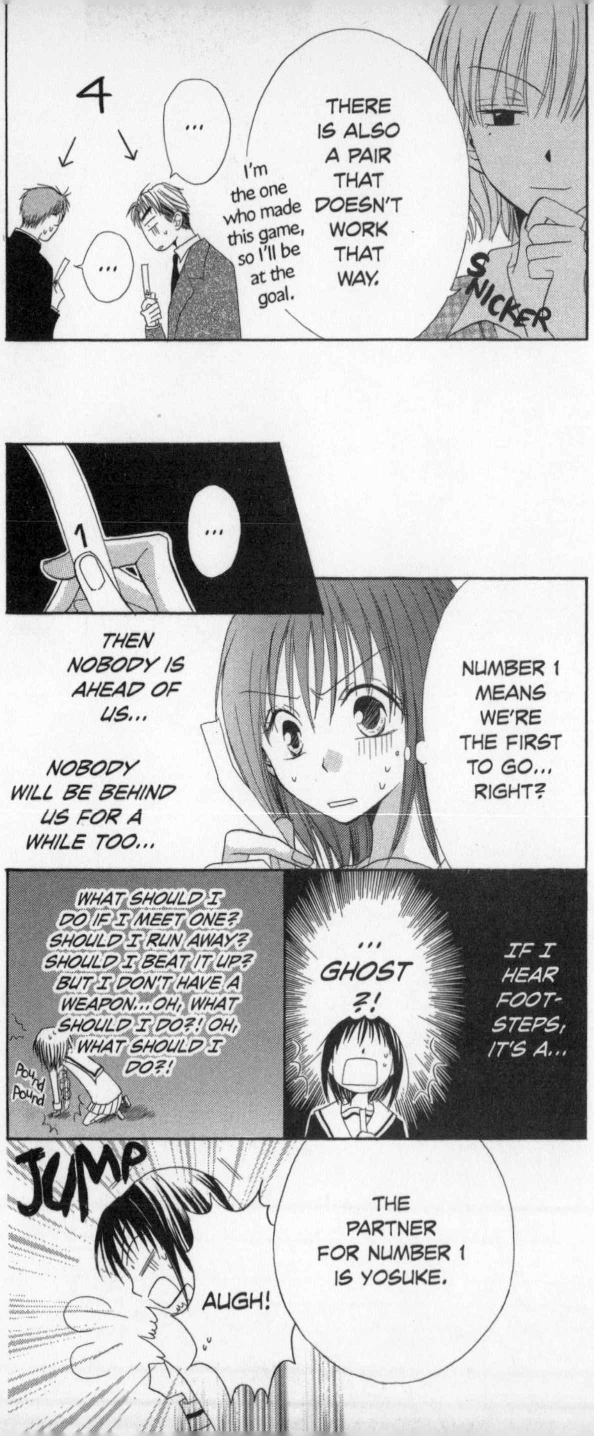
THERE IS ALSO A PAIR THAT DOESN'T WORK THAT WAY.
I'm the one who made this game, so I'll be at the goal.
SNICKER
4
...
...
...
1
NUMBER 1 MEANS WE'RE THE FIRST TO GO... RIGHT?
THEN NOBODY IS AHEAD OF US...
NOBODY WILL BE BEHIND US FOR A WHILE TOO...
IF I HEAR FOOTSTEPS, IT'S A...
...GHOST?!
WHAT SHOULD I DO IF I MEET ONE? SHOULD I RUN AWAY? SHOULD I BEAT IT UP? BUT I DON'T HAVE A WEAPON...OH, WHAT SHOULD I DO?! OH, WHAT SHOULD I DO?!
Pound Pound
THE PARTNER FOR NUMBER 1 IS YOSUKE.
AUGH!
JUMP

Plots, Part 1

Because I found lots of stories that I wrote in the past while I was cleaning my room, I would like to talk about plots this time.

To begin with, a plot is supposed to mean "story, outline or idea of a novel or a script." In other words, it becomes the foundation for a manga.

I believe the ordinary process is to make a broad version of the story in the plot and then divide it into frames during the "name" (rough draft). But because my plots were so weird, I would like to introduce them a little bit.

(I probably made them when I was in high school.)

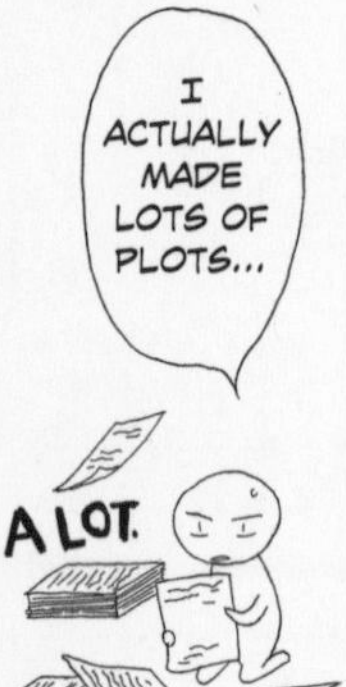
I ACTUALLY MADE LOTS OF PLOTS...
A LOT.

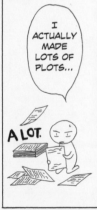

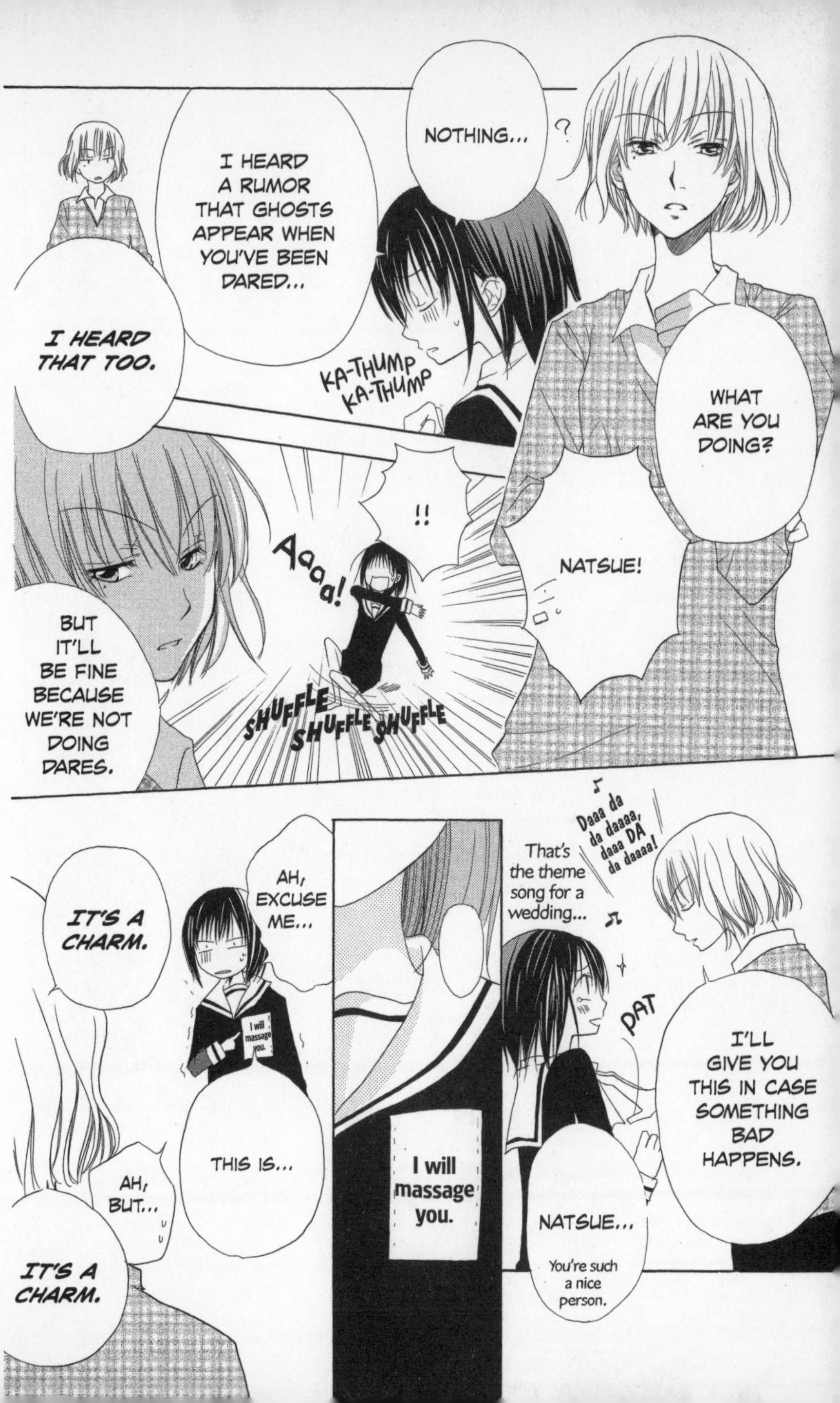
NATSUE!
WHAT ARE YOU DOING?
!!
Aaaa!
SHUFFLE SHUFFLE SHUFFLE
NOTHING...
?
I HEARD A RUMOR THAT GHOSTS APPEAR WHEN YOU'VE BEEN DARED...
KA-THUMP KA-THUMP
I HEARD THAT TOO.
BUT IT'LL BE FINE BECAUSE WE'RE NOT DOING DARES.
Daaa da da daaaa, daaa DA da daaaa!
That's the theme song for a wedding...
PAT
I'LL GIVE YOU THIS IN CASE SOMETHING BAD HAPPENS.
NATSUE...
You're such a nice person.
I will massage you.
AH, EXCUSE ME...
IT'S A CHARM.
I will massage you.
THIS IS...
AH, BUT...
IT'S A CHARM.

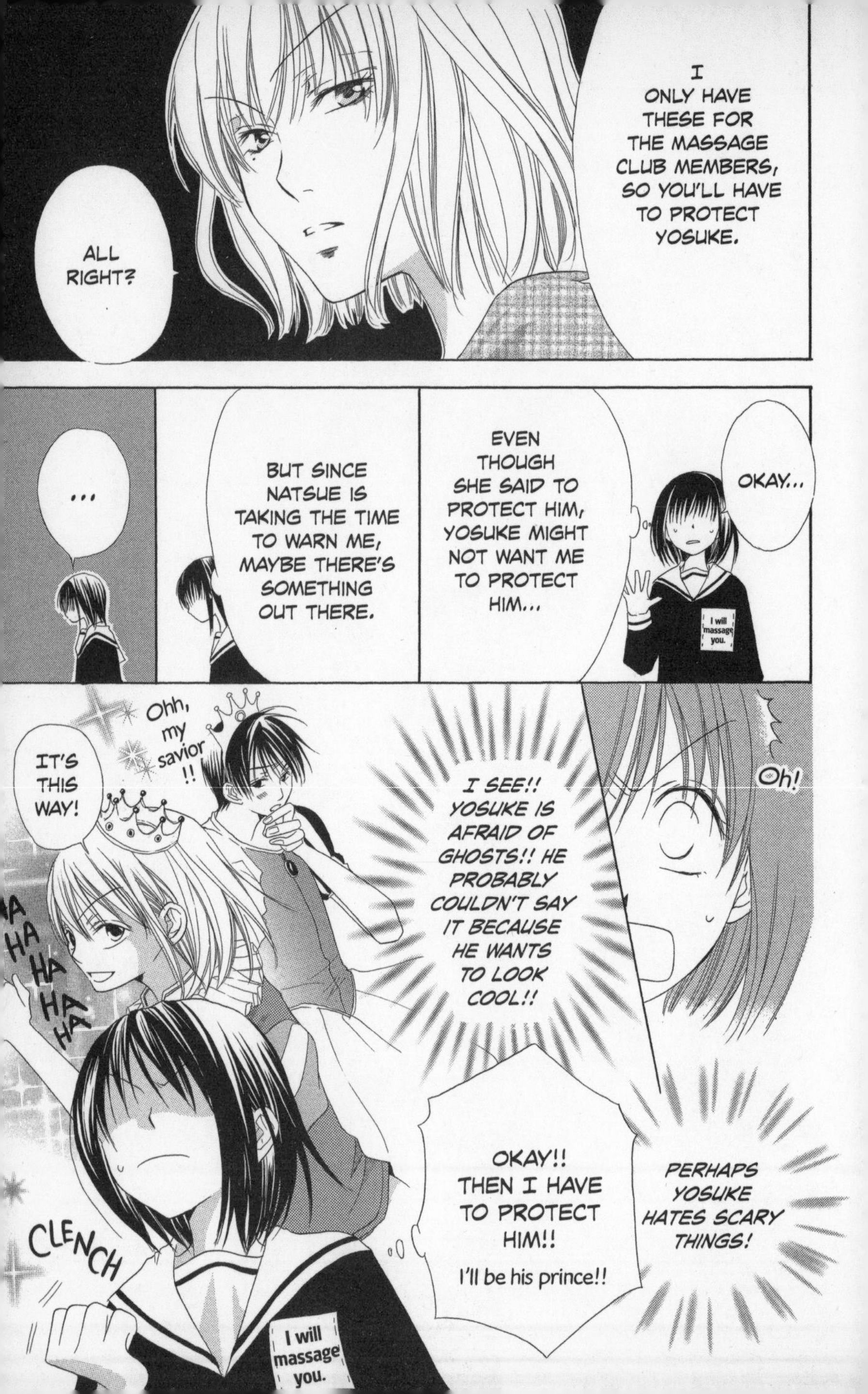
I ONLY HAVE THESE FOR THE MASSAGE CLUB MEMBERS, SO YOU'LL HAVE TO PROTECT YOSUKE.
ALL RIGHT?
OKAY...
EVEN THOUGH SHE SAID TO PROTECT HIM, YOSUKE MIGHT NOT WANT ME TO PROTECT HIM...
I will massage you.
BUT SINCE NATSUE IS TAKING THE TIME TO WARN ME, MAYBE THERE'S SOMETHING OUT THERE.
...
Oh!
I SEE!! YOSUKE IS AFRAID OF GHOSTS!! HE PROBABLY COULDN'T SAY IT BECAUSE HE WANTS TO LOOK COOL!!
PERHAPS YOSUKE HATES SCARY THINGS!
OKAY!! THEN I HAVE TO PROTECT HIM!!
I'll be his prince!!
Ohh, my savior!!
IT'S THIS WAY!
HA HA HA HA HA
CLENCH
I will massage you.

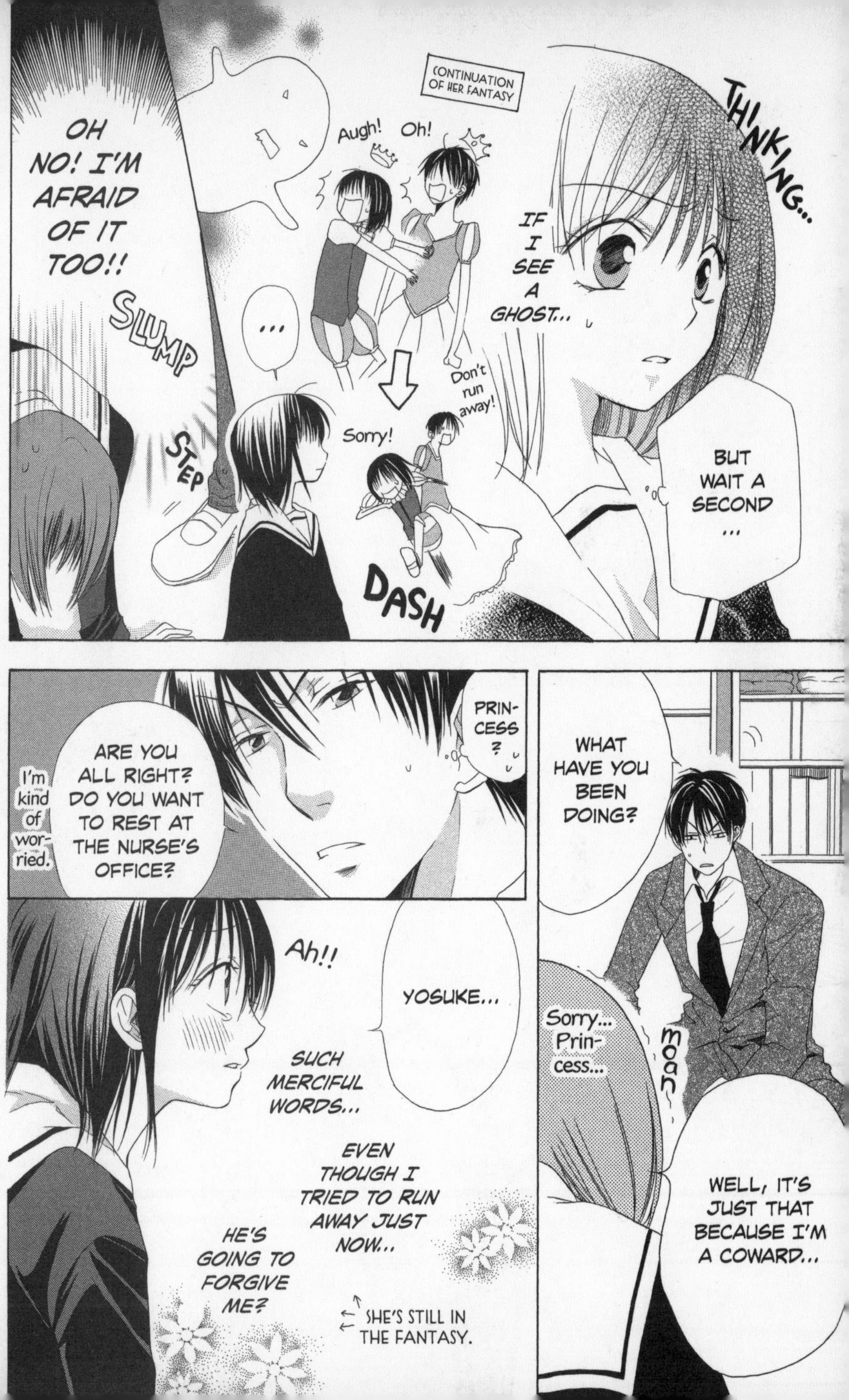
THINKING...
CONTINUATION OF HER FANTASY
IF I SEE A GHOST...
BUT WAIT A SECOND ...
Oh!
Augh!
...
Don't run away!
Sorry!
DASH
OH NO! I'M AFRAID OF IT TOO!!
SLUMP
STEP
WHAT HAVE YOU BEEN DOING?
moan
Sorry... Princess...
WELL, IT'S JUST THAT BECAUSE I'M A COWARD...
PRINCESS?
ARE YOU ALL RIGHT? DO YOU WANT TO REST AT THE NURSE'S OFFICE?
I'm kind of worried.
YOSUKE...
Ah!!
SUCH MERCIFUL WORDS...
EVEN THOUGH I TRIED TO RUN AWAY JUST NOW...
HE'S GOING TO FORGIVE ME?
SHE'S STILL IN THE FANTASY.

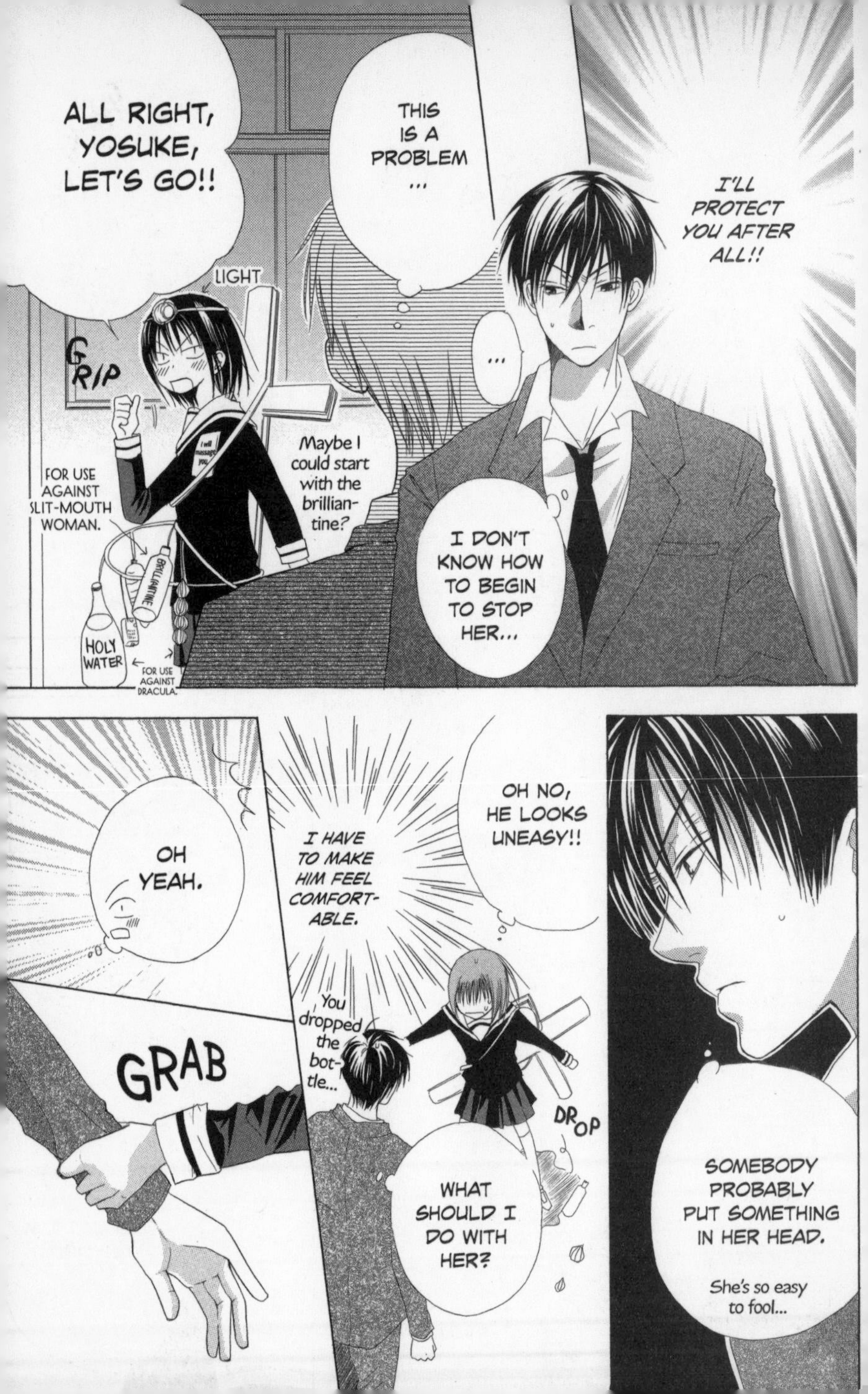
I'LL PROTECT YOU AFTER ALL!!
THIS IS A PROBLEM...
...
I DON'T KNOW HOW TO BEGIN TO STOP HER...
ALL RIGHT, YOSUKE, LET'S GO!!
LIGHT
GRIP
I will massage you
Maybe I could start with the brillian-tine?
FOR USE AGAINST SLIT-MOUTH WOMAN.
BRILLIANTINE
HOLY WATER
FOR USE AGAINST DRACULA.
SOMEBODY PROBABLY PUT SOMETHING IN HER HEAD.
She's so easy to fool...
OH NO, HE LOOKS UNEASY!!
I HAVE TO MAKE HIM FEEL COMFORT-ABLE.
You dropped the bot-tle...
DROP
WHAT SHOULD I DO WITH HER?
OH YEAH.
GRAB

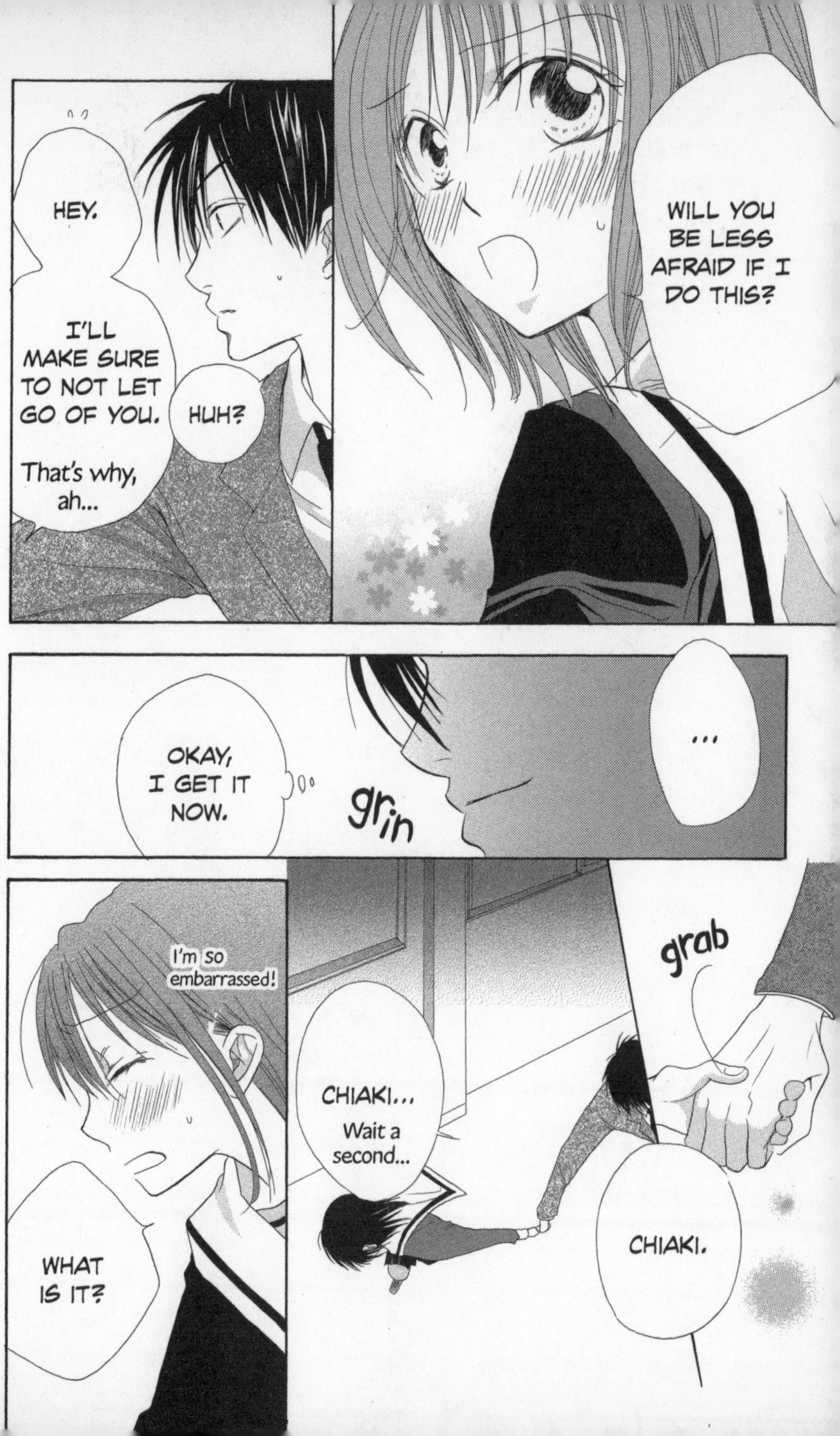
WILL YOU BE LESS AFRAID IF I DO THIS?
HEY.
I'LL MAKE SURE TO NOT LET GO OF YOU.
HUH?
That's why, ah...
...
grin
OKAY, I GET IT NOW.
grab
CHIAKI.
CHIAKI...
Wait a second...
I'm so embarrassed!
WHAT IS IT?

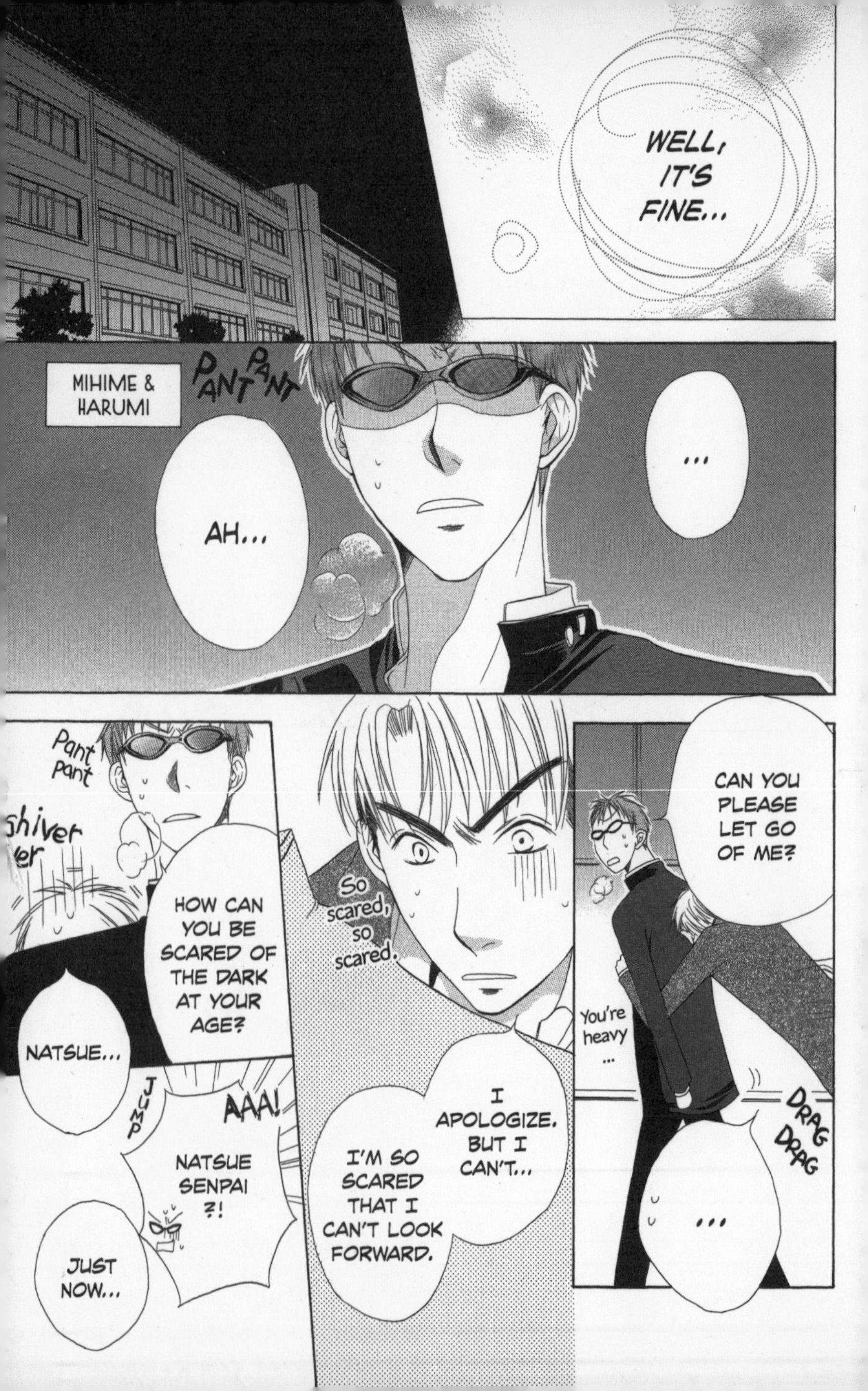
WELL, IT'S FINE...
...
PANT PANT
MIHIME & HARUMI
AH...
CAN YOU PLEASE LET GO OF ME?
You're heavy ...
DRAG DRAG
...
So scared, so scared.
I APOLOGIZE. BUT I CAN'T...
I'M SO SCARED THAT I CAN'T LOOK FORWARD.
Pant pant
shiver ver
HOW CAN YOU BE SCARED OF THE DARK AT YOUR AGE?
NATSUE...
AAA!
JUMP
NATSUE SENPAI ?!
JUST NOW...

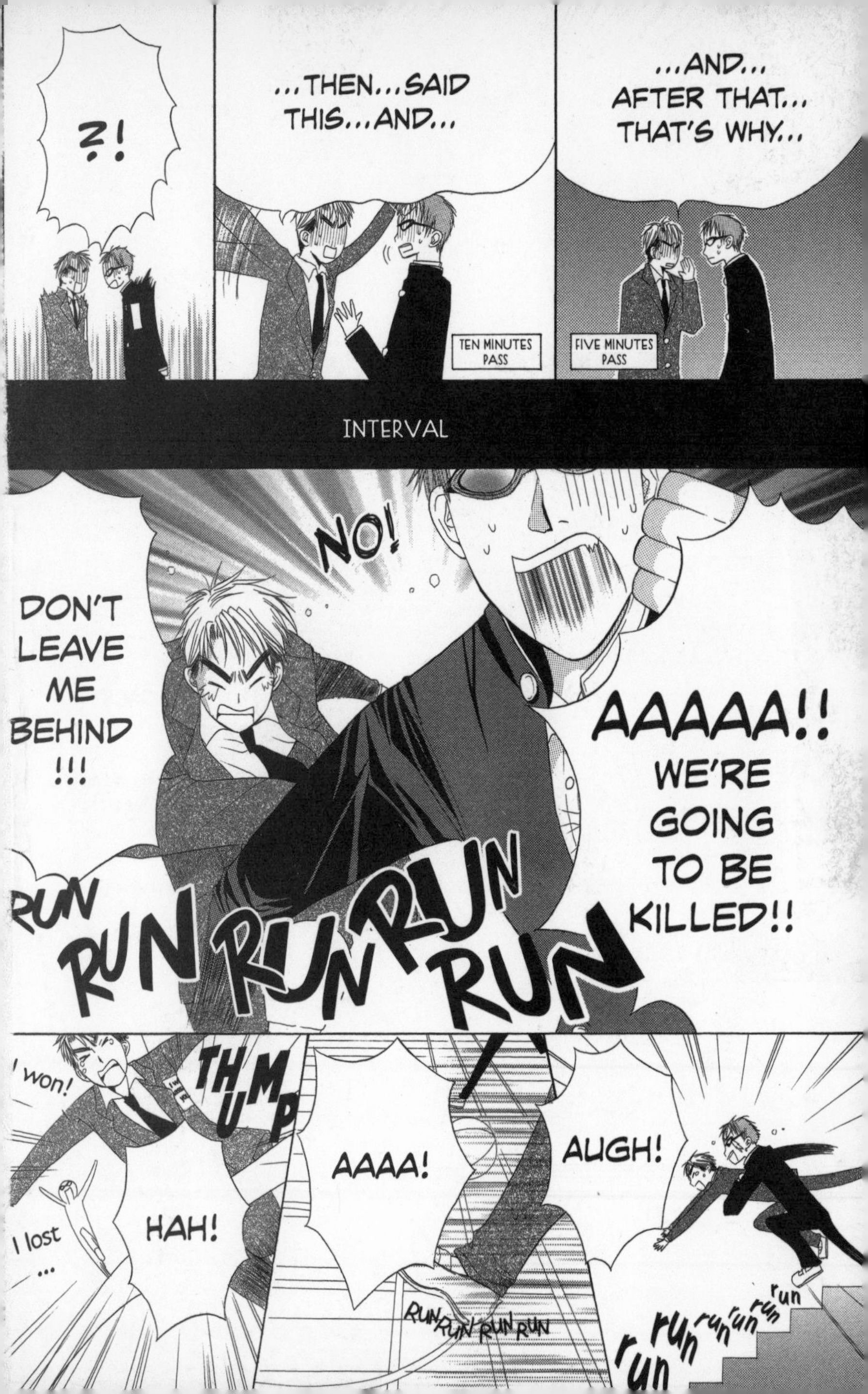
...AND... AFTER THAT... THAT'S WHY...
FIVE MINUTES PASS
...THEN...SAID THIS...AND...
TEN MINUTES PASS
?!
INTERVAL
AAAAA!! WE'RE GOING TO BE KILLED!!
NO!
DON'T LEAVE ME BEHIND !!!
RUN RUN RUN RUN RUN
AUGH!
run run run run run run
AAAA!
RUN RUN RUN RUN
I won!
THUMP
HAH!
I lost ...

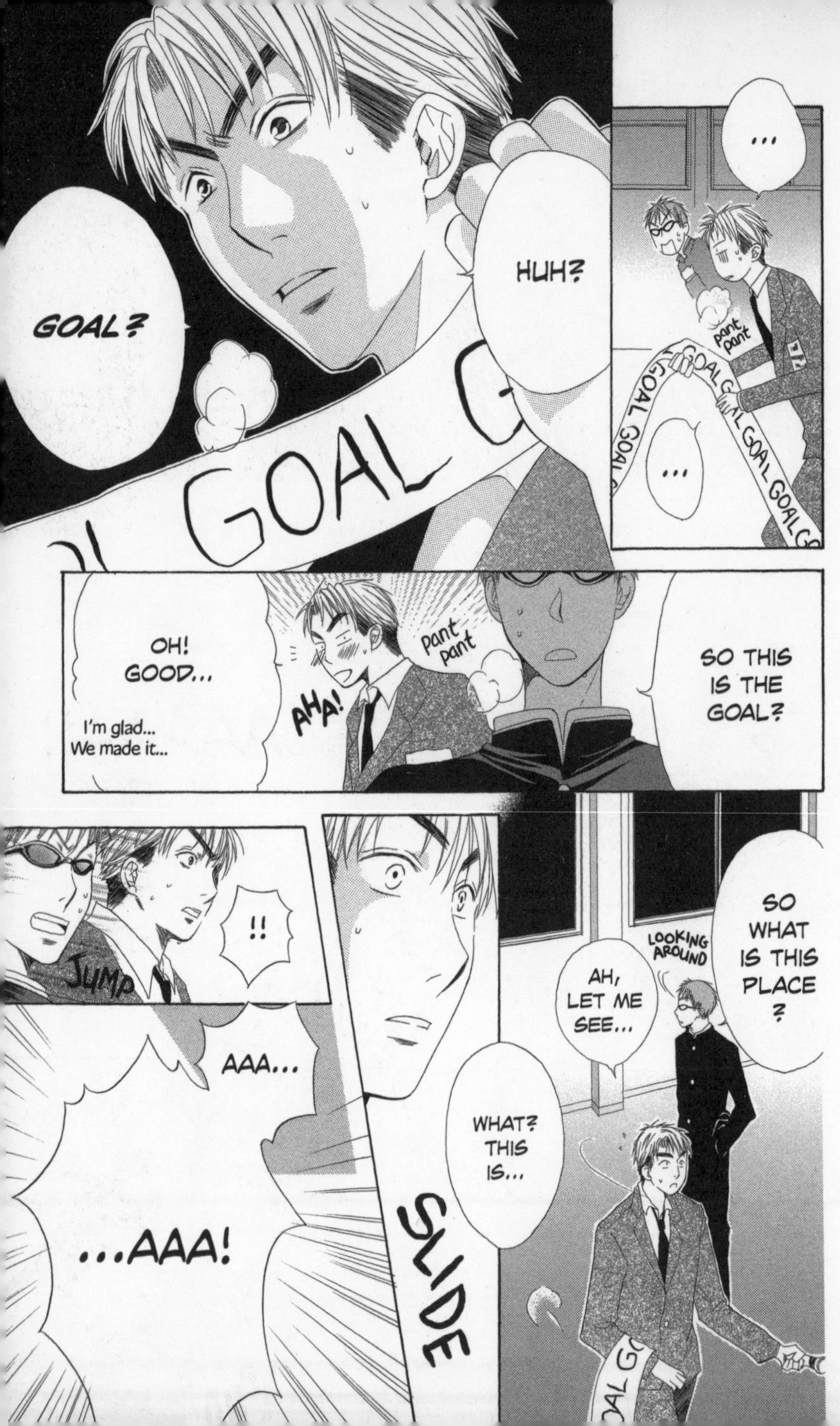
...
pant pant
GOAL
...
HUH?
GOAL?
GOAL
SO THIS IS THE GOAL?
pant pant
AHA!
OH! GOOD...
I'm glad... We made it...
SO WHAT IS THIS PLACE?
LOOKING AROUND
AH, LET ME SEE...
WHAT? THIS IS...
SLIDE
!!
JUMP
AAA...
...AAA!

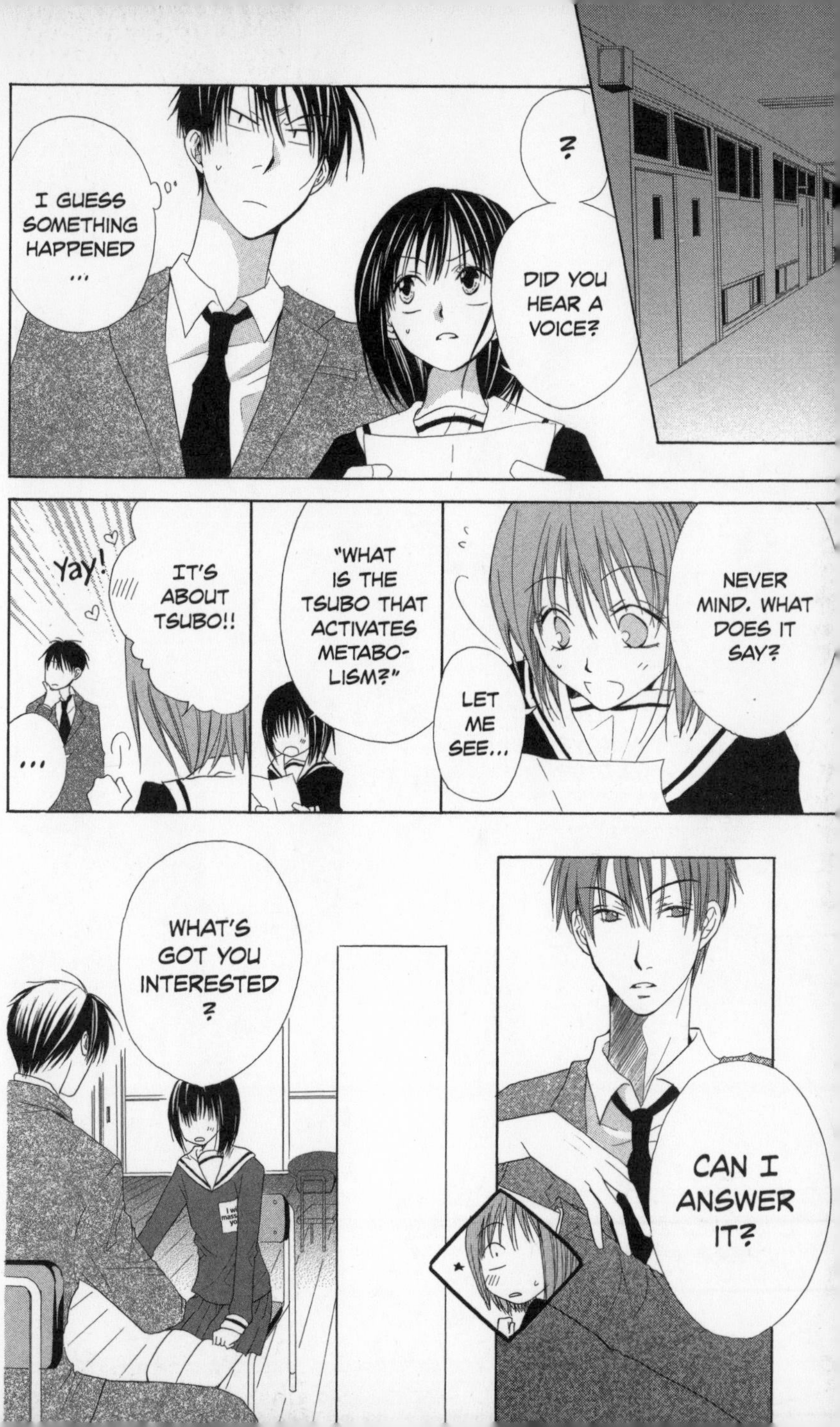
?
DID YOU HEAR A VOICE?
I GUESS SOMETHING HAPPENED ...
NEVER MIND. WHAT DOES IT SAY?
LET ME SEE...
"WHAT IS THE TSUBO THAT ACTIVATES METABOLISM?"
Yay!
IT'S ABOUT TSUBO!!
...
CAN I ANSWER IT?
WHAT'S GOT YOU INTERESTED?

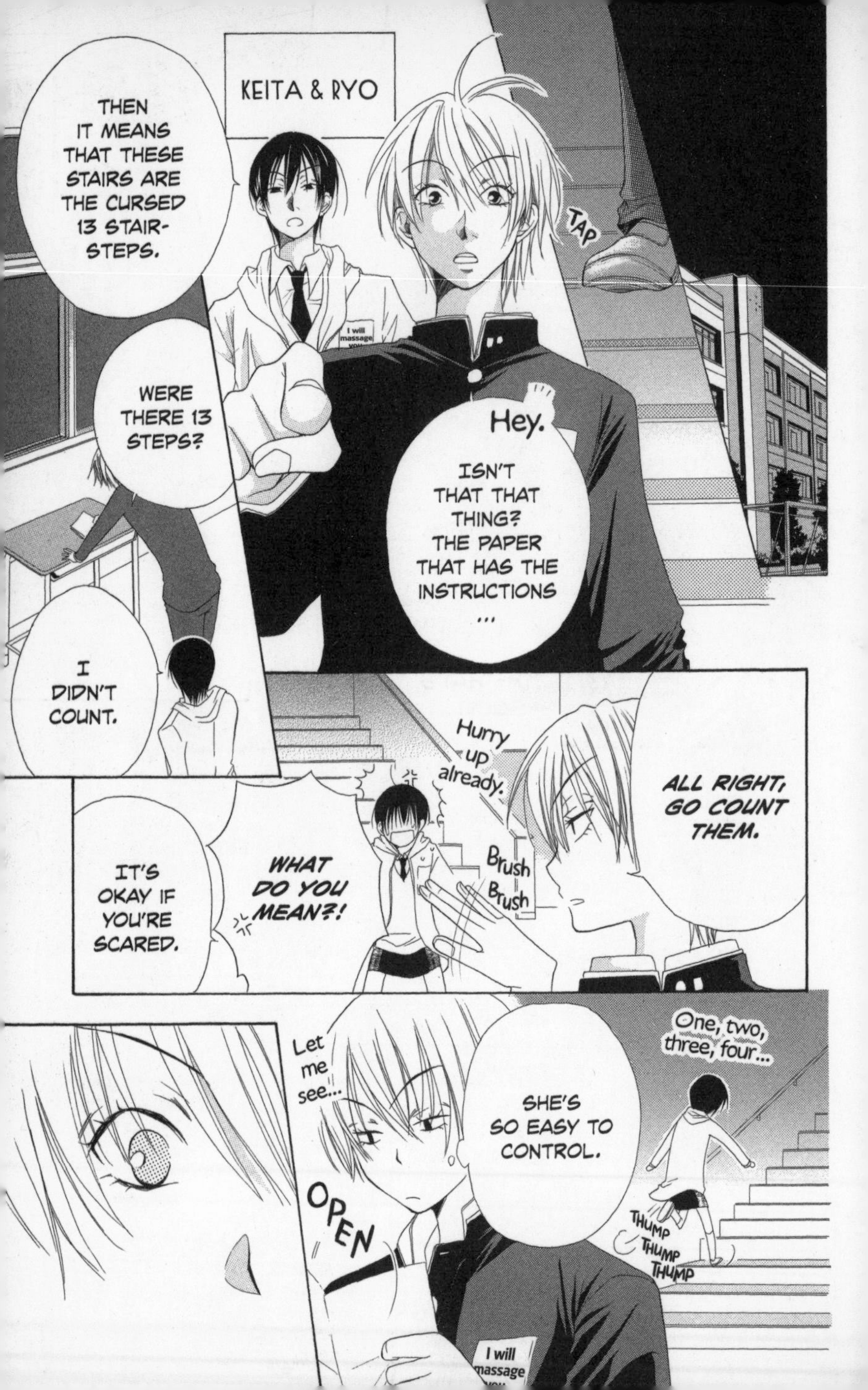
KEITA & RYO
TAP
Hey.
ISN'T THAT THAT THING? THE PAPER THAT HAS THE INSTRUCTIONS ...
I will massage
THEN IT MEANS THAT THESE STAIRS ARE THE CURSED 13 STAIR-STEPS.
WERE THERE 13 STEPS?
I DIDN'T COUNT.
ALL RIGHT, GO COUNT THEM.
Hurry up already.
Brush Brush
WHAT DO YOU MEAN?!
IT'S OKAY IF YOU'RE SCARED.
One, two, three, four...
THUMP THUMP THUMP
SHE'S SO EASY TO CONTROL.
Let me see...
OPEN
I will massage

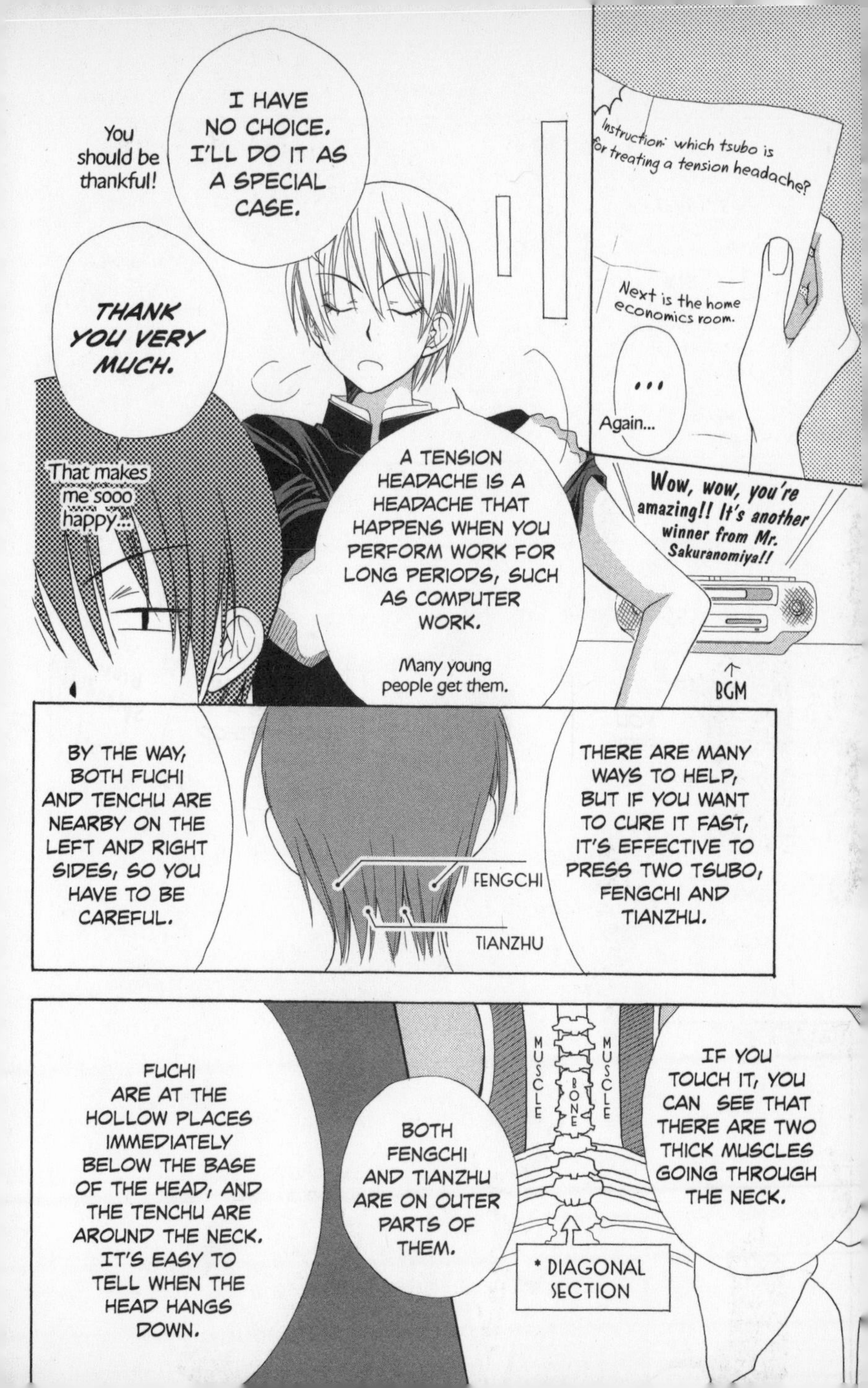

Instruction: which tsubo is for treating a tension headache?
Next is the home economics room.
...
Again...
Wow, wow, you're amazing!! It's another winner from Mr. Sakuranomiya!!
↑ BGM
I HAVE NO CHOICE. I'LL DO IT AS A SPECIAL CASE.
You should be thankful!
THANK YOU VERY MUCH.
A TENSION HEADACHE IS A HEADACHE THAT HAPPENS WHEN YOU PERFORM WORK FOR LONG PERIODS, SUCH AS COMPUTER WORK.
Many young people get them.
That makes me sooo happy...
THERE ARE MANY WAYS TO HELP, BUT IF YOU WANT TO CURE IT FAST, IT'S EFFECTIVE TO PRESS TWO TSUBO, FENGCHI AND TIANZHU.
FENGCHI
TIANZHU
BY THE WAY, BOTH FUCHI AND TENCHU ARE NEARBY ON THE LEFT AND RIGHT SIDES, SO YOU HAVE TO BE CAREFUL.
IF YOU TOUCH IT, YOU CAN SEE THAT THERE ARE TWO THICK MUSCLES GOING THROUGH THE NECK.
MUSCLE
BONE
MUSCLE
* DIAGONAL SECTION
BOTH FENGCHI AND TIANZHU ARE ON OUTER PARTS OF THEM.
FUCHI ARE AT THE HOLLOW PLACES IMMEDIATELY BELOW THE BASE OF THE HEAD, AND THE TENCHU ARE AROUND THE NECK. IT'S EASY TO TELL WHEN THE HEAD HANGS DOWN.

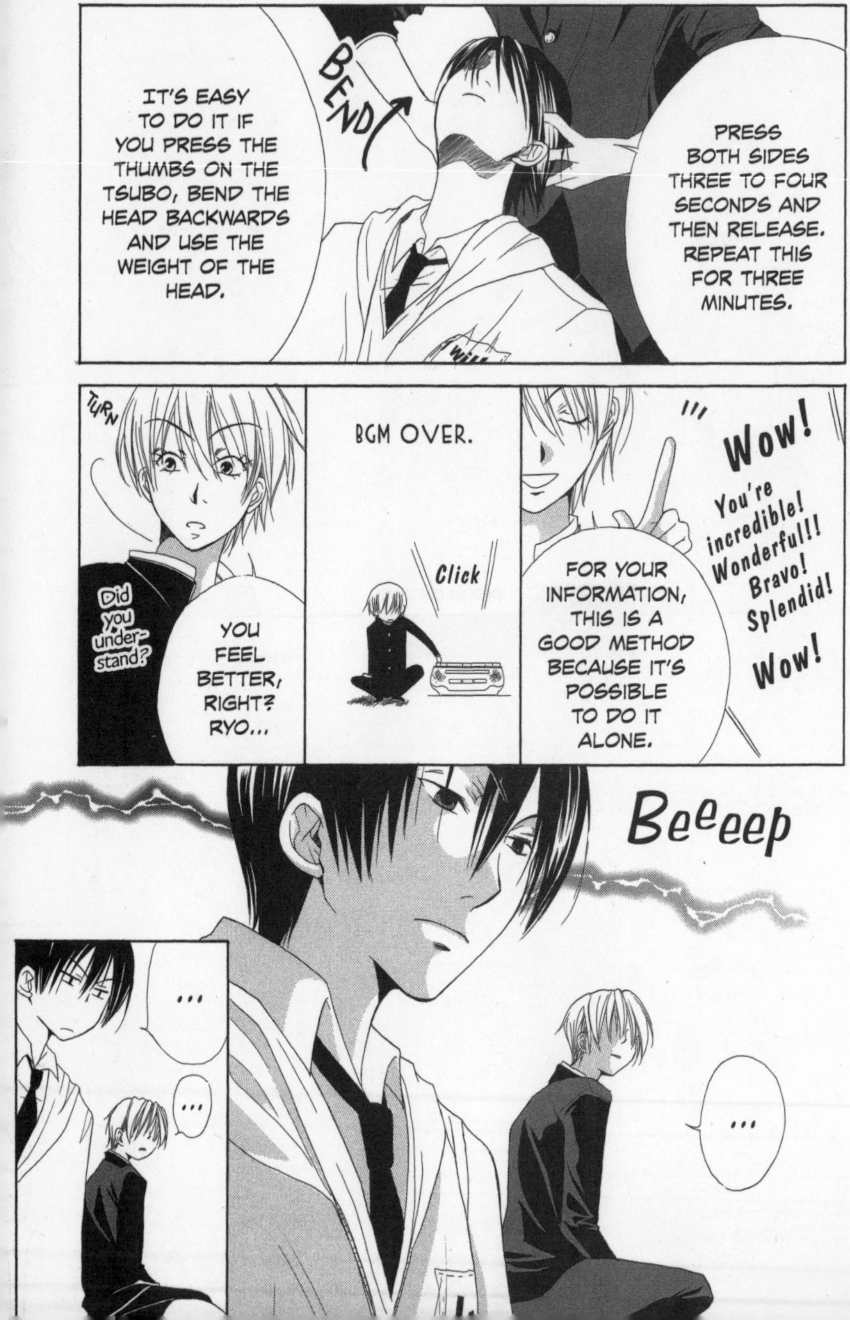
PRESS BOTH SIDES THREE TO FOUR SECONDS AND THEN RELEASE. REPEAT THIS FOR THREE MINUTES.
BEND
IT'S EASY TO DO IT IF YOU PRESS THE THUMBS ON THE TSUBO, BEND THE HEAD BACKWARDS AND USE THE WEIGHT OF THE HEAD.
Wow! You're incredible! Wonderful!! Bravo! Splendid! Wow!
FOR YOUR INFORMATION, THIS IS A GOOD METHOD BECAUSE IT'S POSSIBLE TO DO IT ALONE.
BGM OVER.
Click
TURN
YOU FEEL BETTER, RIGHT? RYO...
Did you under-stand?
Beeeep
...
...
...

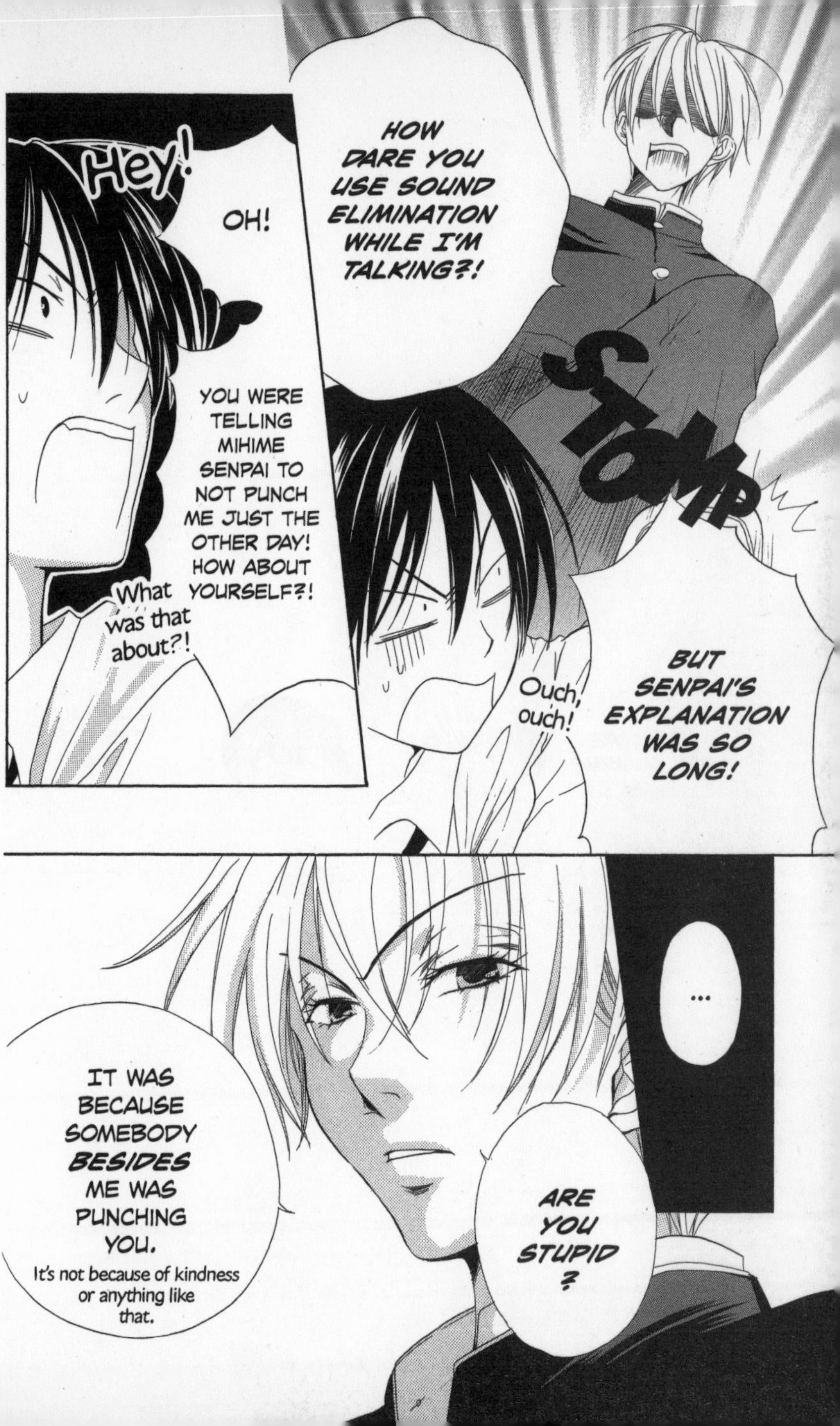
HOW DARE YOU USE SOUND ELIMINATION WHILE I'M TALKING?!
STOMP
BUT SENPAI'S EXPLANATION WAS SO LONG!
Ouch, ouch!
Hey!
OH!
YOU WERE TELLING MIHIME SENPAI TO NOT PUNCH ME JUST THE OTHER DAY! HOW ABOUT YOURSELF?!
What was that about?!
...
ARE YOU STUPID?
IT WAS BECAUSE SOMEBODY *BESIDES* ME WAS PUNCHING YOU.
It's not because of kindness or anything like that.

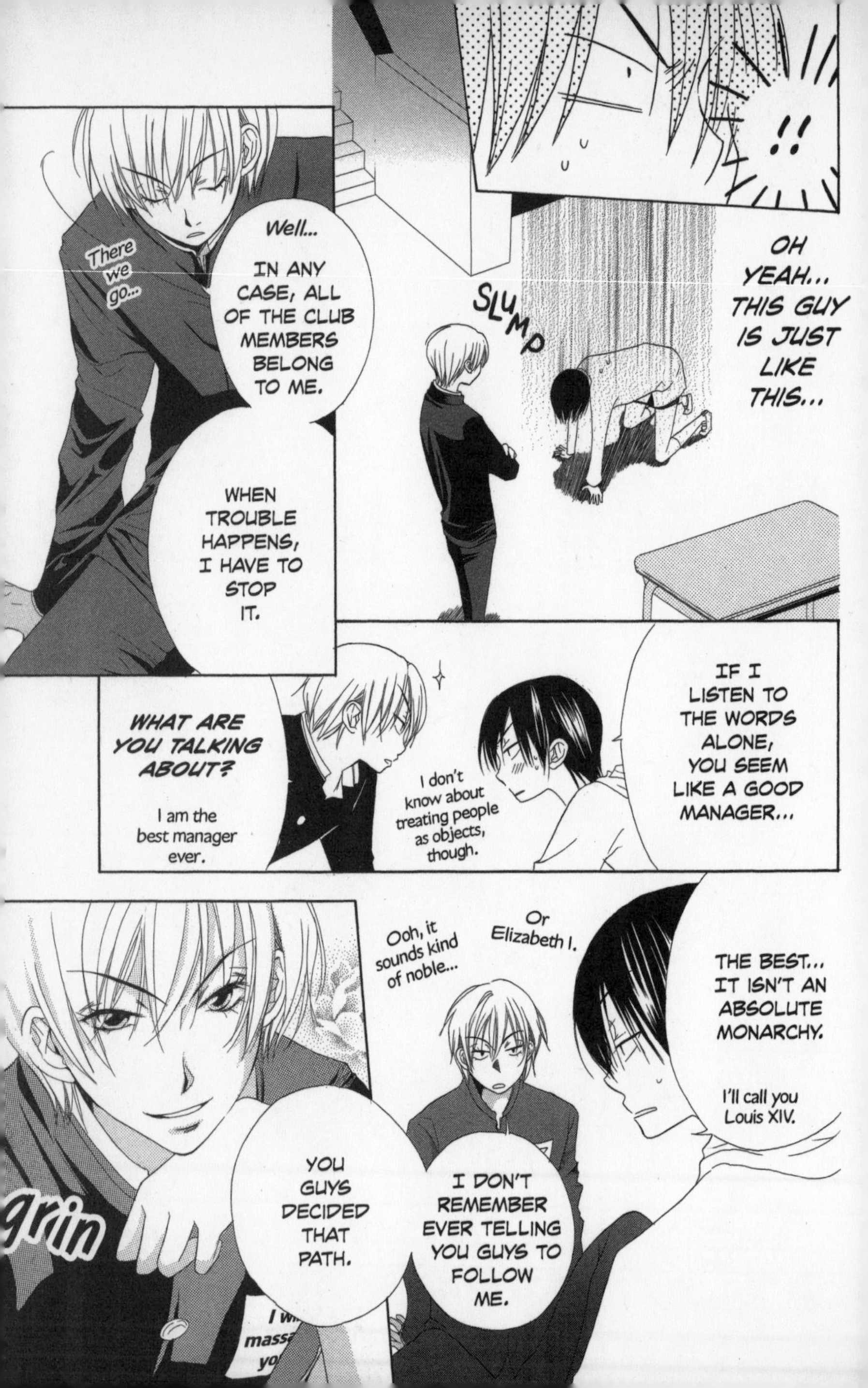
!!
OH YEAH... THIS GUY IS JUST LIKE THIS...
SLUMP
There we go...
Well...
IN ANY CASE, ALL OF THE CLUB MEMBERS BELONG TO ME.
WHEN TROUBLE HAPPENS, I HAVE TO STOP IT.
IF I LISTEN TO THE WORDS ALONE, YOU SEEM LIKE A GOOD MANAGER...
I don't know about treating people as objects, though.
WHAT ARE YOU TALKING ABOUT?
I am the best manager ever.
THE BEST... IT ISN'T AN ABSOLUTE MONARCHY.
I'll call you Louis XIV.
Or Elizabeth I.
Ooh, it sounds kind of noble...
I DON'T REMEMBER EVER TELLING YOU GUYS TO FOLLOW ME.
YOU GUYS DECIDED THAT PATH.
grin

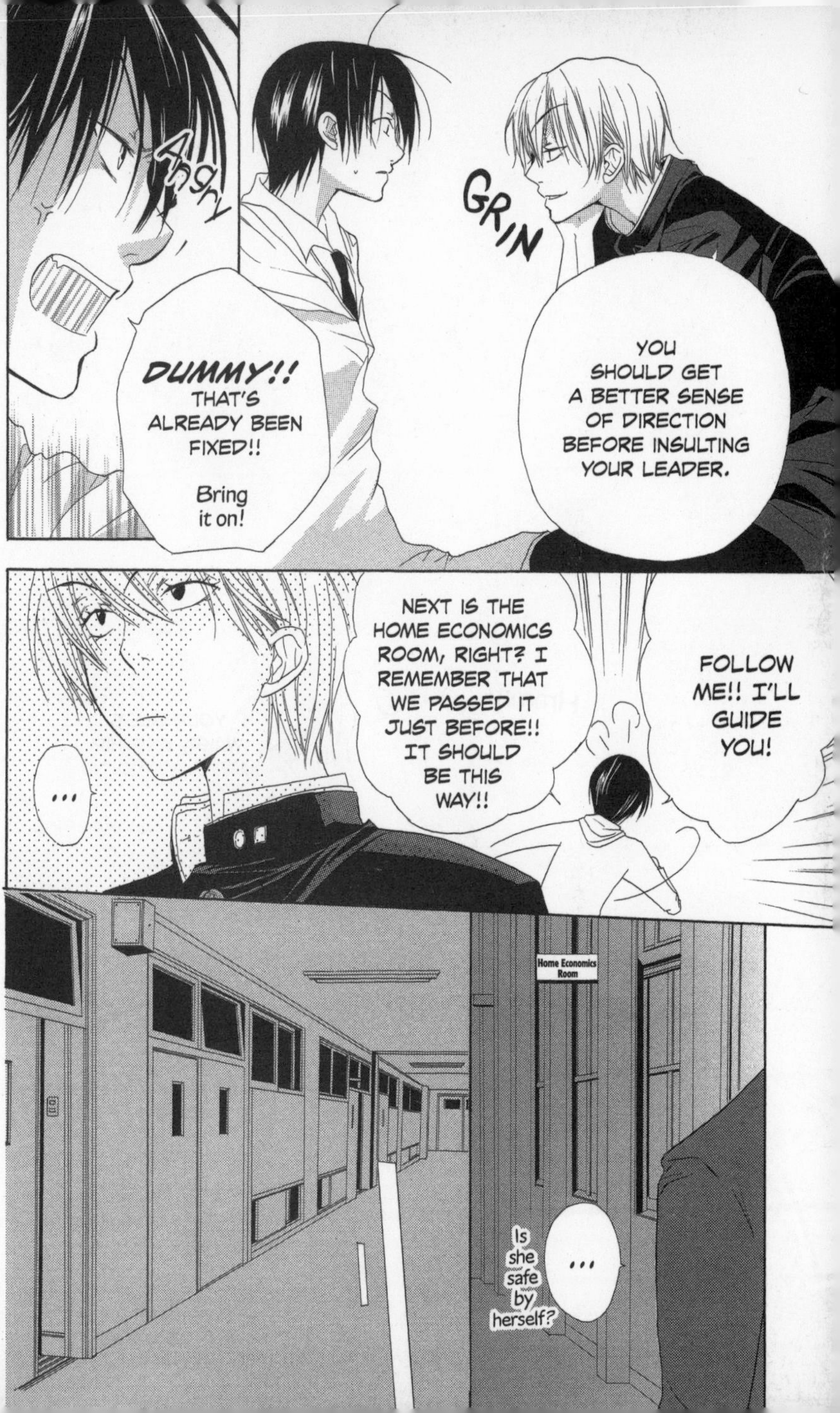
GRIN
YOU SHOULD GET A BETTER SENSE OF DIRECTION BEFORE INSULTING YOUR LEADER.
Angry
DUMMY!! THAT'S ALREADY BEEN FIXED!!
Bring it on!
FOLLOW ME!! I'LL GUIDE YOU!
NEXT IS THE HOME ECONOMICS ROOM, RIGHT? I REMEMBER THAT WE PASSED IT JUST BEFORE!! IT SHOULD BE THIS WAY!!
...
Home Economics Room
...
Is she safe by herself?

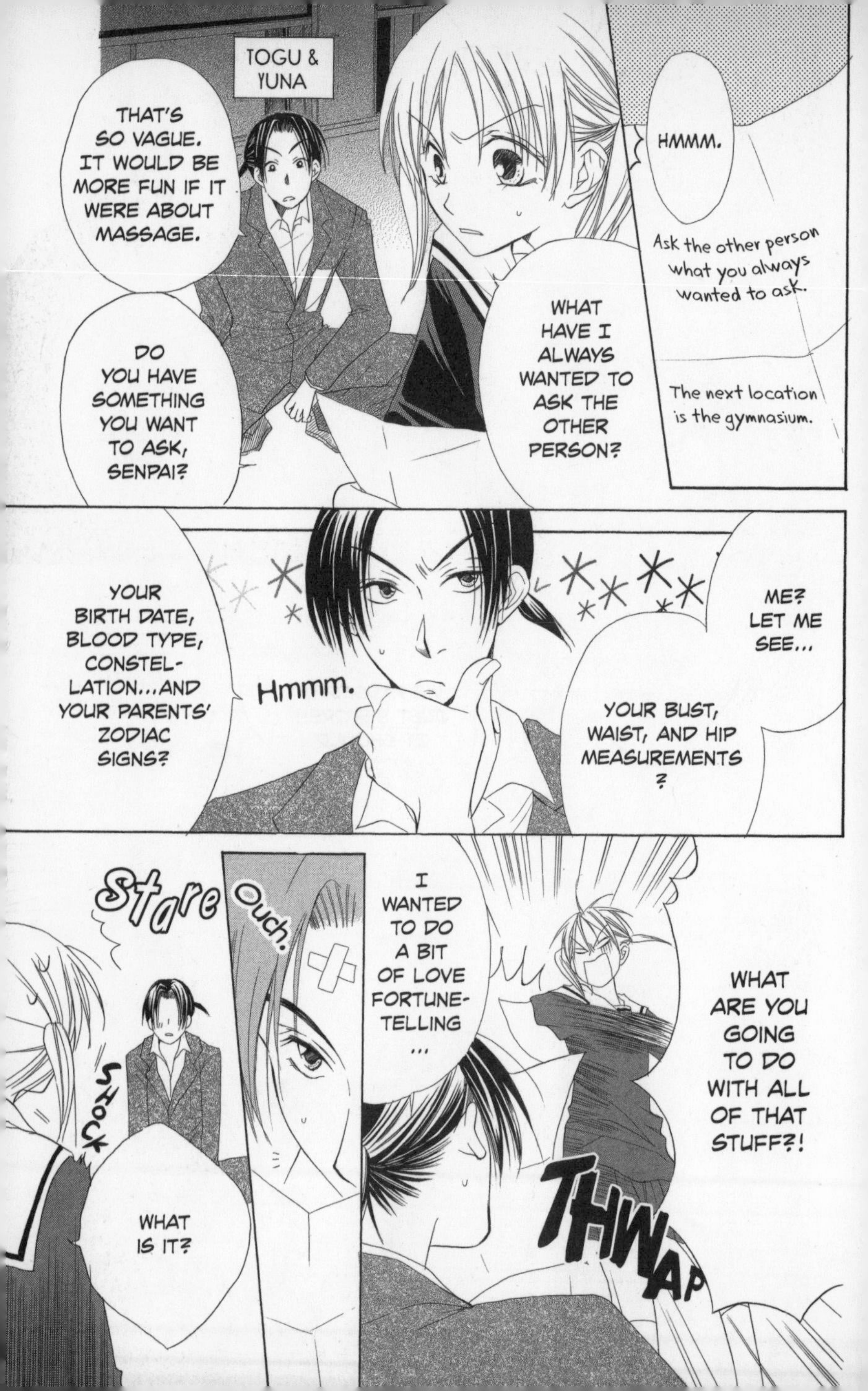
HMMM.
Ask the other person what you always wanted to ask.
The next location is the gymnasium.
TOGU & YUNA
WHAT HAVE I ALWAYS WANTED TO ASK THE OTHER PERSON?
THAT'S SO VAGUE. IT WOULD BE MORE FUN IF IT WERE ABOUT MASSAGE.
DO YOU HAVE SOMETHING YOU WANT TO ASK, SENPAI?
ME? LET ME SEE...
YOUR BUST, WAIST, AND HIP MEASUREMENTS?
Hmmm.
YOUR BIRTH DATE, BLOOD TYPE, CONSTEL-LATION...AND YOUR PARENTS' ZODIAC SIGNS?
WHAT ARE YOU GOING TO DO WITH ALL OF THAT STUFF?!
THWAP
I WANTED TO DO A BIT OF LOVE FORTUNE-TELLING...
Ouch.
Stare
SHOCK
WHAT IS IT?

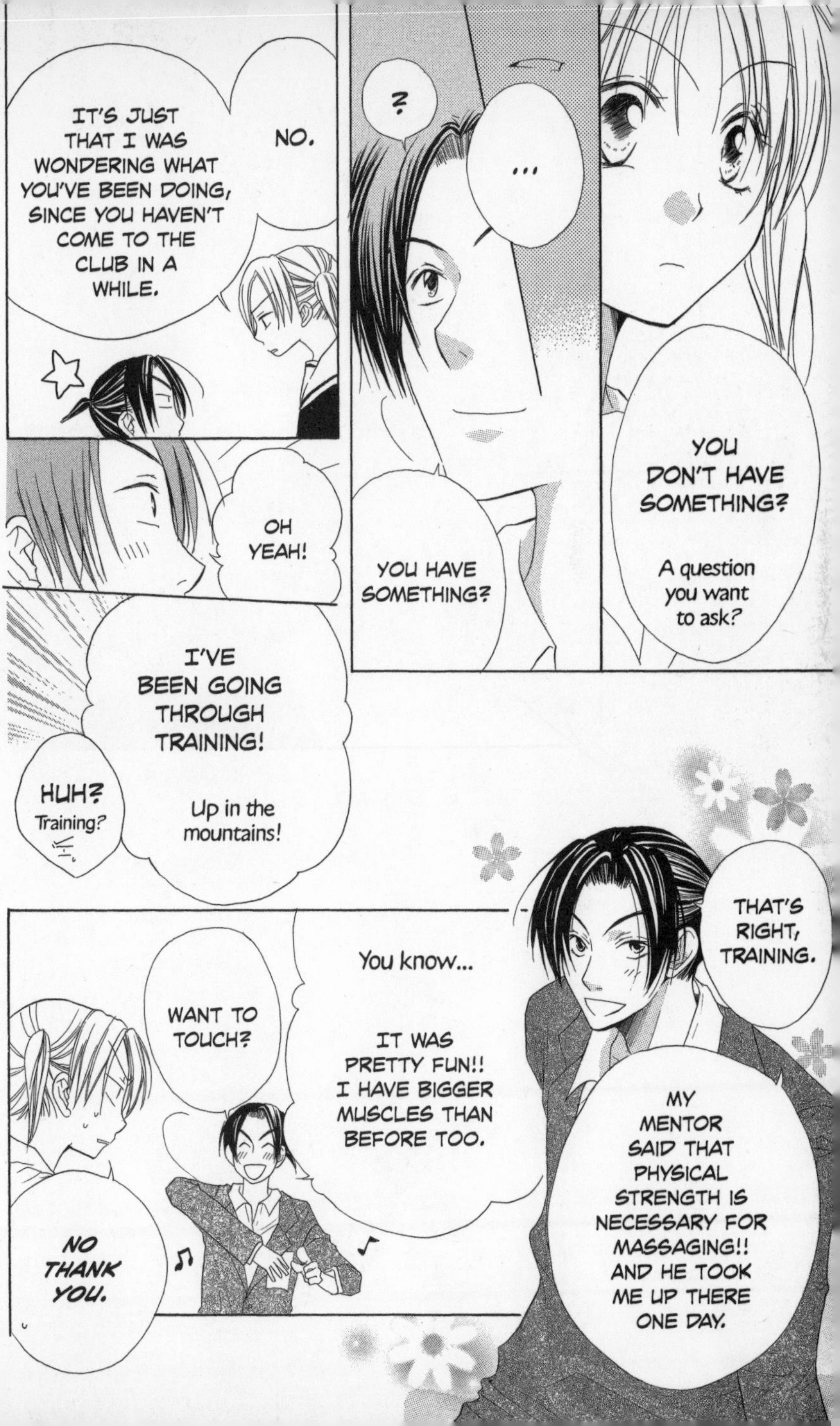
YOU DON'T HAVE SOMETHING?
A question you want to ask?
?
...
YOU HAVE SOMETHING?
NO.
IT'S JUST THAT I WAS WONDERING WHAT YOU'VE BEEN DOING, SINCE YOU HAVEN'T COME TO THE CLUB IN A WHILE.
OH YEAH!
I'VE BEEN GOING THROUGH TRAINING!
Up in the mountains!
HUH?
Training?
THAT'S RIGHT, TRAINING.
MY MENTOR SAID THAT PHYSICAL STRENGTH IS NECESSARY FOR MASSAGING!! AND HE TOOK ME UP THERE ONE DAY.
You know...
IT WAS PRETTY FUN!! I HAVE BIGGER MUSCLES THAN BEFORE TOO.
WANT TO TOUCH?
NO THANK YOU.

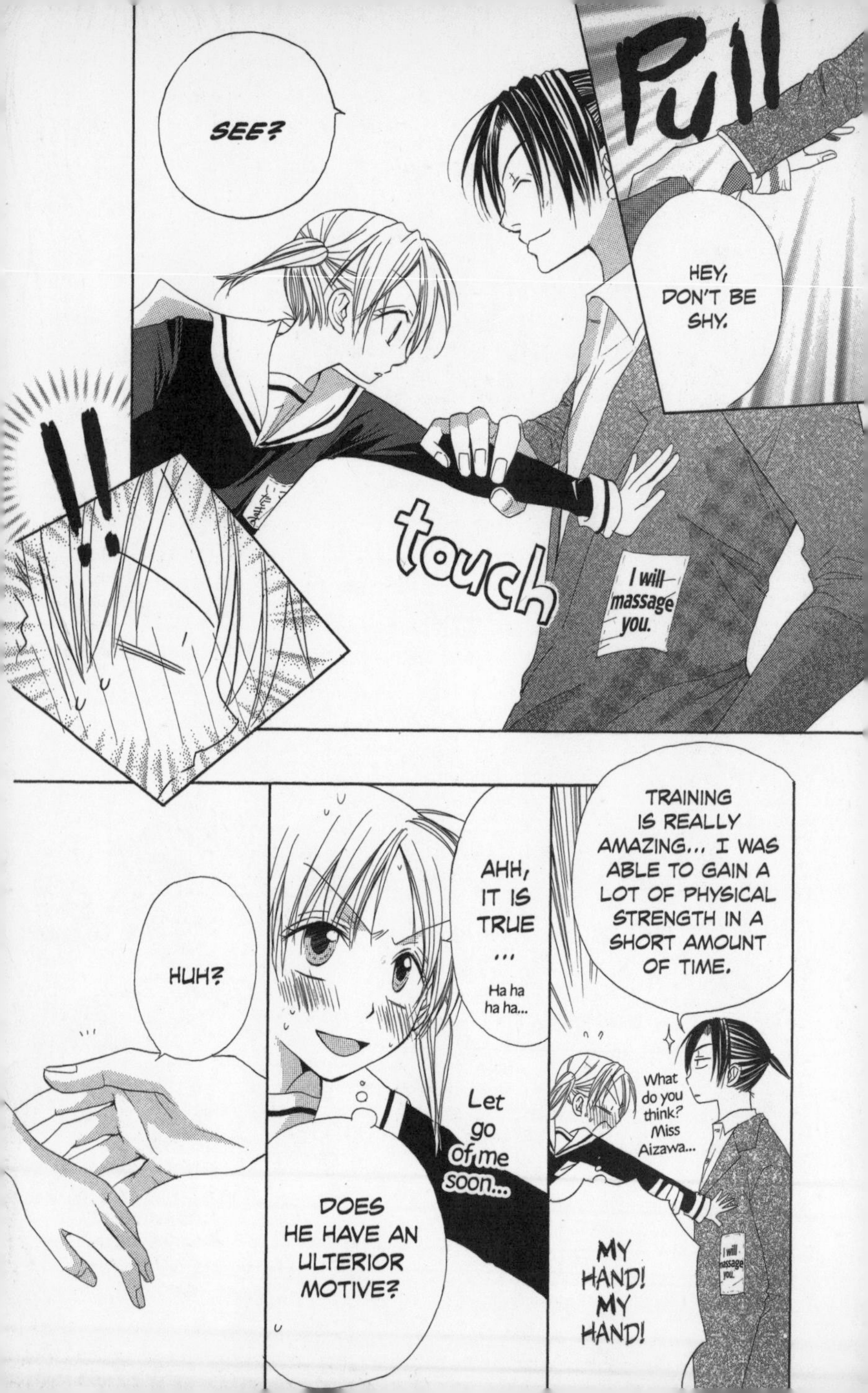
Pull
HEY, DON'T BE SHY.
SEE?
touch
I will massage you.
!!
TRAINING IS REALLY AMAZING... I WAS ABLE TO GAIN A LOT OF PHYSICAL STRENGTH IN A SHORT AMOUNT OF TIME.
What do you think? Miss Aizawa...
MY HAND! MY HAND!
I will massage you.
AHH, IT IS TRUE...
Ha ha ha ha...
Let go of me soon...
DOES HE HAVE AN ULTERIOR MOTIVE?
HUH?

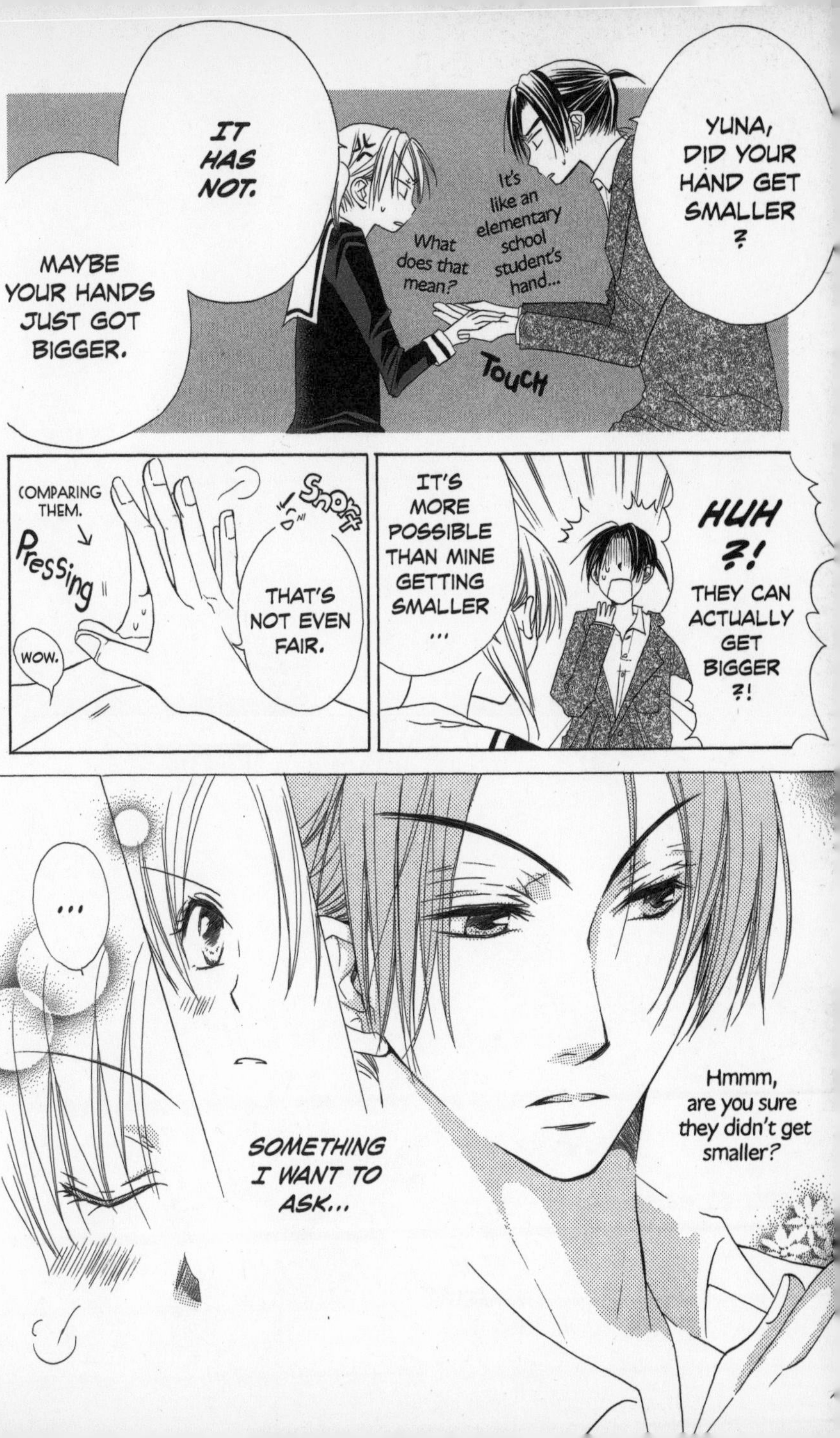
YUNA, DID YOUR HAND GET SMALLER?
It's like an elementary school student's hand...
What does that mean?
IT HAS NOT.
MAYBE YOUR HANDS JUST GOT BIGGER.
TOUCH
HUH?! THEY CAN ACTUALLY GET BIGGER?!
IT'S MORE POSSIBLE THAN MINE GETTING SMALLER...
Snort
THAT'S NOT EVEN FAIR.
COMPARING THEM.
Pressing
WOW.
Hmmm, are you sure they didn't get smaller?
SOMETHING I WANT TO ASK...
...

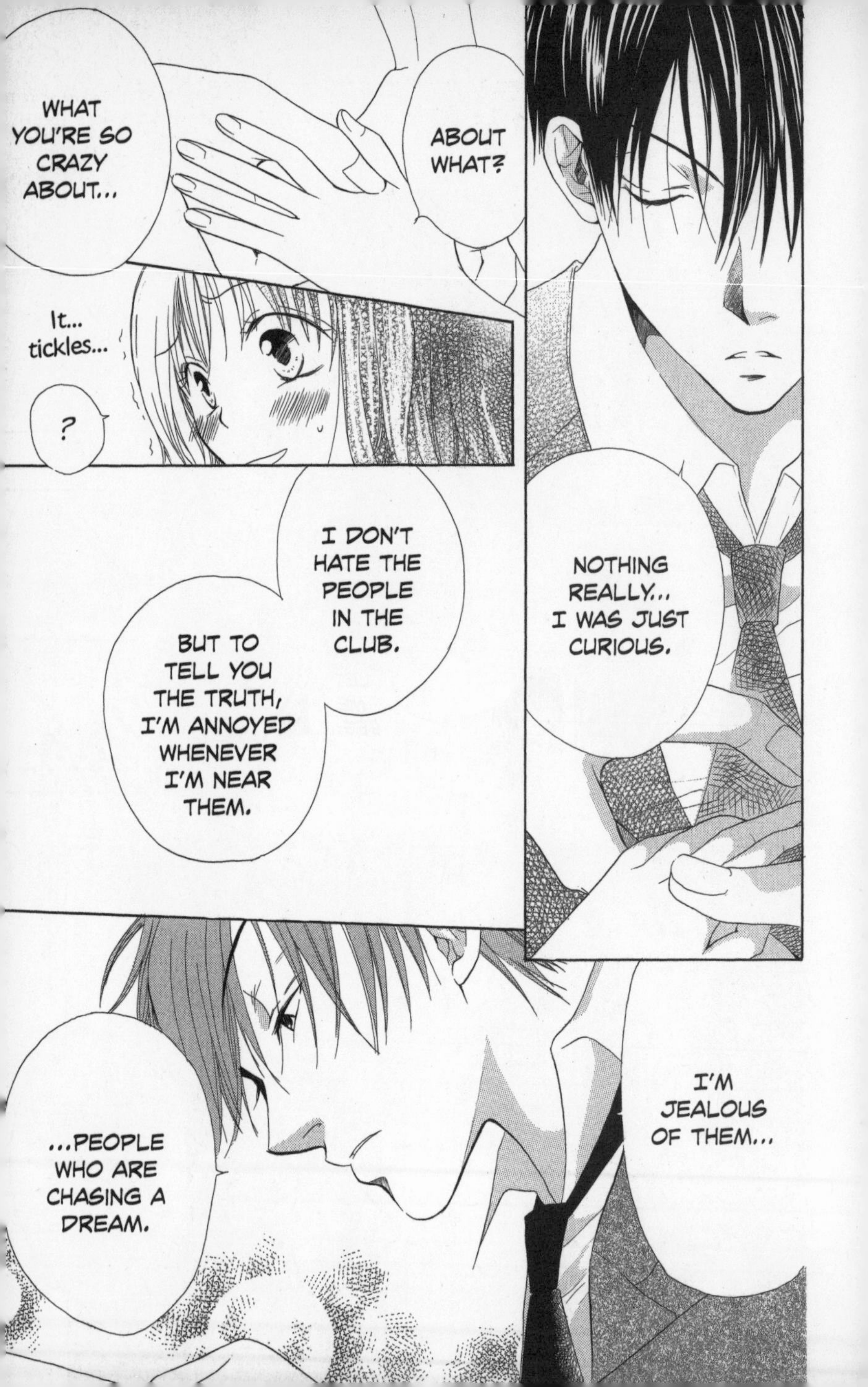
NOTHING REALLY... I WAS JUST CURIOUS.
ABOUT WHAT?
WHAT YOU'RE SO CRAZY ABOUT...
It... tickles...
?
I DON'T HATE THE PEOPLE IN THE CLUB.
BUT TO TELL YOU THE TRUTH, I'M ANNOYED WHENEVER I'M NEAR THEM.
I'M JEALOUS OF THEM...
...PEOPLE WHO ARE CHASING A DREAM.

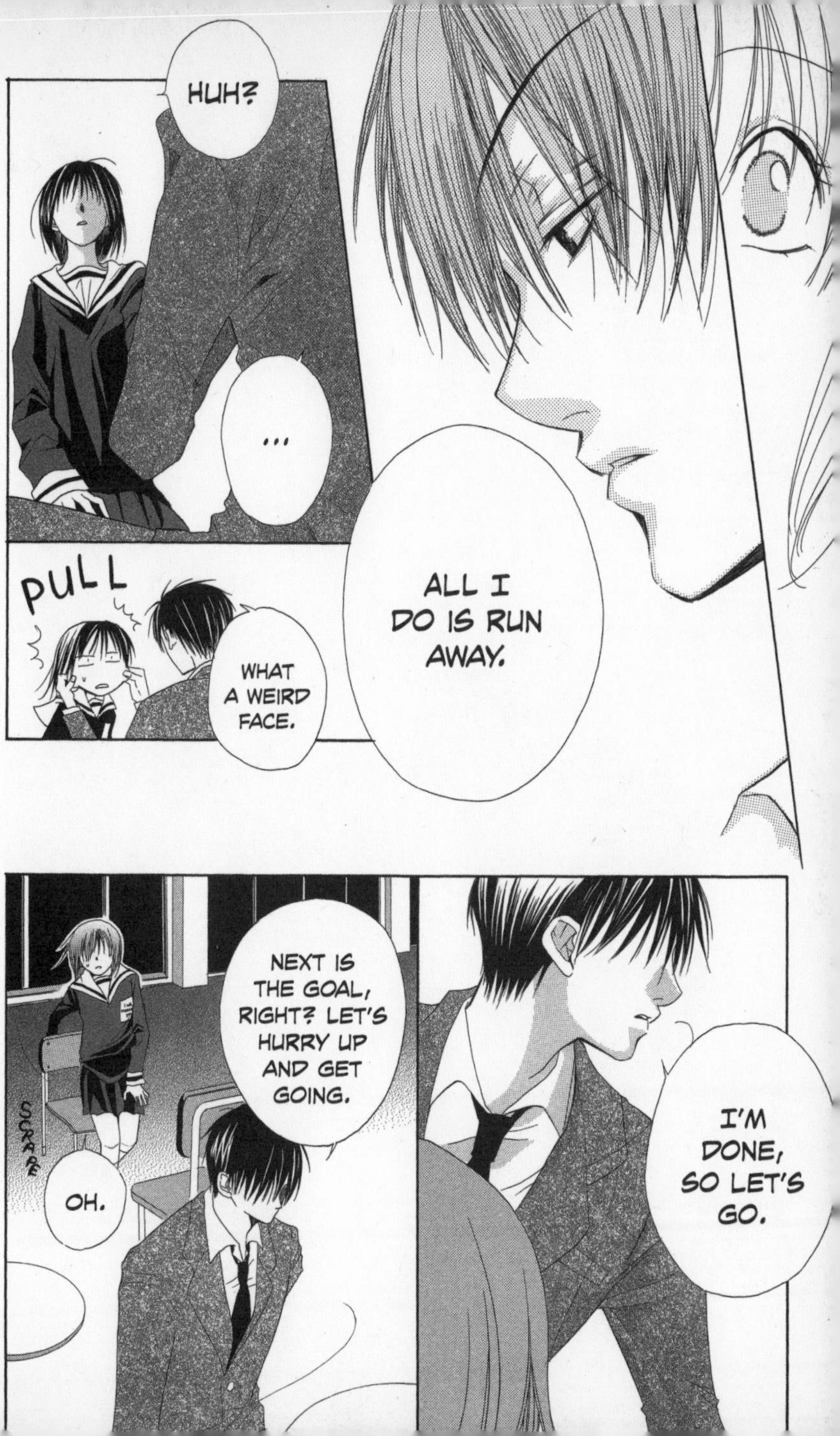
ALL I DO IS RUN AWAY.
HUH?
...
PULL
WHAT A WEIRD FACE.
I'M DONE, SO LET'S GO.
NEXT IS THE GOAL, RIGHT? LET'S HURRY UP AND GET GOING.
SCRAPE
OH.

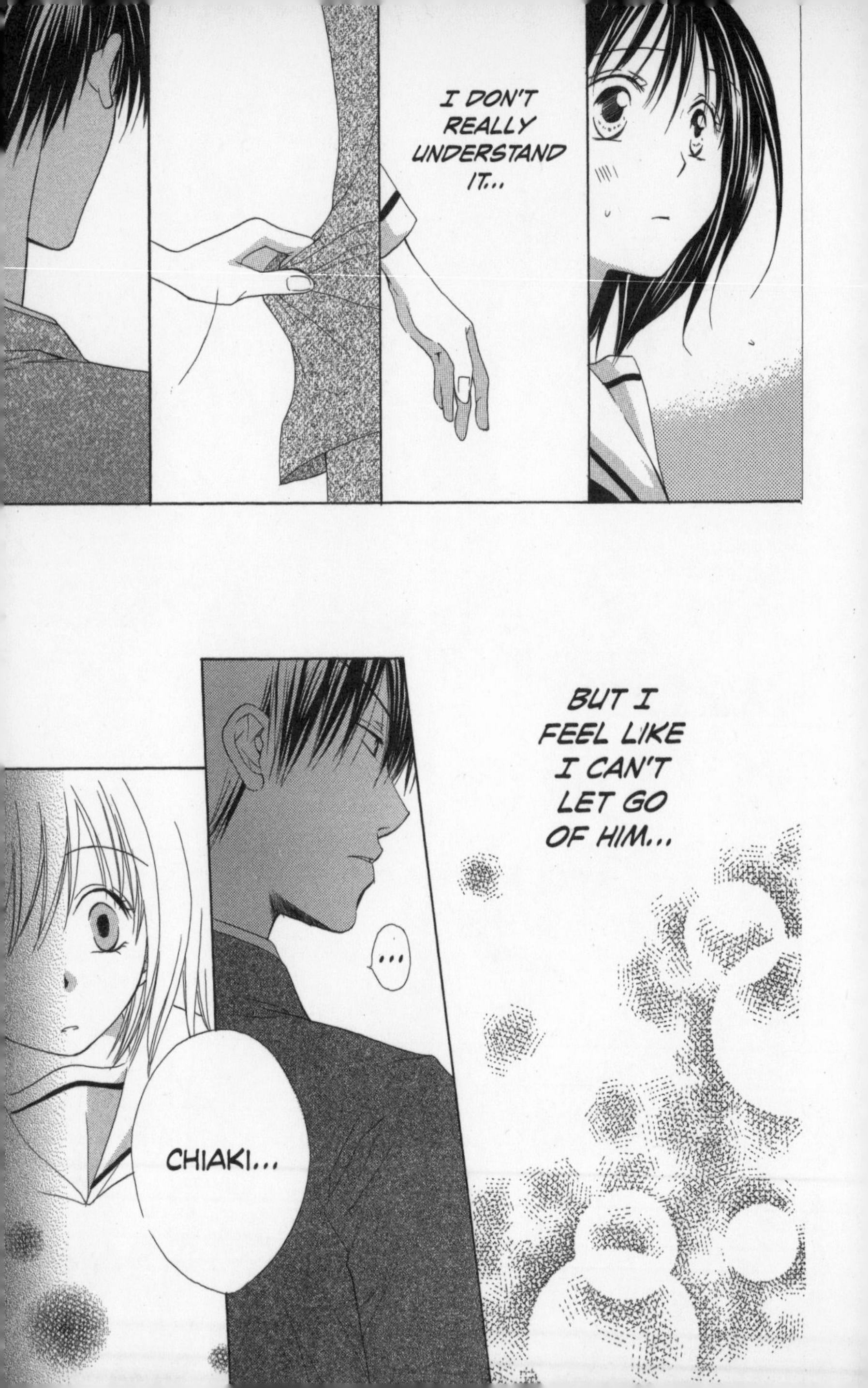
I DON'T REALLY UNDERSTAND IT...
BUT I FEEL LIKE I CAN'T LET GO OF HIM...
...
CHIAKI...

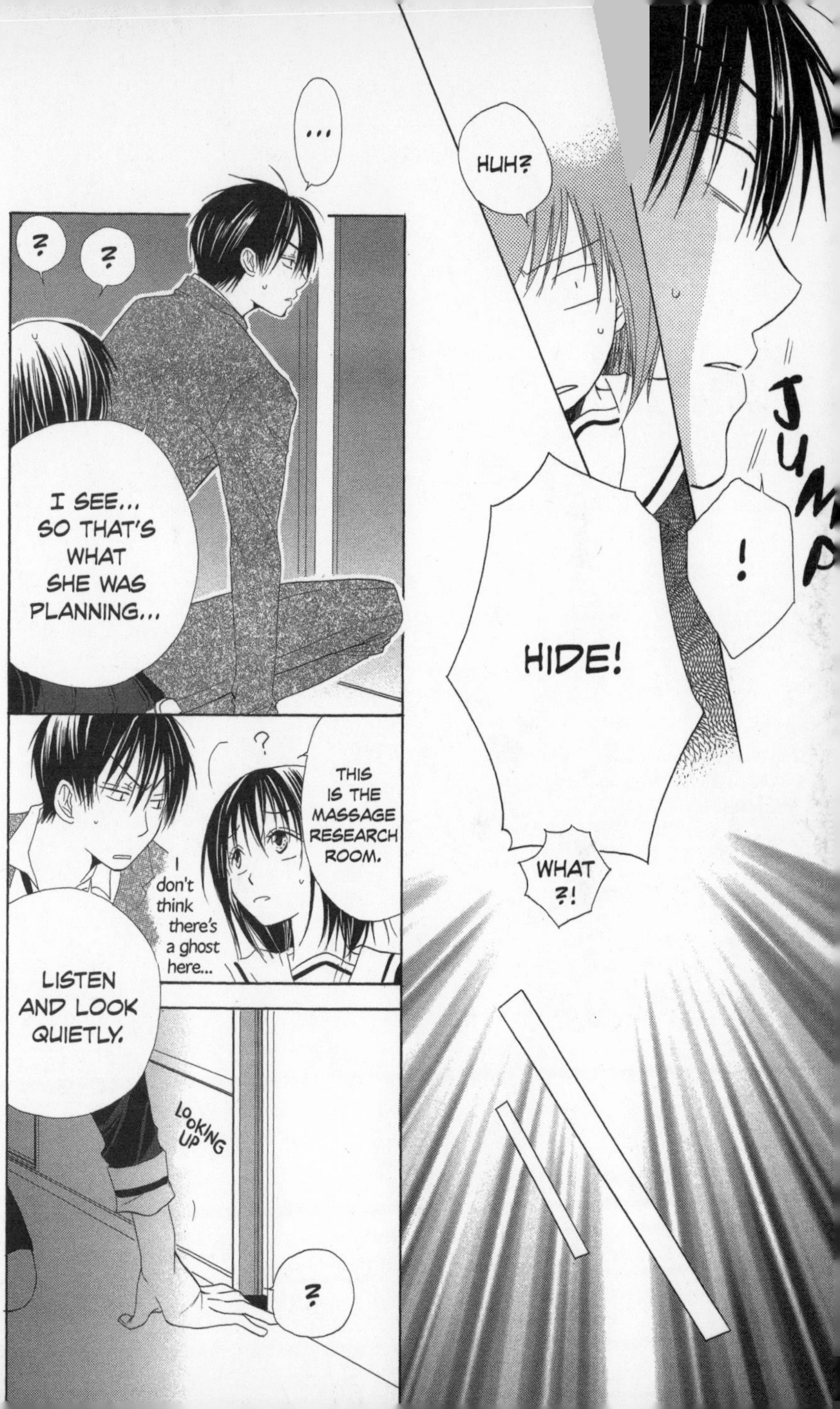
HUH?
JUMP
!
HIDE!
WHAT?!
...
?
?
I SEE... SO THAT'S WHAT SHE WAS PLANNING...
THIS IS THE MASSAGE RESEARCH ROOM.
I don't think there's a ghost here...
LISTEN AND LOOK QUIETLY.
LOOKING UP
?

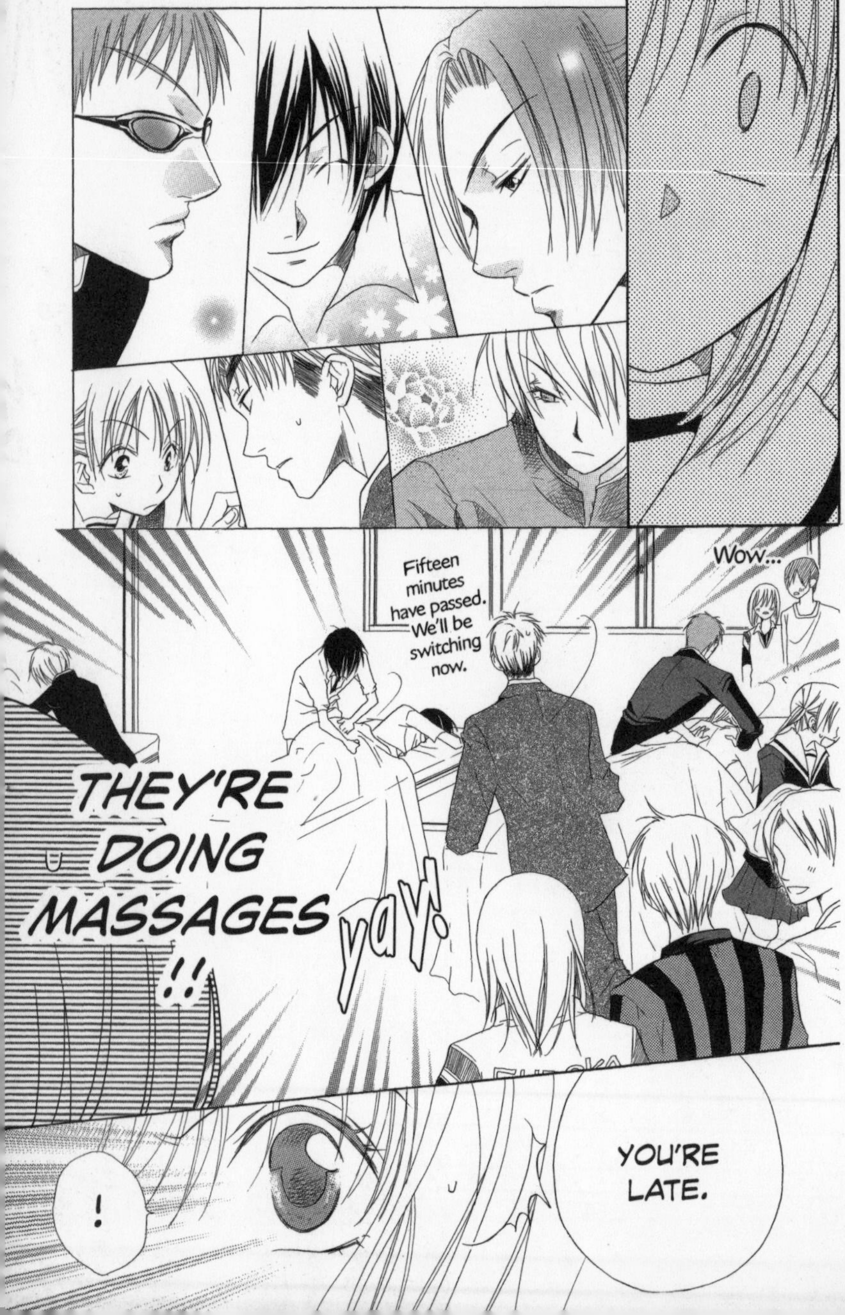
Wow...
Fifteen minutes have passed. We'll be switching now.
THEY'RE DOING MASSAGES!!
yay!
YOU'RE LATE.
!

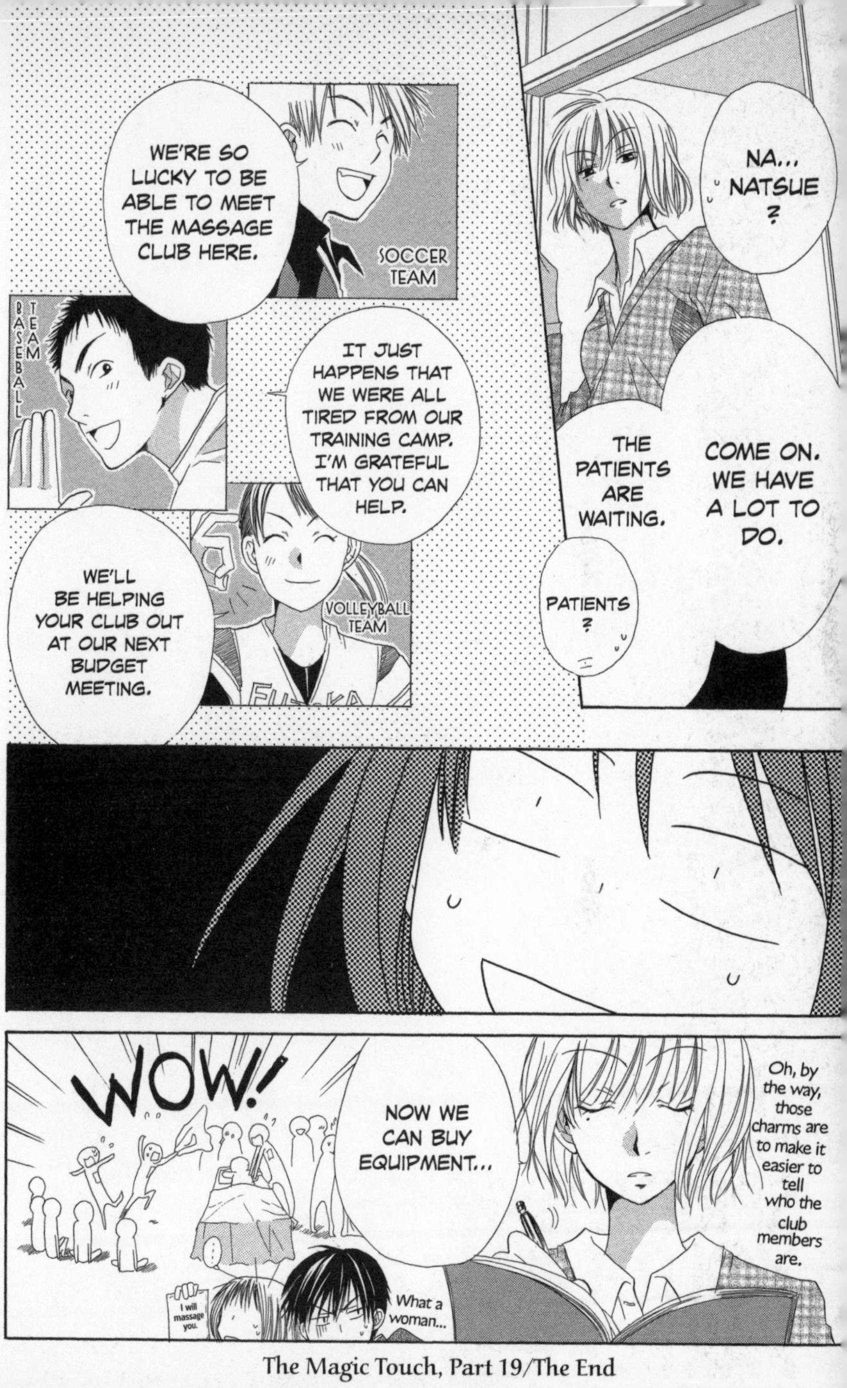
NA... NATSUE?
COME ON. WE HAVE A LOT TO DO.
THE PATIENTS ARE WAITING.
PATIENTS?
WE'RE SO LUCKY TO BE ABLE TO MEET THE MASSAGE CLUB HERE.
SOCCER TEAM
BASEBALL TEAM
IT JUST HAPPENS THAT WE WERE ALL TIRED FROM OUR TRAINING CAMP. I'M GRATEFUL THAT YOU CAN HELP.
VOLLEYBALL TEAM
WE'LL BE HELPING YOUR CLUB OUT AT OUR NEXT BUDGET MEETING.
Oh, by the way, those charms are to make it easier to tell who the club members are.
NOW WE CAN BUY EQUIPMENT...
WOW!
What a woman...
I will massage you.

The Magic Touch, Part 19/The End

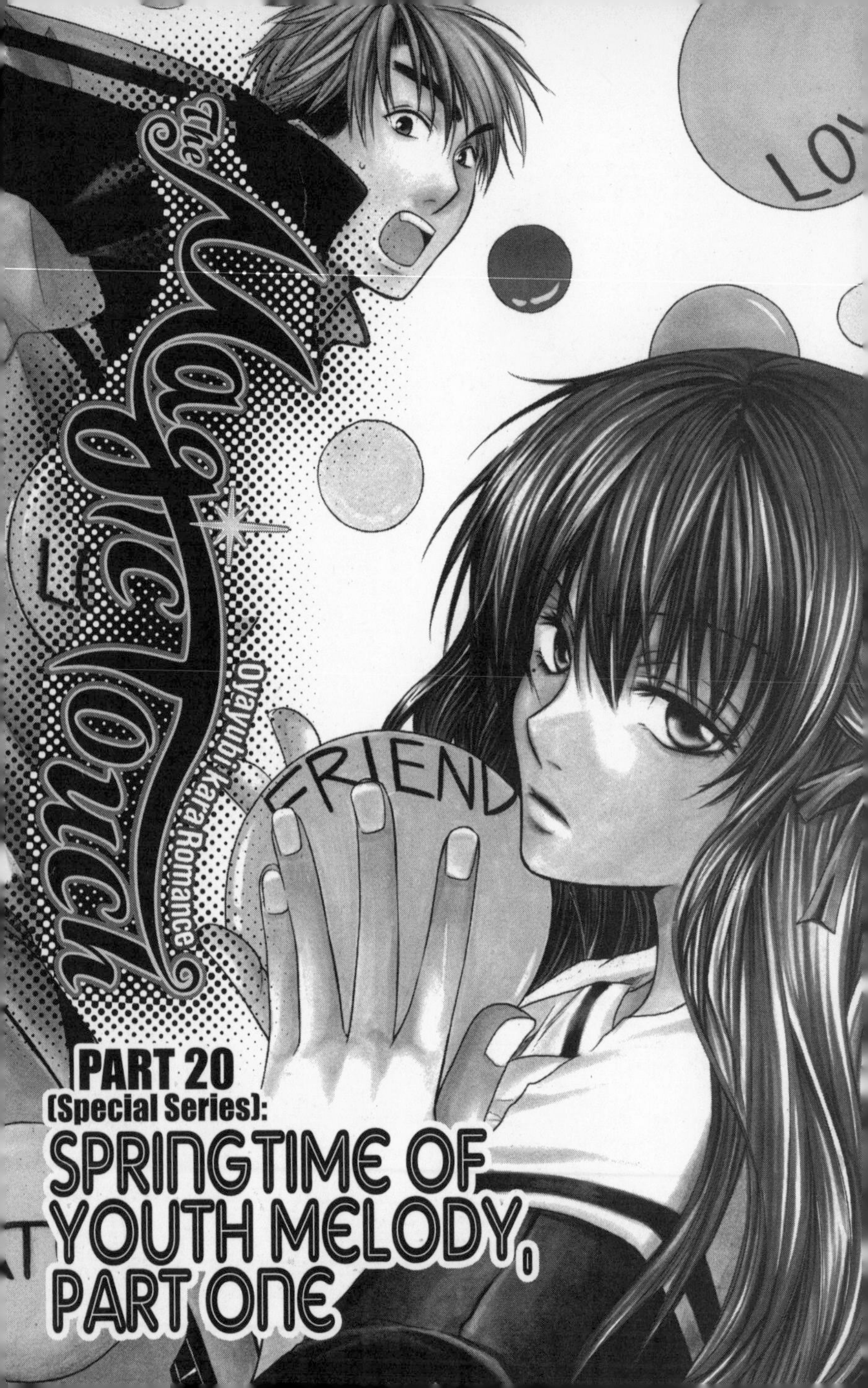
The Magic Touch
Oyayubi Kara Romance
LOV
FRIEND
PART 20
(Special Series):
SPRINGTIME OF YOUTH MELODY, PART ONE

Yuna Aizawa

Birthday: December 21

Blood Type: A

Grade: First-Year Student, Futouka Academy

Height: 159 cm (5' 2")

Hobbies: Observing Handsome Boys, Collecting Information

Special Talents: All Sports

What She Likes: Good-Looking People, Spaghetti

What She Hates: Sea Urchins

Siblings: A Little Sister

Club Activity in Middle School: Badminton Club (Captain)

Ryo Kuromatsu

HER USUAL CLOTHES WERE HANDED DOWN FROM HER OLDER BROTHERS.

Birthday: March 14

Blood Type: O

Grade: First-Year Student, Sazanka High School

Height: 171 cm (5' 7")

Hobby: Watching Pro Wrestling

Special Talents: Concentration

What She Likes: Sweets, the Hanshin Tigers Baseball Team

What She Hates: Gaudy Clothes

Siblings: Two Older Brothers

Club Activity in Middle School: Karate Team

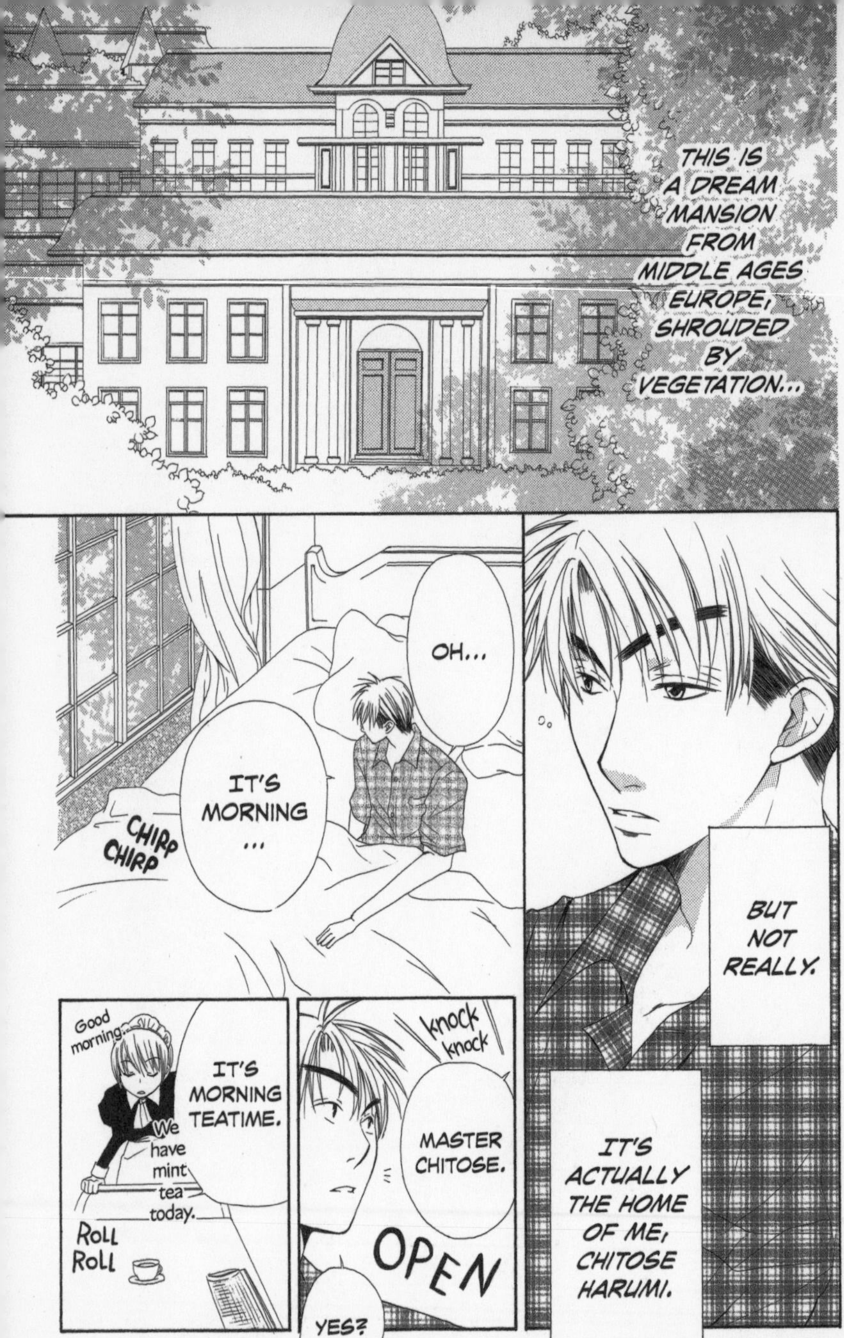
THIS IS A DREAM MANSION FROM MIDDLE AGES EUROPE, SHROUDED BY VEGETATION...
BUT NOT REALLY.
IT'S ACTUALLY THE HOME OF ME, CHITOSE HARUMI.
OH...
IT'S MORNING ...
CHIRP CHIRP
knock knock
MASTER CHITOSE.
OPEN
YES?
IT'S MORNING TEATIME.
Good morning...
We have mint tea today.
ROLL ROLL

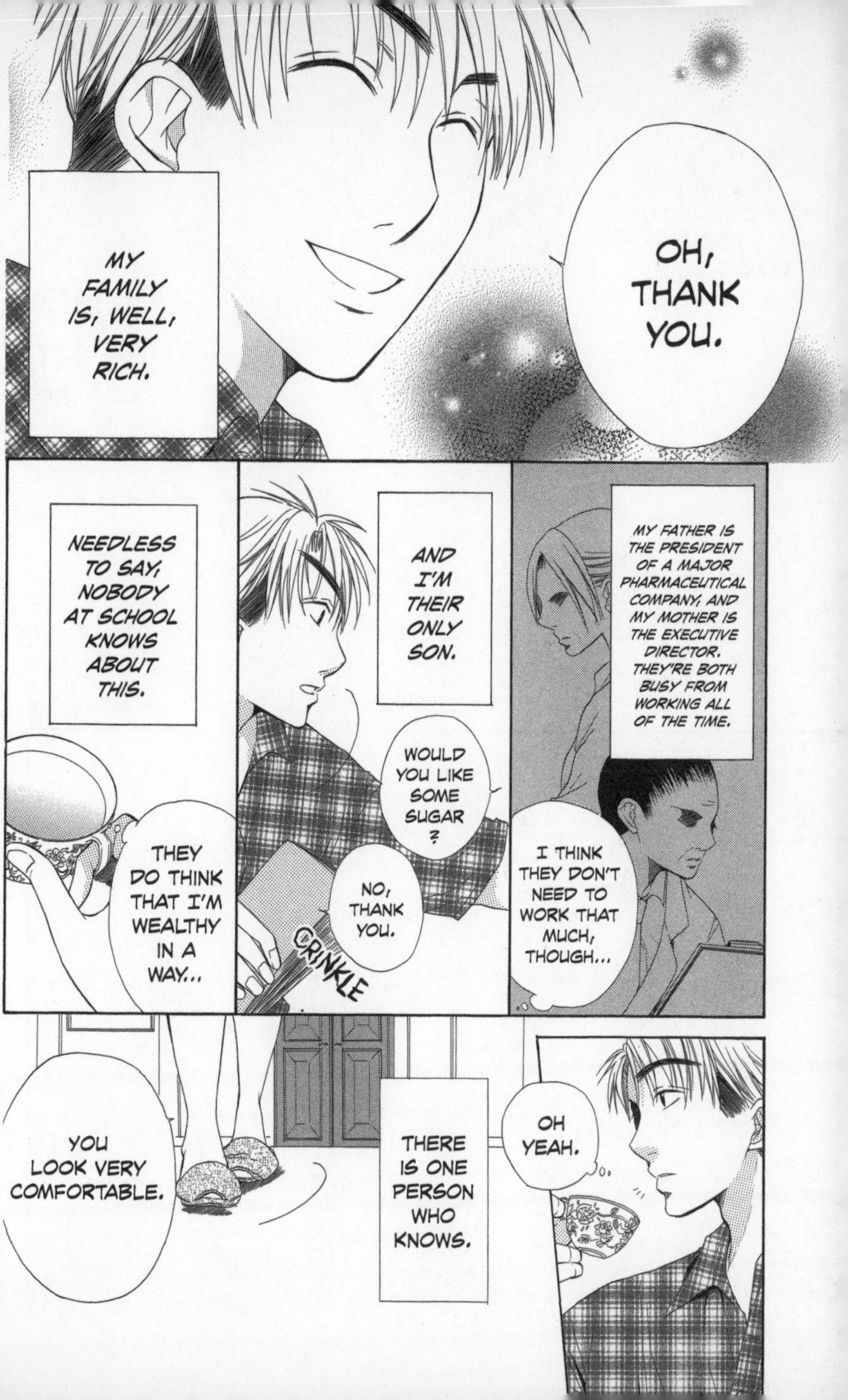
OH, THANK YOU.
MY FAMILY IS, WELL, VERY RICH.
MY FATHER IS THE PRESIDENT OF A MAJOR PHARMACEUTICAL COMPANY, AND MY MOTHER IS THE EXECUTIVE DIRECTOR. THEY'RE BOTH BUSY FROM WORKING ALL OF THE TIME.
I THINK THEY DON'T NEED TO WORK THAT MUCH, THOUGH...
AND I'M THEIR ONLY SON.
WOULD YOU LIKE SOME SUGAR?
NO, THANK YOU.
CRINKLE
NEEDLESS TO SAY, NOBODY AT SCHOOL KNOWS ABOUT THIS.
THEY DO THINK THAT I'M WEALTHY IN A WAY...
OH YEAH.
THERE IS ONE PERSON WHO KNOWS.
YOU LOOK VERY COMFORTABLE.

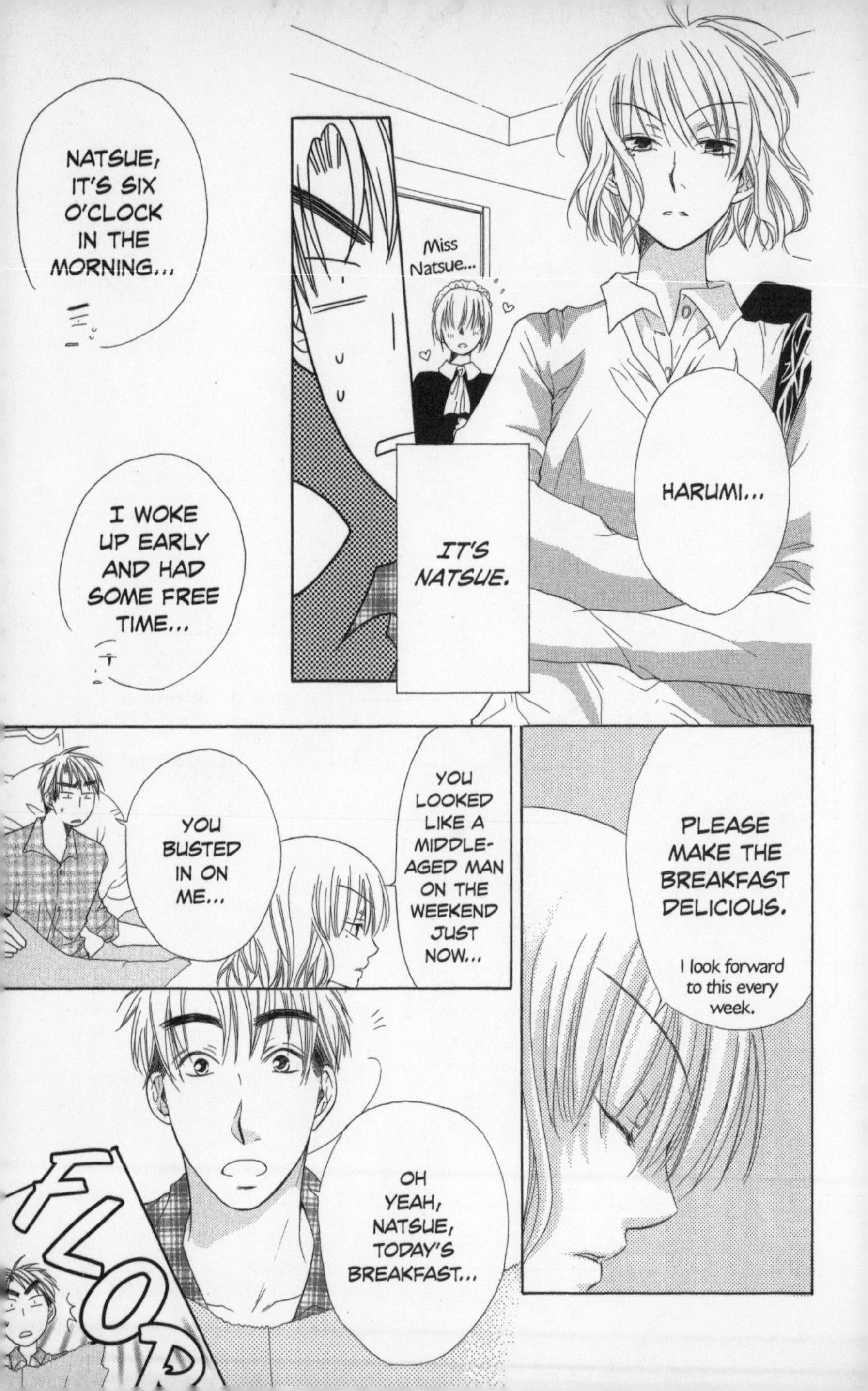
HARUMI...
Miss Natsue...
IT'S NATSUE.
NATSUE, IT'S SIX O'CLOCK IN THE MORNING...
I WOKE UP EARLY AND HAD SOME FREE TIME...
PLEASE MAKE THE BREAKFAST DELICIOUS.
I look forward to this every week.
YOU LOOKED LIKE A MIDDLE-AGED MAN ON THE WEEKEND JUST NOW...
YOU BUSTED IN ON ME...
OH YEAH, NATSUE, TODAY'S BREAKFAST...
FLOP

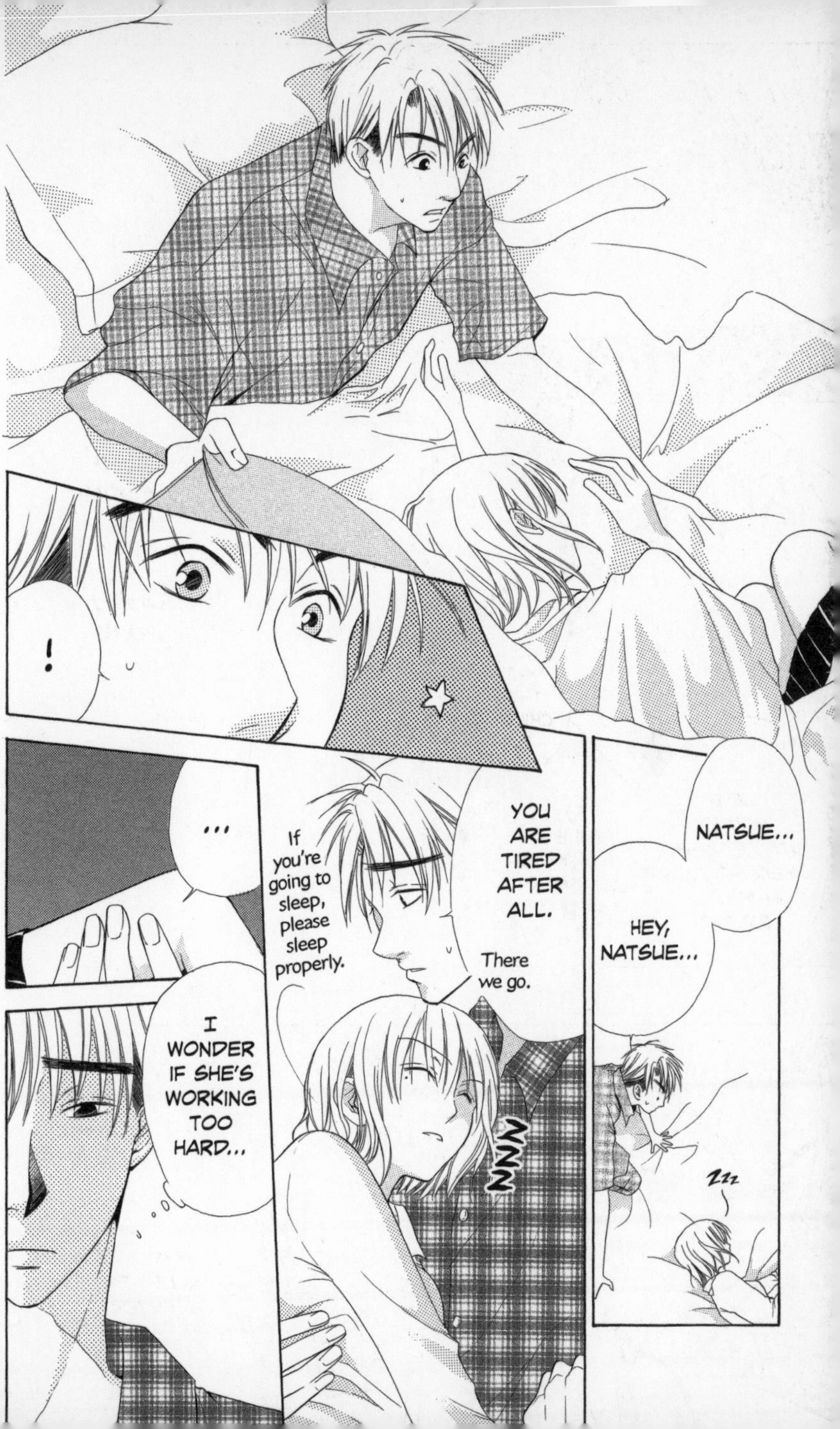
!
NATSUE...
HEY, NATSUE...
Zzz
YOU ARE TIRED AFTER ALL.
There we go.
If you're going to sleep, please sleep properly.
...
I WONDER IF SHE'S WORKING TOO HARD...

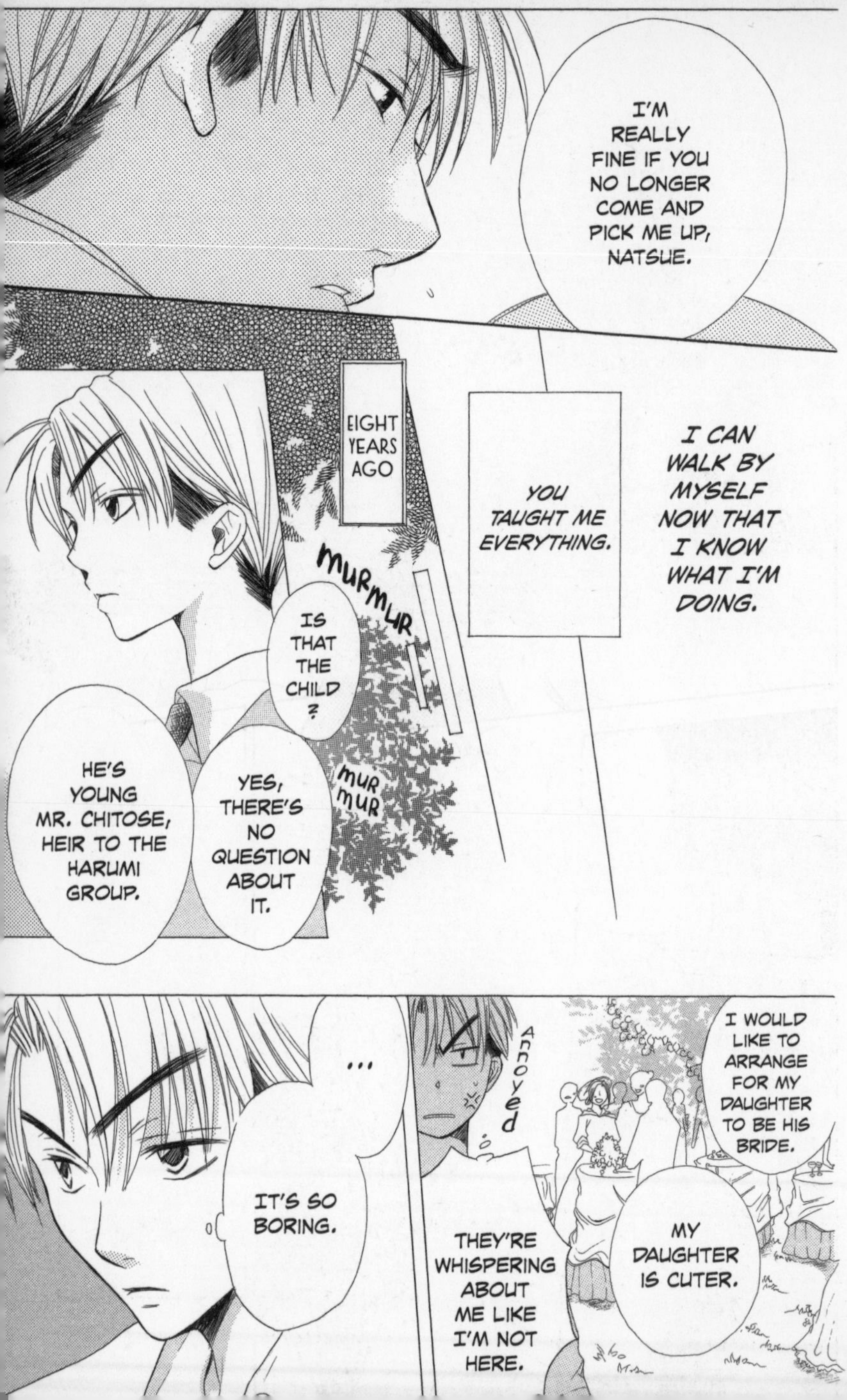
I'M REALLY FINE IF YOU NO LONGER COME AND PICK ME UP, NATSUE.
I CAN WALK BY MYSELF NOW THAT I KNOW WHAT I'M DOING.
YOU TAUGHT ME EVERYTHING.
EIGHT YEARS AGO
murmur
IS THAT THE CHILD?
mur mur
YES, THERE'S NO QUESTION ABOUT IT.
HE'S YOUNG MR. CHITOSE, HEIR TO THE HARUMI GROUP.
I WOULD LIKE TO ARRANGE FOR MY DAUGHTER TO BE HIS BRIDE.
MY DAUGHTER IS CUTER.
THEY'RE WHISPERING ABOUT ME LIKE I'M NOT HERE.
Annoyed
...
IT'S SO BORING.

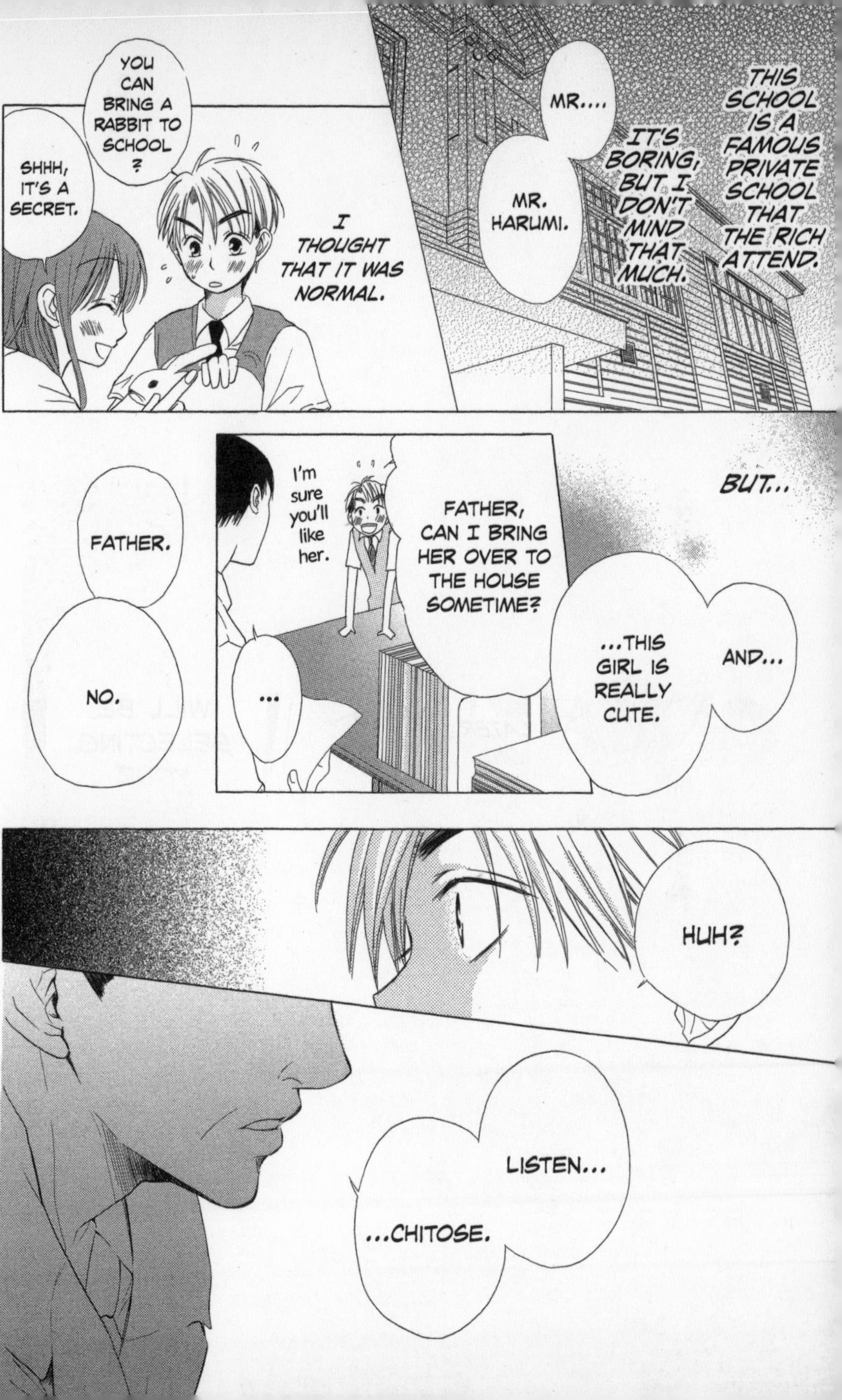
THIS SCHOOL IS A FAMOUS PRIVATE SCHOOL THAT THE RICH ATTEND.
IT'S BORING, BUT I DON'T MIND THAT MUCH.
MR....
MR. HARUMI.
I THOUGHT THAT IT WAS NORMAL.
YOU CAN BRING A RABBIT TO SCHOOL?
SHHH, IT'S A SECRET.
BUT...
AND...
...THIS GIRL IS REALLY CUTE.
FATHER, CAN I BRING HER OVER TO THE HOUSE SOMETIME?
I'm sure you'll like her.
...
FATHER.
NO.
HUH?
LISTEN...
...CHITOSE.

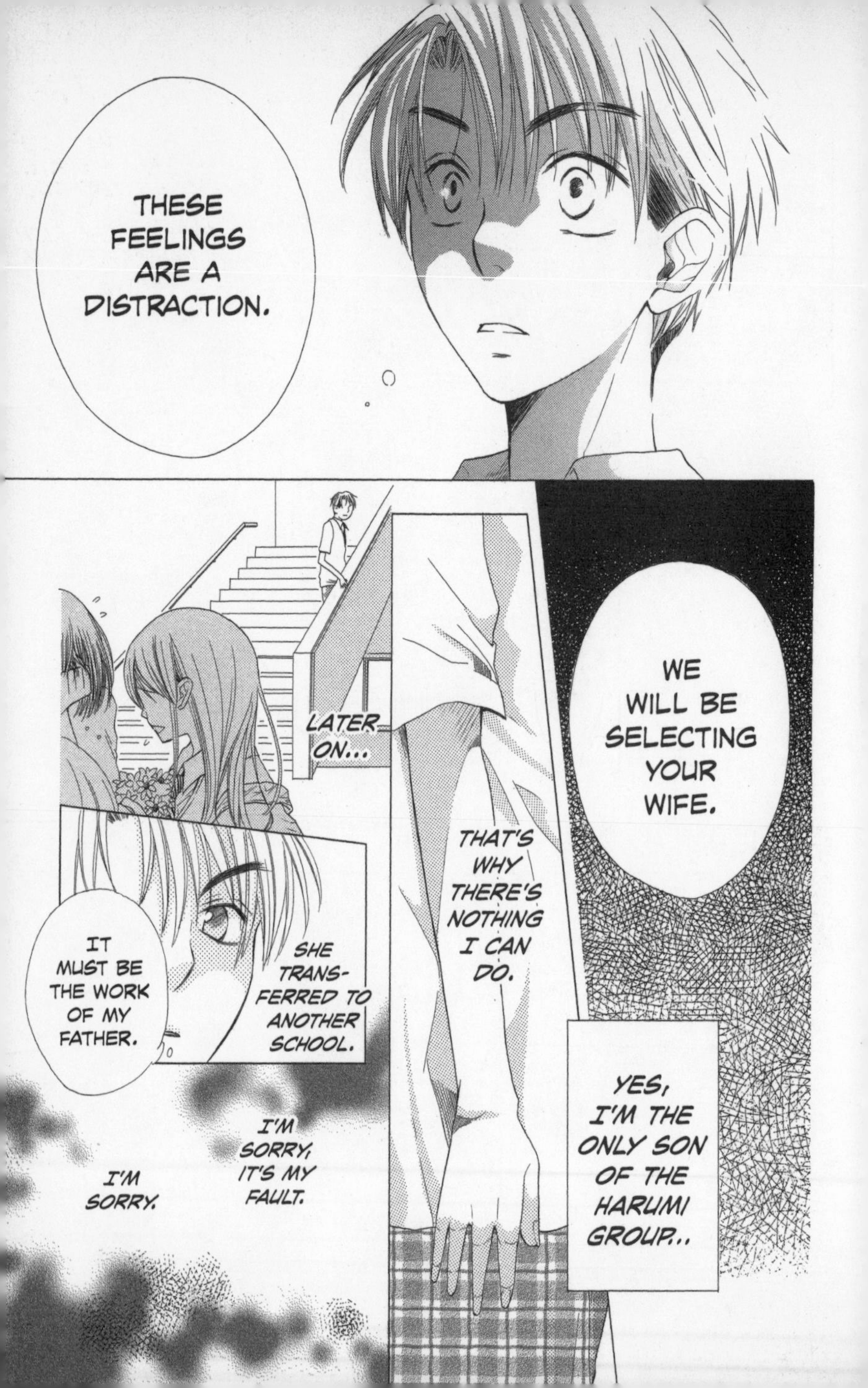
THESE FEELINGS ARE A DISTRACTION.
WE WILL BE SELECTING YOUR WIFE.
YES, I'M THE ONLY SON OF THE HARUMI GROUP...
THAT'S WHY THERE'S NOTHING I CAN DO.
LATER ON...
SHE TRANS-FERRED TO ANOTHER SCHOOL.
IT MUST BE THE WORK OF MY FATHER.
I'M SORRY, IT'S MY FAULT.
I'M SORRY.

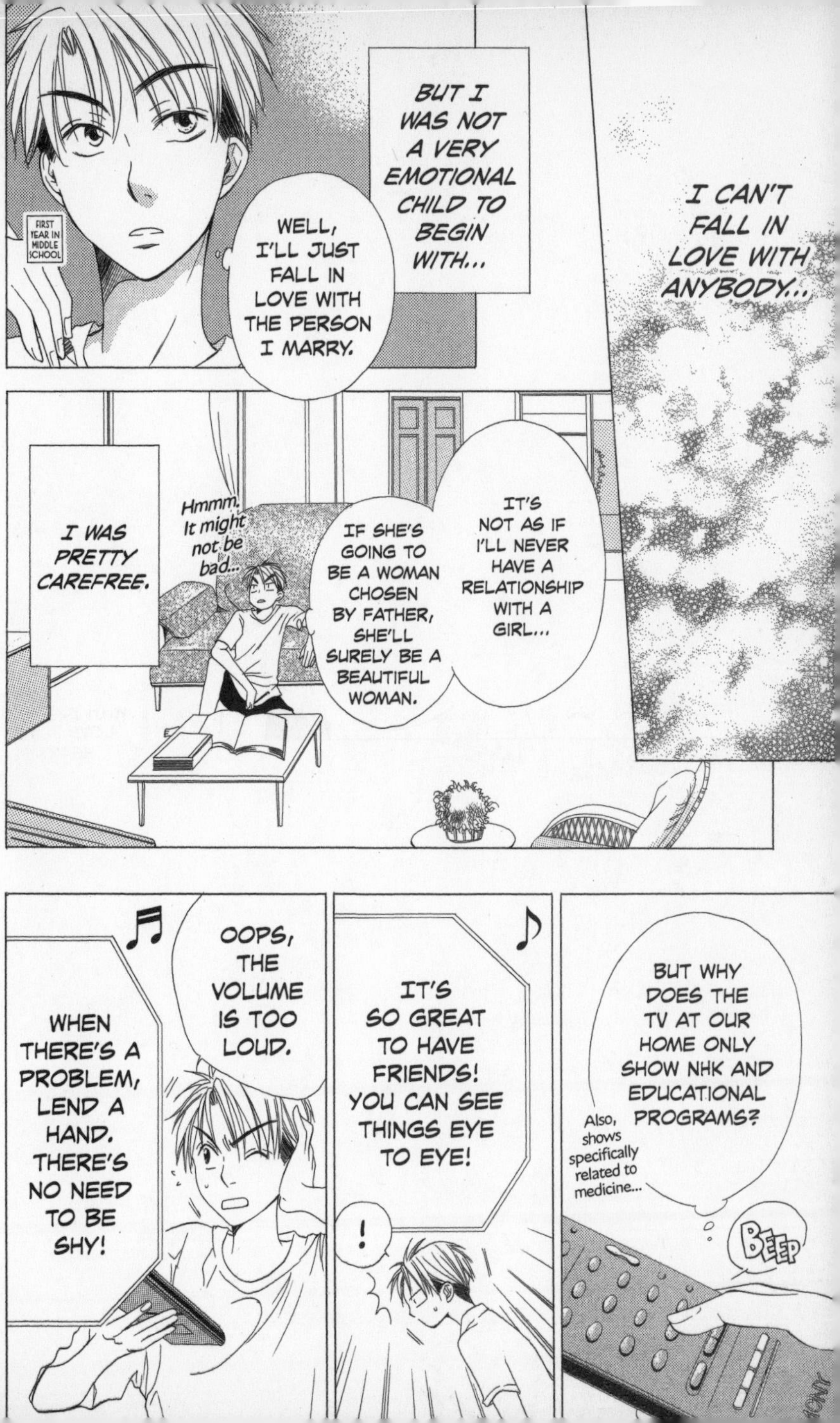
I CAN'T FALL IN LOVE WITH ANYBODY...
BUT I WAS NOT A VERY EMOTIONAL CHILD TO BEGIN WITH...
FIRST YEAR IN MIDDLE SCHOOL
WELL, I'LL JUST FALL IN LOVE WITH THE PERSON I MARRY.
IT'S NOT AS IF I'LL NEVER HAVE A RELATIONSHIP WITH A GIRL...
IF SHE'S GOING TO BE A WOMAN CHOSEN BY FATHER, SHE'LL SURELY BE A BEAUTIFUL WOMAN.
Hmmm. It might not be bad...
I WAS PRETTY CAREFREE.
BUT WHY DOES THE TV AT OUR HOME ONLY SHOW NHK AND EDUCATIONAL PROGRAMS?
Also, shows specifically related to medicine...
BEEP
IT'S SO GREAT TO HAVE FRIENDS! YOU CAN SEE THINGS EYE TO EYE!
!
OOPS, THE VOLUME IS TOO LOUD.
WHEN THERE'S A PROBLEM, LEND A HAND. THERE'S NO NEED TO BE SHY!

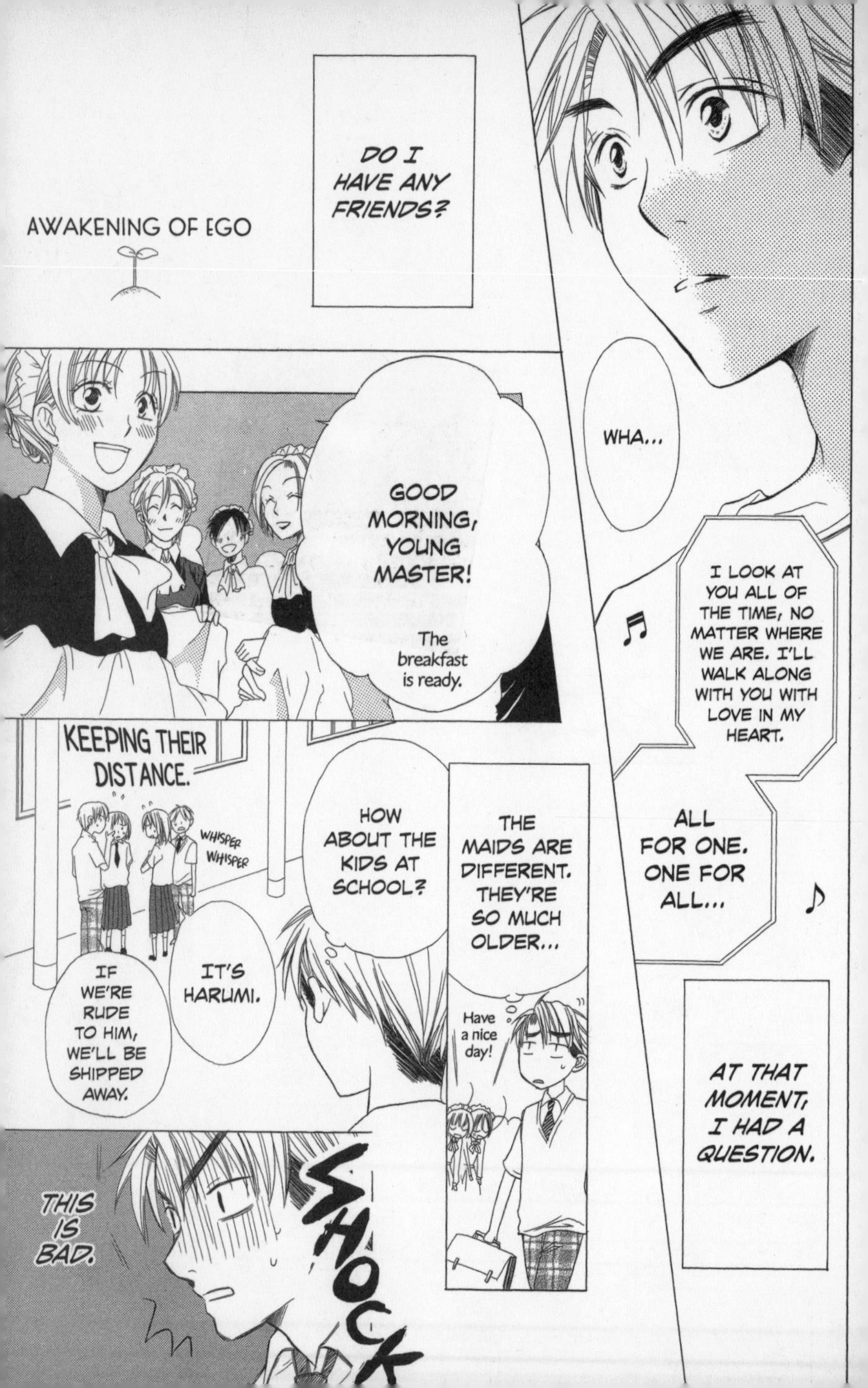

WHA...
I LOOK AT YOU ALL OF THE TIME, NO MATTER WHERE WE ARE. I'LL WALK ALONG WITH YOU WITH LOVE IN MY HEART.
ALL FOR ONE. ONE FOR ALL... ♪
AT THAT MOMENT, I HAD A QUESTION.
DO I HAVE ANY FRIENDS?
AWAKENING OF EGO
GOOD MORNING, YOUNG MASTER!
The breakfast is ready.
THE MAIDS ARE DIFFERENT. THEY'RE SO MUCH OLDER...
Have a nice day!
HOW ABOUT THE KIDS AT SCHOOL?
KEEPING THEIR DISTANCE.
WHISPER WHISPER
IT'S HARUMI.
IF WE'RE RUDE TO HIM, WE'LL BE SHIPPED AWAY.
SHOCK
THIS IS BAD.

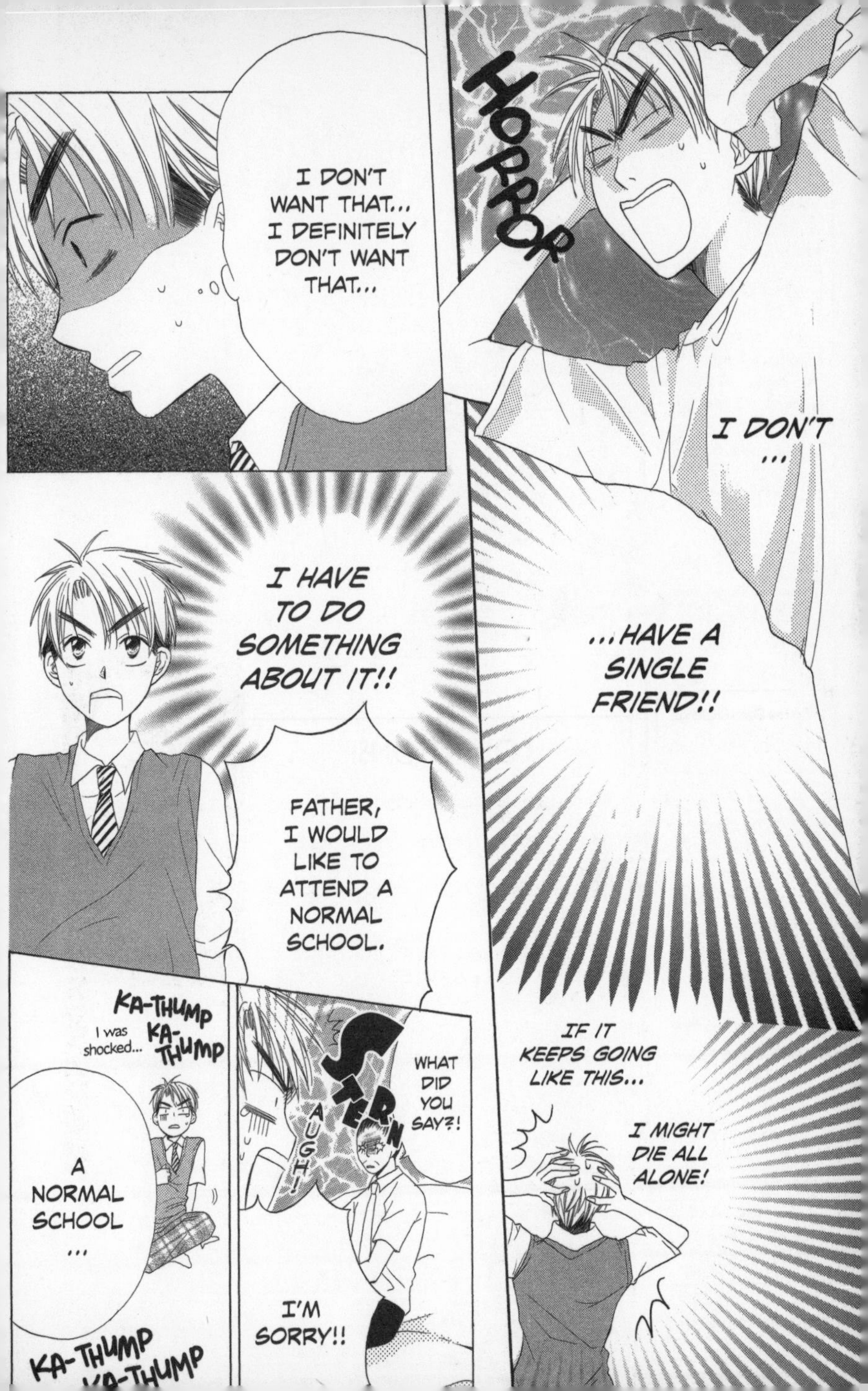
HORROR
I DON'T ...
...HAVE A SINGLE FRIEND!!
I DON'T WANT THAT... I DEFINITELY DON'T WANT THAT...
IF IT KEEPS GOING LIKE THIS...
I MIGHT DIE ALL ALONE!
I HAVE TO DO SOMETHING ABOUT IT!!
FATHER, I WOULD LIKE TO ATTEND A NORMAL SCHOOL.
STERN
WHAT DID YOU SAY?!
AUGH!
I'M SORRY!!
KA-THUMP KA-THUMP
I was shocked...
A NORMAL SCHOOL ...
KA-THUMP KA-THUMP

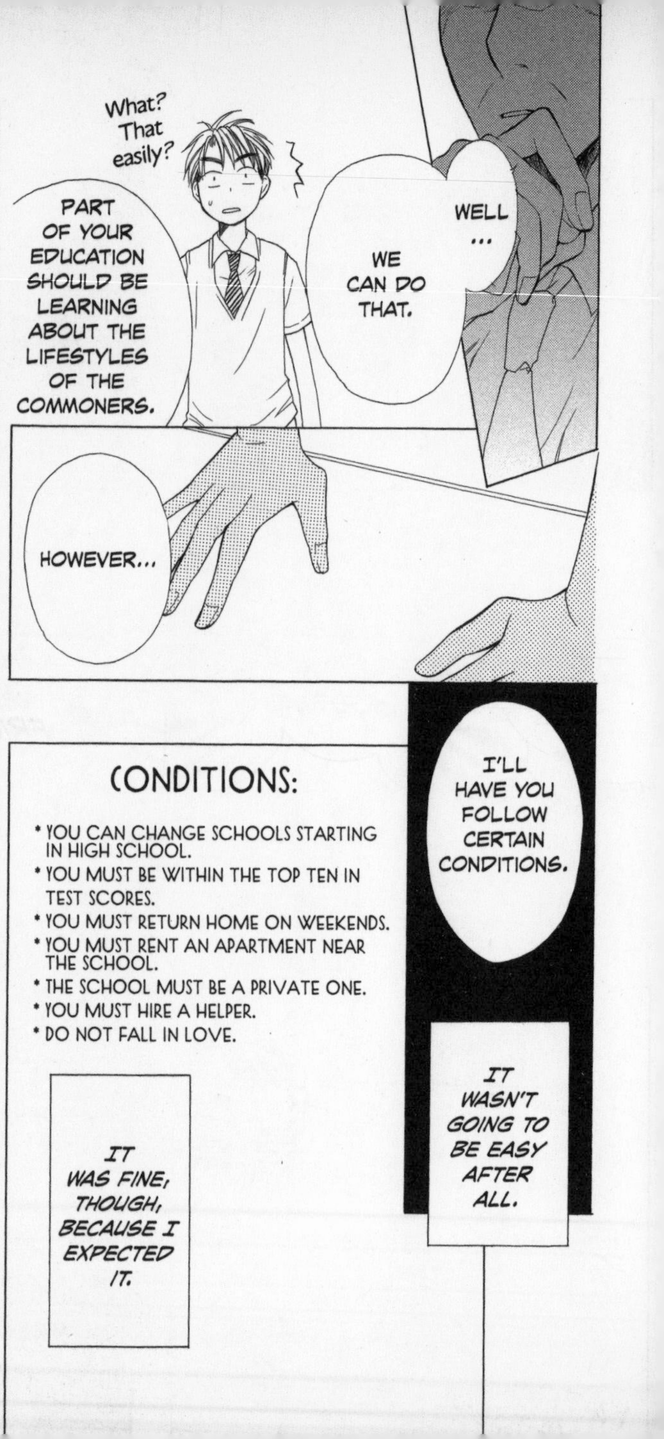
WELL ...
WE CAN DO THAT.
What? That easily?
PART OF YOUR EDUCATION SHOULD BE LEARNING ABOUT THE LIFESTYLES OF THE COMMONERS.
HOWEVER...
I'LL HAVE YOU FOLLOW CERTAIN CONDITIONS.
CONDITIONS:
* YOU CAN CHANGE SCHOOLS STARTING IN HIGH SCHOOL.
* YOU MUST BE WITHIN THE TOP TEN IN TEST SCORES.
* YOU MUST RETURN HOME ON WEEKENDS.
* YOU MUST RENT AN APARTMENT NEAR THE SCHOOL.
* THE SCHOOL MUST BE A PRIVATE ONE.
* YOU MUST HIRE A HELPER.
* DO NOT FALL IN LOVE.
IT WASN'T GOING TO BE EASY AFTER ALL.
IT WAS FINE, THOUGH, BECAUSE I EXPECTED IT.

Plots, Part 2

Weird Plots

Example 1

The taste of miso soup is different in each household. After tasting the miso soup of another family, one understands that there are many different flavors, just by that one tasting.

I wonder what kind of story I was trying to write. Terrifyingly, there are more.

Example 2

"Do the Bean Challenge"

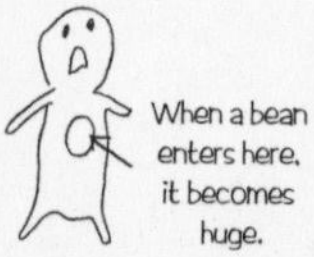
When a bean enters here, it becomes huge.

* The Bean Challenge is to make a creature at the train station eat the beans and make it huge in order to receive a fabulous prize.

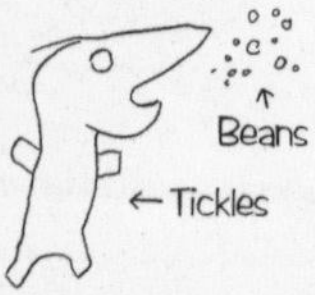
Beans
←Tickles

Anyway, they're not manga for girls...

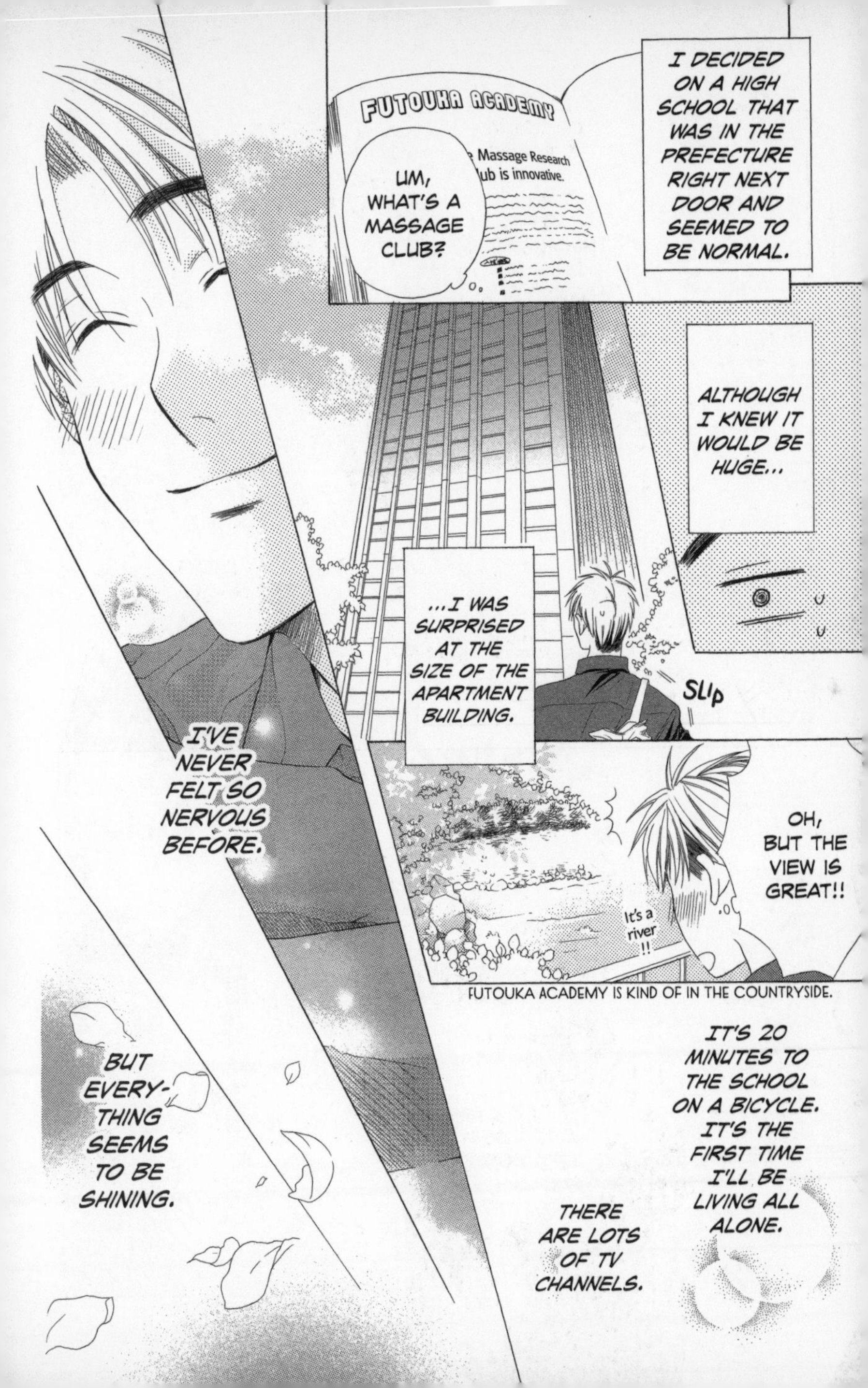
I DECIDED ON A HIGH SCHOOL THAT WAS IN THE PREFECTURE RIGHT NEXT DOOR AND SEEMED TO BE NORMAL.
FUTOUKA ACADEMY
Massage Research
is innovative.
UM, WHAT'S A MASSAGE CLUB?
ALTHOUGH I KNEW IT WOULD BE HUGE...
...I WAS SURPRISED AT THE SIZE OF THE APARTMENT BUILDING.
SLIP
OH, BUT THE VIEW IS GREAT!!
It's a river!!
FUTOUKA ACADEMY IS KIND OF IN THE COUNTRYSIDE.
IT'S 20 MINUTES TO THE SCHOOL ON A BICYCLE. IT'S THE FIRST TIME I'LL BE LIVING ALL ALONE.
THERE ARE LOTS OF TV CHANNELS.
I'VE NEVER FELT SO NERVOUS BEFORE.
BUT EVERY-THING SEEMS TO BE SHINING.

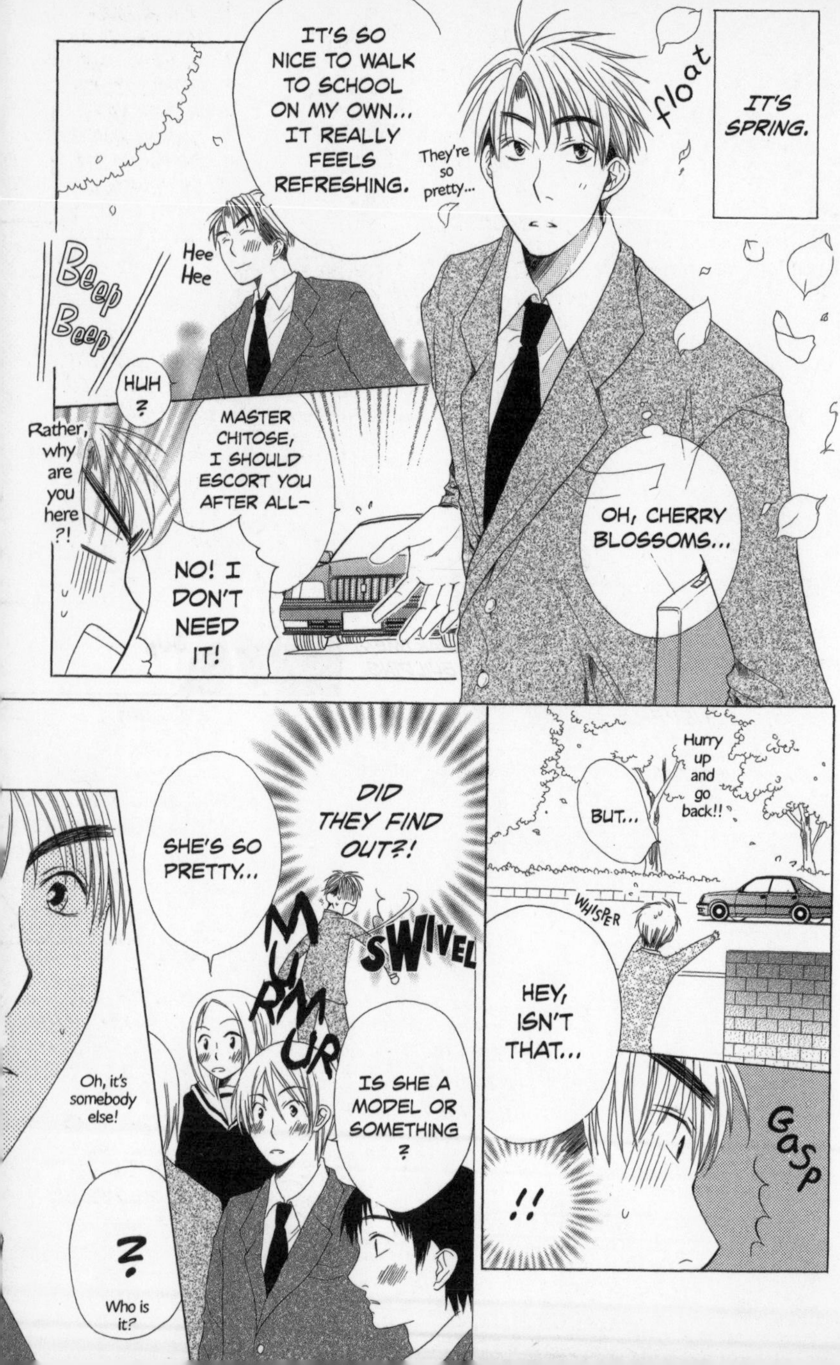
IT'S SPRING.
float
IT'S SO NICE TO WALK TO SCHOOL ON MY OWN... IT REALLY FEELS REFRESHING.
They're so pretty...
OH, CHERRY BLOSSOMS...
Beep Beep
Hee Hee
HUH?
MASTER CHITOSE, I SHOULD ESCORT YOU AFTER ALL–
NO! I DON'T NEED IT!
Rather, why are you here?!
Hurry up and go back!!
BUT...
WHISPER
HEY, ISN'T THAT...
GASP
!!
DID THEY FIND OUT?!
SWIVEL
MURMUR
SHE'S SO PRETTY...
IS SHE A MODEL OR SOMETHING?
Oh, it's somebody else!
?
Who is it?

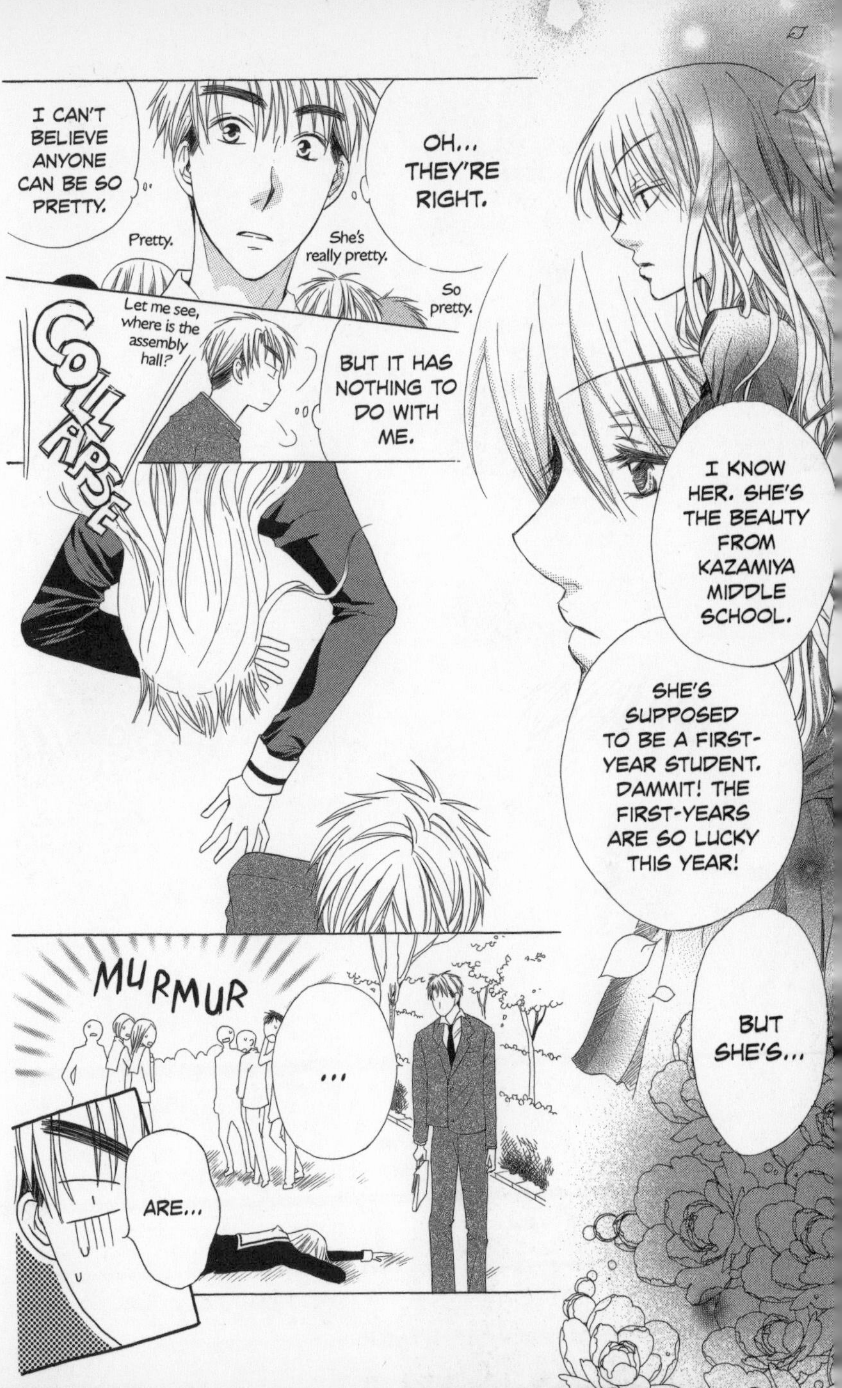
I KNOW HER. SHE'S THE BEAUTY FROM KAZAMIYA MIDDLE SCHOOL.
SHE'S SUPPOSED TO BE A FIRST-YEAR STUDENT. DAMMIT! THE FIRST-YEARS ARE SO LUCKY THIS YEAR!
BUT SHE'S...
OH... THEY'RE RIGHT.
She's really pretty.
So pretty.
I CAN'T BELIEVE ANYONE CAN BE SO PRETTY.
Pretty.
BUT IT HAS NOTHING TO DO WITH ME.
Let me see, where is the assembly hall?
COLLAPSE
MURMUR
...
ARE...

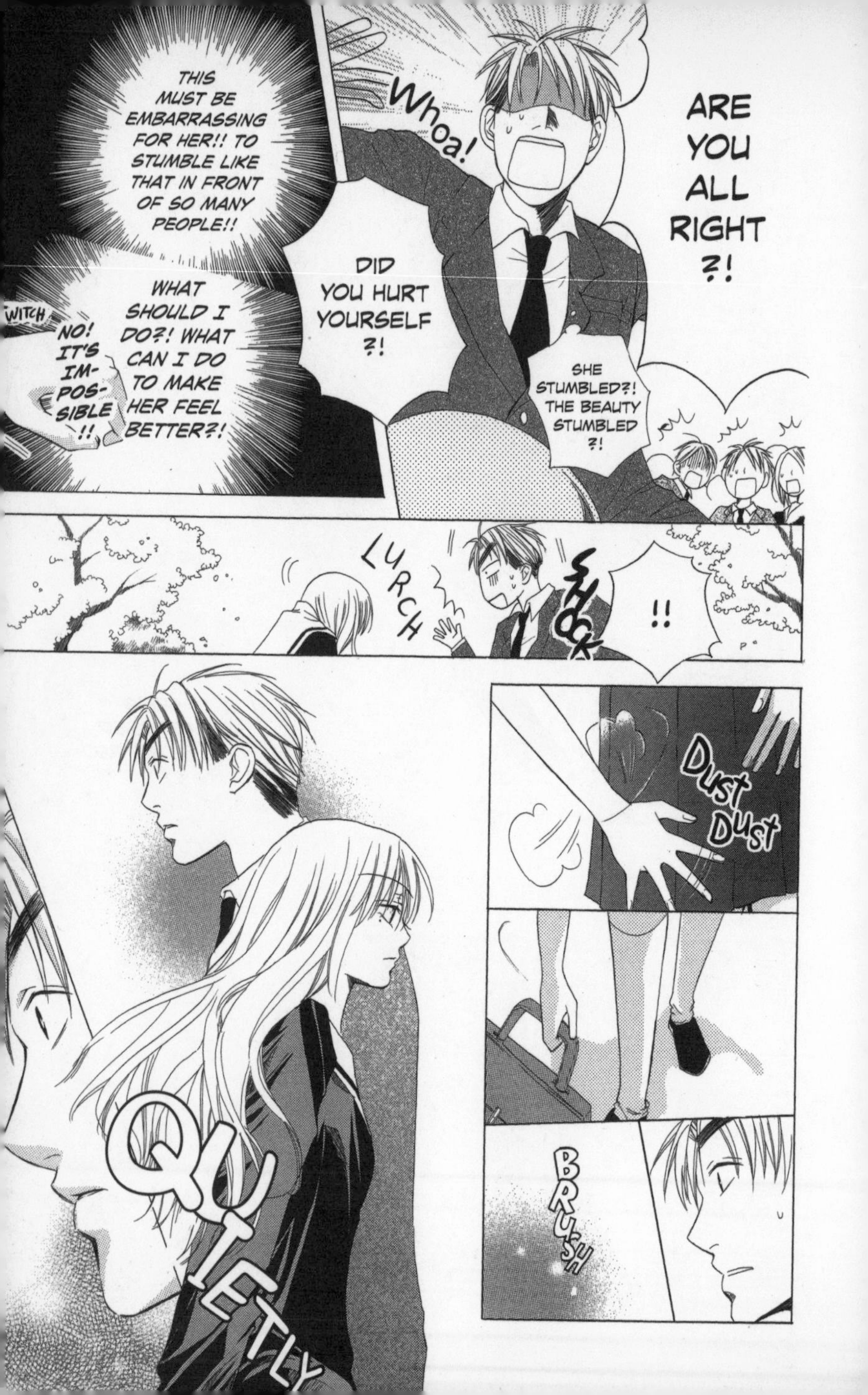
ARE YOU ALL RIGHT?!
Whoa!
SHE STUMBLED?! THE BEAUTY STUMBLED?!
DID YOU HURT YOURSELF?!
THIS MUST BE EMBARRASSING FOR HER!! TO STUMBLE LIKE THAT IN FRONT OF SO MANY PEOPLE!!
WHAT SHOULD I DO?! WHAT CAN I DO TO MAKE HER FEEL BETTER?!
NO! IT'S IMPOSSIBLE!!
WITCH
!!
SHOCK
LURCH
Dust Dust
BRUSH
QUIETLY

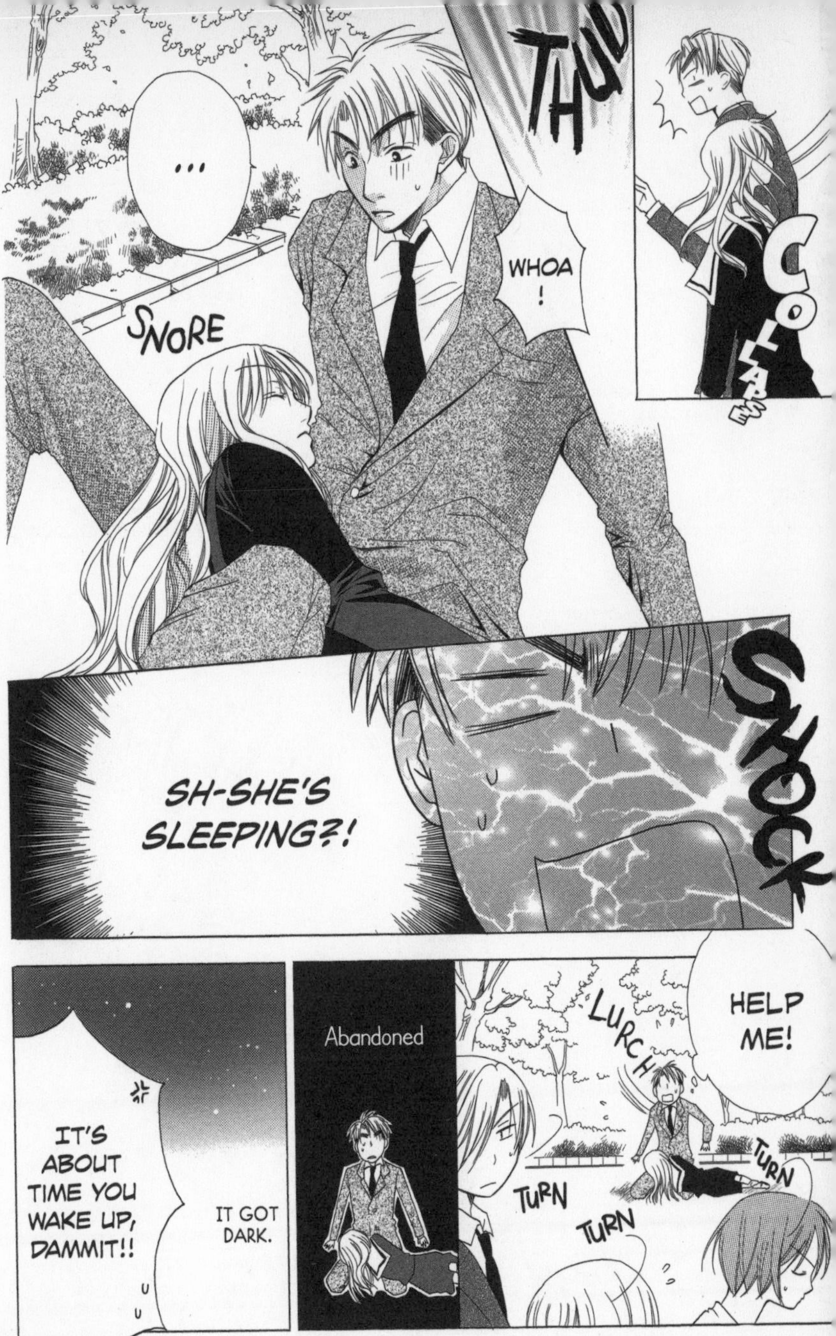
THUD
COLLAPSE
WHOA!
...
SNORE
SHOCK
SH-SHE'S SLEEPING?!
HELP ME!
LURCH
TURN
TURN
TURN
Abandoned
IT GOT DARK.
IT'S ABOUT TIME YOU WAKE UP, DAMMIT!!

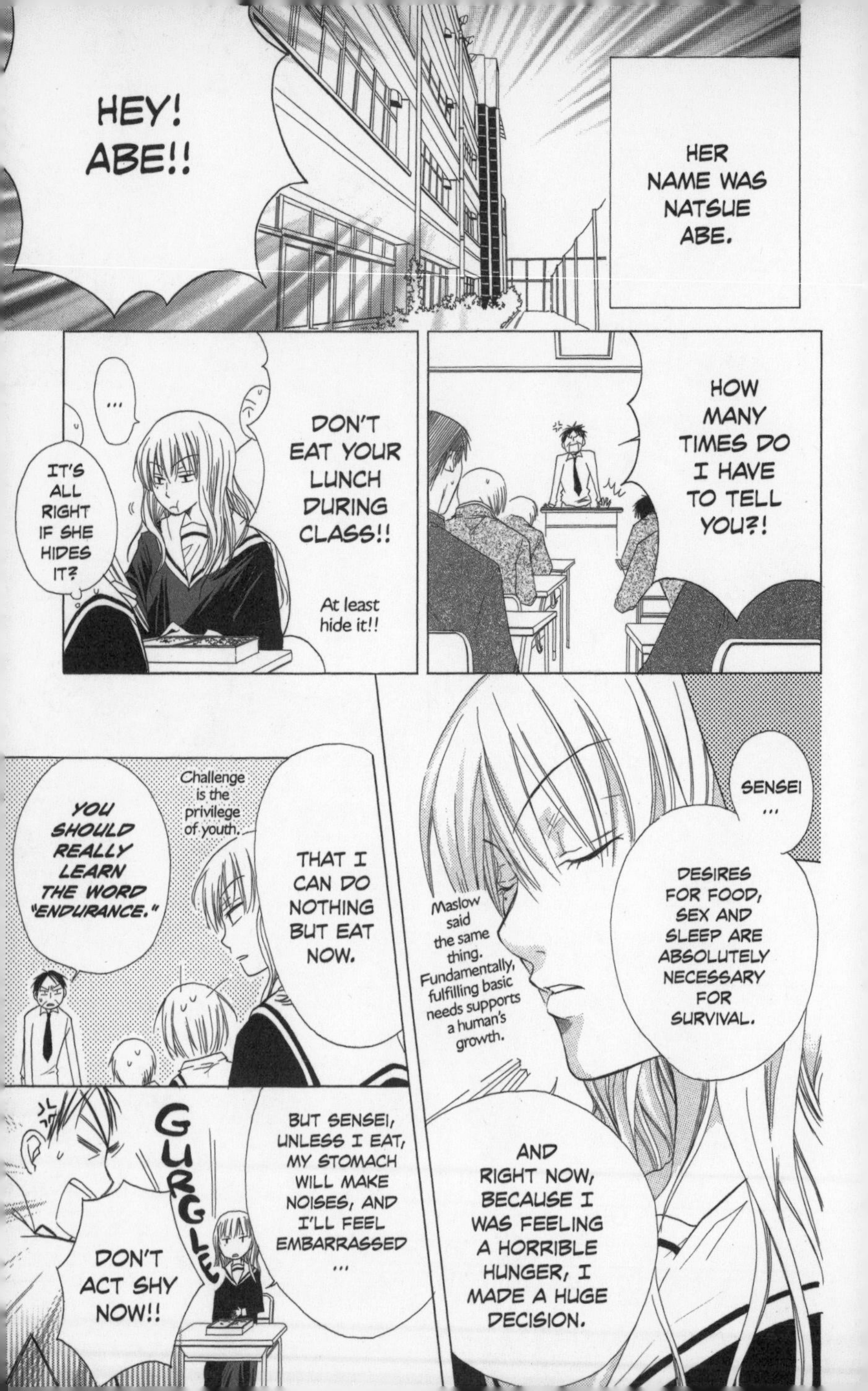
HER NAME WAS NATSUE ABE.
HEY! ABE!!
HOW MANY TIMES DO I HAVE TO TELL YOU?!
DON'T EAT YOUR LUNCH DURING CLASS!!
...
At least hide it!!
IT'S ALL RIGHT IF SHE HIDES IT?
SENSEI ...
DESIRES FOR FOOD, SEX AND SLEEP ARE ABSOLUTELY NECESSARY FOR SURVIVAL.
Maslow said the same thing. Fundamentally, fulfilling basic needs supports a human's growth.
AND RIGHT NOW, BECAUSE I WAS FEELING A HORRIBLE HUNGER, I MADE A HUGE DECISION.
THAT I CAN DO NOTHING BUT EAT NOW.
Challenge is the privilege of youth.
YOU SHOULD REALLY LEARN THE WORD "ENDURANCE."
BUT SENSEI, UNLESS I EAT, MY STOMACH WILL MAKE NOISES, AND I'LL FEEL EMBARRASSED ...
GURGLE
DON'T ACT SHY NOW!!

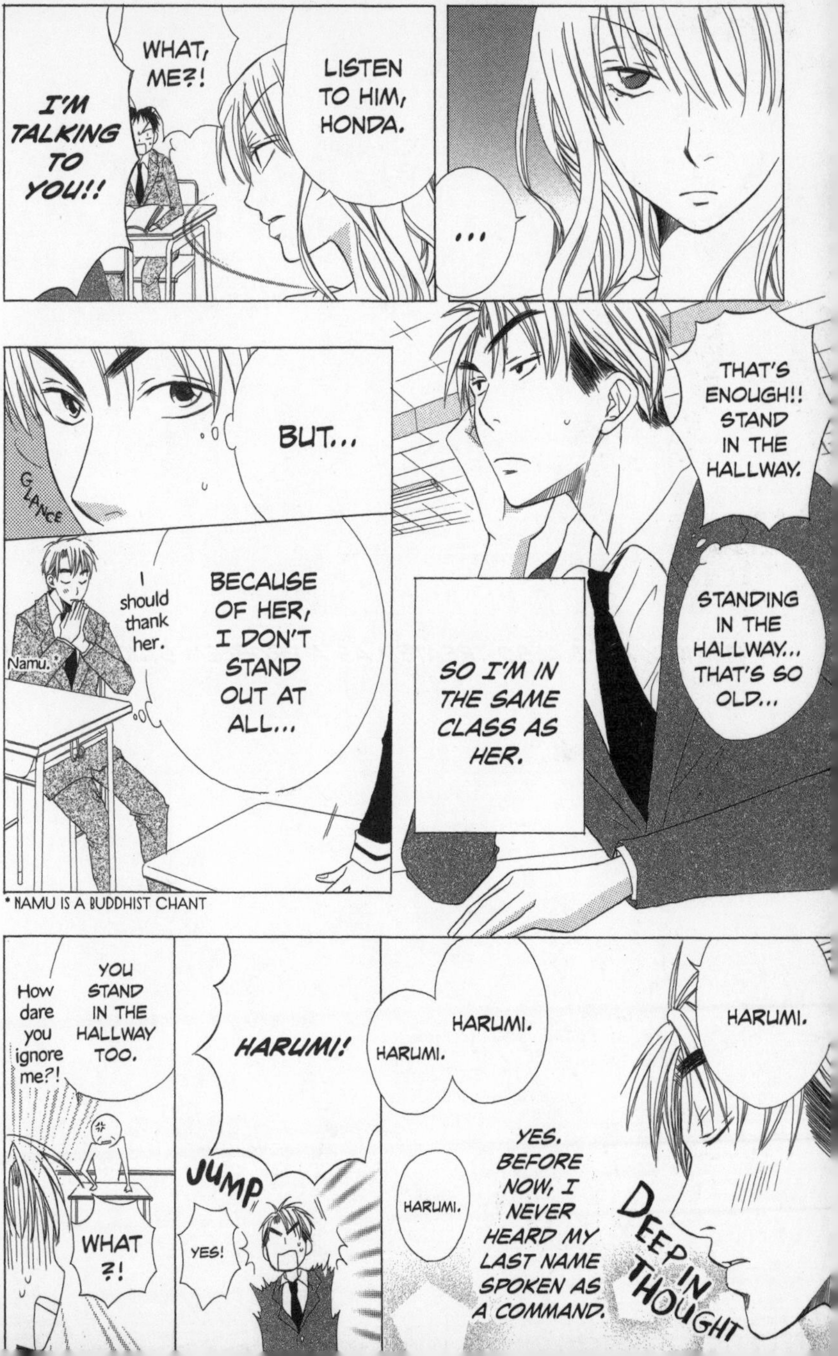
...
LISTEN TO HIM, HONDA.
WHAT, ME?!
I'M TALKING TO YOU!!
THAT'S ENOUGH!! STAND IN THE HALLWAY.
STANDING IN THE HALLWAY... THAT'S SO OLD...
SO I'M IN THE SAME CLASS AS HER.
BUT...
GLANCE
BECAUSE OF HER, I DON'T STAND OUT AT ALL...
I should thank her.
Namu.*
HARUMI.
HARUMI.
HARUMI.
YES. BEFORE NOW, I NEVER HEARD MY LAST NAME SPOKEN AS A COMMAND.
DEEP IN THOUGHT
HARUMI.
HARUMI!
JUMP
YES!
YOU STAND IN THE HALLWAY TOO.
How dare you ignore me?!
WHAT?!

* NAMU IS A BUDDHIST CHANT

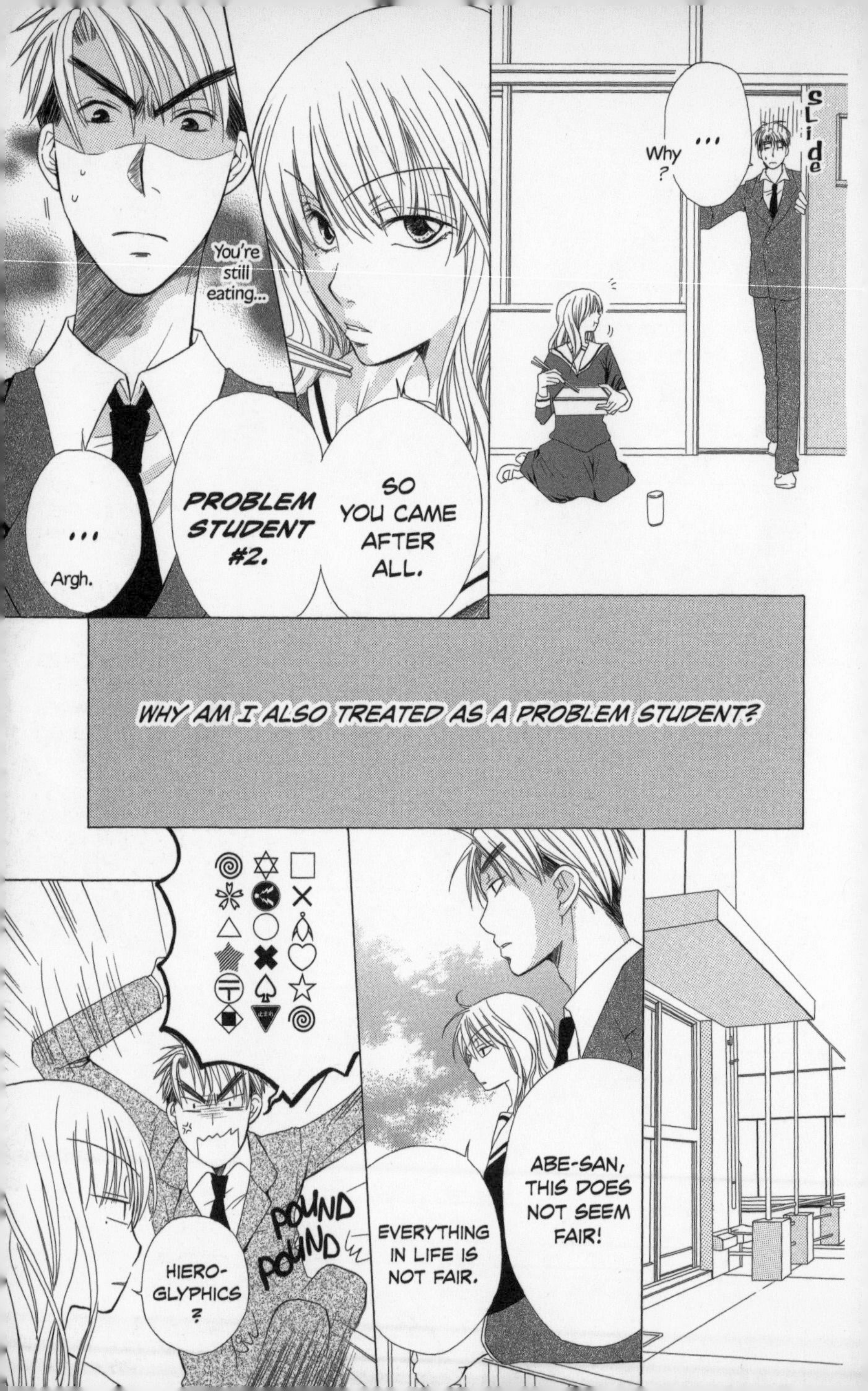
Slide
Why? ...
SO YOU CAME AFTER ALL.
PROBLEM STUDENT #2.
You're still eating...
... Argh.
WHY AM I ALSO TREATED AS A PROBLEM STUDENT?
ABE-SAN, THIS DOES NOT SEEM FAIR!
EVERYTHING IN LIFE IS NOT FAIR.
POUND POUND
HIERO-GLYPHICS?

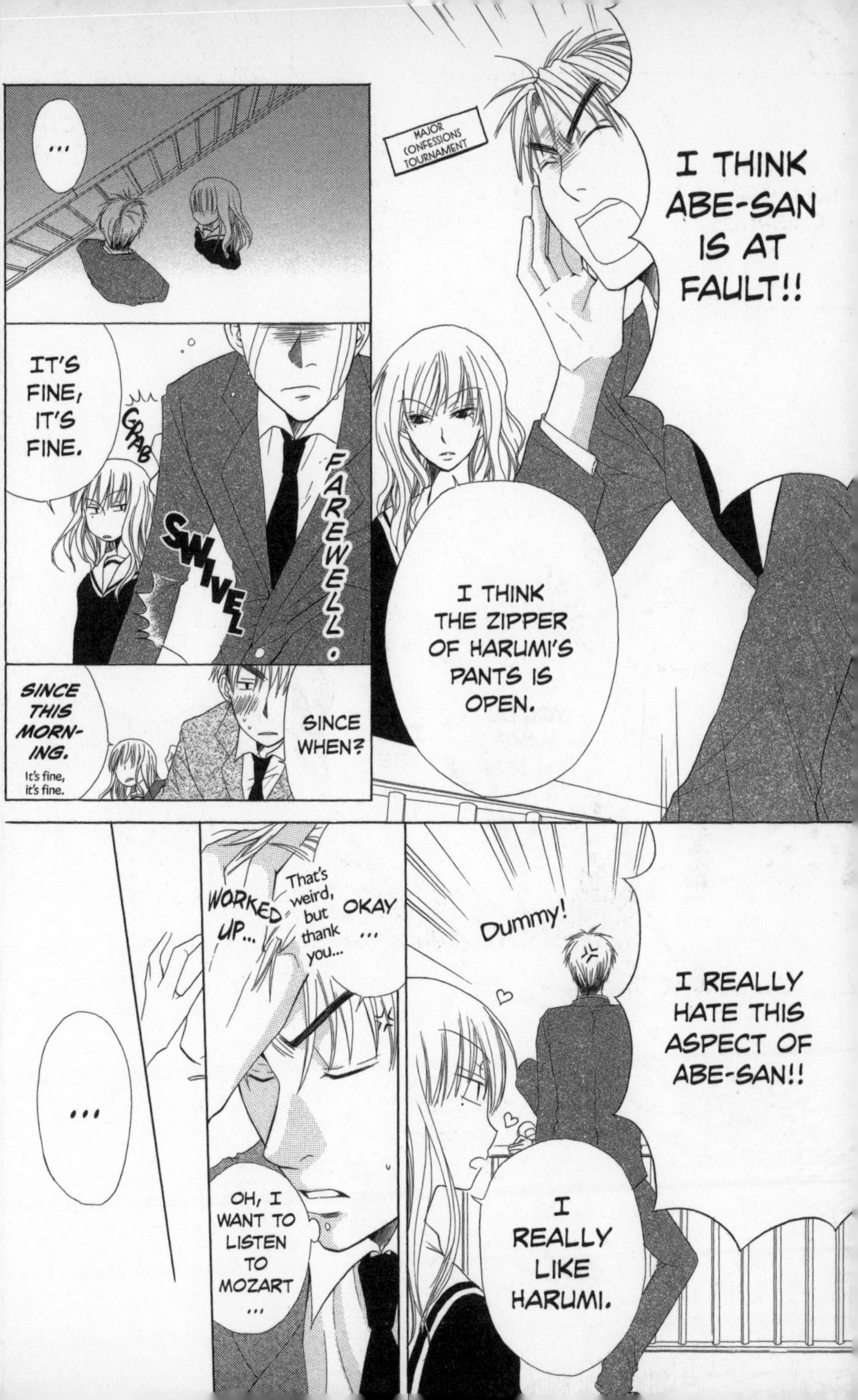
I THINK ABE-SAN IS AT FAULT!!
MAJOR CONFESSIONS TOURNAMENT
I THINK THE ZIPPER OF HARUMI'S PANTS IS OPEN.
...
FAREWELL.
SWIVEL
GRAB
IT'S FINE, IT'S FINE.
SINCE WHEN?
SINCE THIS MORNING.
It's fine, it's fine.
I REALLY HATE THIS ASPECT OF ABE-SAN!!
Dummy!
I REALLY LIKE HARUMI.
OKAY ...
That's weird, but thank you...
WORKED UP...
OH, I WANT TO LISTEN TO MOZART ...
...

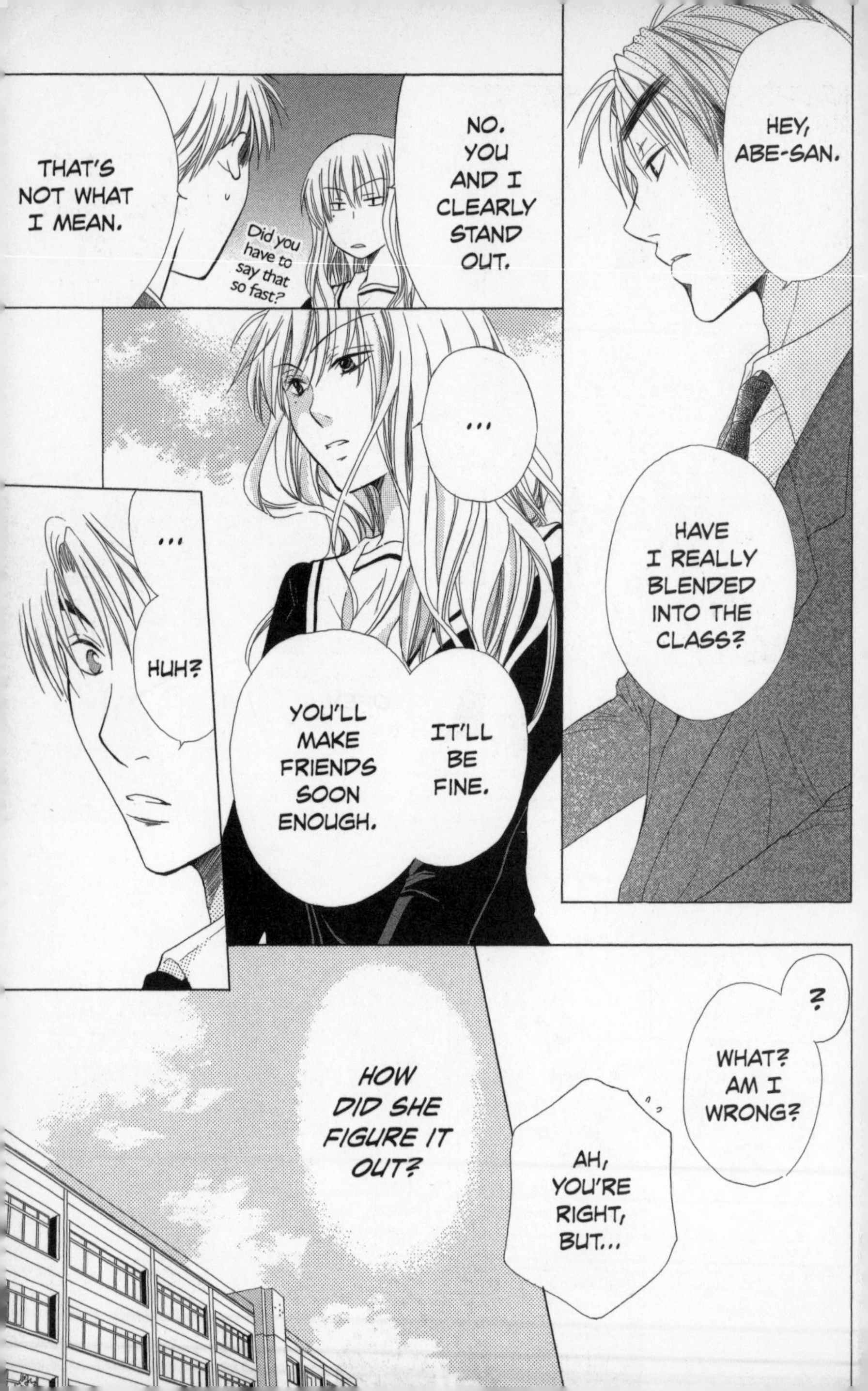
HEY, ABE-SAN.
HAVE I REALLY BLENDED INTO THE CLASS?
NO. YOU AND I CLEARLY STAND OUT.
THAT'S NOT WHAT I MEAN.
Did you have to say that so fast?
...
IT'LL BE FINE.
YOU'LL MAKE FRIENDS SOON ENOUGH.
...
HUH?
?
WHAT? AM I WRONG?
AH, YOU'RE RIGHT, BUT...
HOW DID SHE FIGURE IT OUT?

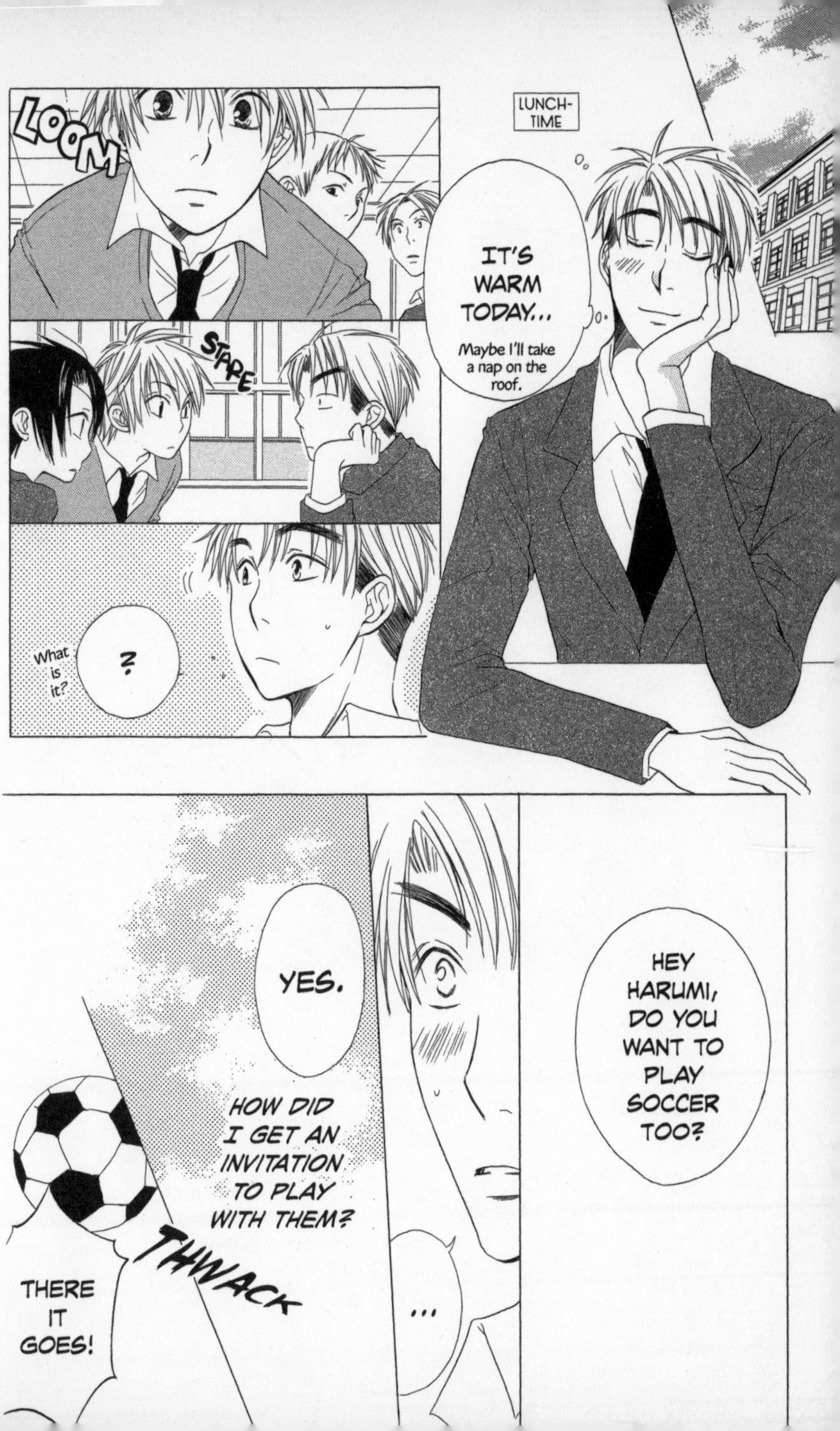
LUNCH-TIME
IT'S WARM TODAY... Maybe I'll take a nap on the roof.
LOOM
STARE
?
What is it?
HEY HARUMI, DO YOU WANT TO PLAY SOCCER TOO?
YES.
...
HOW DID I GET AN INVITATION TO PLAY WITH THEM?
THWACK
THERE IT GOES!

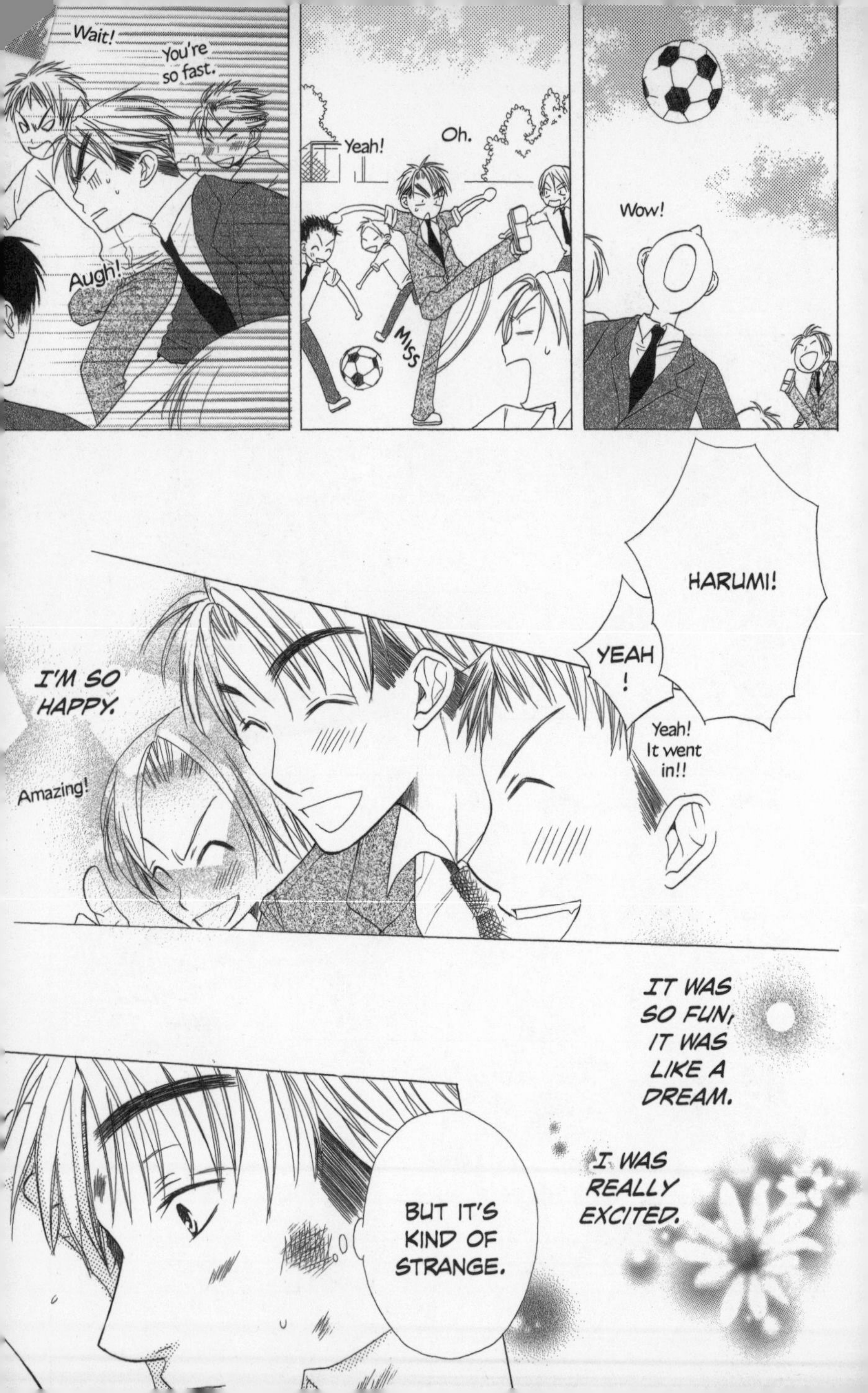
Wow!
Oh.
Yeah!
MISS
Wait!
You're so fast.
Augh!
HARUMI!
YEAH!
Yeah! It went in!!
I'M SO HAPPY.
Amazing!
IT WAS SO FUN, IT WAS LIKE A DREAM.
I WAS REALLY EXCITED.
BUT IT'S KIND OF STRANGE.

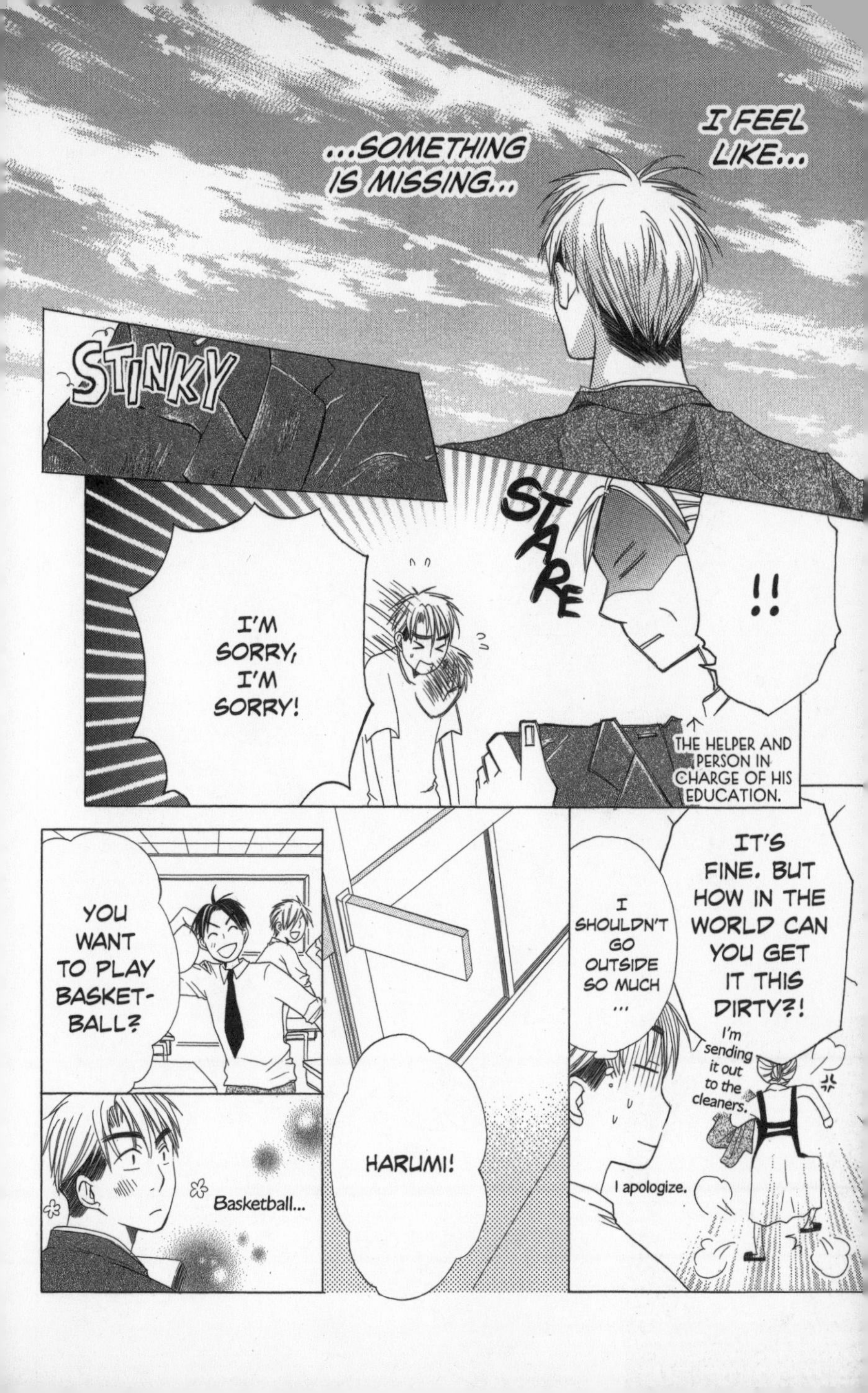
I FEEL LIKE...
...SOMETHING IS MISSING...
STINKY
!!
STARE
THE HELPER AND PERSON IN CHARGE OF HIS EDUCATION.
I'M SORRY, I'M SORRY!
IT'S FINE. BUT HOW IN THE WORLD CAN YOU GET IT THIS DIRTY?!
I'm sending it out to the cleaners.
I SHOULDN'T GO OUTSIDE SO MUCH ...
I apologize.
HARUMI!
YOU WANT TO PLAY BASKET-BALL?
Basketball...

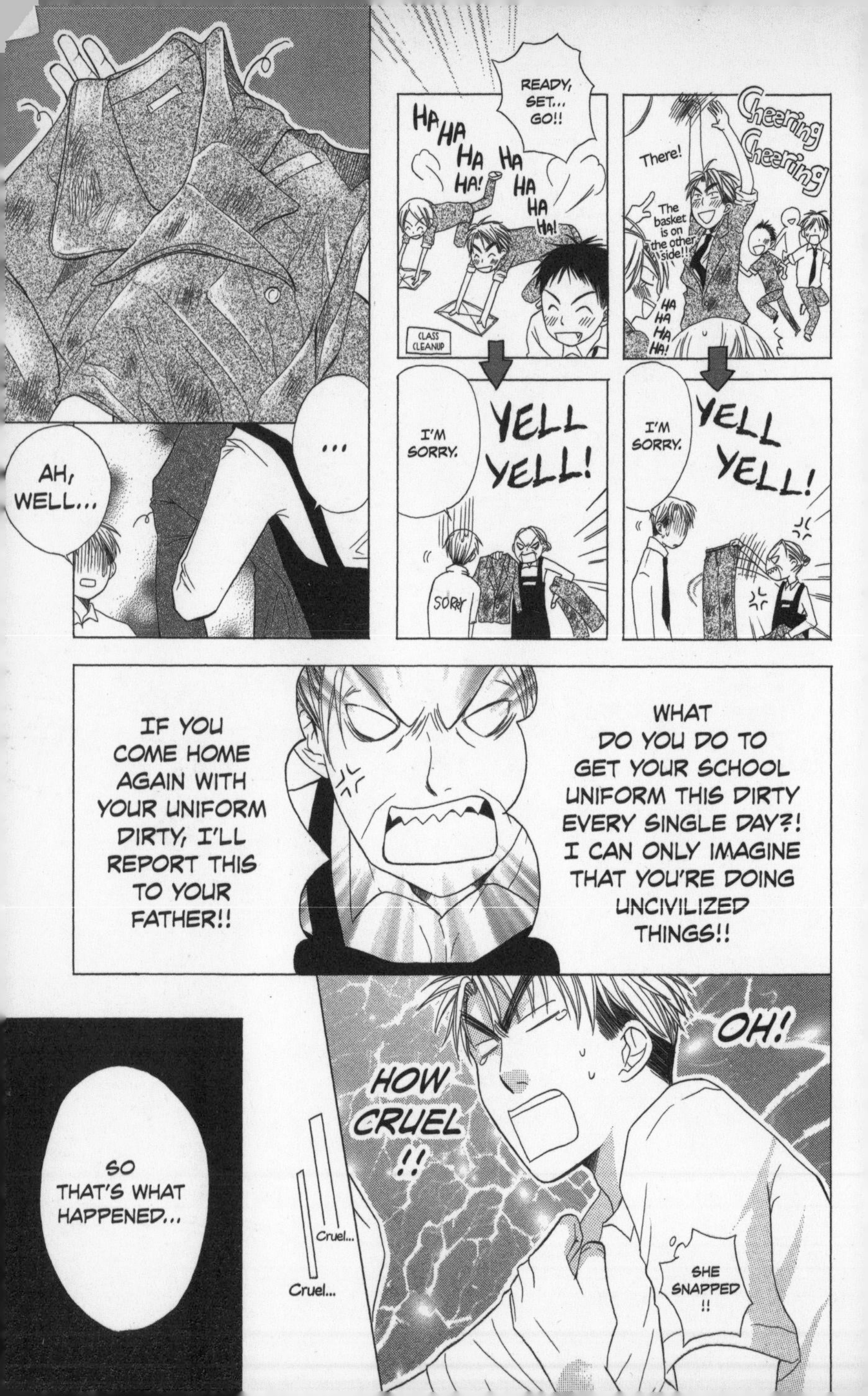
Cheering
Cheering
There!
The basket is on the other side!!
HA HA HA HA!
READY, SET... GO!!
HA HA HA HA HA! HA HA HA HA!
CLASS CLEANUP
I'M SORRY.
YELL YELL!
I'M SORRY.
YELL YELL!
SORRY
...
AH, WELL...
WHAT DO YOU DO TO GET YOUR SCHOOL UNIFORM THIS DIRTY EVERY SINGLE DAY?! I CAN ONLY IMAGINE THAT YOU'RE DOING UNCIVILIZED THINGS!!
IF YOU COME HOME AGAIN WITH YOUR UNIFORM DIRTY, I'LL REPORT THIS TO YOUR FATHER!!
OH!
HOW CRUEL!!
SHE SNAPPED!!
Cruel...
Cruel...
SO THAT'S WHAT HAPPENED...

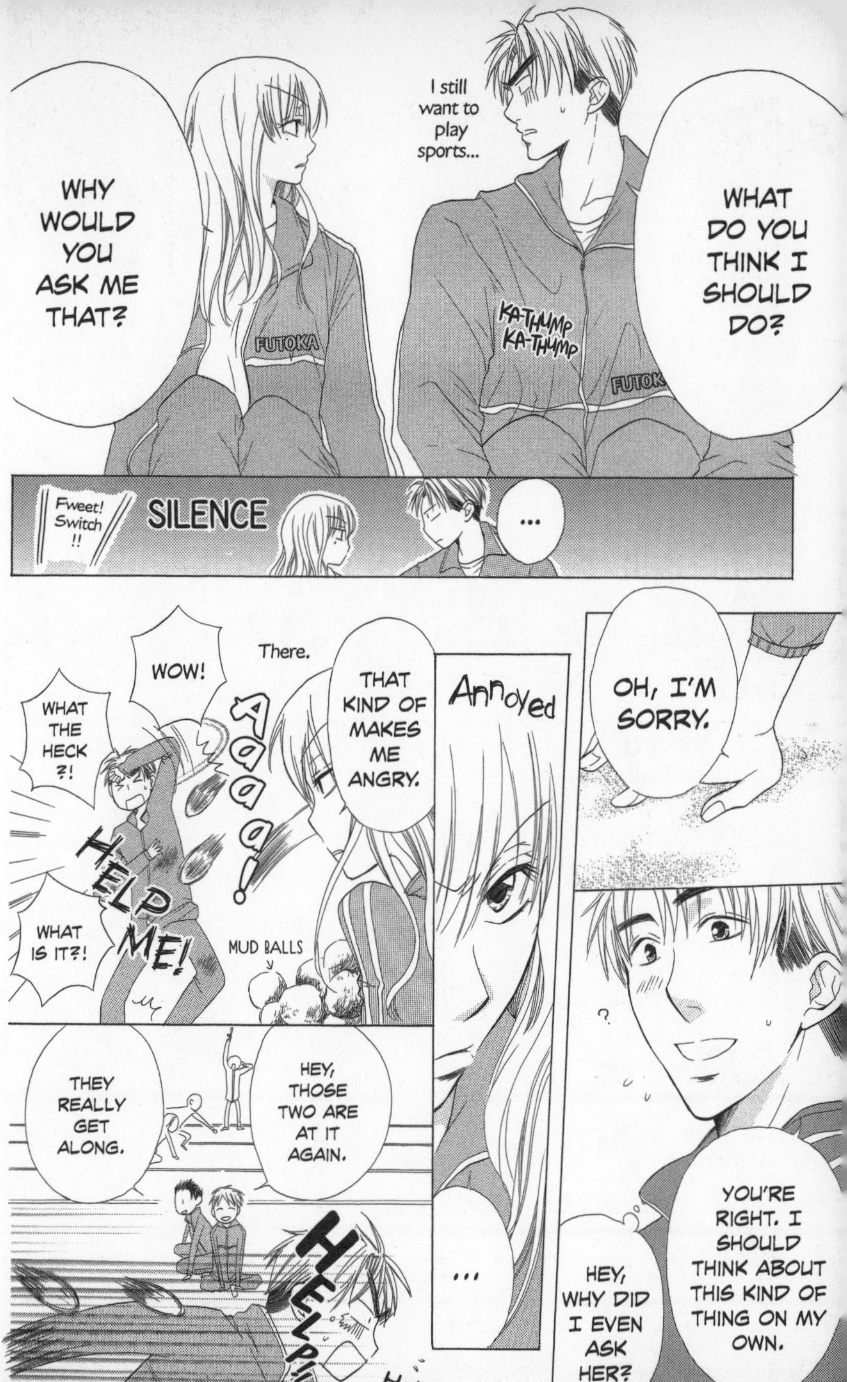
WHAT DO YOU THINK I SHOULD DO?
I still want to play sports...
KA-THUMP KA-THUMP
FUTOKA
WHY WOULD YOU ASK ME THAT?
FUTOKA
...
SILENCE
Fweet! Switch !!
OH, I'M SORRY.
YOU'RE RIGHT. I SHOULD THINK ABOUT THIS KIND OF THING ON MY OWN.
HEY, WHY DID I EVEN ASK HER?
Annoyed
...
THAT KIND OF MAKES ME ANGRY.
There.
Aaaaa!
WOW!
WHAT THE HECK ?!
HELP ME!
WHAT IS IT?!
MUD BALLS
HEY, THOSE TWO ARE AT IT AGAIN.
THEY REALLY GET ALONG.
HELP!!
Help me!

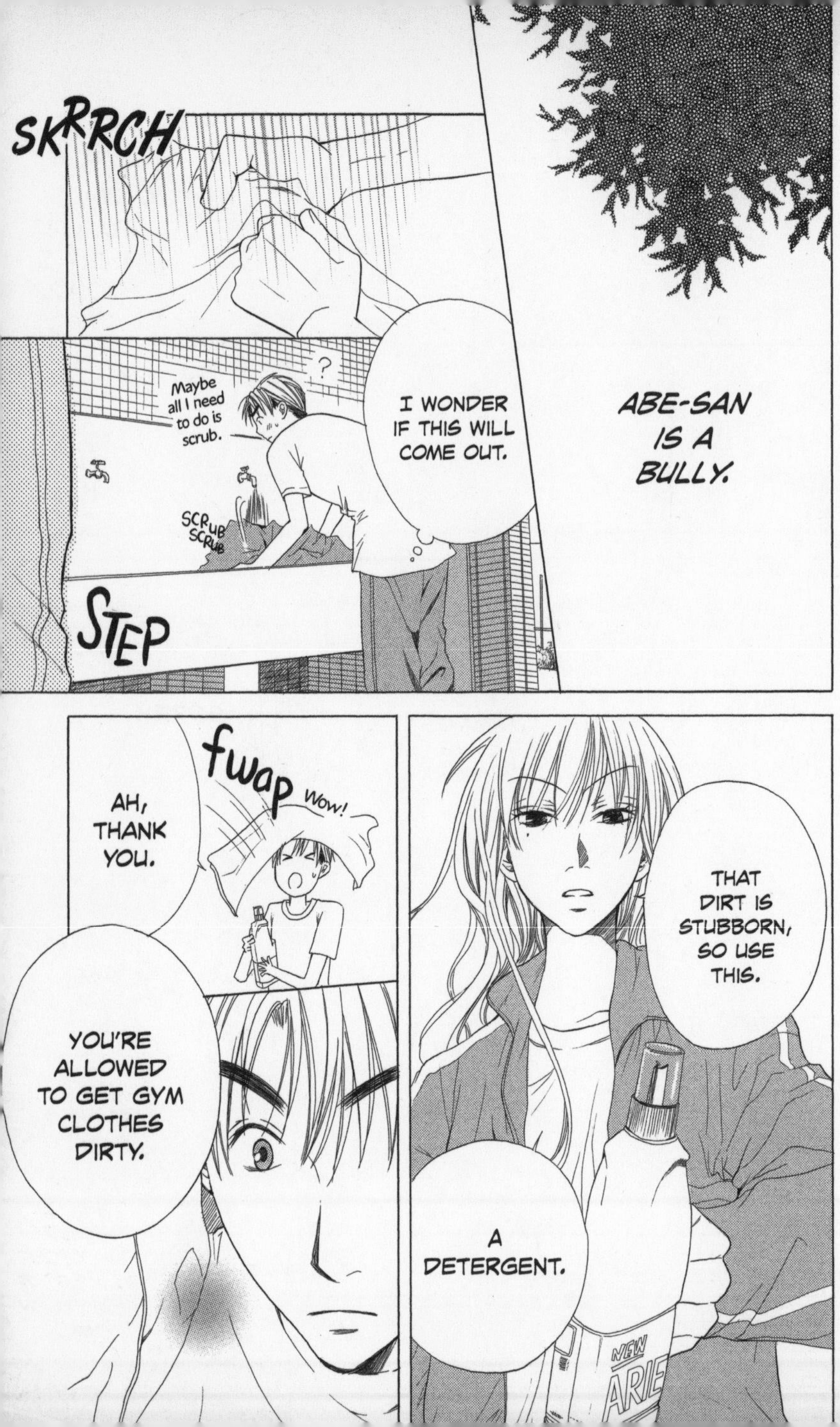
ABE-SAN IS A BULLY.
SKRRCH
I WONDER IF THIS WILL COME OUT.
?
Maybe all I need to do is scrub.
SCRUB SCRUB
STEP
THAT DIRT IS STUBBORN, SO USE THIS.
A DETERGENT.
NEW ARIE
fwap
Wow!
AH, THANK YOU.
YOU'RE ALLOWED TO GET GYM CLOTHES DIRTY.

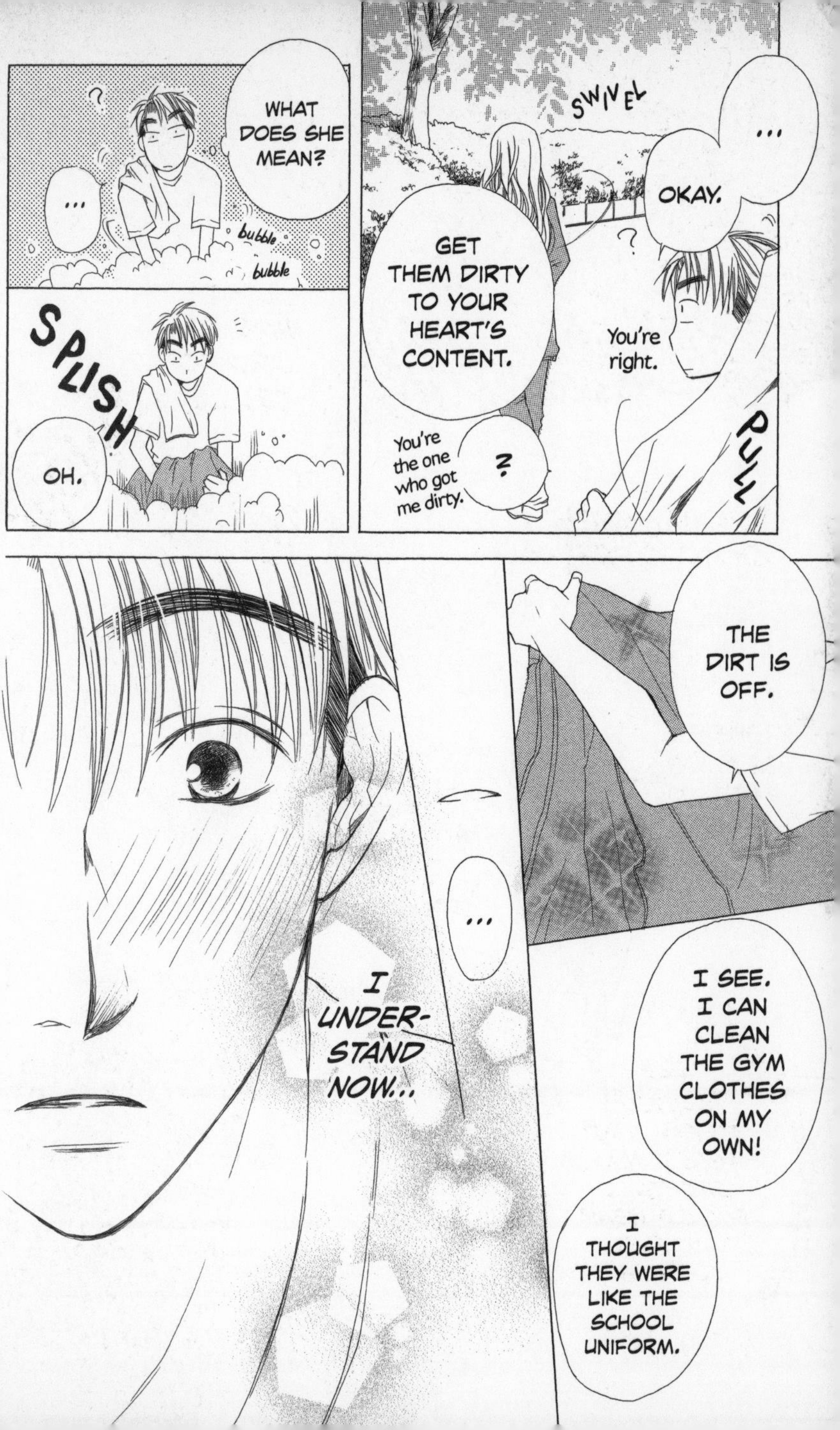
...
OKAY.
SWIVEL
?
GET THEM DIRTY TO YOUR HEART'S CONTENT.
You're right.
PULL
?
You're the one who got me dirty.
WHAT DOES SHE MEAN?
?
...
bubble
bubble
SPLISH
OH.
THE DIRT IS OFF.
I SEE. I CAN CLEAN THE GYM CLOTHES ON MY OWN!
I THOUGHT THEY WERE LIKE THE SCHOOL UNIFORM.
...
I UNDER-STAND NOW...

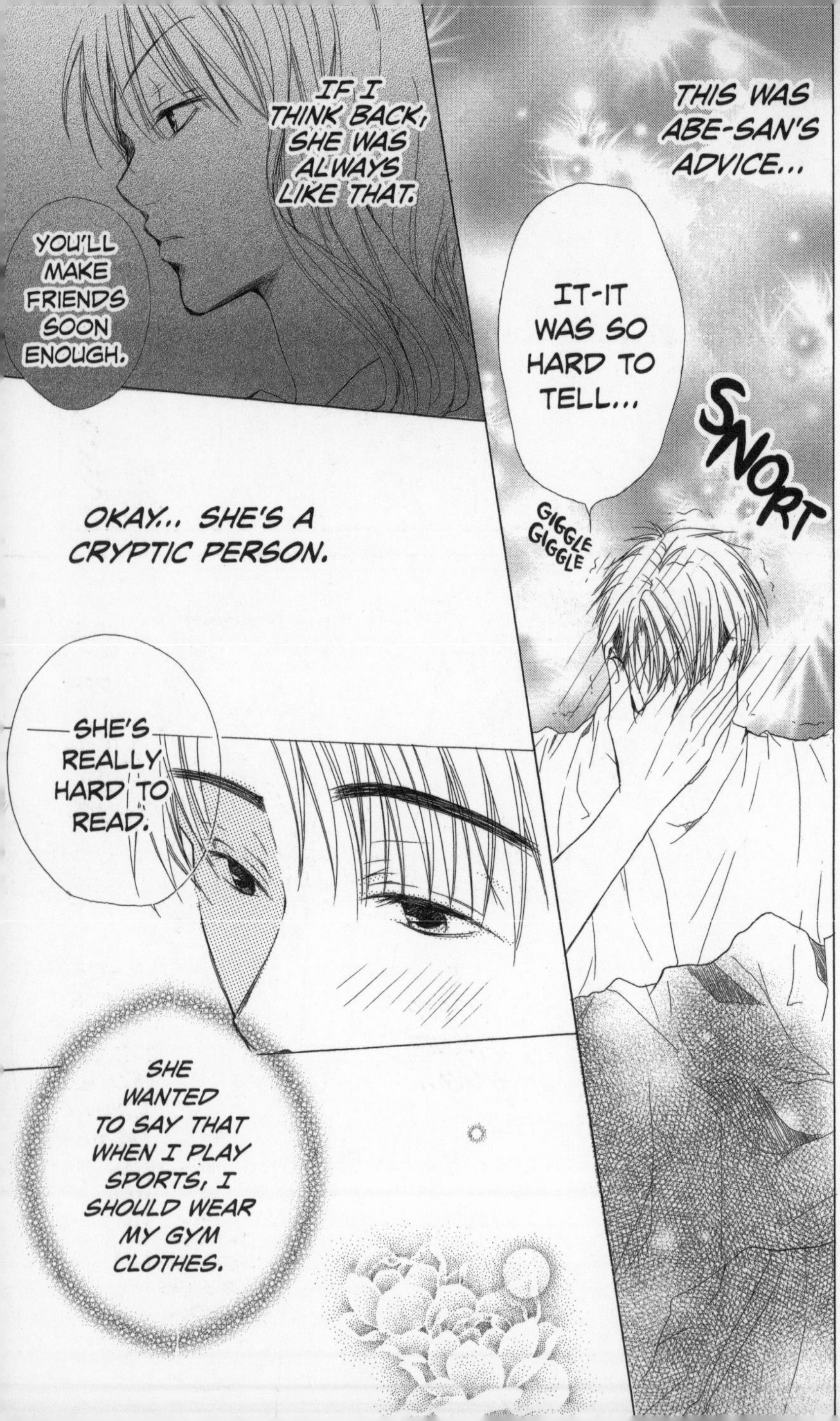
THIS WAS ABE-SAN'S ADVICE...
IT-IT WAS SO HARD TO TELL...
SNORT
GIGGLE GIGGLE
IF I THINK BACK, SHE WAS ALWAYS LIKE THAT.
YOU'LL MAKE FRIENDS SOON ENOUGH.
OKAY.. SHE'S A CRYPTIC PERSON.
SHE'S REALLY HARD TO READ.
SHE WANTED TO SAY THAT WHEN I PLAY SPORTS, I SHOULD WEAR MY GYM CLOTHES.

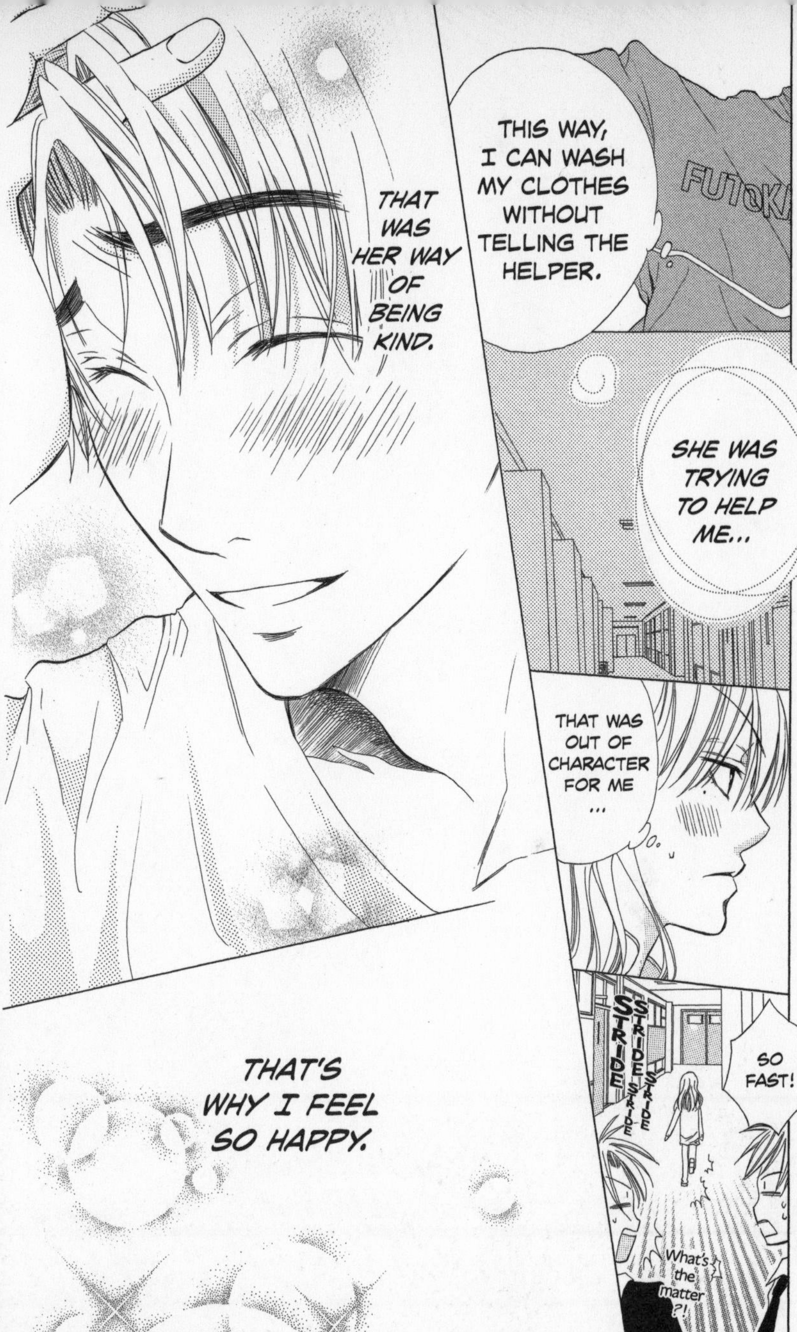
THIS WAY, I CAN WASH MY CLOTHES WITHOUT TELLING THE HELPER.
FUTOKI
SHE WAS TRYING TO HELP ME...
THAT WAS OUT OF CHARACTER FOR ME ...
SO FAST!
STRIDE STRIDE STRIDE STRIDE
What's the matter?!
THAT WAS HER WAY OF BEING KIND.
THAT'S WHY I FEEL SO HAPPY.

The Magic Touch, Part 20/The End

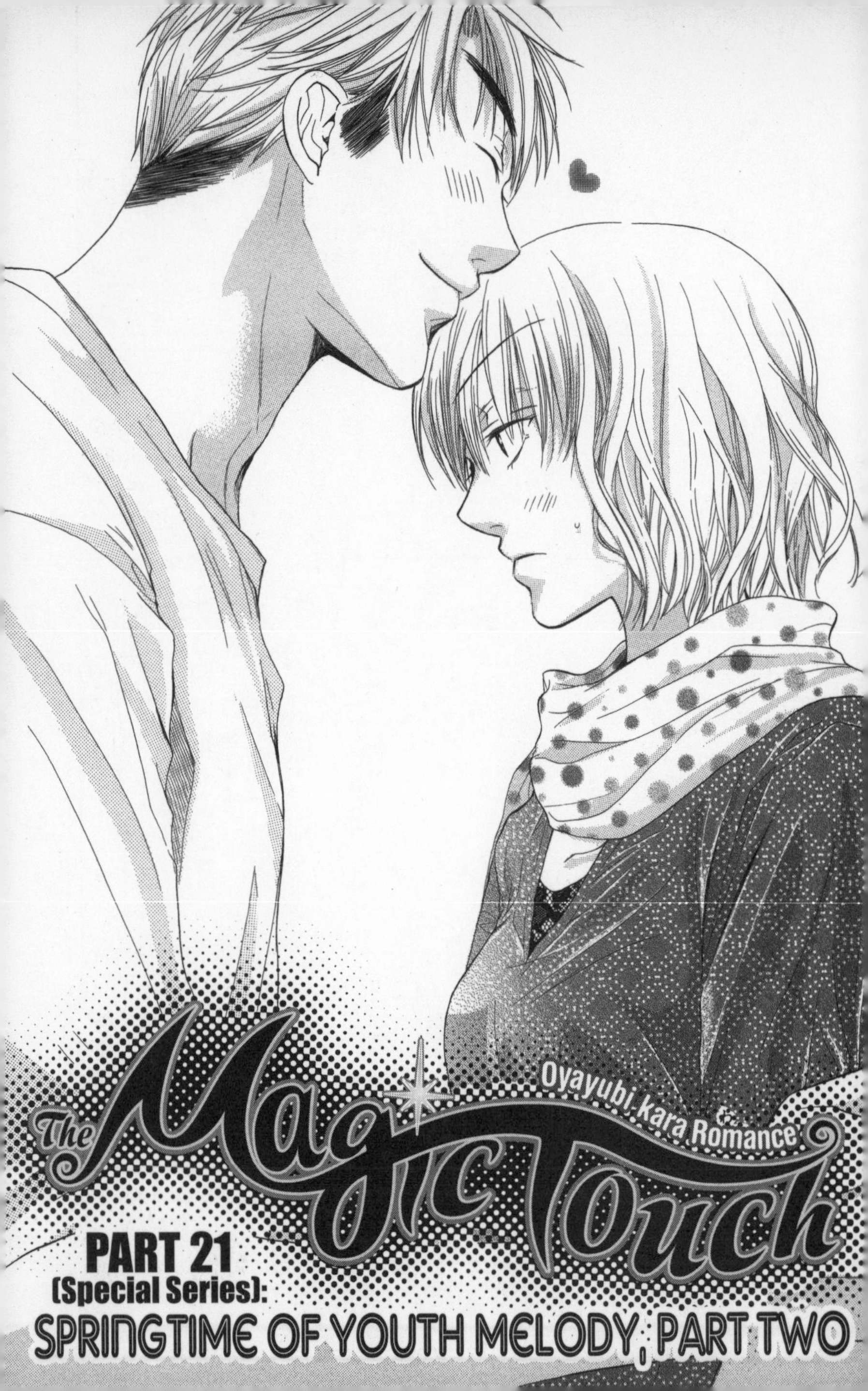
The Magic Touch
Oyayubi kara Romance
PART 21
(Special Series):
SPRINGTIME OF YOUTH MELODY, PART TWO

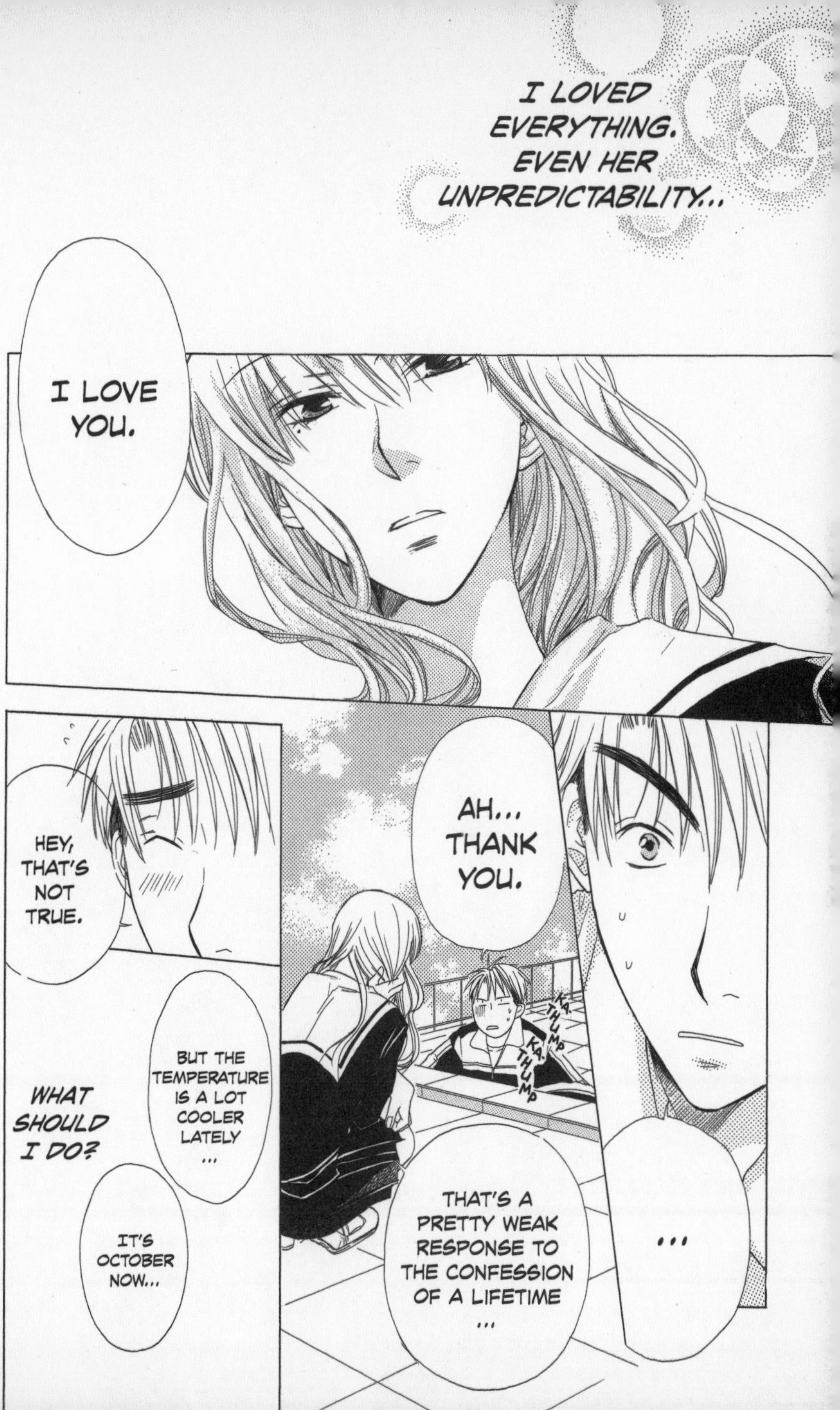
I LOVED EVERYTHING. EVEN HER UNPREDICTABILITY...
I LOVE YOU.
AH... THANK YOU.
...
KA-THUMP KA-THUMP
THAT'S A PRETTY WEAK RESPONSE TO THE CONFESSION OF A LIFETIME ...
HEY, THAT'S NOT TRUE.
BUT THE TEMPERATURE IS A LOT COOLER LATELY ...
WHAT SHOULD I DO?
IT'S OCTOBER NOW...

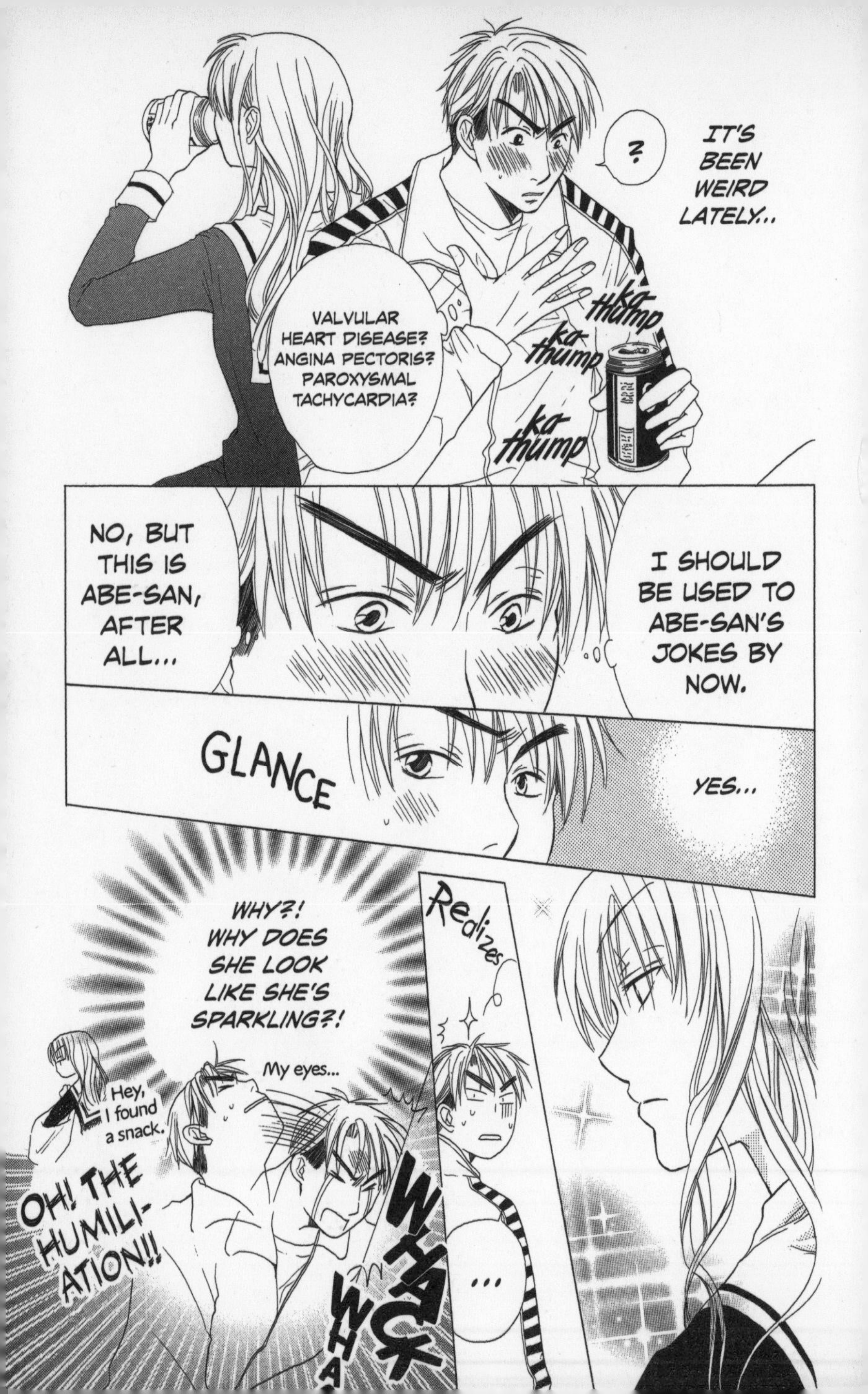

IT'S BEEN WEIRD LATELY...
?
ka-thump
ka-thump
ka-thump
VALVULAR HEART DISEASE? ANGINA PECTORIS? PAROXYSMAL TACHYCARDIA?
I SHOULD BE USED TO ABE-SAN'S JOKES BY NOW.
NO, BUT THIS IS ABE-SAN, AFTER ALL...
YES...
GLANCE
Realizes
...
WHY?! WHY DOES SHE LOOK LIKE SHE'S SPARKLING?!
My eyes...
Hey, I found a snack.
OH! THE HUMILI-ATION!!
WHACK

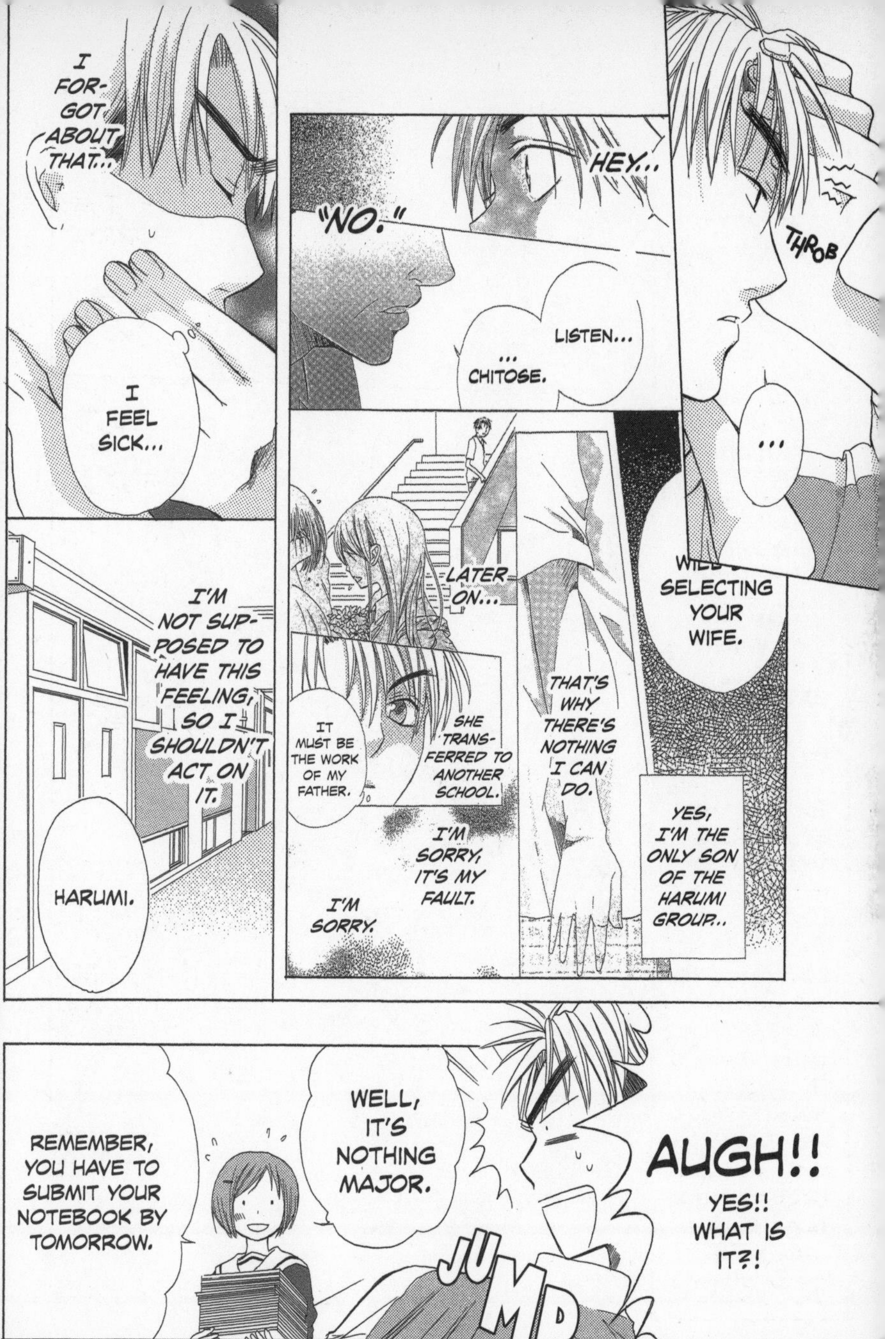
THROB
...
HEY...
"NO."
LISTEN... ...CHITOSE.
I FOR-GOT ABOUT THAT...
I FEEL SICK...
SELECTING YOUR WIFE.
YES, I'M THE ONLY SON OF THE HARUMI GROUP...
THAT'S WHY THERE'S NOTHING I CAN DO.
LATER ON...
SHE TRANS-FERRED TO ANOTHER SCHOOL.
IT MUST BE THE WORK OF MY FATHER.
I'M SORRY, IT'S MY FAULT.
I'M SORRY.
I'M NOT SUP-POSED TO HAVE THIS FEELING, SO I SHOULDN'T ACT ON IT.
HARUMI.
AUGH!!
YES!! WHAT IS IT?!
JUMP
WELL, IT'S NOTHING MAJOR.
REMEMBER, YOU HAVE TO SUBMIT YOUR NOTEBOOK BY TOMORROW.

Plots, Part 3

A better plot appears.

↓

What is it?
It's nonchalant!!
That?
You're going to give up the seat?
Then you're going to give up the seat?
You're going to lend the notebook?

School.
Yes.

Skipping class?

For some reason, it's all in questions. Which makes me want to ask, "What is it?" The content is not clear at all. I wonder why giving up the seat was so shocking. I don't really care, but what does "It's nonchalant!!" mean? Although I wrote it in my high school years, it's as if another person is responsible. After years pass by, a person changes.

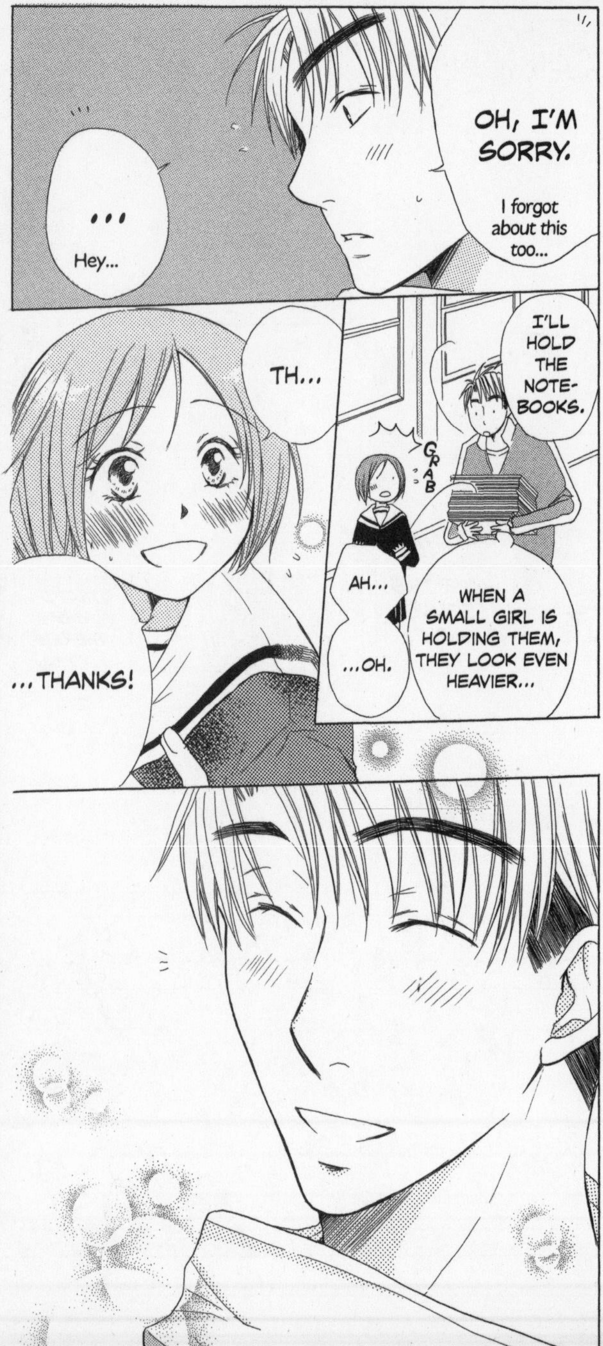
OH, I'M SORRY.
I forgot about this too...
...
Hey...
I'LL HOLD THE NOTE-BOOKS.
GRAB
WHEN A SMALL GIRL IS HOLDING THEM, THEY LOOK EVEN HEAVIER...
AH...
...OH.
TH...
...THANKS!

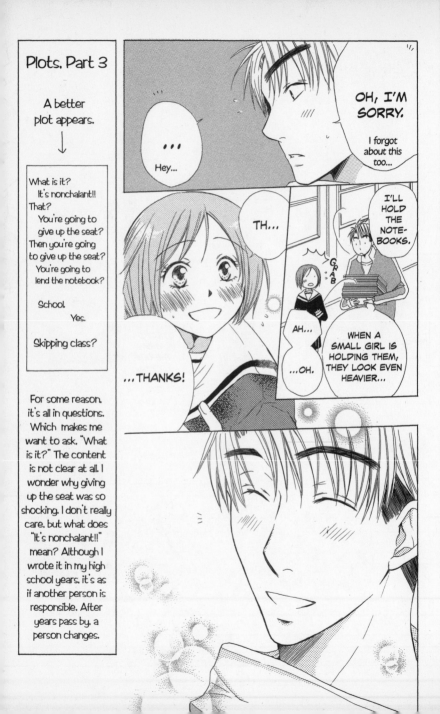

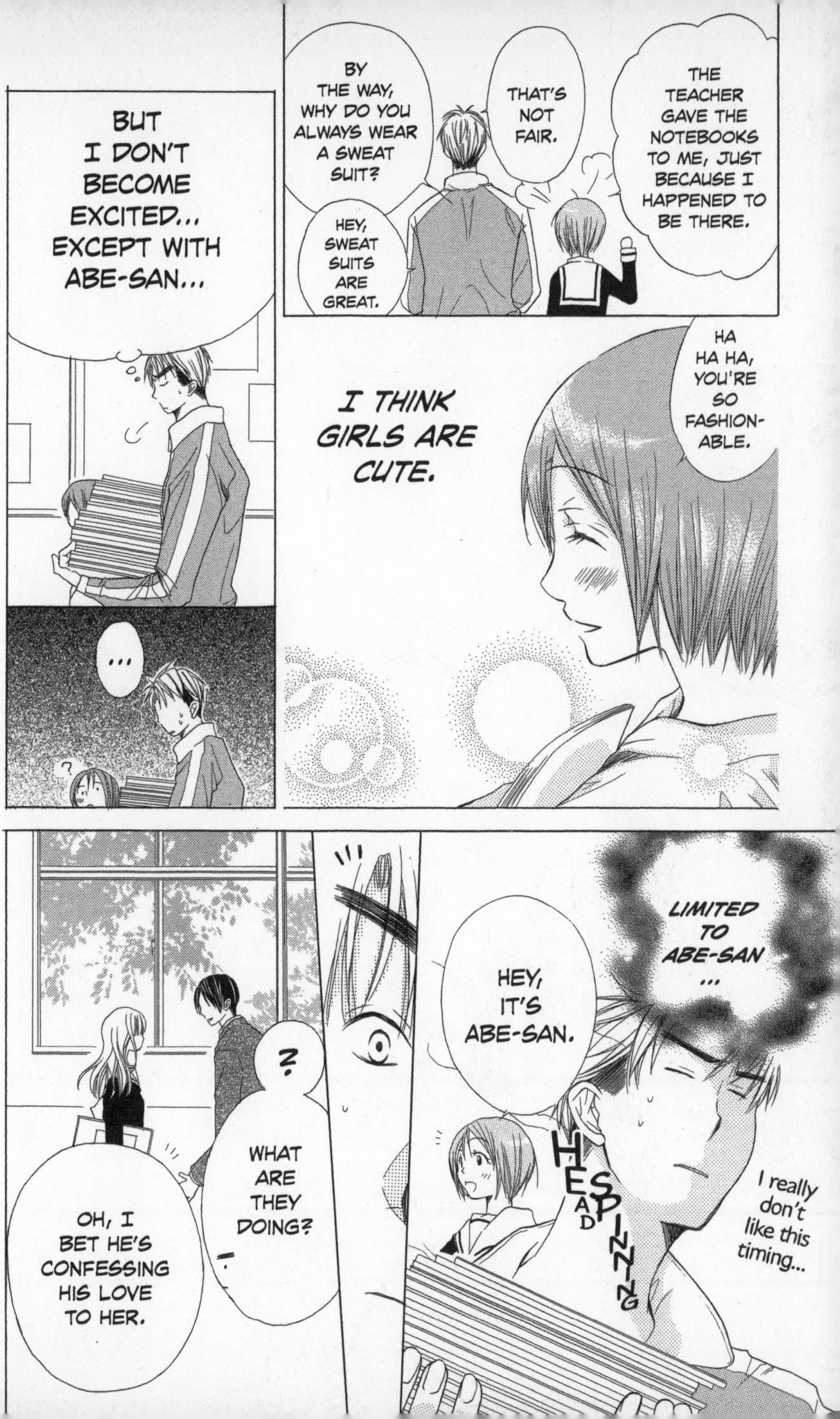
THE TEACHER GAVE THE NOTEBOOKS TO ME, JUST BECAUSE I HAPPENED TO BE THERE.
THAT'S NOT FAIR.
BY THE WAY, WHY DO YOU ALWAYS WEAR A SWEAT SUIT?
HEY, SWEAT SUITS ARE GREAT.
HA HA HA, YOU'RE SO FASHION-ABLE.
I THINK GIRLS ARE CUTE.
BUT I DON'T BECOME EXCITED... EXCEPT WITH ABE-SAN...
...
LIMITED TO ABE-SAN ...
HEY, IT'S ABE-SAN.
HEAD SPINNING
I really don't like this timing...
?
WHAT ARE THEY DOING?
OH, I BET HE'S CONFESSING HIS LOVE TO HER.

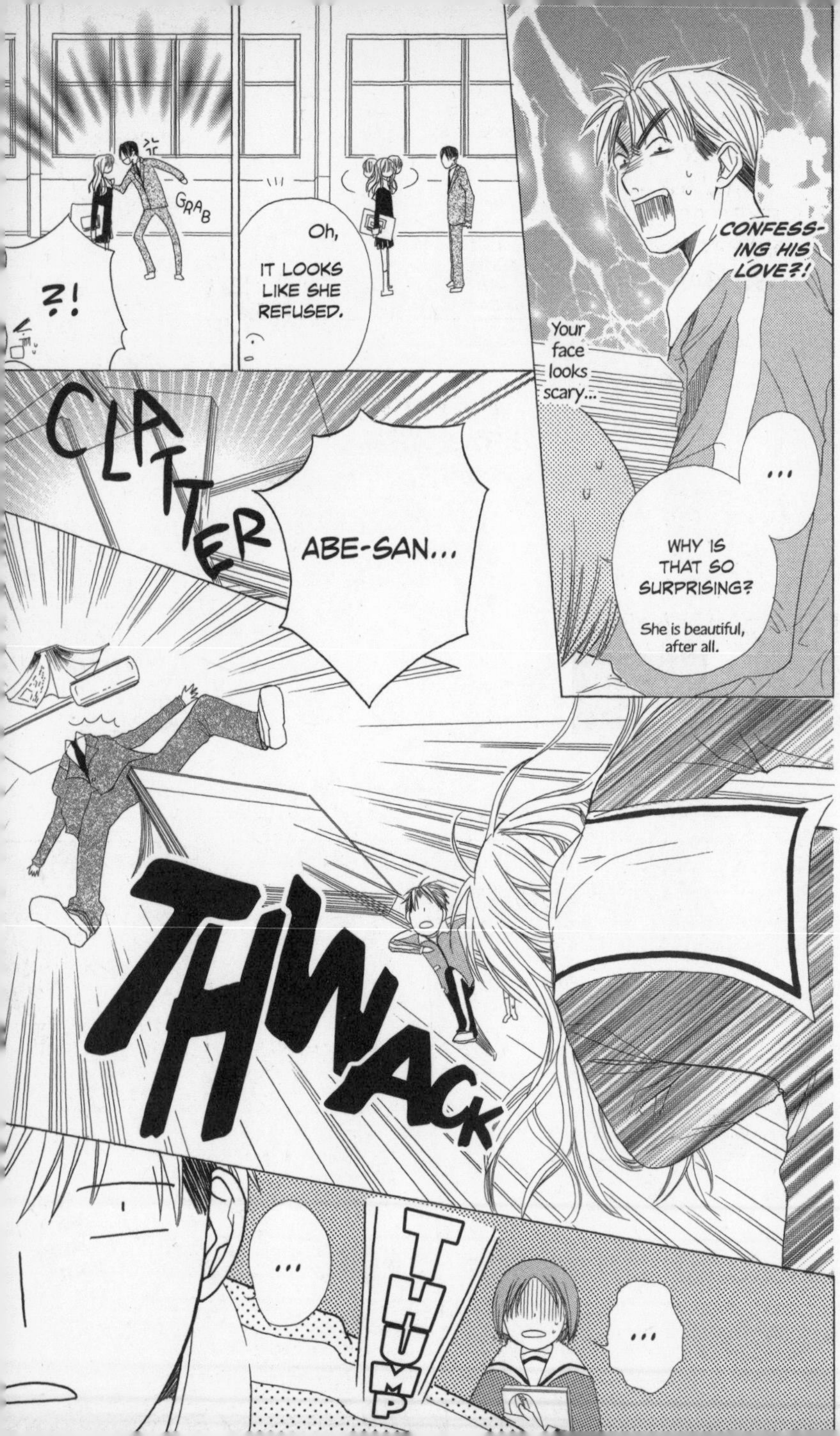
CONFESSING HIS LOVE?!
Your face looks scary...
...
WHY IS THAT SO SURPRISING?
She is beautiful, after all.
Oh,
IT LOOKS LIKE SHE REFUSED.
GRAB
?!
CLATTER
ABE-SAN...
THWACK
...
THUMP
...

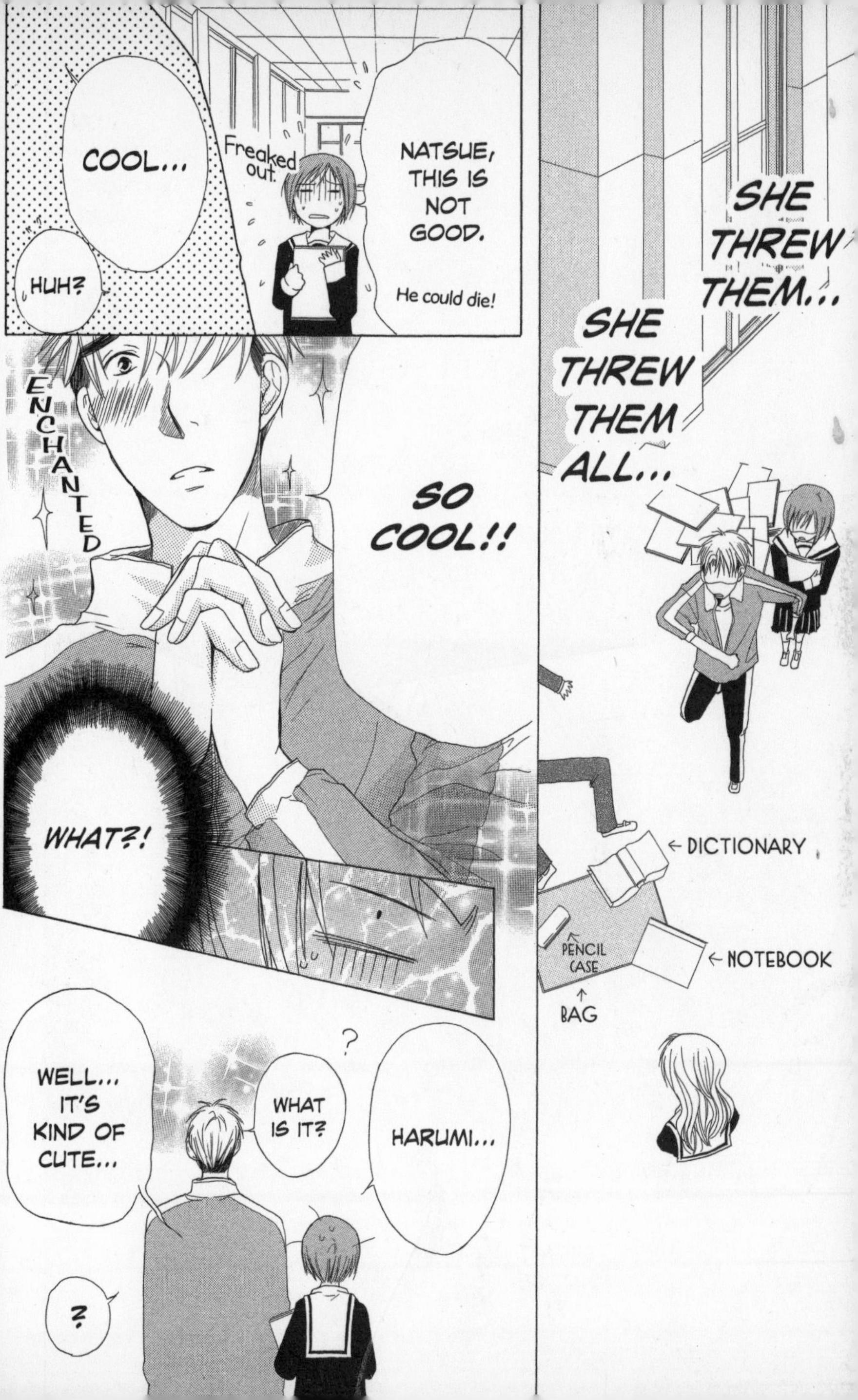
SHE THREW THEM...
SHE THREW THEM ALL...
← DICTIONARY
← NOTEBOOK
PENCIL CASE
BAG
NATSUE, THIS IS NOT GOOD.
He could die!
Freaked out.
COOL...
HUH?
SO COOL!!
ENCHANTED
WHAT?!
HARUMI...
?
WHAT IS IT?
WELL... IT'S KIND OF CUTE...
?

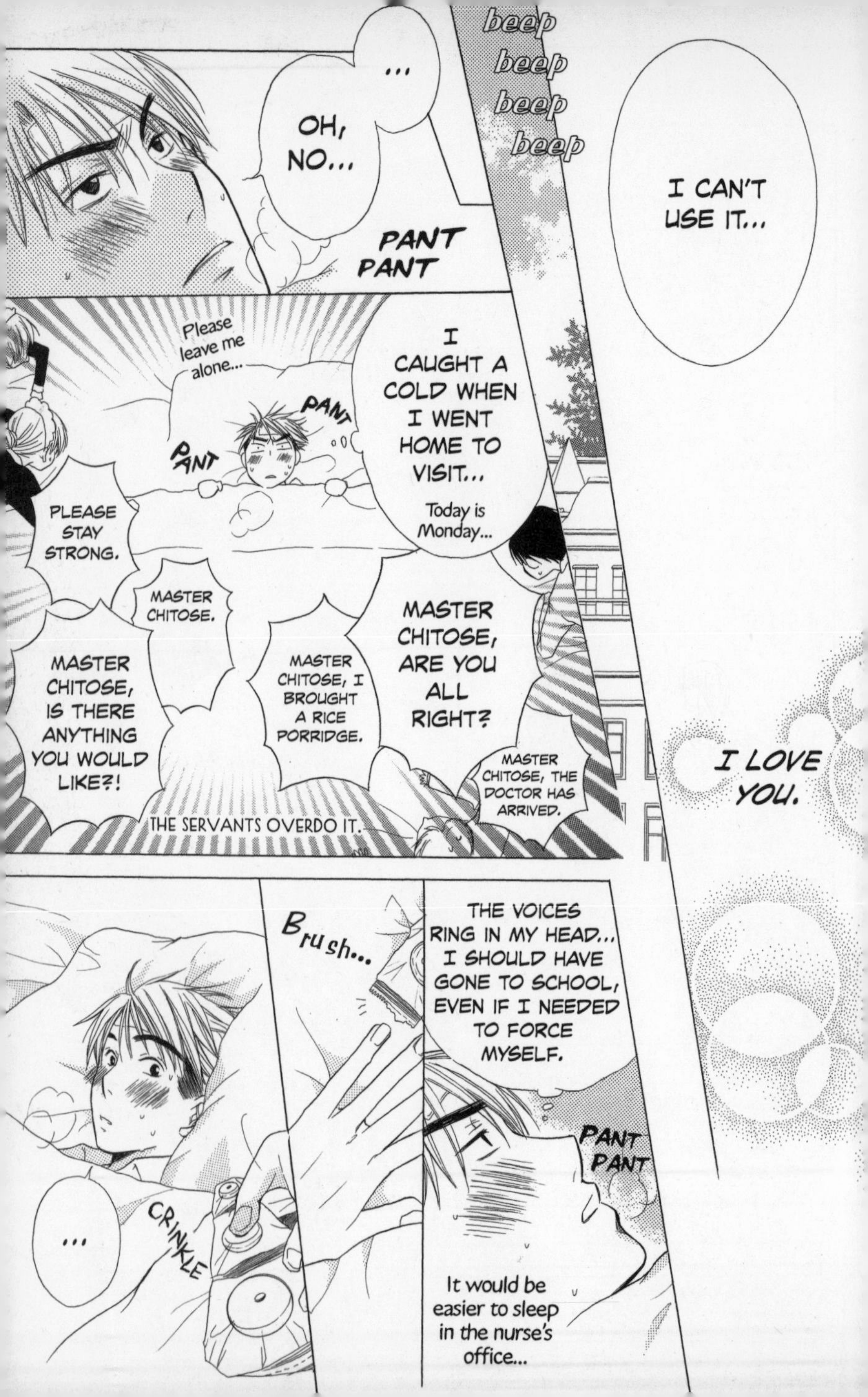
I CAN'T USE IT...
I LOVE YOU.
beep beep beep beep
...
OH, NO...
PANT PANT
I CAUGHT A COLD WHEN I WENT HOME TO VISIT...
Today is Monday...
Please leave me alone...
PANT
PANT
MASTER CHITOSE, ARE YOU ALL RIGHT?
MASTER CHITOSE, THE DOCTOR HAS ARRIVED.
MASTER CHITOSE, I BROUGHT A RICE PORRIDGE.
MASTER CHITOSE.
PLEASE STAY STRONG.
MASTER CHITOSE, IS THERE ANYTHING YOU WOULD LIKE?!
THE SERVANTS OVERDO IT.
THE VOICES RING IN MY HEAD... I SHOULD HAVE GONE TO SCHOOL, EVEN IF I NEEDED TO FORCE MYSELF.
PANT PANT
It would be easier to sleep in the nurse's office...
Brush...
...
CRINKLE

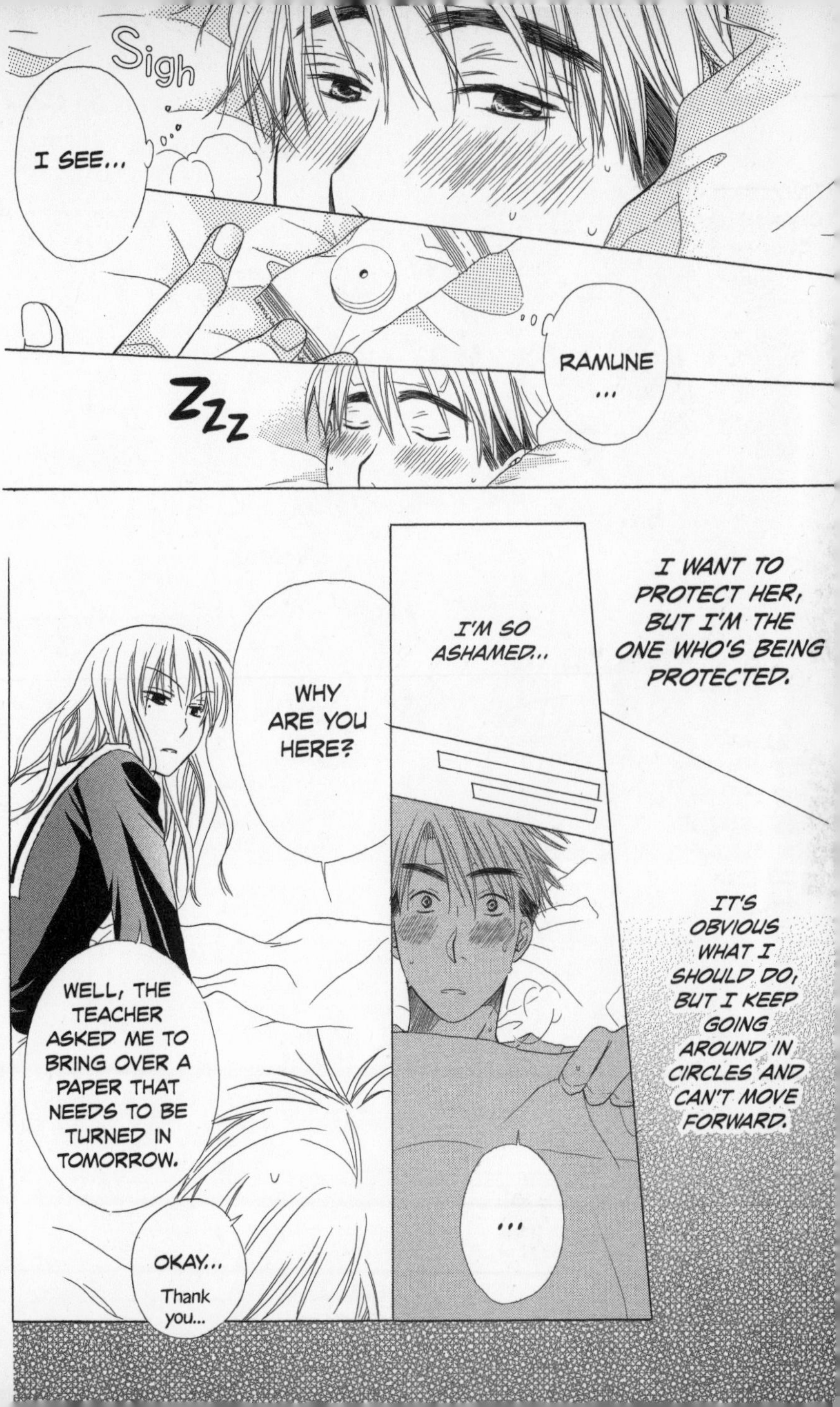
Sigh
I SEE...
RAMUNE...
ZZZ
I WANT TO PROTECT HER, BUT I'M THE ONE WHO'S BEING PROTECTED.
I'M SO ASHAMED...
IT'S OBVIOUS WHAT I SHOULD DO, BUT I KEEP GOING AROUND IN CIRCLES AND CAN'T MOVE FORWARD.
...
WHY ARE YOU HERE?
WELL, THE TEACHER ASKED ME TO BRING OVER A PAPER THAT NEEDS TO BE TURNED IN TOMORROW.
OKAY... Thank you...

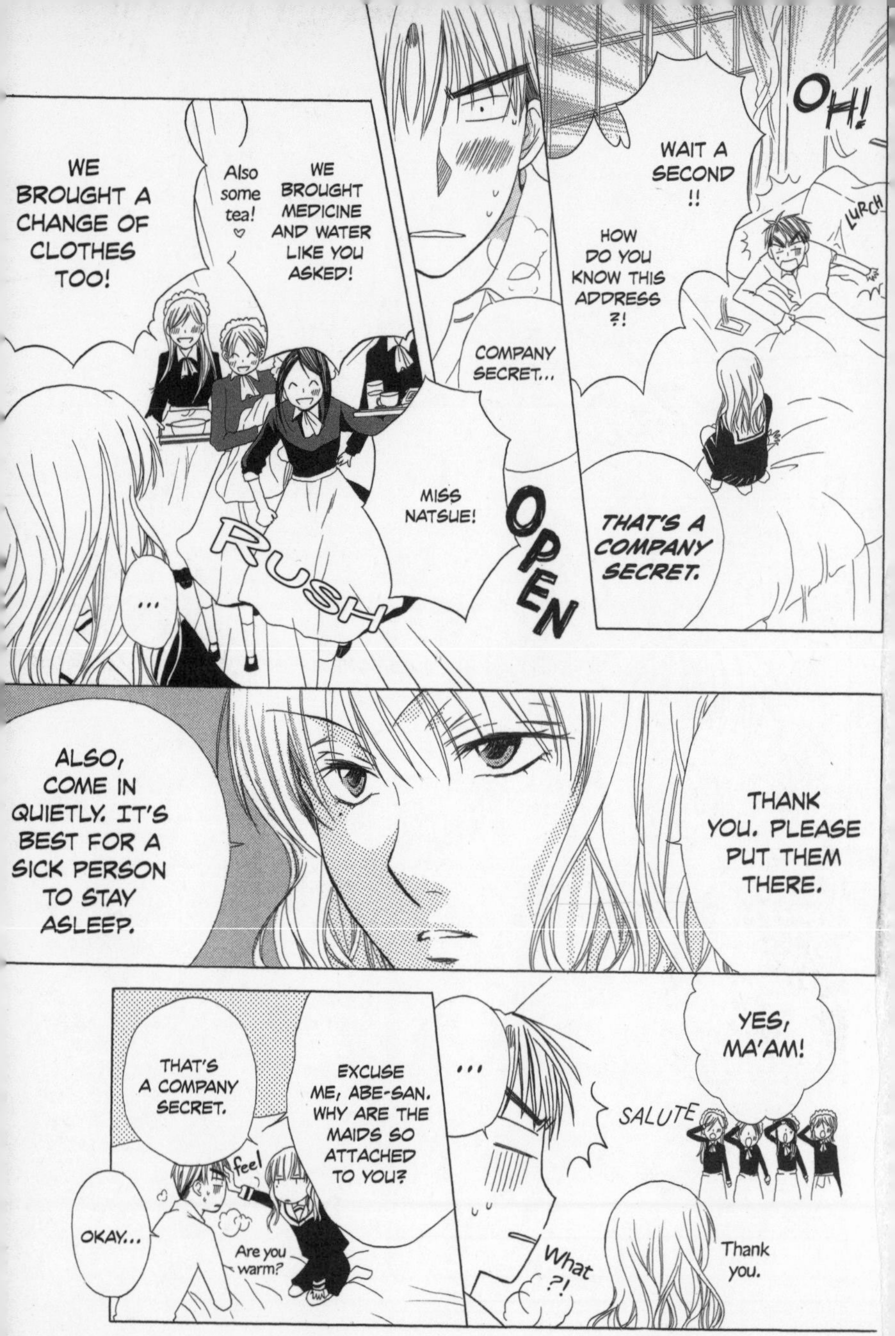
OH!
WAIT A SECOND !!
LURCH
HOW DO YOU KNOW THIS ADDRESS ?!
THAT'S A COMPANY SECRET.
COMPANY SECRET...
OPEN
MISS NATSUE!
WE BROUGHT MEDICINE AND WATER LIKE YOU ASKED!
Also some tea! ♡
WE BROUGHT A CHANGE OF CLOTHES TOO!
RUSH
...
THANK YOU. PLEASE PUT THEM THERE.
ALSO, COME IN QUIETLY. IT'S BEST FOR A SICK PERSON TO STAY ASLEEP.
YES, MA'AM!
SALUTE
Thank you.
...
What ?!
EXCUSE ME, ABE-SAN. WHY ARE THE MAIDS SO ATTACHED TO YOU?
THAT'S A COMPANY SECRET.
feel
Are you warm?
OKAY...

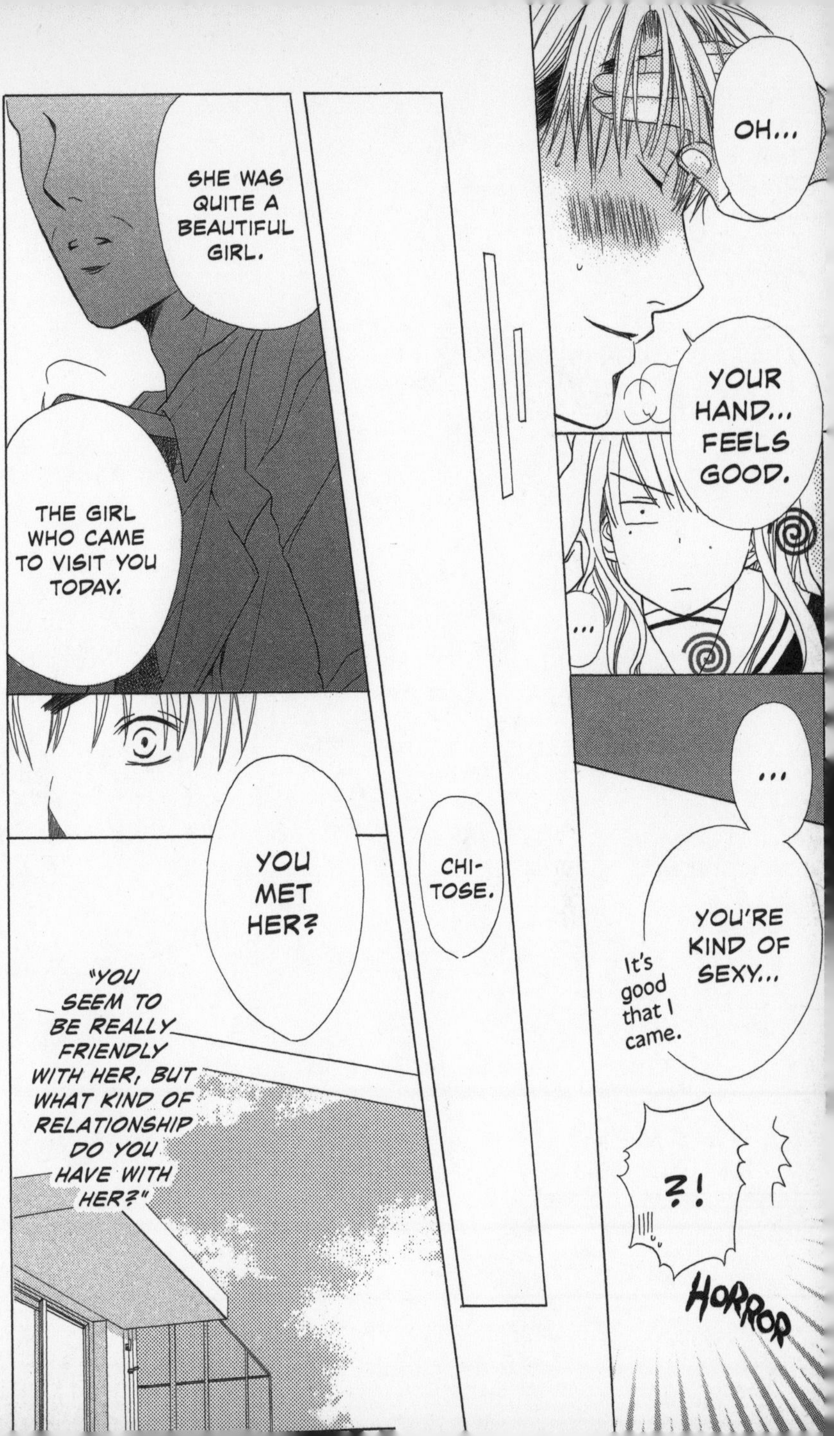

OH...
YOUR HAND... FEELS GOOD.
...
...
YOU'RE KIND OF SEXY...
It's good that I came.
?!
HORROR
CHI-TOSE.
SHE WAS QUITE A BEAUTIFUL GIRL.
THE GIRL WHO CAME TO VISIT YOU TODAY.
YOU MET HER?
"YOU SEEM TO BE REALLY FRIENDLY WITH HER, BUT WHAT KIND OF RELATIONSHIP DO YOU HAVE WITH HER?"

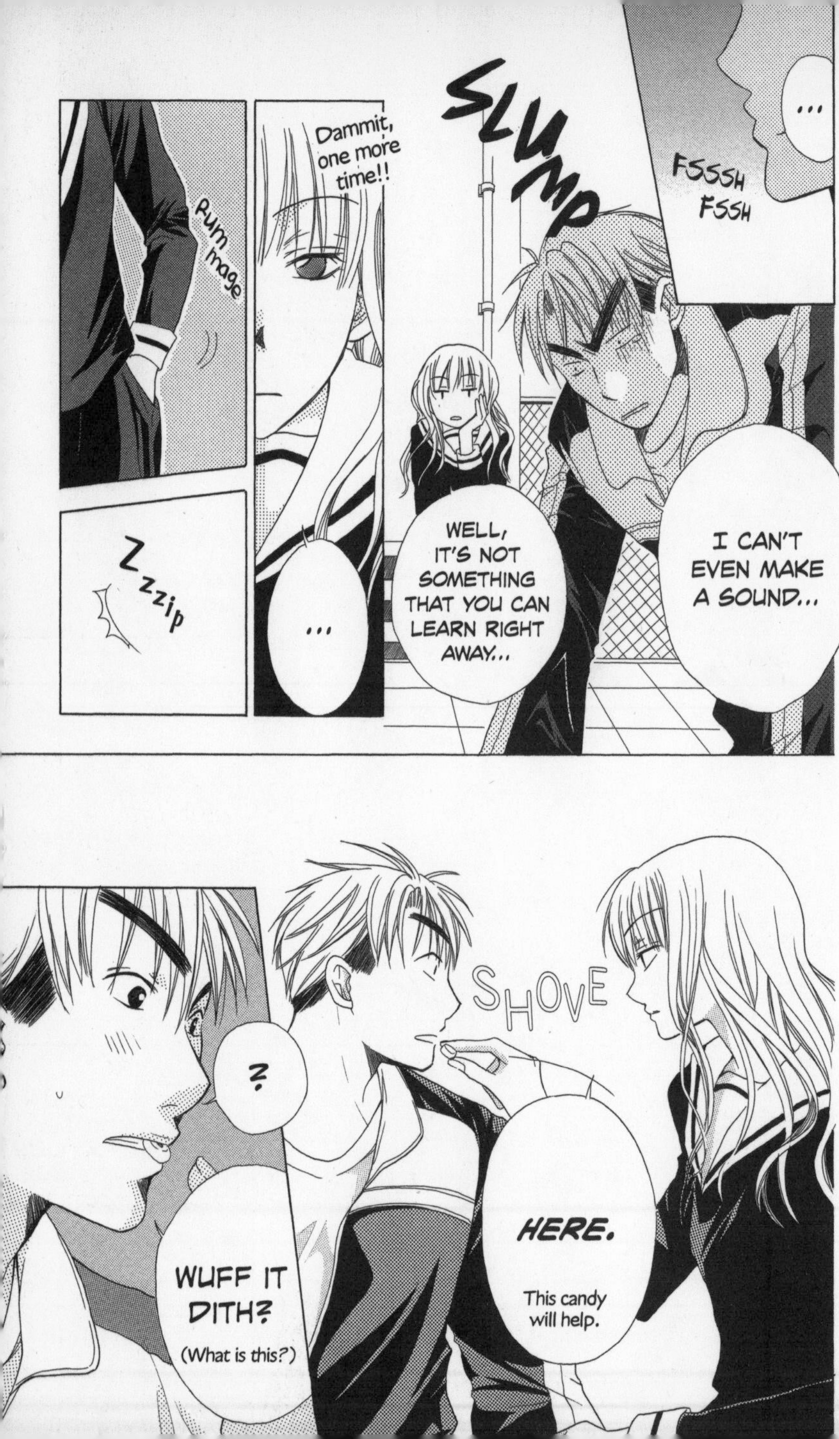
...
FSSSH
FSSH
SLUMP
I CAN'T EVEN MAKE A SOUND...
WELL, IT'S NOT SOMETHING THAT YOU CAN LEARN RIGHT AWAY...
Dammit, one more time!!
...
Rummage
Zzzip
SHOVE
HERE.
This candy will help.
?
WUFF IT DITH?
(What is this?)

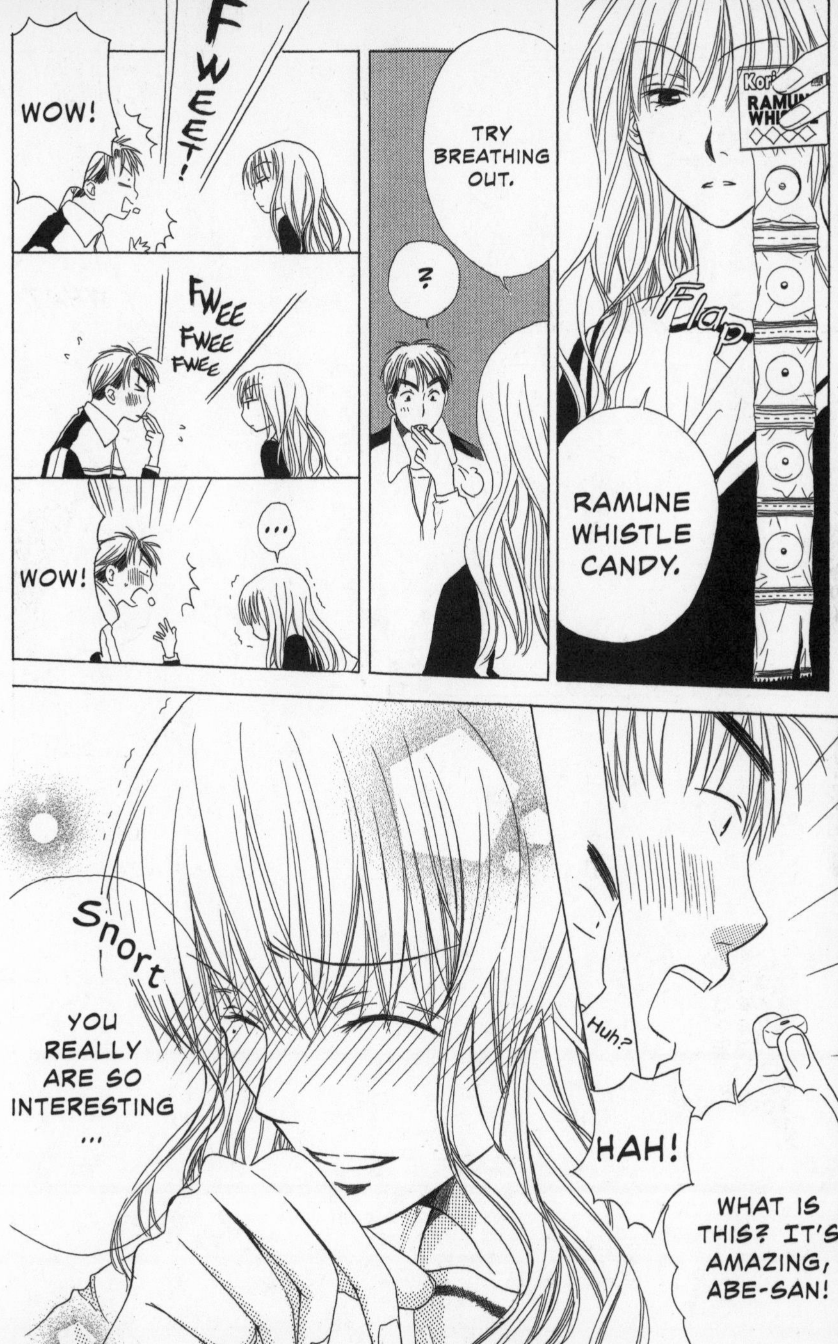
Flap
RAMUNE WHISTLE CANDY.
TRY BREATHING OUT.
?
FWEET!
WOW!
FWEE FWEE FWEE
WOW!
...
Huh?
HAH!
WHAT IS THIS? IT'S AMAZING, ABE-SAN!
Snort
YOU REALLY ARE SO INTERESTING ...

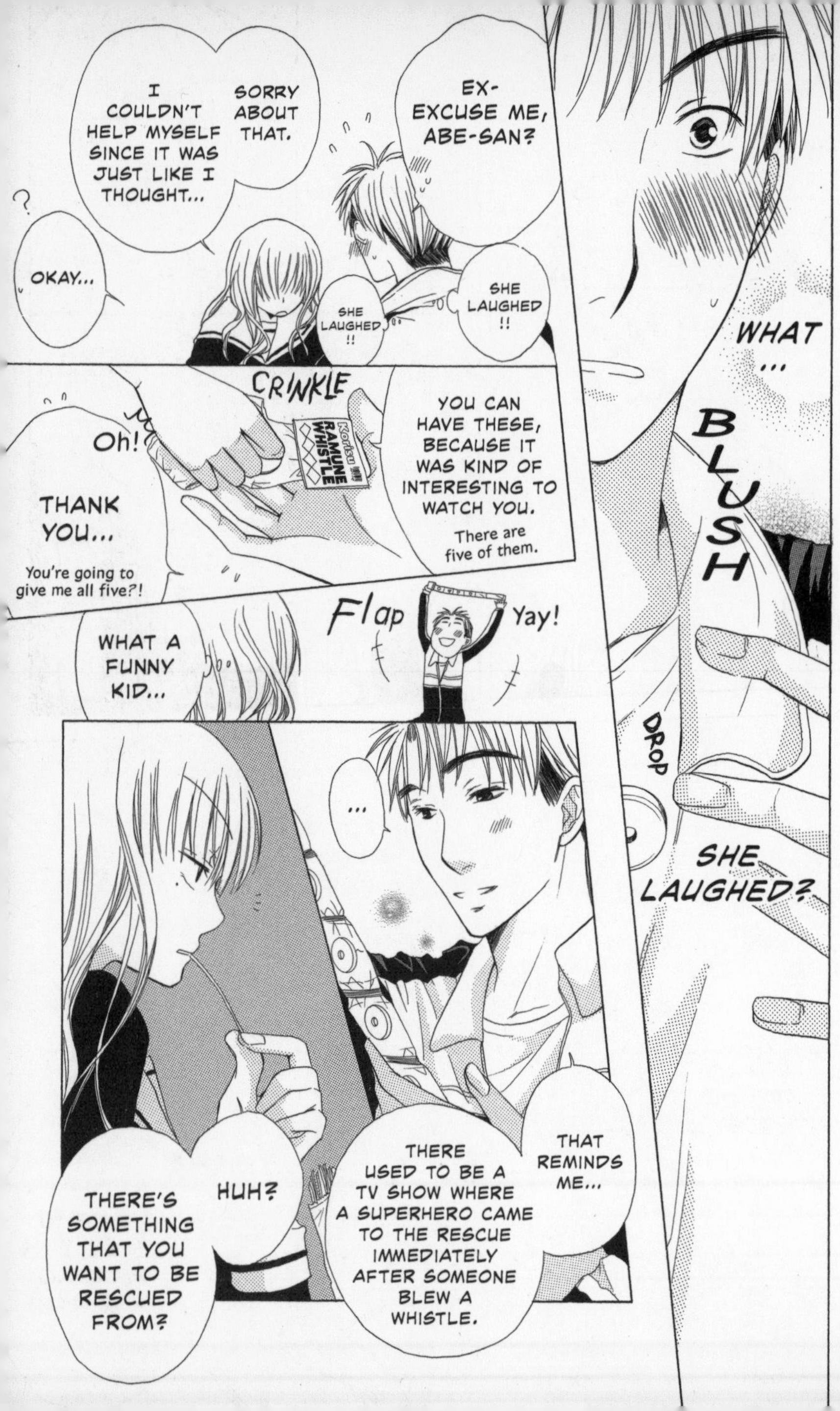
WHAT ...
BLUSH
DROP
SHE LAUGHED?
EX- EXCUSE ME, ABE-SAN?
SHE LAUGHED !!
SHE LAUGHED !!
SORRY ABOUT THAT.
I COULDN'T HELP MYSELF SINCE IT WAS JUST LIKE I THOUGHT...
OKAY...
CRINKLE
YOU CAN HAVE THESE, BECAUSE IT WAS KIND OF INTERESTING TO WATCH YOU.
There are five of them.
RAMUNE WHISTLE
Oh!
THANK YOU...
You're going to give me all five?!
Yay!
Flap
WHAT A FUNNY KID...
...
THAT REMINDS ME...
THERE USED TO BE A TV SHOW WHERE A SUPERHERO CAME TO THE RESCUE IMMEDIATELY AFTER SOMEONE BLEW A WHISTLE.
HUH?
THERE'S SOMETHING THAT YOU WANT TO BE RESCUED FROM?

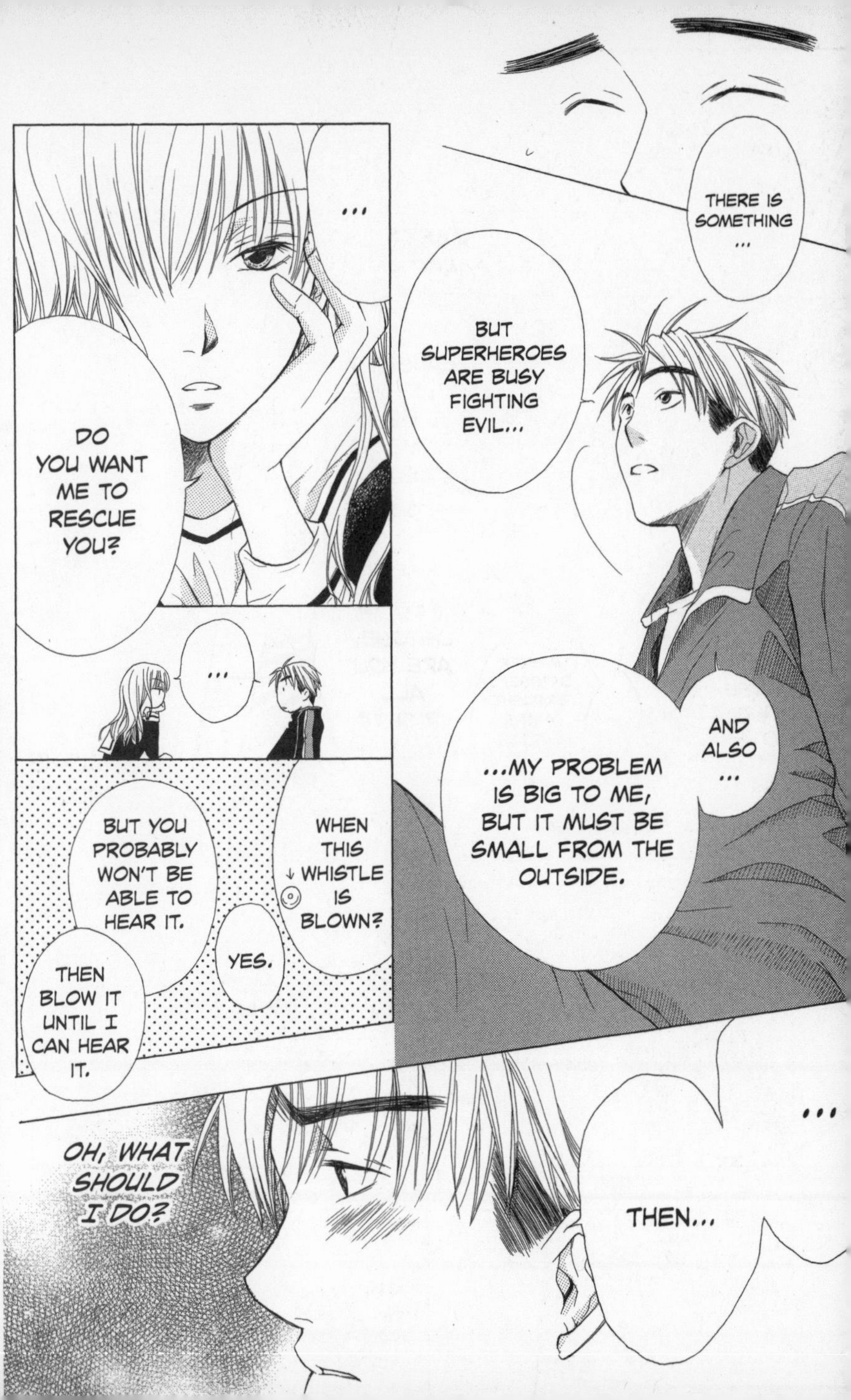
THERE IS SOMETHING ...
BUT SUPERHEROES ARE BUSY FIGHTING EVIL...
AND ALSO ...
...MY PROBLEM IS BIG TO ME, BUT IT MUST BE SMALL FROM THE OUTSIDE.
...
DO YOU WANT ME TO RESCUE YOU?
...
WHEN THIS WHISTLE IS BLOWN?
YES.
BUT YOU PROBABLY WON'T BE ABLE TO HEAR IT.
THEN BLOW IT UNTIL I CAN HEAR IT.
...
THEN...
OH, WHAT SHOULD I DO?

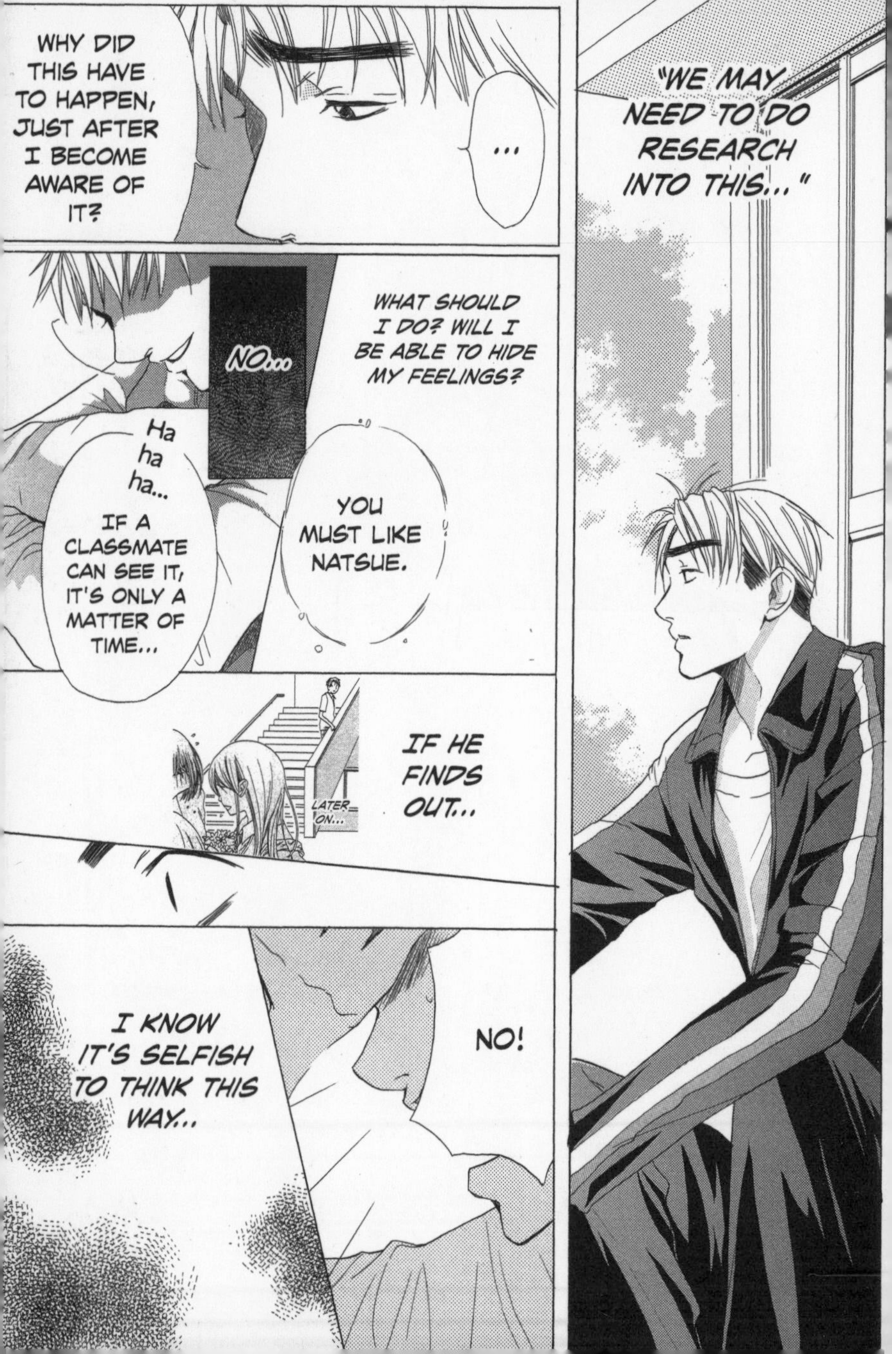
"WE MAY NEED TO DO RESEARCH INTO THIS..."
...
WHY DID THIS HAVE TO HAPPEN, JUST AFTER I BECOME AWARE OF IT?
WHAT SHOULD I DO? WILL I BE ABLE TO HIDE MY FEELINGS?
NO...
YOU MUST LIKE NATSUE.
Ha ha ha... IF A CLASSMATE CAN SEE IT, IT'S ONLY A MATTER OF TIME...
IF HE FINDS OUT...
LATER ON...
NO!
I KNOW IT'S SELFISH TO THINK THIS WAY..

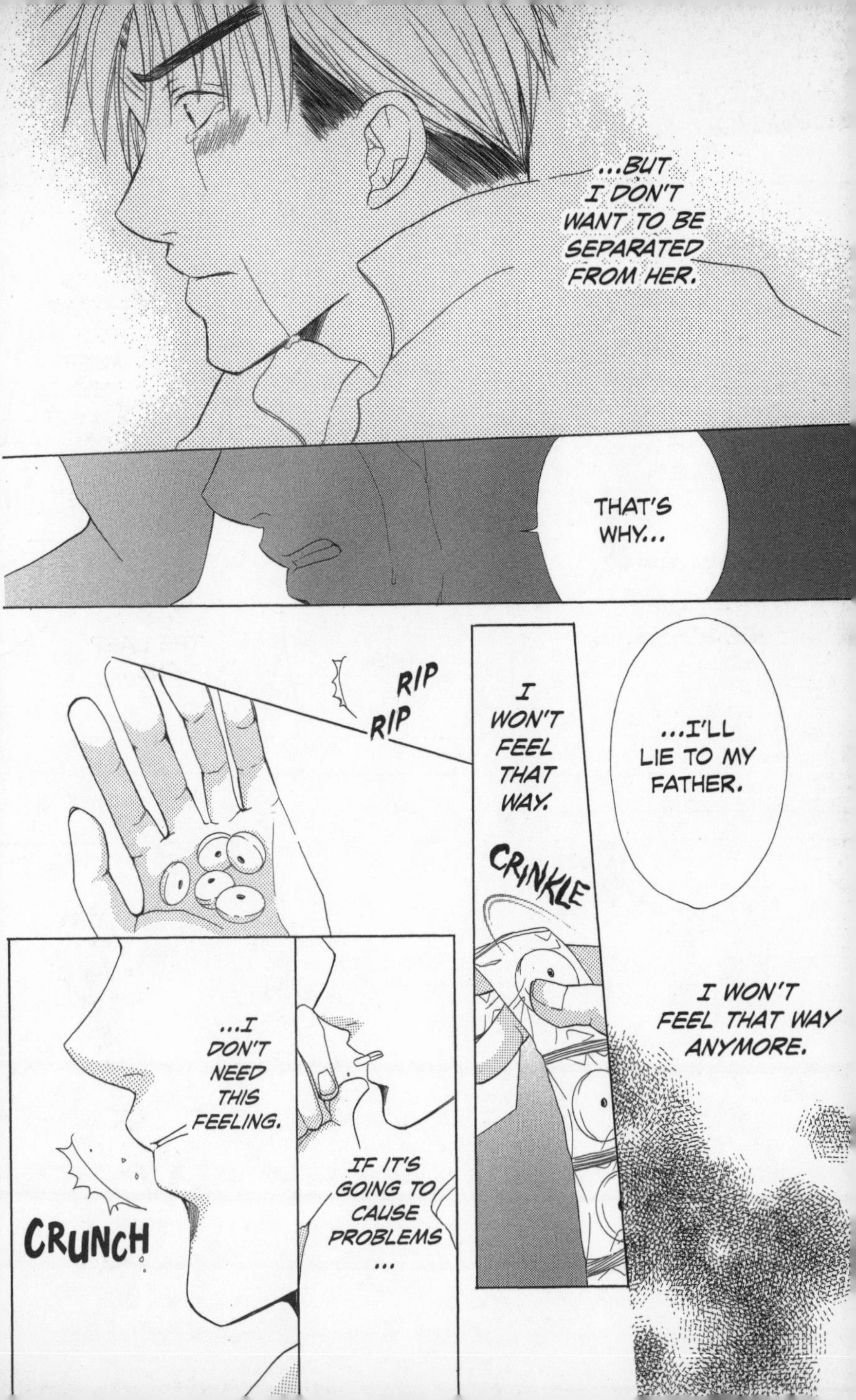
...BUT I DON'T WANT TO BE SEPARATED FROM HER.
THAT'S WHY...
...I'LL LIE TO MY FATHER.
I WON'T FEEL THAT WAY.
CRINKLE
I WON'T FEEL THAT WAY ANYMORE.
RIP
RIP
IF IT'S GOING TO CAUSE PROBLEMS ...
...I DON'T NEED THIS FEELING.
CRUNCH

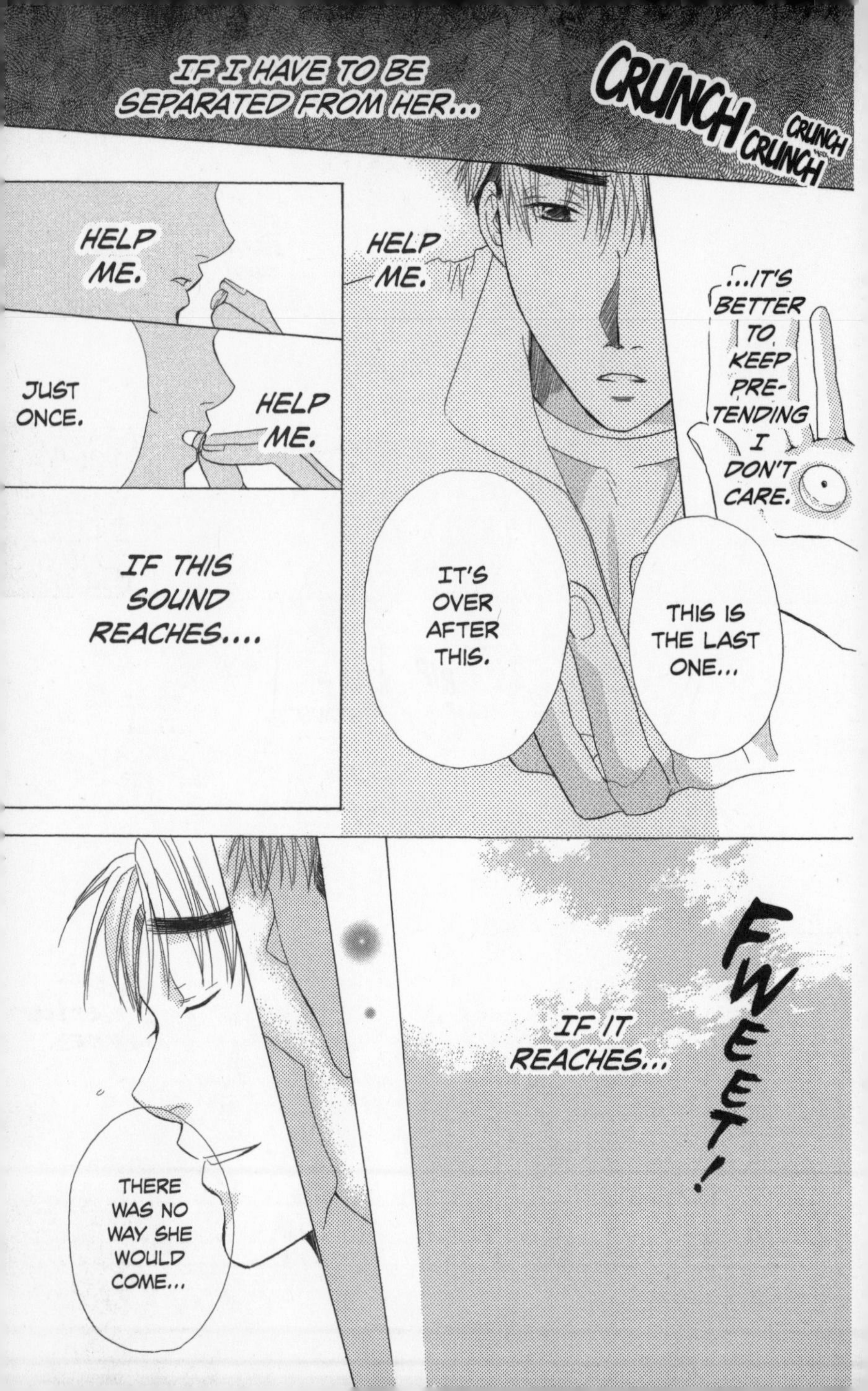
CRUNCH
CRUNCH CRUNCH
IF I HAVE TO BE SEPARATED FROM HER...
...IT'S BETTER TO KEEP PRE-TENDING I DON'T CARE.
HELP ME.
THIS IS THE LAST ONE...
IT'S OVER AFTER THIS.
HELP ME.
HELP ME.
JUST ONCE.
IF THIS SOUND REACHES....
FWEET!
IF IT REACHES...
THERE WAS NO WAY SHE WOULD COME...

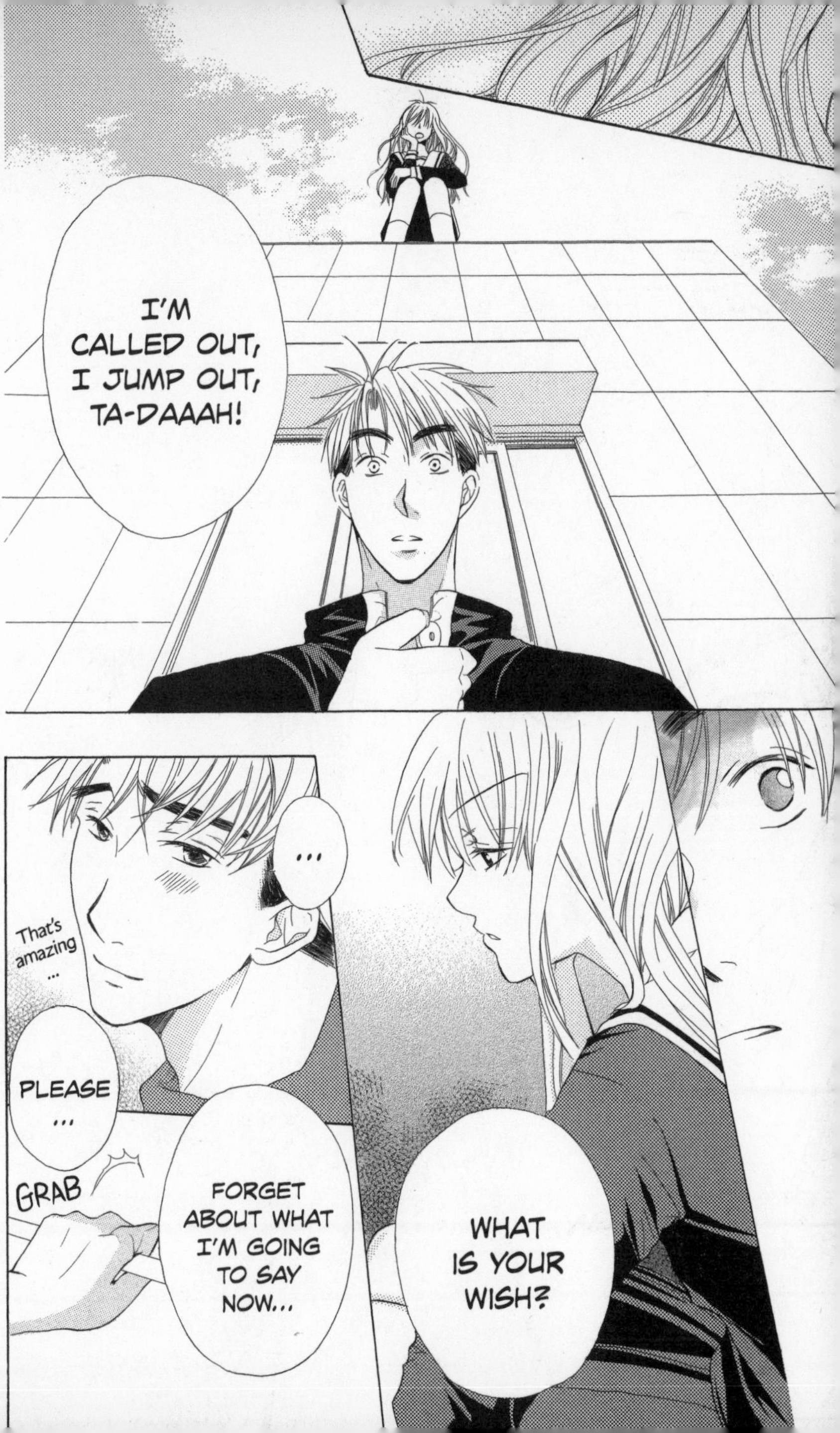
I'M CALLED OUT, I JUMP OUT, TA-DAAAH!
WHAT IS YOUR WISH?
...
That's amazing ...
PLEASE ...
FORGET ABOUT WHAT I'M GOING TO SAY NOW...
GRAB

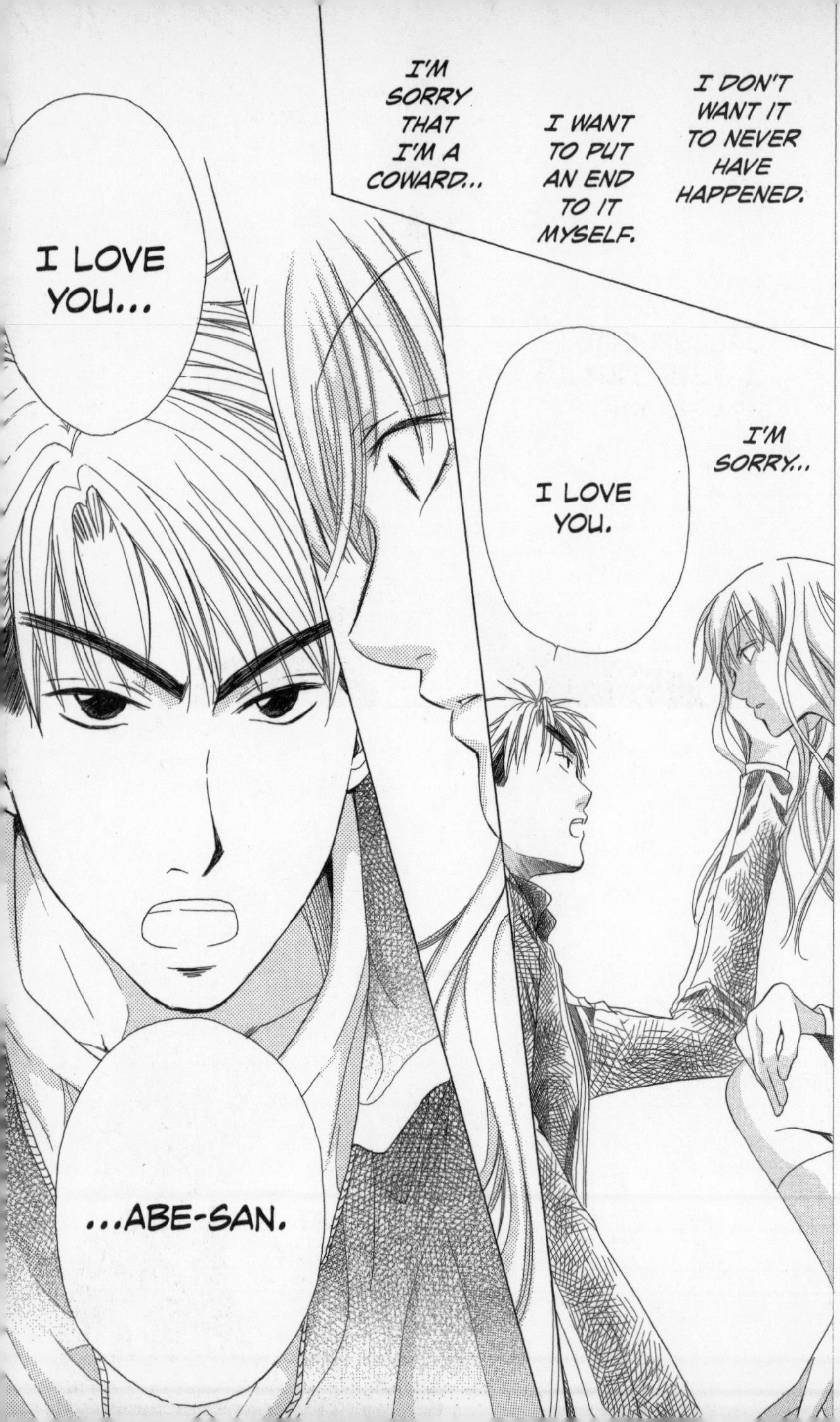
I DON'T WANT IT TO NEVER HAVE HAPPENED.
I WANT TO PUT AN END TO IT MYSELF.
I'M SORRY THAT I'M A COWARD...
I'M SORRY...
I LOVE YOU.
I LOVE YOU...
...ABE-SAN.

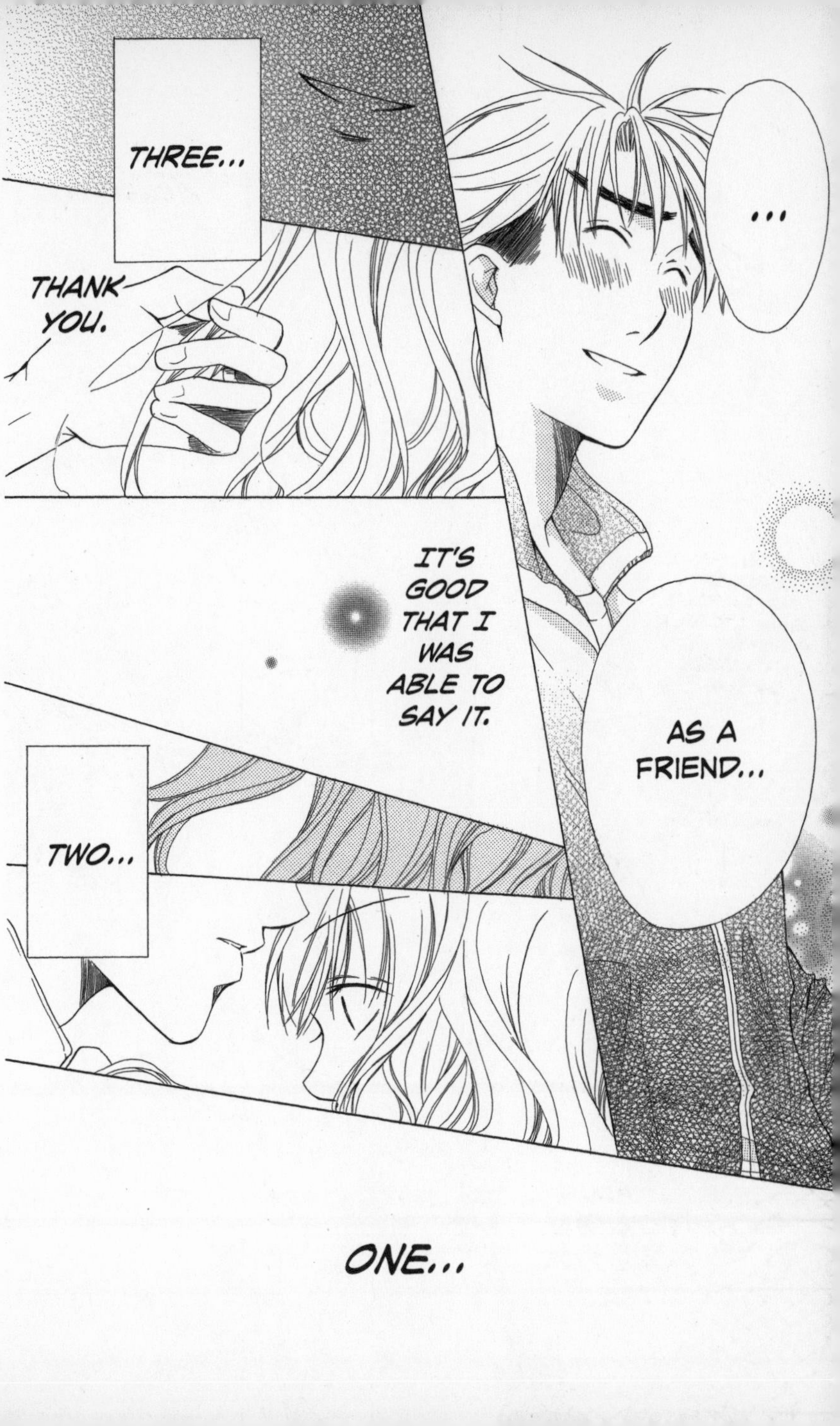
...
AS A FRIEND...
THREE...
THANK YOU.
IT'S GOOD THAT I WAS ABLE TO SAY IT.
TWO...
ONE...

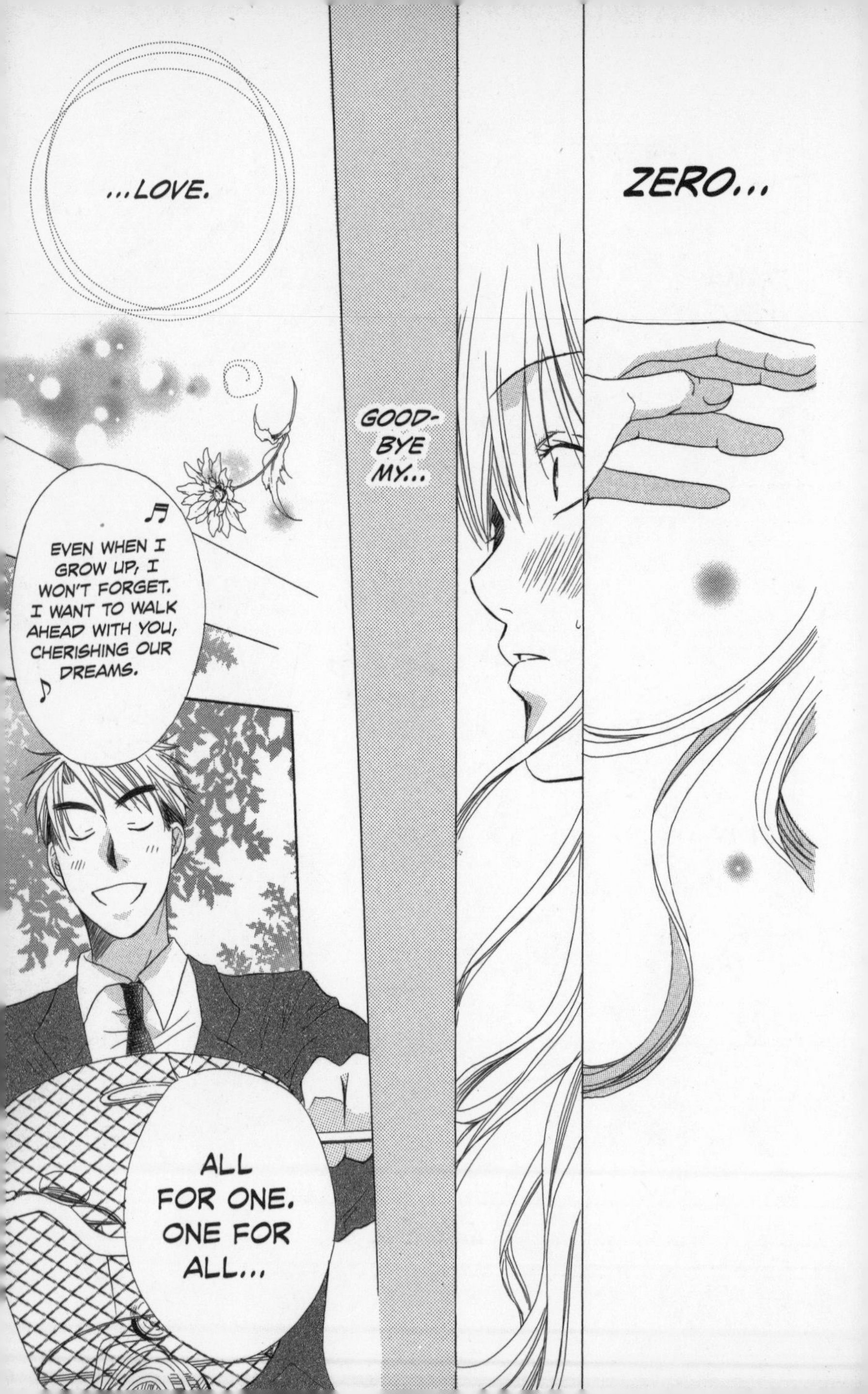
ZERO...
GOOD-BYE MY...
...LOVE.
EVEN WHEN I GROW UP, I WON'T FORGET. I WANT TO WALK AHEAD WITH YOU, CHERISHING OUR DREAMS.
ALL FOR ONE. ONE FOR ALL...

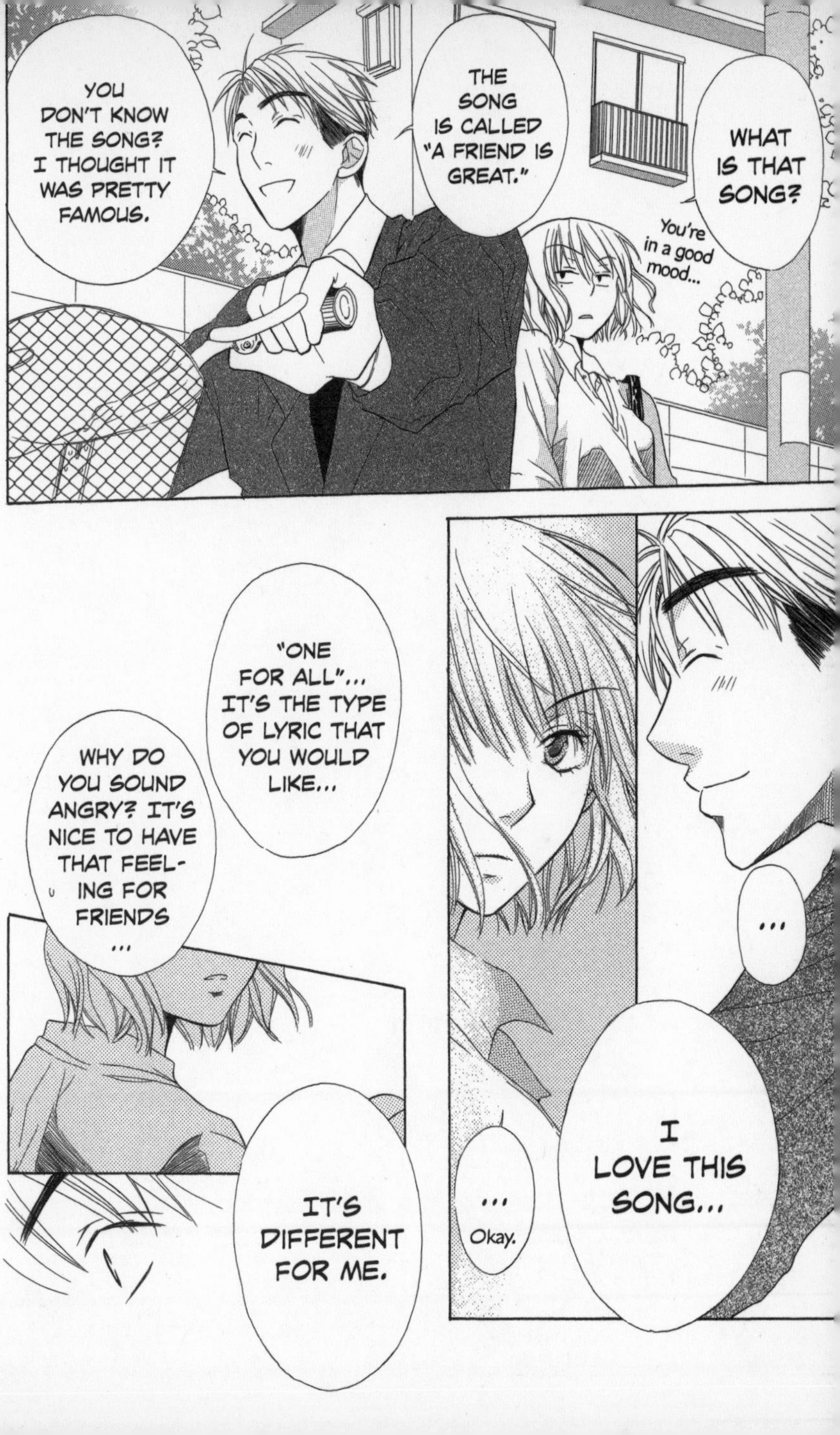
WHAT IS THAT SONG?
You're in a good mood...
THE SONG IS CALLED "A FRIEND IS GREAT."
YOU DON'T KNOW THE SONG? I THOUGHT IT WAS PRETTY FAMOUS.
...
I LOVE THIS SONG...
... Okay.
"ONE FOR ALL"... IT'S THE TYPE OF LYRIC THAT YOU WOULD LIKE...
WHY DO YOU SOUND ANGRY? IT'S NICE TO HAVE THAT FEEL-ING FOR FRIENDS ...
IT'S DIFFERENT FOR ME.

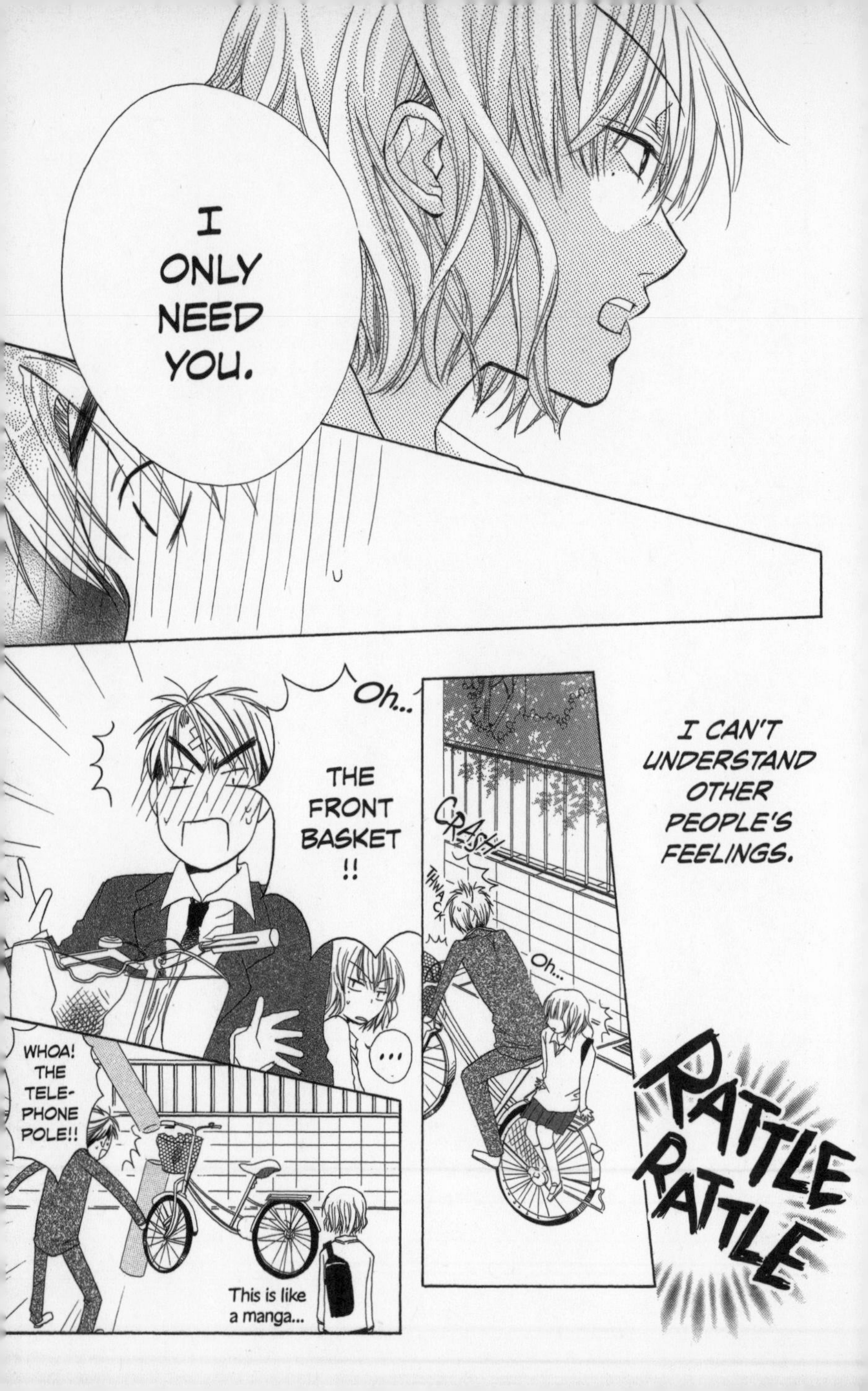
I ONLY NEED YOU.
I CAN'T UNDERSTAND OTHER PEOPLE'S FEELINGS.
CRASH
THWACK
Oh...
RATTLE RATTLE
Oh...
THE FRONT BASKET!!
...
WHOA! THE TELEPHONE POLE!!
This is like a manga...

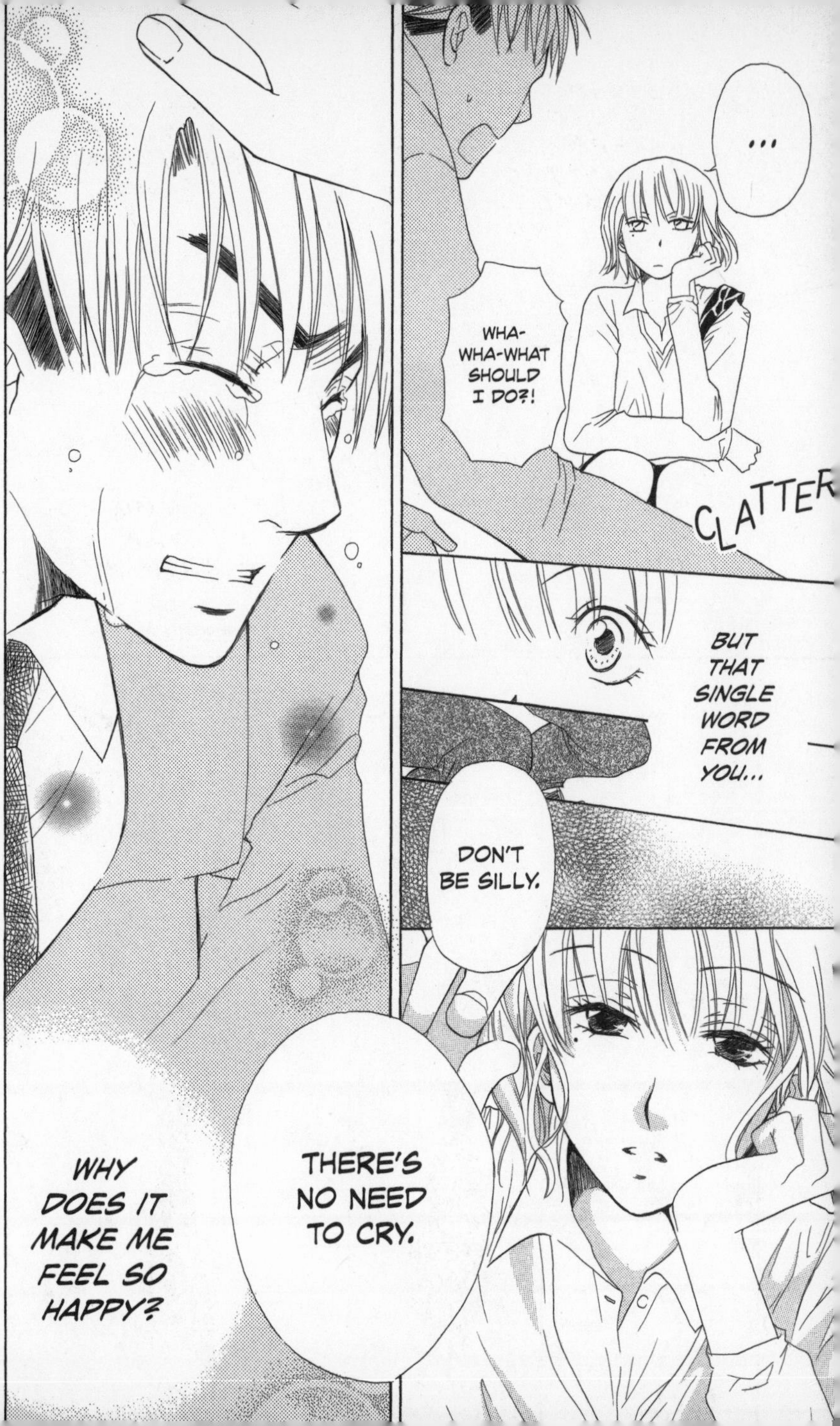
...
WHA-WHA-WHAT SHOULD I DO?!
CLATTER
BUT THAT SINGLE WORD FROM YOU...
DON'T BE SILLY.
THERE'S NO NEED TO CRY.
WHY DOES IT MAKE ME FEEL SO HAPPY?

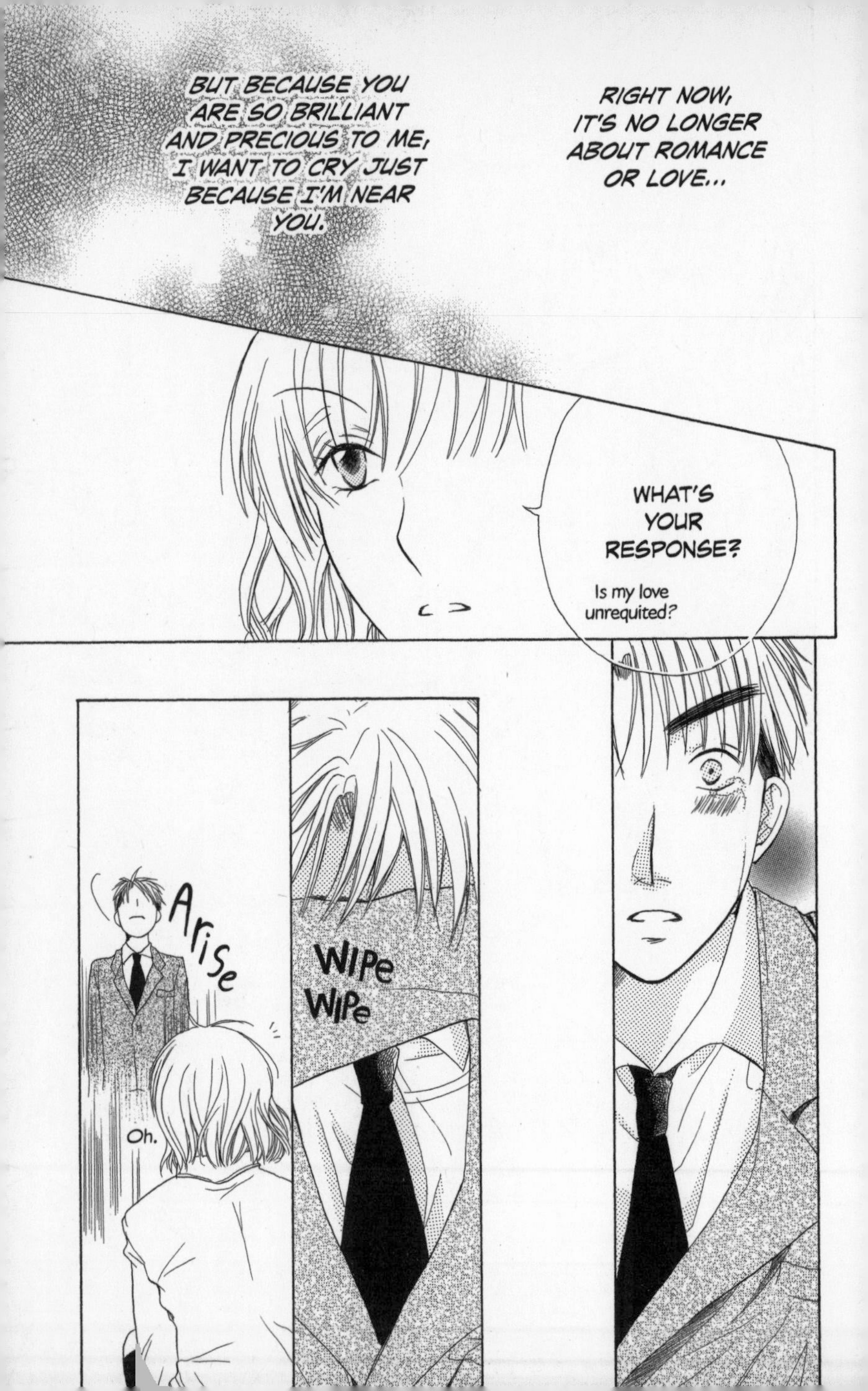
RIGHT NOW, IT'S NO LONGER ABOUT ROMANCE OR LOVE...
BUT BECAUSE YOU ARE SO BRILLIANT AND PRECIOUS TO ME, I WANT TO CRY JUST BECAUSE I'M NEAR YOU.
WHAT'S YOUR RESPONSE?
Is my love unrequited?
WIPE WIPE
Arise
Oh.

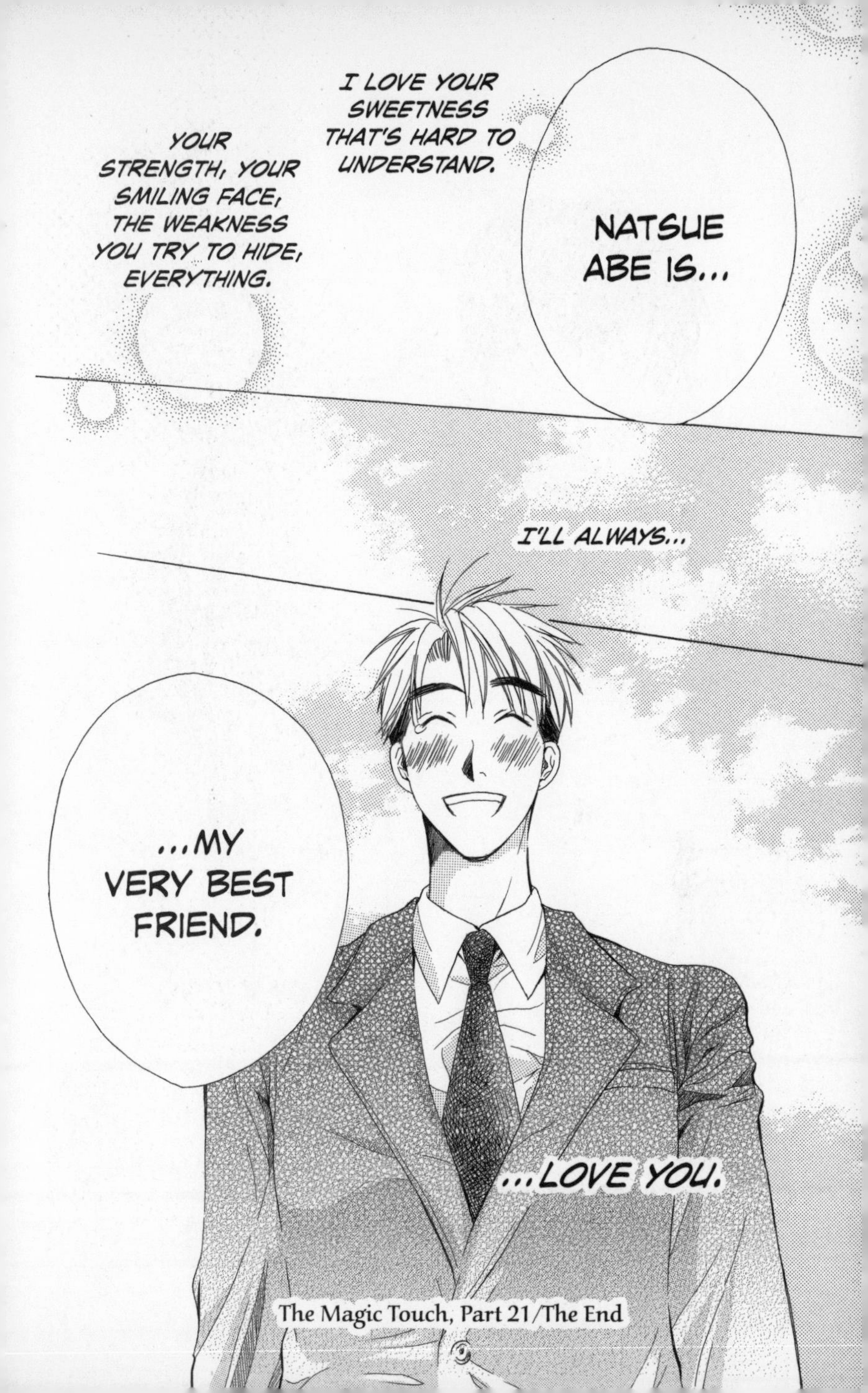
NATSUE ABE IS...
I LOVE YOUR SWEETNESS THAT'S HARD TO UNDERSTAND.
YOUR STRENGTH, YOUR SMILING FACE, THE WEAKNESS YOU TRY TO HIDE, EVERYTHING.
I'LL ALWAYS...
...MY VERY BEST FRIEND.
...LOVE YOU.

The Magic Touch, Part 21/The End

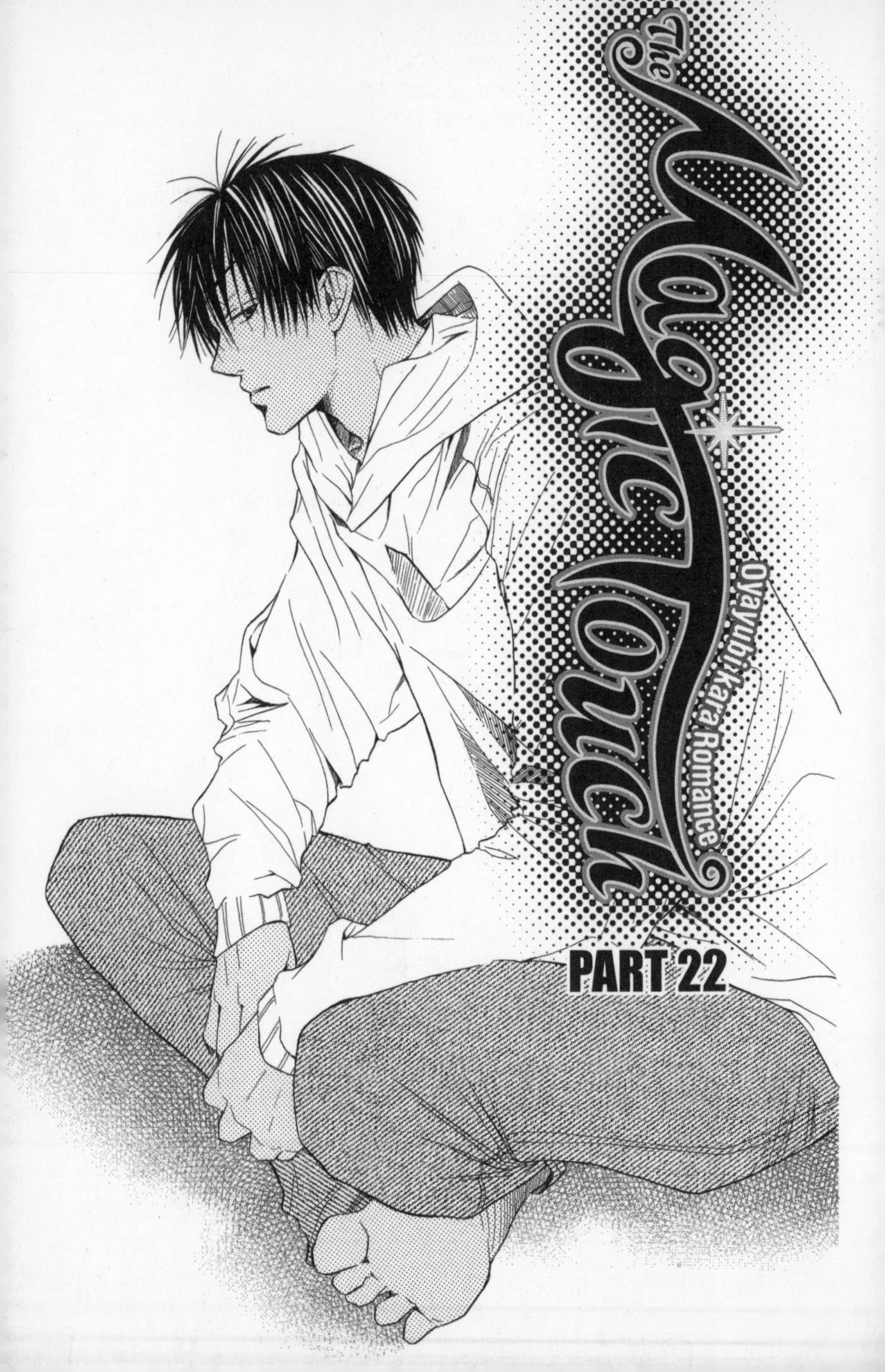
The Magic Touch
Oyayubi kara Romance
PART 22

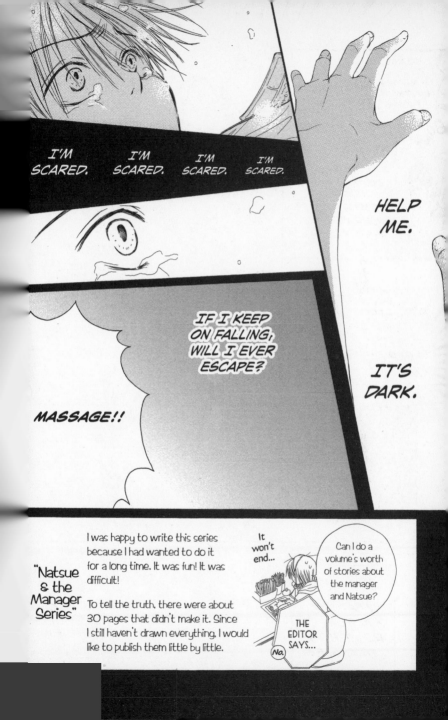

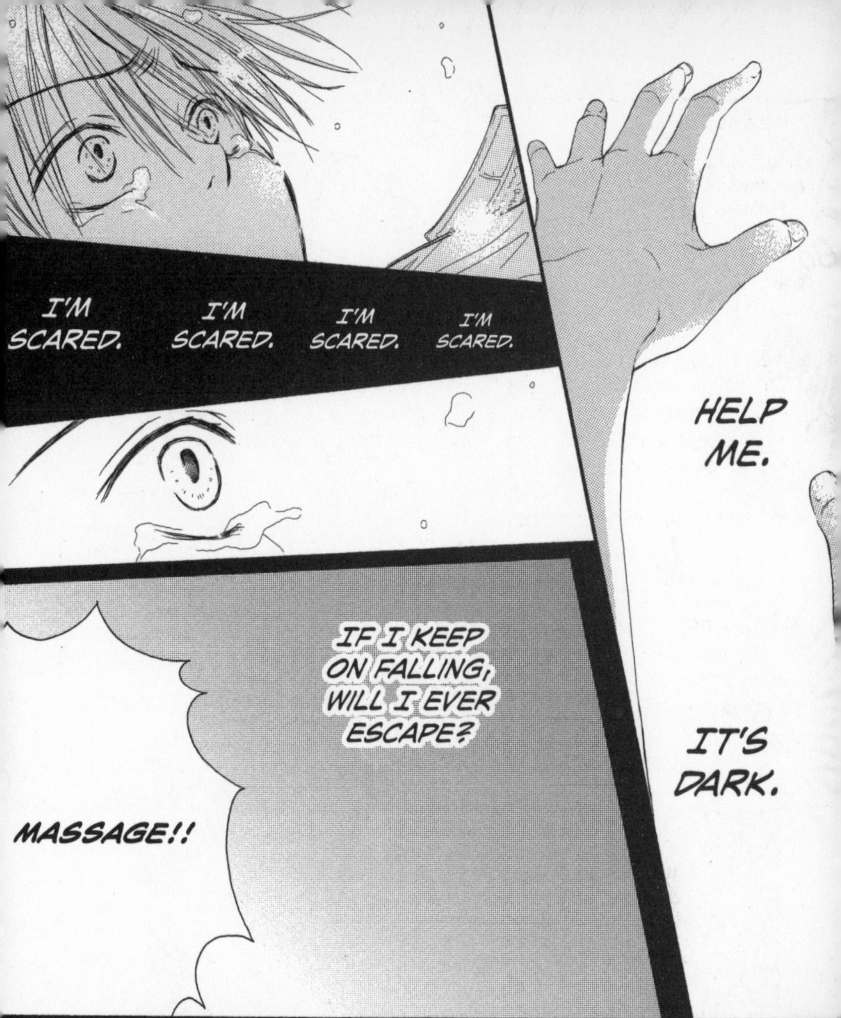
HELP ME.
IT'S DARK.
I'M SCARED.
I'M SCARED.
I'M SCARED.
I'M SCARED.
IF I KEEP ON FALLING, WILL I EVER ESCAPE?
MASSAGE!!

"Natsue & the Manager Series"

I was happy to write this series because I had wanted to do it for a long time. It was fun! It was difficult!

To tell the truth, there were about 30 pages that didn't make it. Since I still haven't drawn everything, I would like to publish them little by little.

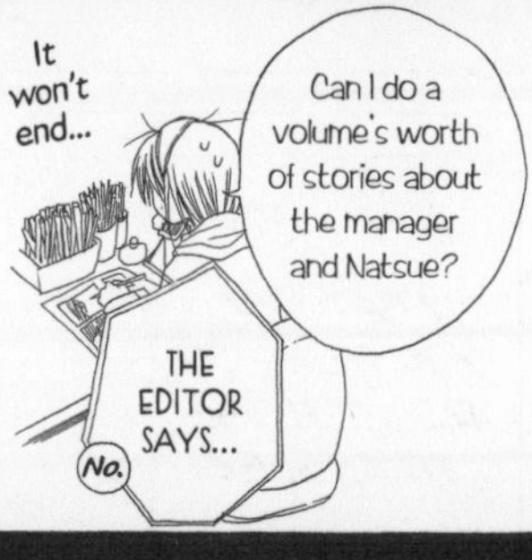
Can I do a volume's worth of stories about the manager and Natsue?
It won't end...
THE EDITOR SAYS...
No.

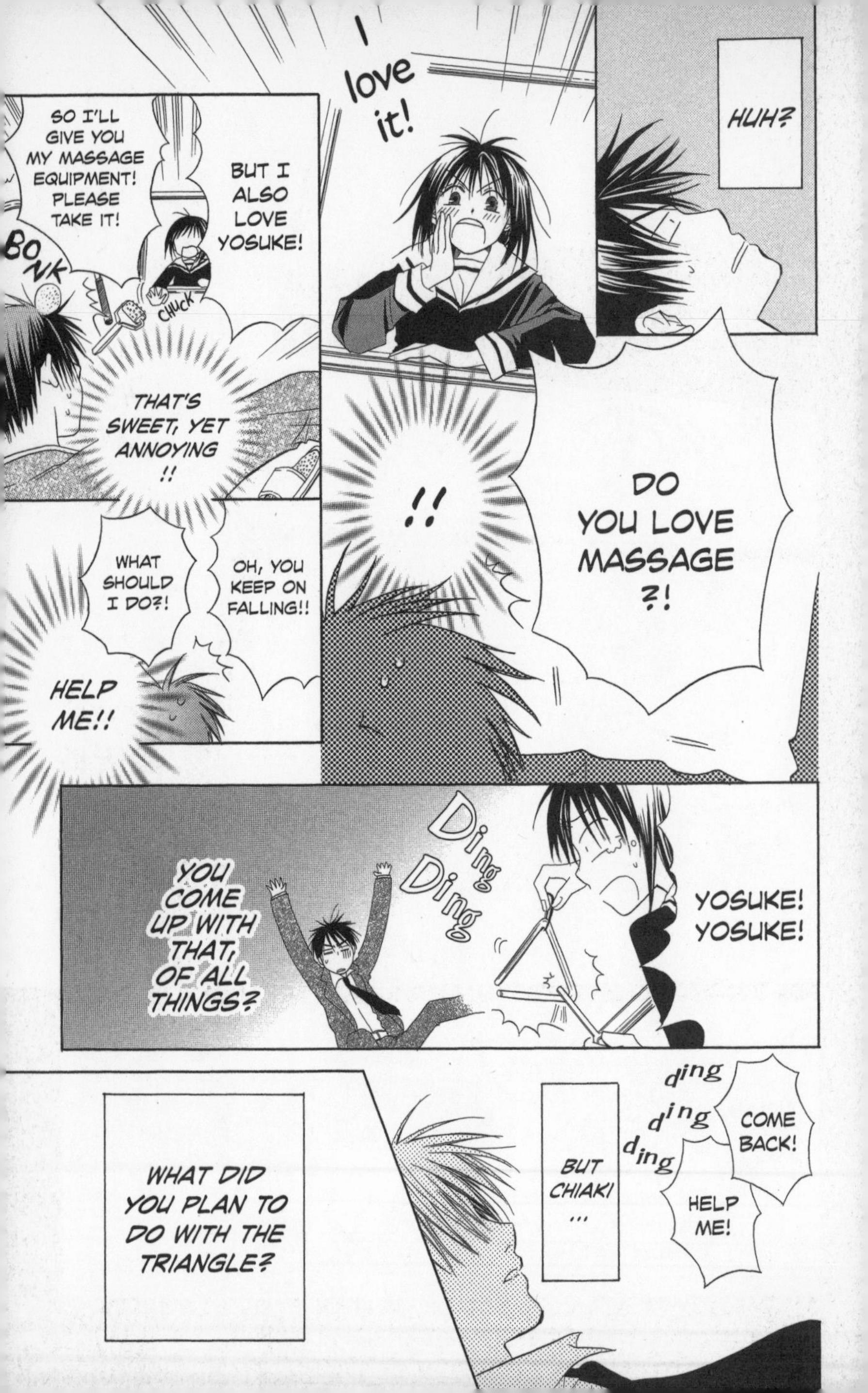
HUH?
I love it!
!!
DO YOU LOVE MASSAGE?!
BUT I ALSO LOVE YOSUKE!
SO I'LL GIVE YOU MY MASSAGE EQUIPMENT! PLEASE TAKE IT!
BONK
CHUCK
THAT'S SWEET, YET ANNOYING!!
OH, YOU KEEP ON FALLING!!
WHAT SHOULD I DO?!
HELP ME!!
YOSUKE! YOSUKE!
Ding Ding
YOU COME UP WITH THAT, OF ALL THINGS?
COME BACK!
HELP ME!
ding ding ding
BUT CHIAKI...
WHAT DID YOU PLAN TO DO WITH THE TRIANGLE?

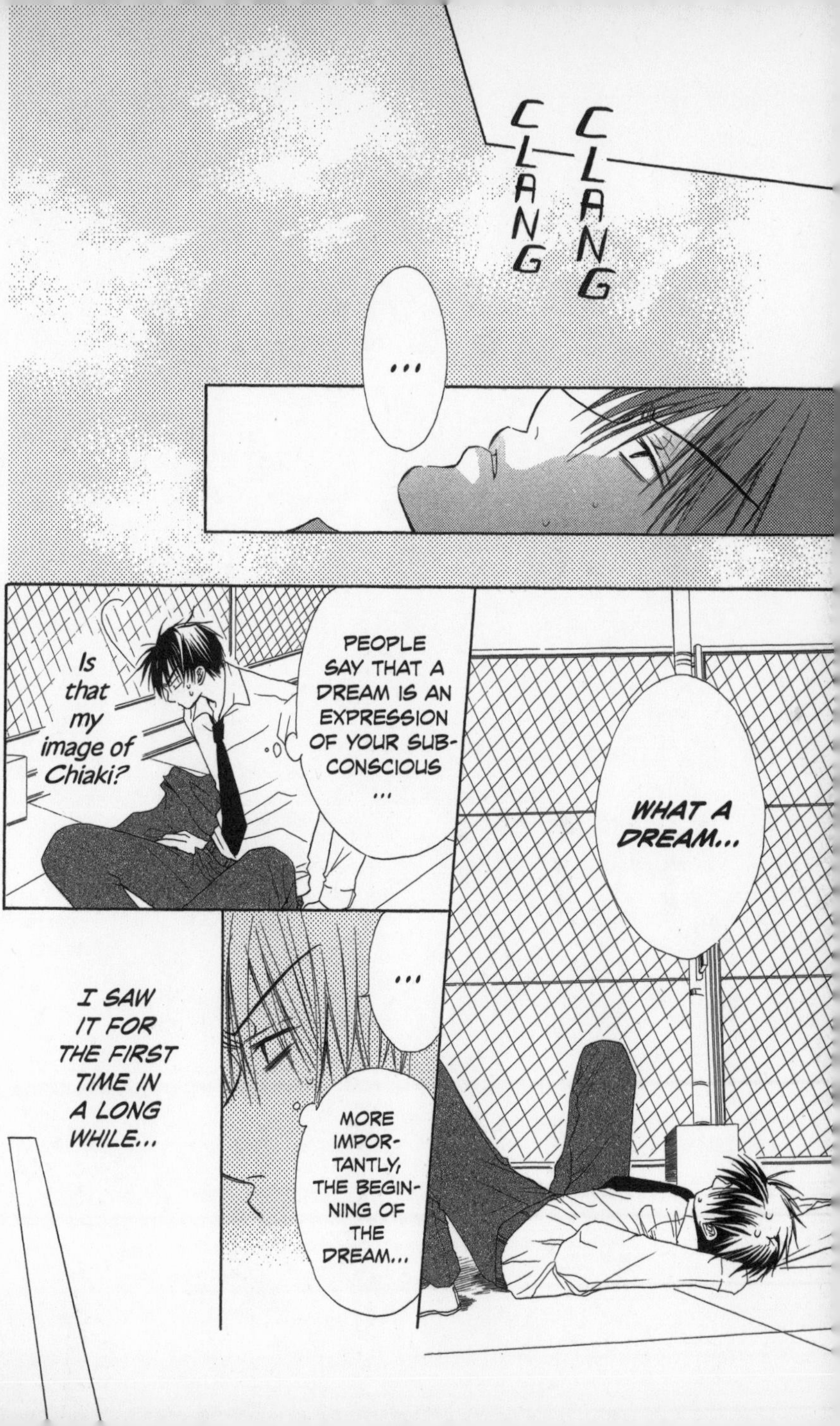
CLANG CLANG
...
WHAT A DREAM...
PEOPLE SAY THAT A DREAM IS AN EXPRESSION OF YOUR SUB-CONSCIOUS ...
Is that my image of Chiaki?
...
MORE IMPORTANTLY, THE BEGINNING OF THE DREAM...
I SAW IT FOR THE FIRST TIME IN A LONG WHILE...

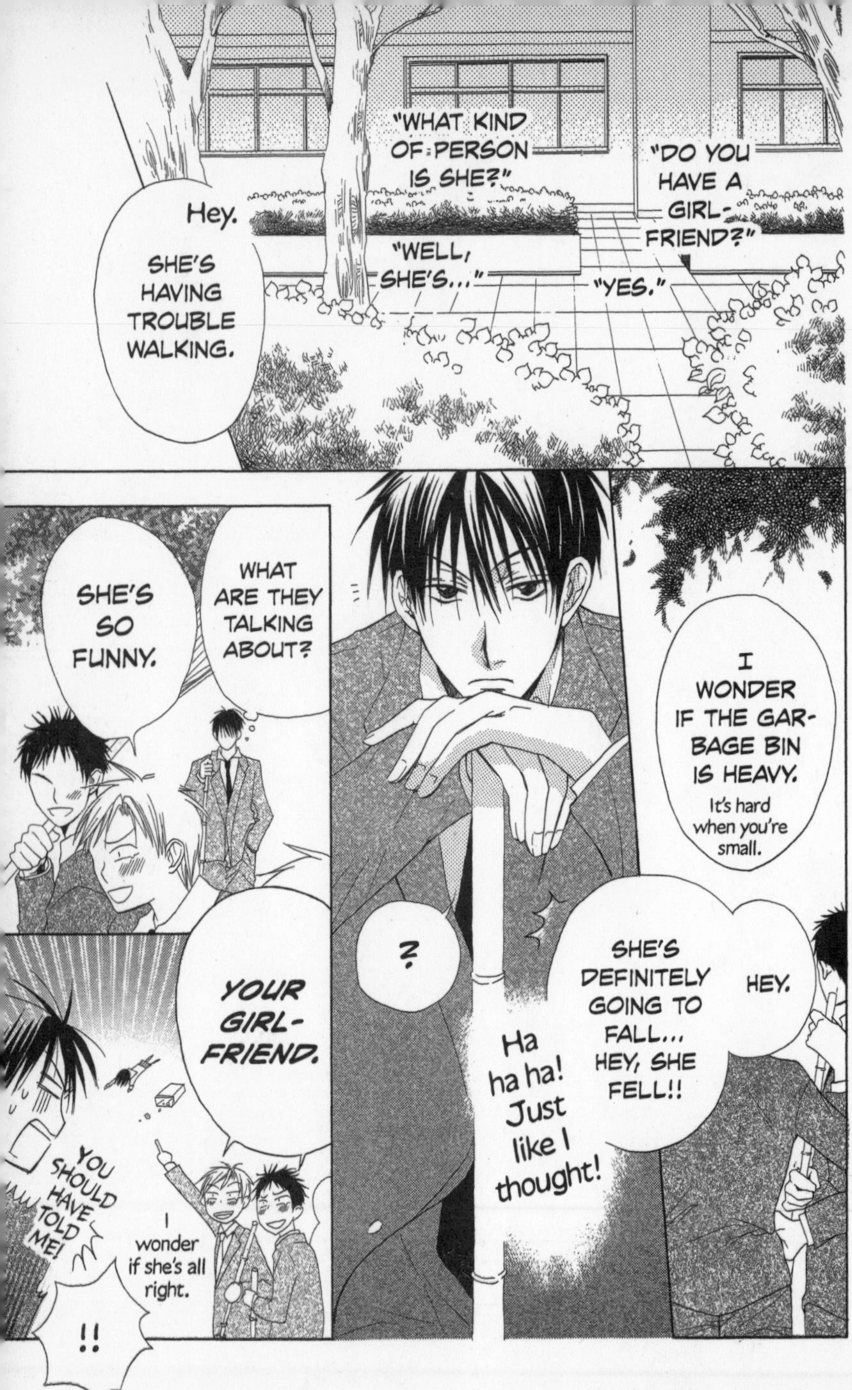
"DO YOU HAVE A GIRL-FRIEND?"
"WHAT KIND OF PERSON IS SHE?"
"YES."
"WELL, SHE'S..."
Hey.
SHE'S HAVING TROUBLE WALKING.
I WONDER IF THE GAR-BAGE BIN IS HEAVY.
It's hard when you're small.
HEY.
SHE'S DEFINITELY GOING TO FALL... HEY, SHE FELL!!
Ha ha ha! Just like I thought!
?
WHAT ARE THEY TALKING ABOUT?
SHE'S SO FUNNY.
YOUR GIRL-FRIEND.
I wonder if she's all right.
YOU SHOULD HAVE TOLD ME!
!!

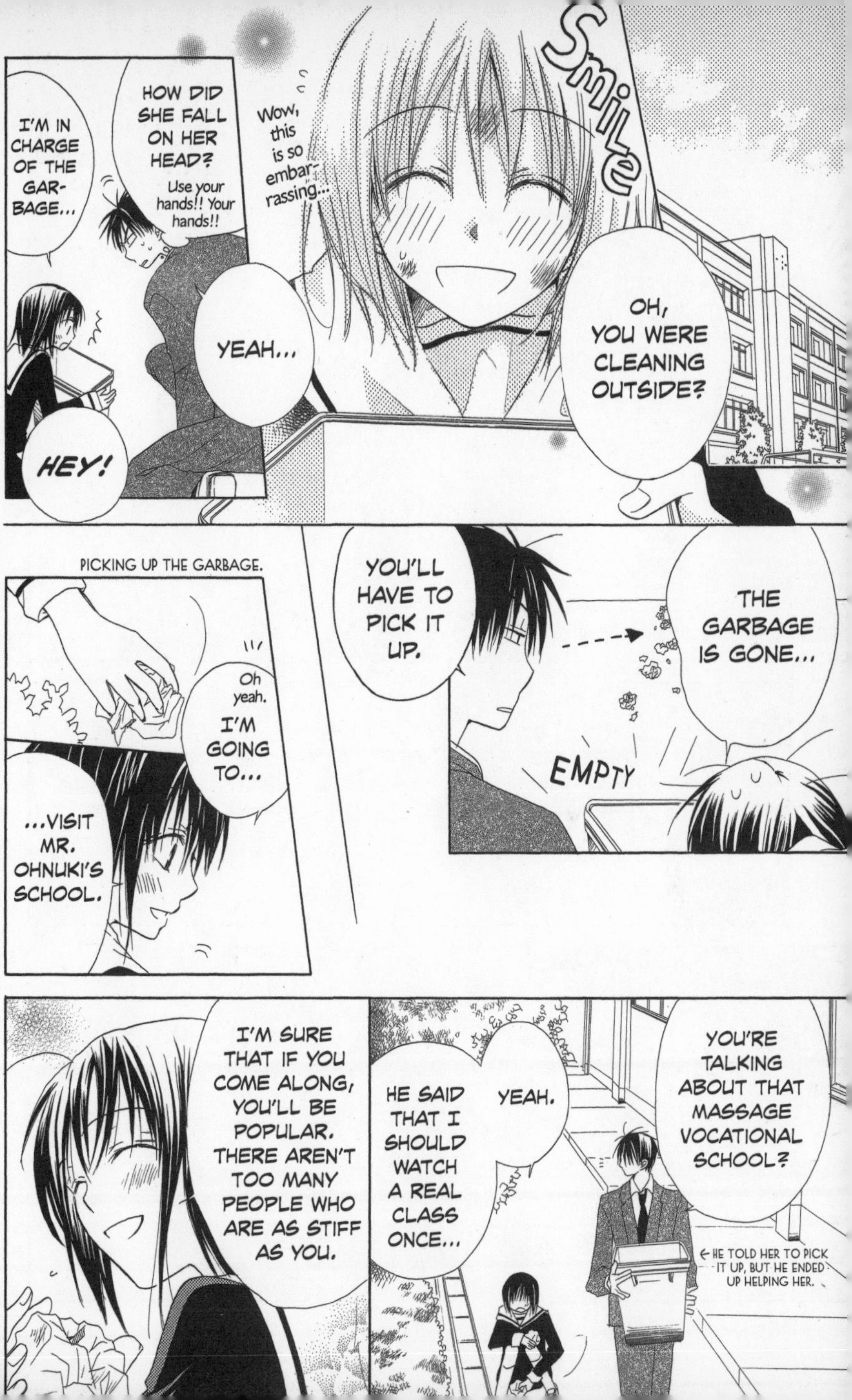
Smile
OH, YOU WERE CLEANING OUTSIDE?
Wow, this is so embarrassing...
YEAH...
HOW DID SHE FALL ON HER HEAD?
Use your hands!! Your hands!!
I'M IN CHARGE OF THE GARBAGE...
HEY!
THE GARBAGE IS GONE...
EMPTY
YOU'LL HAVE TO PICK IT UP.
PICKING UP THE GARBAGE.
Oh yeah.
I'M GOING TO...
...VISIT MR. OHNUKI'S SCHOOL.
YOU'RE TALKING ABOUT THAT MASSAGE VOCATIONAL SCHOOL?
YEAH.
HE SAID THAT I SHOULD WATCH A REAL CLASS ONCE...
← HE TOLD HER TO PICK IT UP, BUT HE ENDED UP HELPING HER.
I'M SURE THAT IF YOU COME ALONG, YOU'LL BE POPULAR. THERE AREN'T TOO MANY PEOPLE WHO ARE AS STIFF AS YOU.

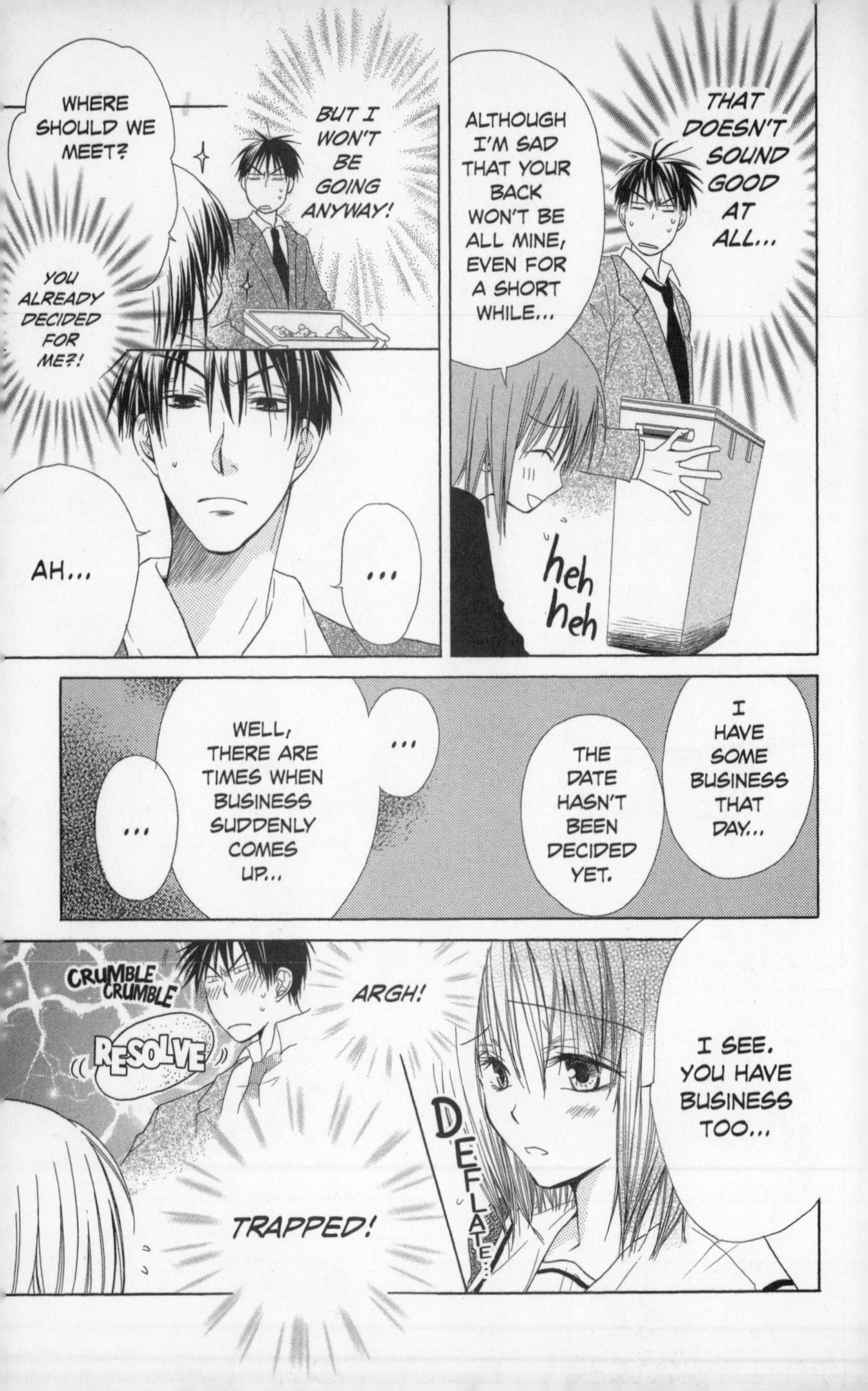
THAT DOESN'T SOUND GOOD AT ALL...
ALTHOUGH I'M SAD THAT YOUR BACK WON'T BE ALL MINE, EVEN FOR A SHORT WHILE...
heh heh
WHERE SHOULD WE MEET?
YOU ALREADY DECIDED FOR ME?!
BUT I WON'T BE GOING ANYWAY!
...
AH...
I HAVE SOME BUSINESS THAT DAY...
THE DATE HASN'T BEEN DECIDED YET.
...
WELL, THERE ARE TIMES WHEN BUSINESS SUDDENLY COMES UP...
...
I SEE. YOU HAVE BUSINESS TOO...
DEFLATE...
ARGH!
CRUMBLE CRUMBLE
RESOLVE
TRAPPED!

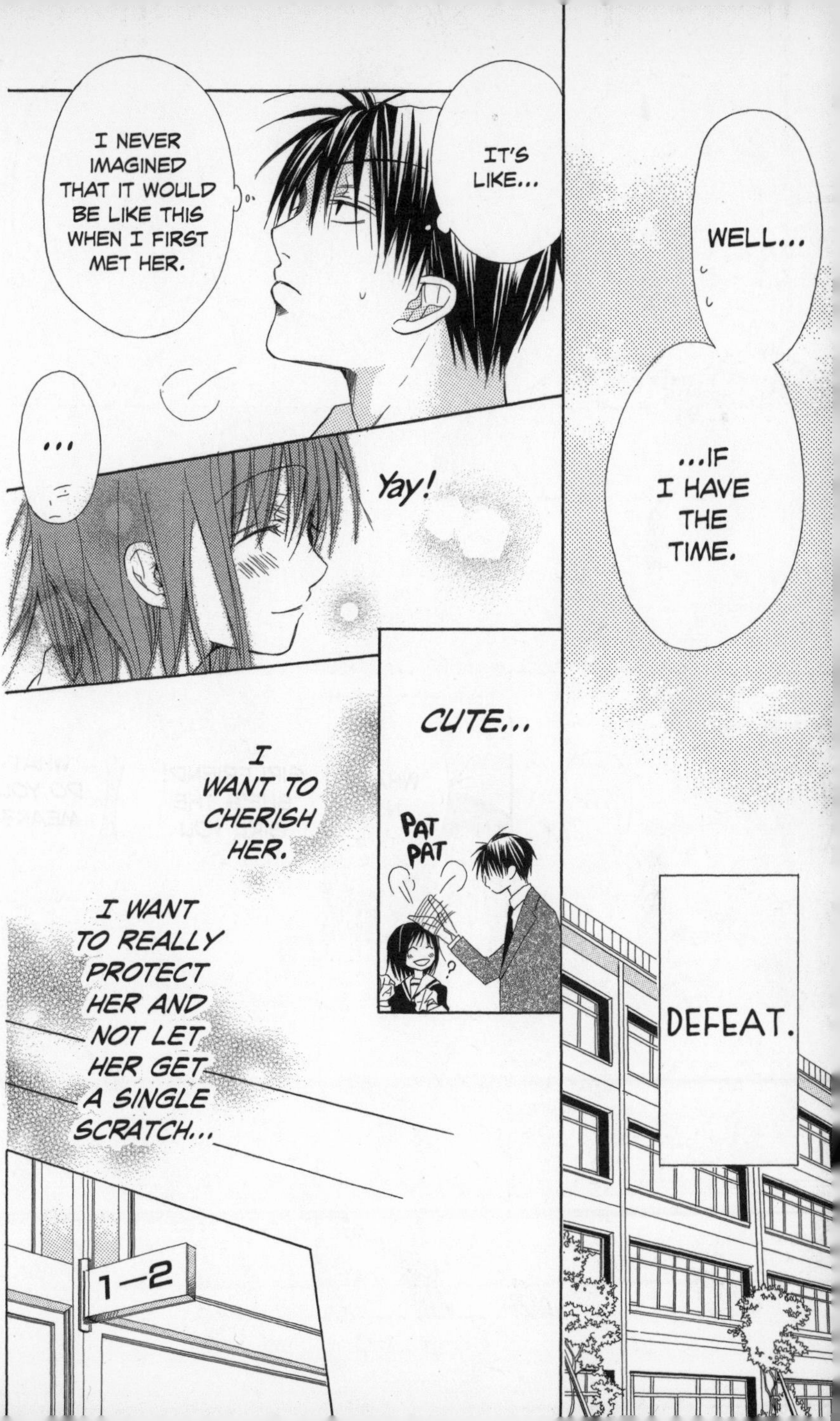
WELL...
...IF I HAVE THE TIME.
IT'S LIKE...
I NEVER IMAGINED THAT IT WOULD BE LIKE THIS WHEN I FIRST MET HER.
...
Yay!
CUTE...
PAT PAT
DEFEAT.
I WANT TO CHERISH HER.
I WANT TO REALLY PROTECT HER AND NOT LET HER GET A SINGLE SCRATCH...
1-2

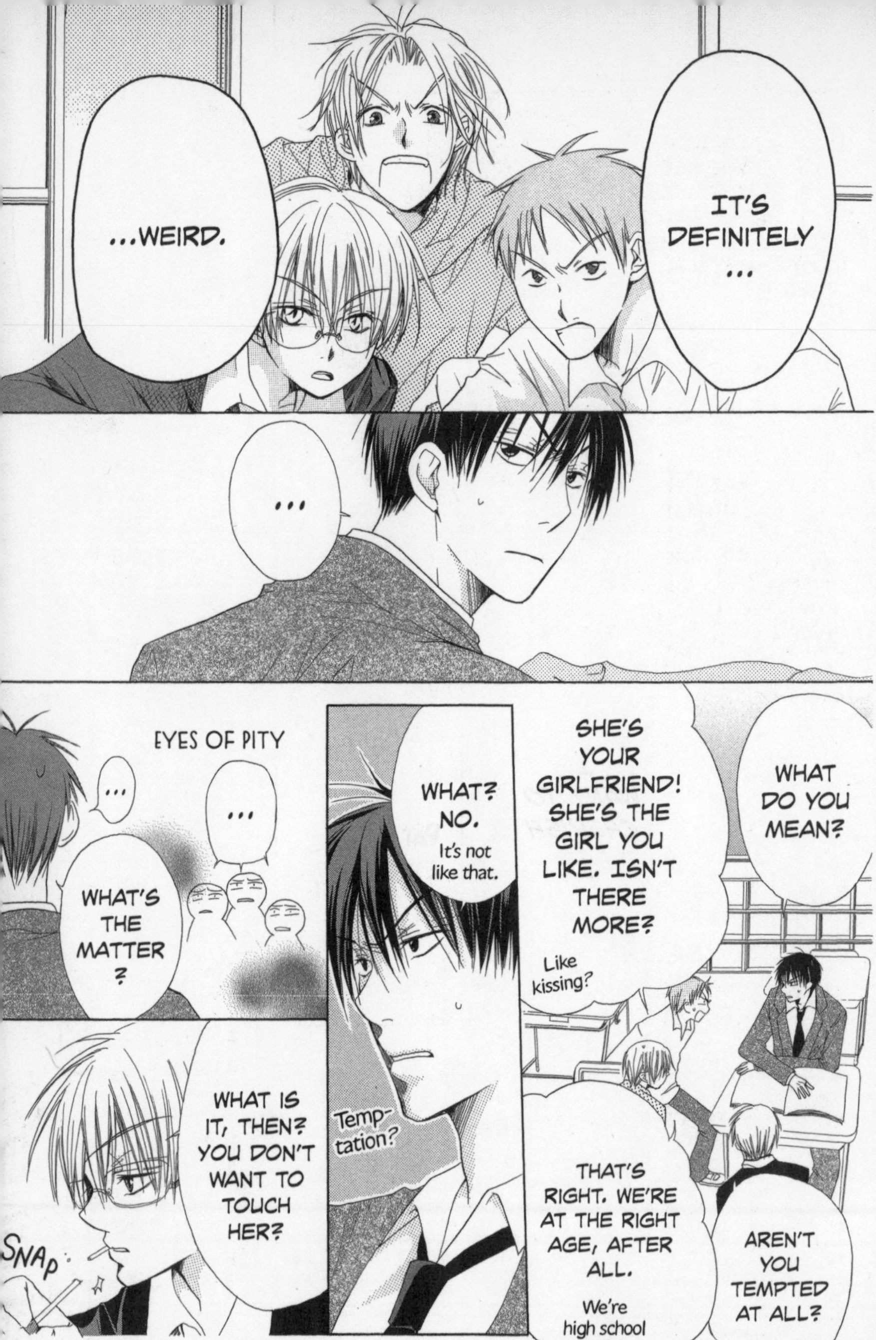
IT'S DEFINITELY ...
...WEIRD.
...
WHAT DO YOU MEAN?
SHE'S YOUR GIRLFRIEND! SHE'S THE GIRL YOU LIKE. ISN'T THERE MORE?
Like kissing?
AREN'T YOU TEMPTED AT ALL?
THAT'S RIGHT. WE'RE AT THE RIGHT AGE, AFTER ALL.
We're high school kids!
WHAT? NO.
It's not like that.
Temp-tation?
EYES OF PITY
...
...
WHAT'S THE MATTER?
WHAT IS IT, THEN? YOU DON'T WANT TO TOUCH HER?
SNAP

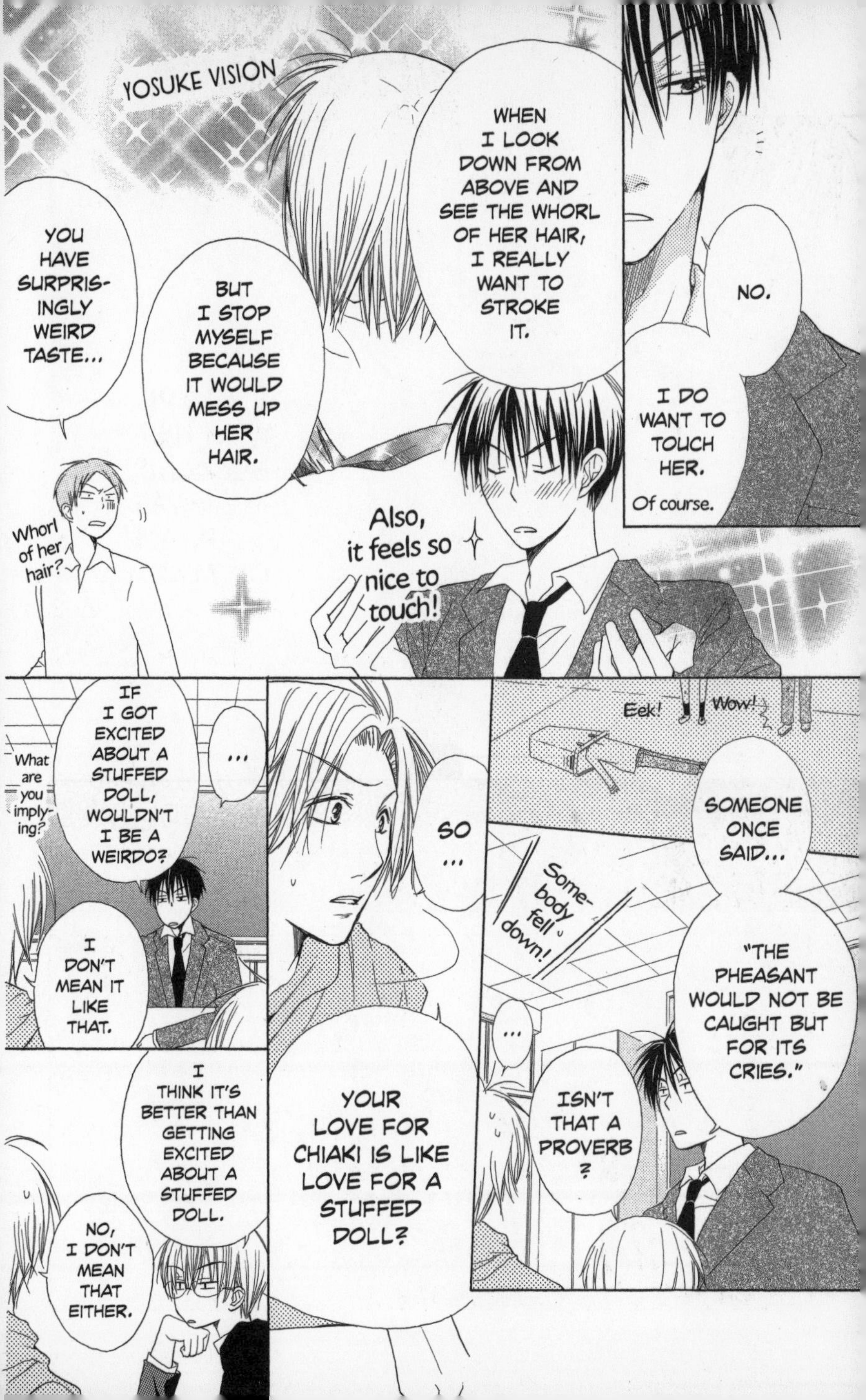
NO.
I DO WANT TO TOUCH HER.
Of course.
YOSUKE VISION
WHEN I LOOK DOWN FROM ABOVE AND SEE THE WHORL OF HER HAIR, I REALLY WANT TO STROKE IT.
BUT I STOP MYSELF BECAUSE IT WOULD MESS UP HER HAIR.
YOU HAVE SURPRISINGLY WEIRD TASTE...
Also, it feels so nice to touch!
Whorl of her hair?
Eek!
Wow!
SOMEONE ONCE SAID...
Somebody fell down!
"THE PHEASANT WOULD NOT BE CAUGHT BUT FOR ITS CRIES."
...
ISN'T THAT A PROVERB?
SO ...
YOUR LOVE FOR CHIAKI IS LIKE LOVE FOR A STUFFED DOLL?
...
IF I GOT EXCITED ABOUT A STUFFED DOLL, WOULDN'T I BE A WEIRDO?
What are you implying?
I DON'T MEAN IT LIKE THAT.
I THINK IT'S BETTER THAN GETTING EXCITED ABOUT A STUFFED DOLL.
NO, I DON'T MEAN THAT EITHER.

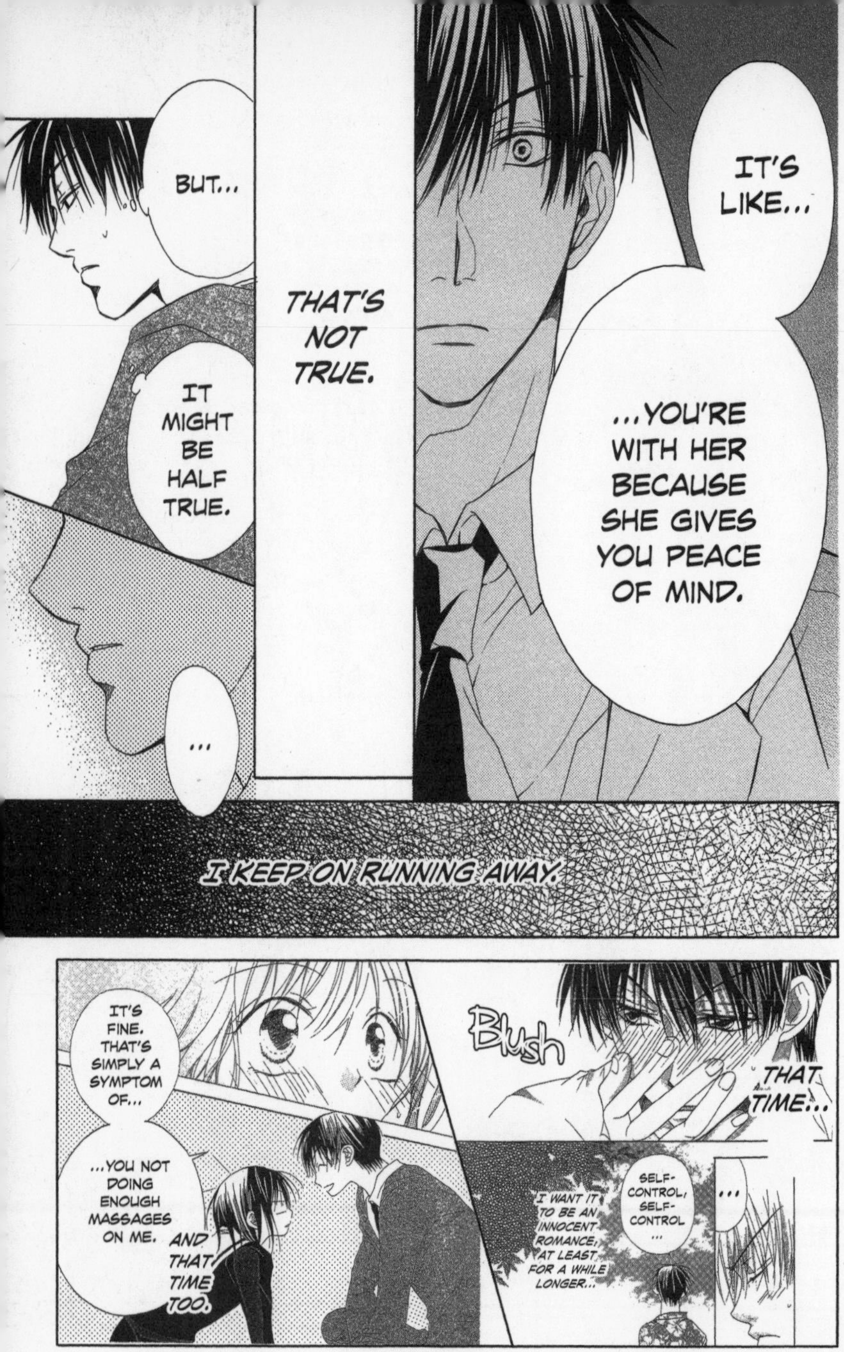
IT'S LIKE...
...YOU'RE WITH HER BECAUSE SHE GIVES YOU PEACE OF MIND.
THAT'S NOT TRUE.
BUT...
IT MIGHT BE HALF TRUE.
...
I KEEP ON RUNNING AWAY.
Blush
THAT TIME...
...
SELF-CONTROL, SELF-CONTROL...
I WANT IT TO BE AN INNOCENT ROMANCE, AT LEAST FOR A WHILE LONGER...
IT'S FINE. THAT'S SIMPLY A SYMPTOM OF...
...YOU NOT DOING ENOUGH MASSAGES ON ME.
AND THAT TIME TOO.

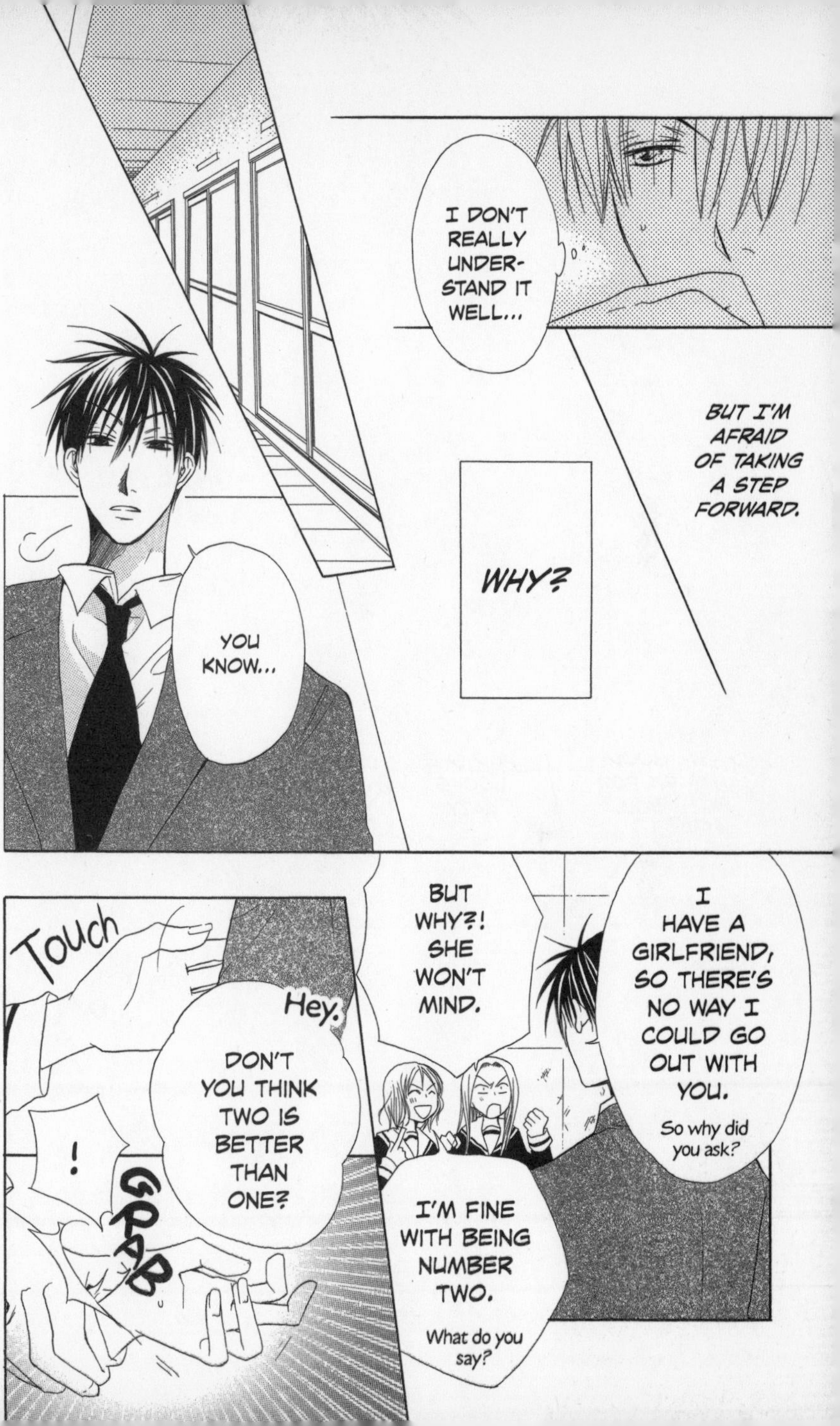
I DON'T REALLY UNDERSTAND IT WELL...
BUT I'M AFRAID OF TAKING A STEP FORWARD.
WHY?
YOU KNOW...
I HAVE A GIRLFRIEND, SO THERE'S NO WAY I COULD GO OUT WITH YOU.
So why did you ask?
BUT WHY?! SHE WON'T MIND.
I'M FINE WITH BEING NUMBER TWO.
What do you say?
Touch
Hey.
DON'T YOU THINK TWO IS BETTER THAN ONE?
!
GRAB

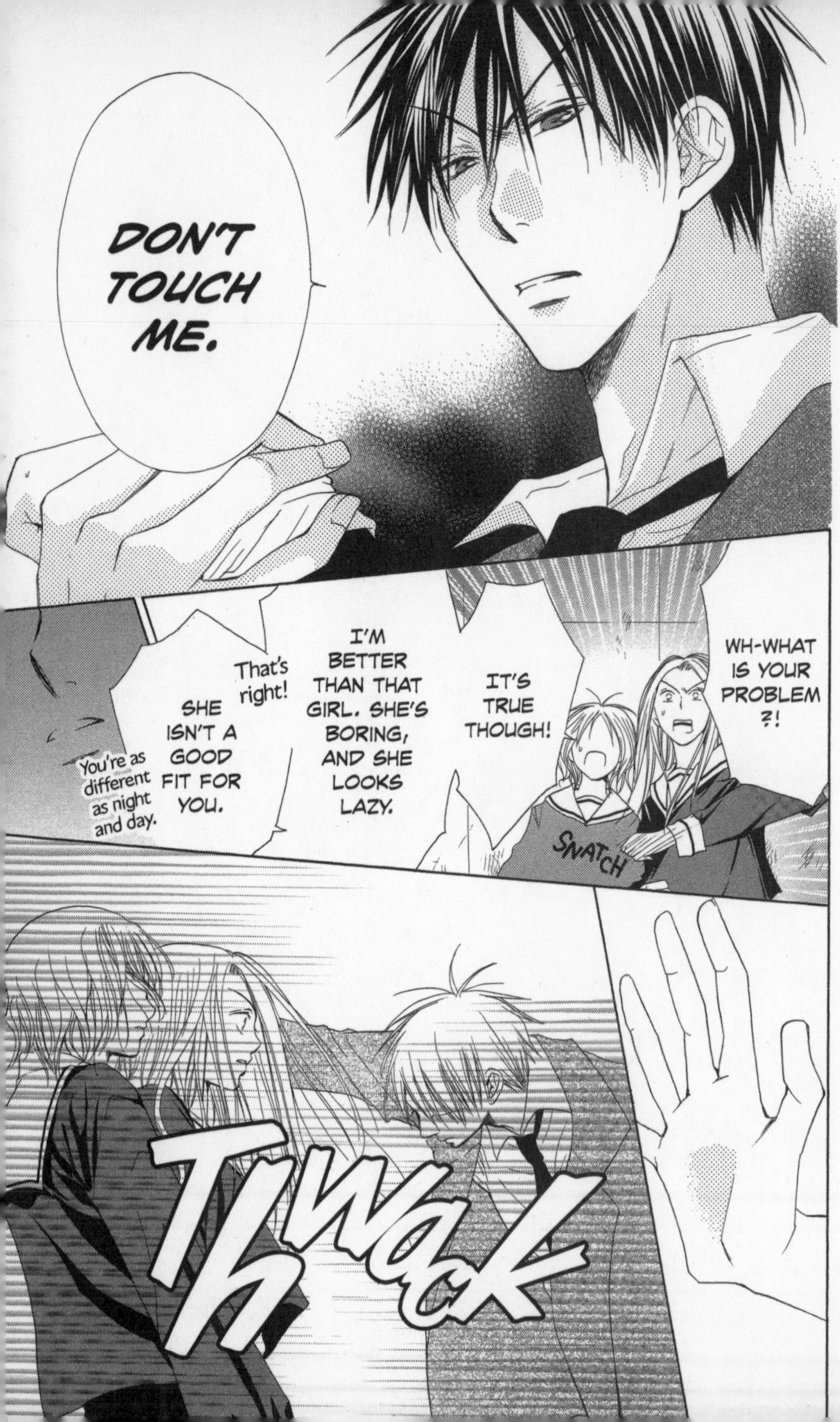
DON'T TOUCH ME.
WH-WHAT IS YOUR PROBLEM?!
IT'S TRUE THOUGH!
SNATCH
I'M BETTER THAN THAT GIRL. SHE'S BORING, AND SHE LOOKS LAZY.
That's right!
SHE ISN'T A GOOD FIT FOR YOU.
You're as different as night and day.
THWACK

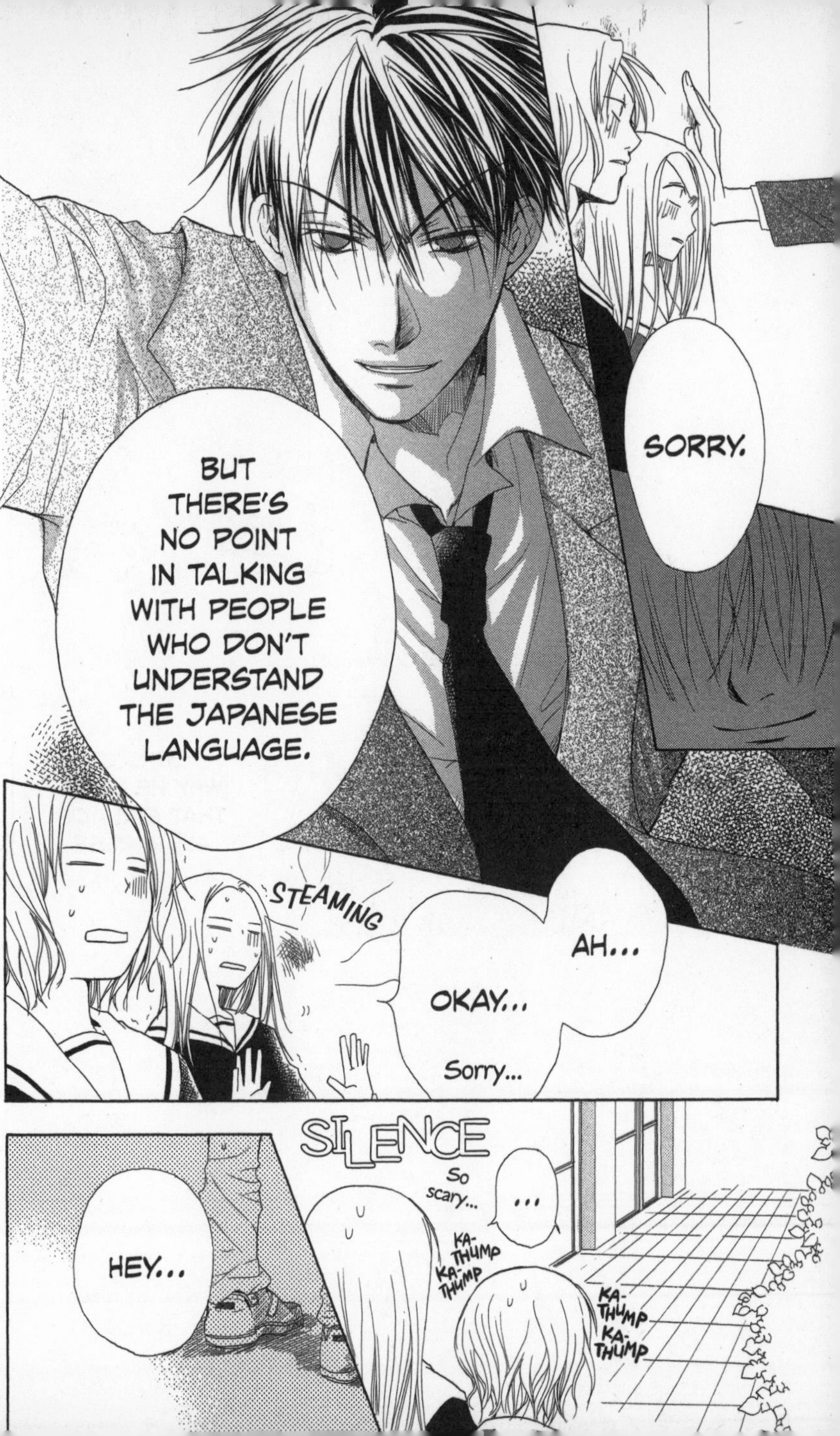
SORRY.
BUT THERE'S NO POINT IN TALKING WITH PEOPLE WHO DON'T UNDERSTAND THE JAPANESE LANGUAGE.
AH... OKAY...
Sorry...
STEAMING
SILENCE
...
So scary...
KA-THUMP KA-THUMP
KA-THUMP KA-THUMP
HEY...

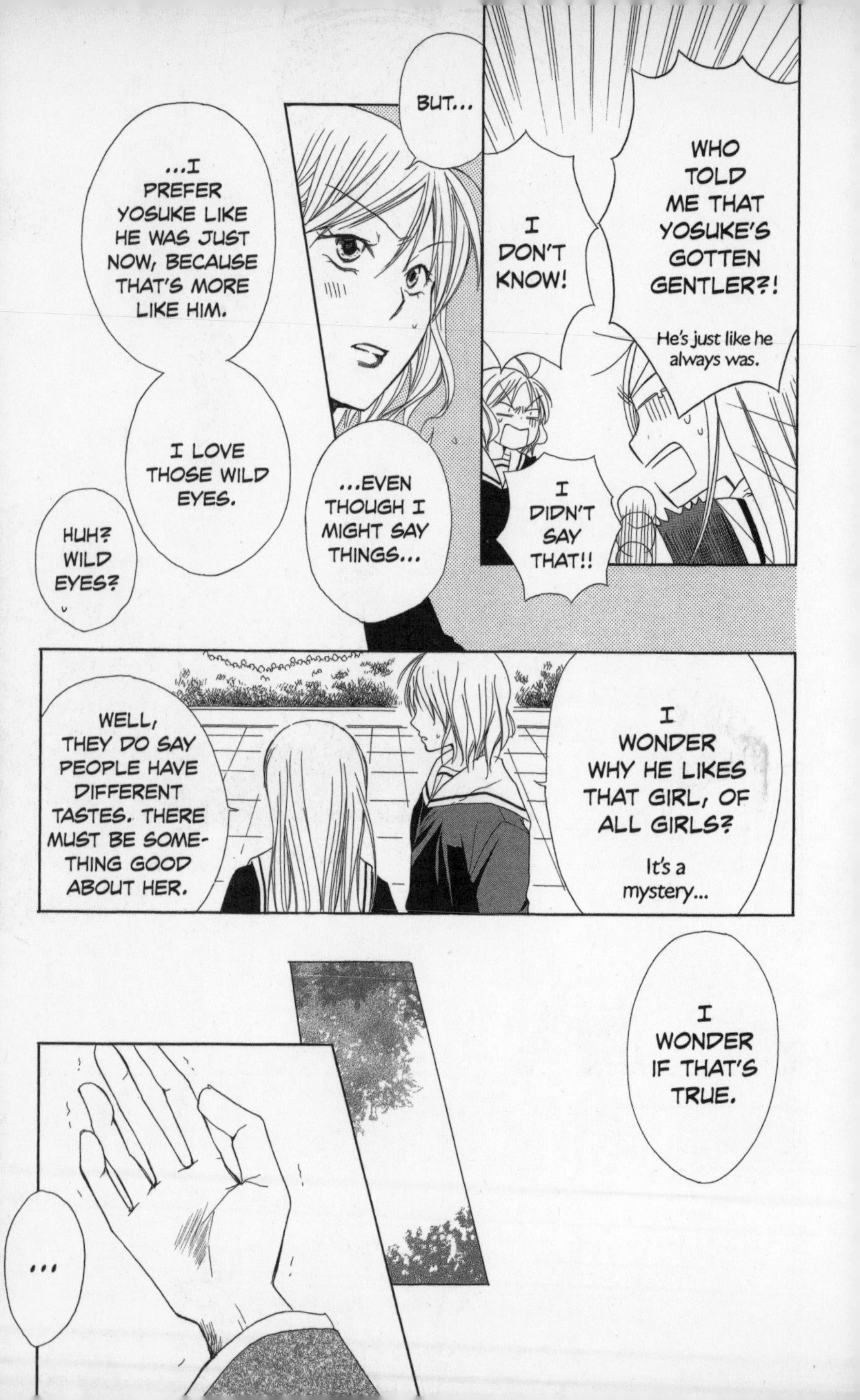
WHO TOLD ME THAT YOSUKE'S GOTTEN GENTLER?!
He's just like he always was.
I DON'T KNOW!
I DIDN'T SAY THAT!!
BUT...
...EVEN THOUGH I MIGHT SAY THINGS...
...I PREFER YOSUKE LIKE HE WAS JUST NOW, BECAUSE THAT'S MORE LIKE HIM.
I LOVE THOSE WILD EYES.
HUH? WILD EYES?
I WONDER WHY HE LIKES THAT GIRL, OF ALL GIRLS?
It's a mystery...
WELL, THEY DO SAY PEOPLE HAVE DIFFERENT TASTES. THERE MUST BE SOMETHING GOOD ABOUT HER.
I WONDER IF THAT'S TRUE.
...

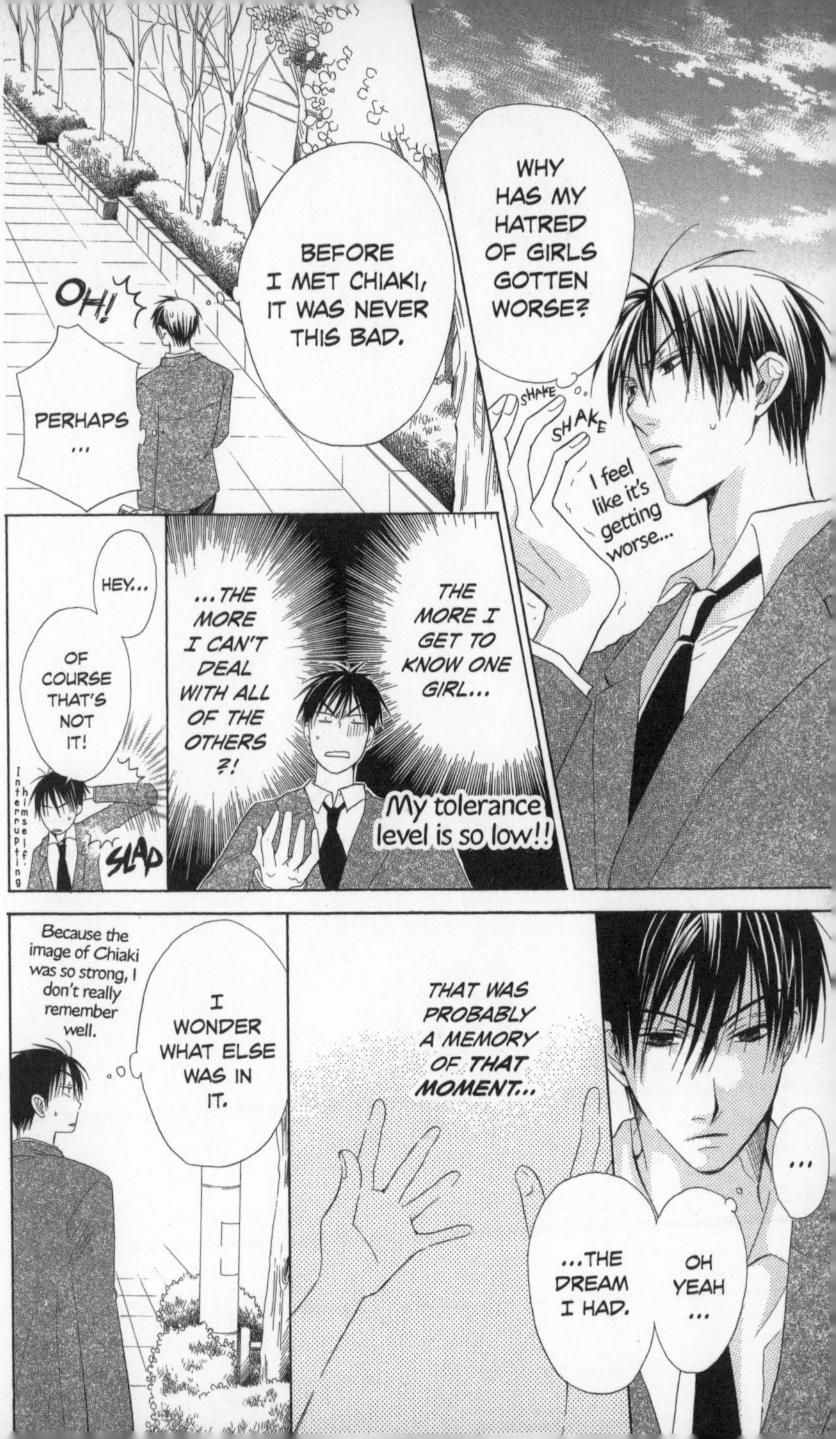
WHY HAS MY HATRED OF GIRLS GOTTEN WORSE?
SHAKE SHAKE
I feel like it's getting worse...
BEFORE I MET CHIAKI, IT WAS NEVER THIS BAD.
OH!
PERHAPS ...
THE MORE I GET TO KNOW ONE GIRL...
...THE MORE I CAN'T DEAL WITH ALL OF THE OTHERS?!
My tolerance level is so low!!
HEY...
OF COURSE THAT'S NOT IT!
Interrupting himself.
SLAP
THAT WAS PROBABLY A MEMORY OF THAT MOMENT...
...
OH YEAH ...
...THE DREAM I HAD.
I WONDER WHAT ELSE WAS IN IT.
Because the image of Chiaki was so strong, I don't really remember well.

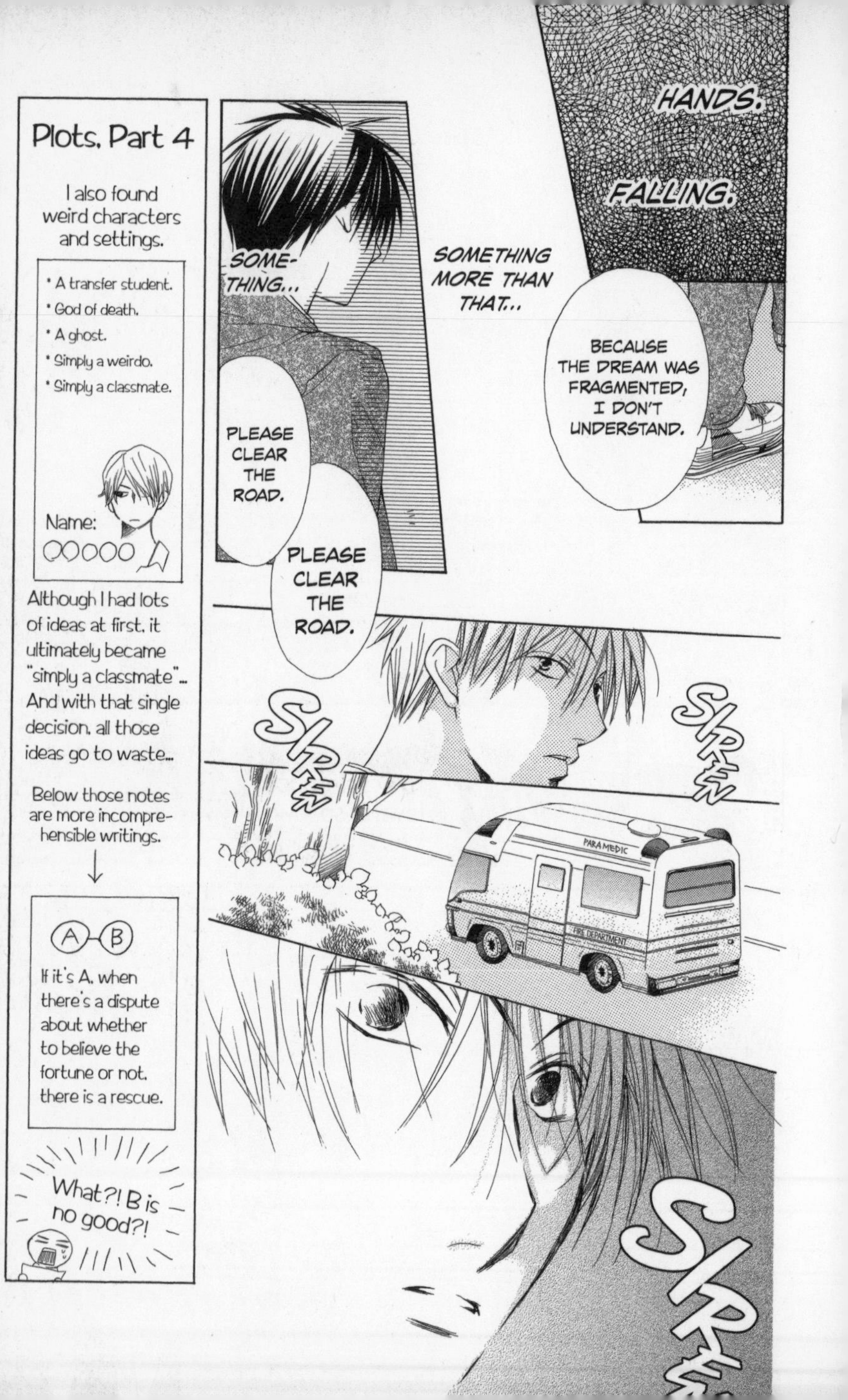
HANDS.
FALLING.
SOMETHING MORE THAN THAT...
BECAUSE THE DREAM WAS FRAGMENTED, I DON'T UNDERSTAND.
SOME-THING...
PLEASE CLEAR THE ROAD.
PLEASE CLEAR THE ROAD.
SIREN
SIREN
PARAMEDIC
FIRE DEPARTMENT
SIREN

Plots, Part 4

I also found weird characters and settings.

- A transfer student.
- God of death.
- A ghost.
- Simply a weirdo.
- Simply a classmate.

Name: ○○○○○

Although I had lots of ideas at first, it ultimately became "simply a classmate"... And with that single decision, all those ideas go to waste...

Below those notes are more incomprehensible writings.

↓

Ⓐ-Ⓑ

If it's A, when there's a dispute about whether to believe the fortune or not, there is a rescue.

What?! B is no good?!

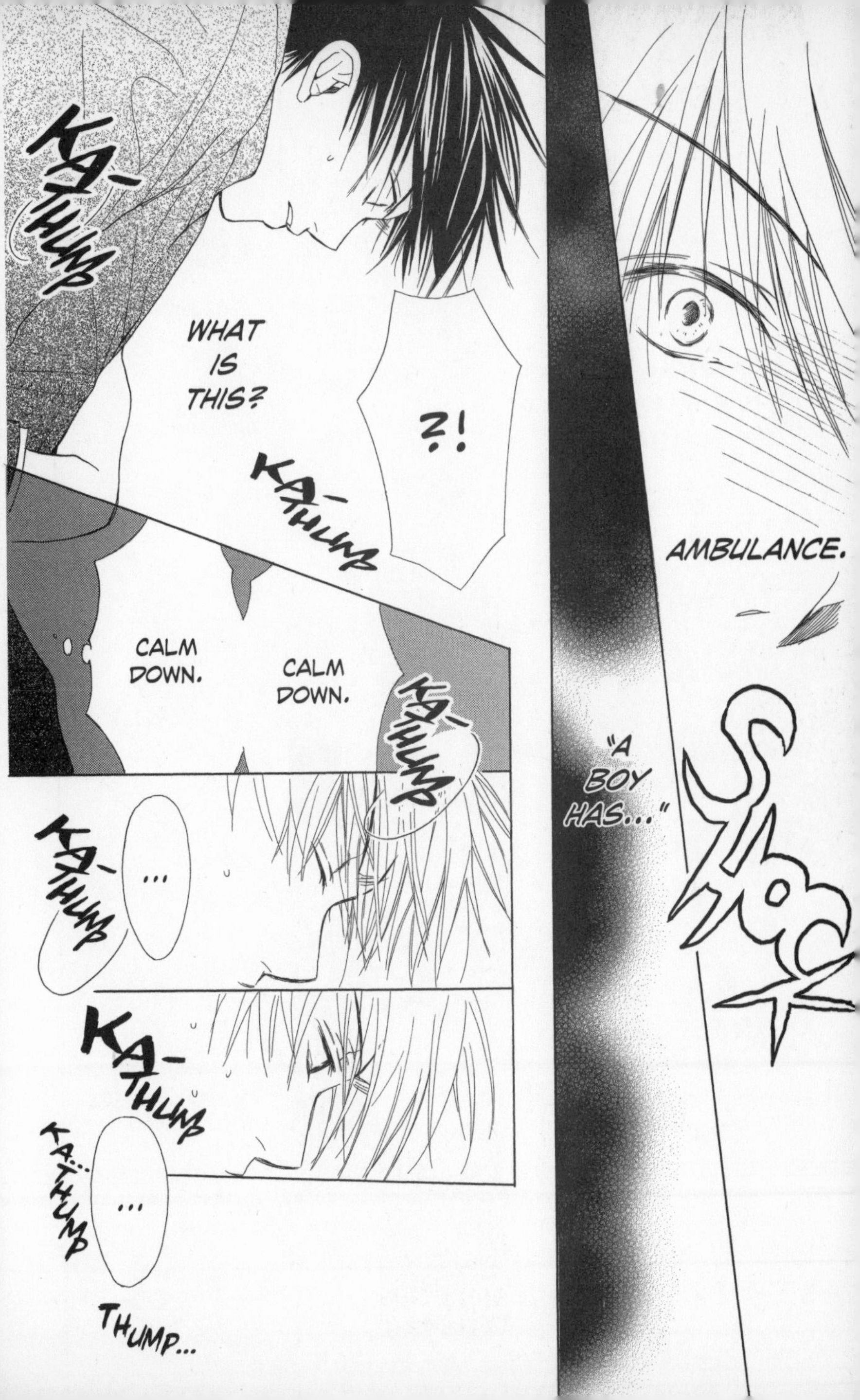
AMBULANCE.
SHOCK
"A BOY HAS..."
?!
KA-THUMP
WHAT IS THIS?
KA-THUMP
KA-THUMP
CALM DOWN.
CALM DOWN.
...
KA-THUMP
KA-THUMP
...
KA-THUMP
THUMP...

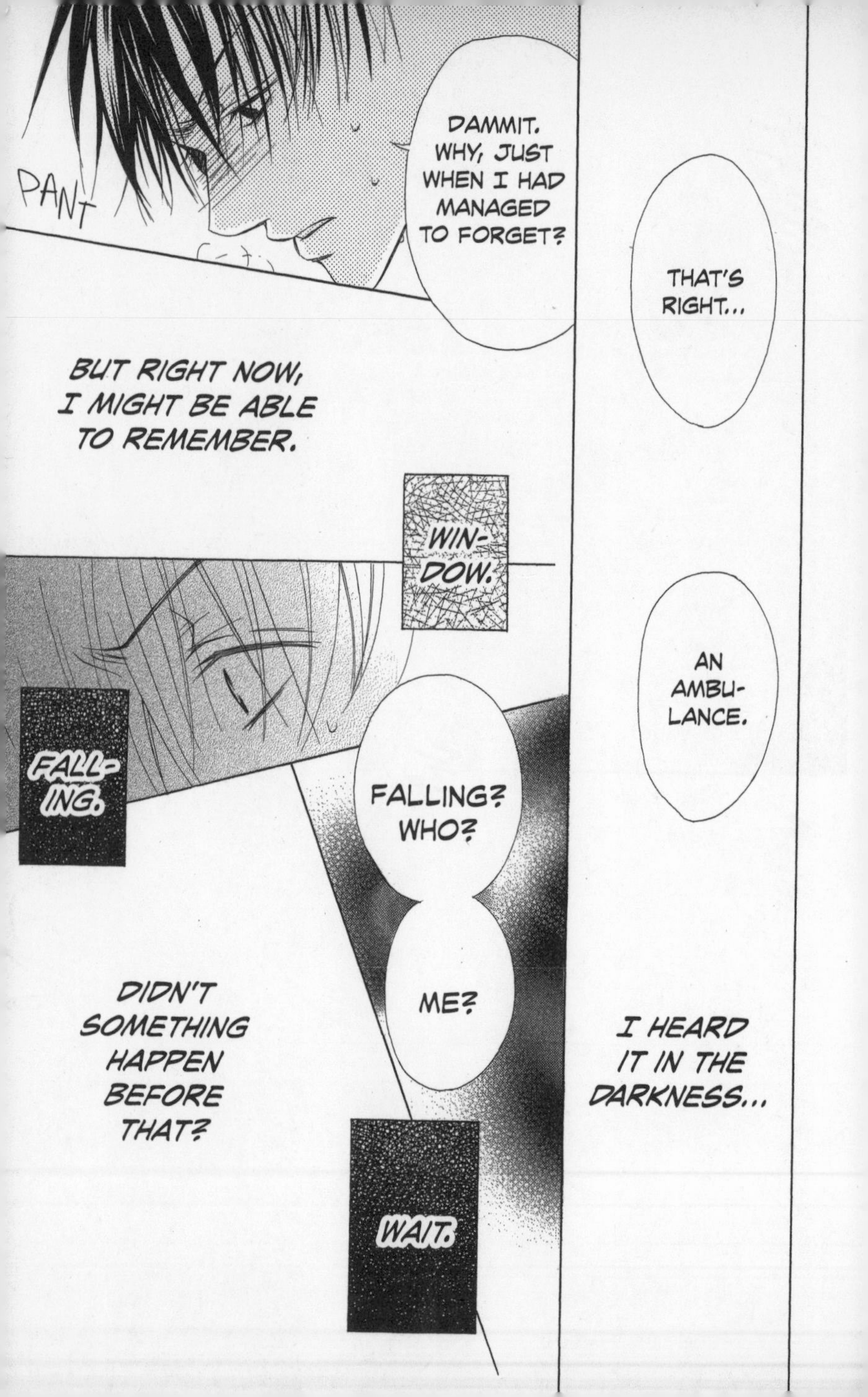
THAT'S RIGHT...
AN AMBULANCE.
I HEARD IT IN THE DARKNESS...
DAMMIT. WHY, JUST WHEN I HAD MANAGED TO FORGET?
PANT
BUT RIGHT NOW, I MIGHT BE ABLE TO REMEMBER.
WIN-DOW.
FALLING? WHO?
FALL-ING.
ME?
DIDN'T SOMETHING HAPPEN BEFORE THAT?
WAIT.

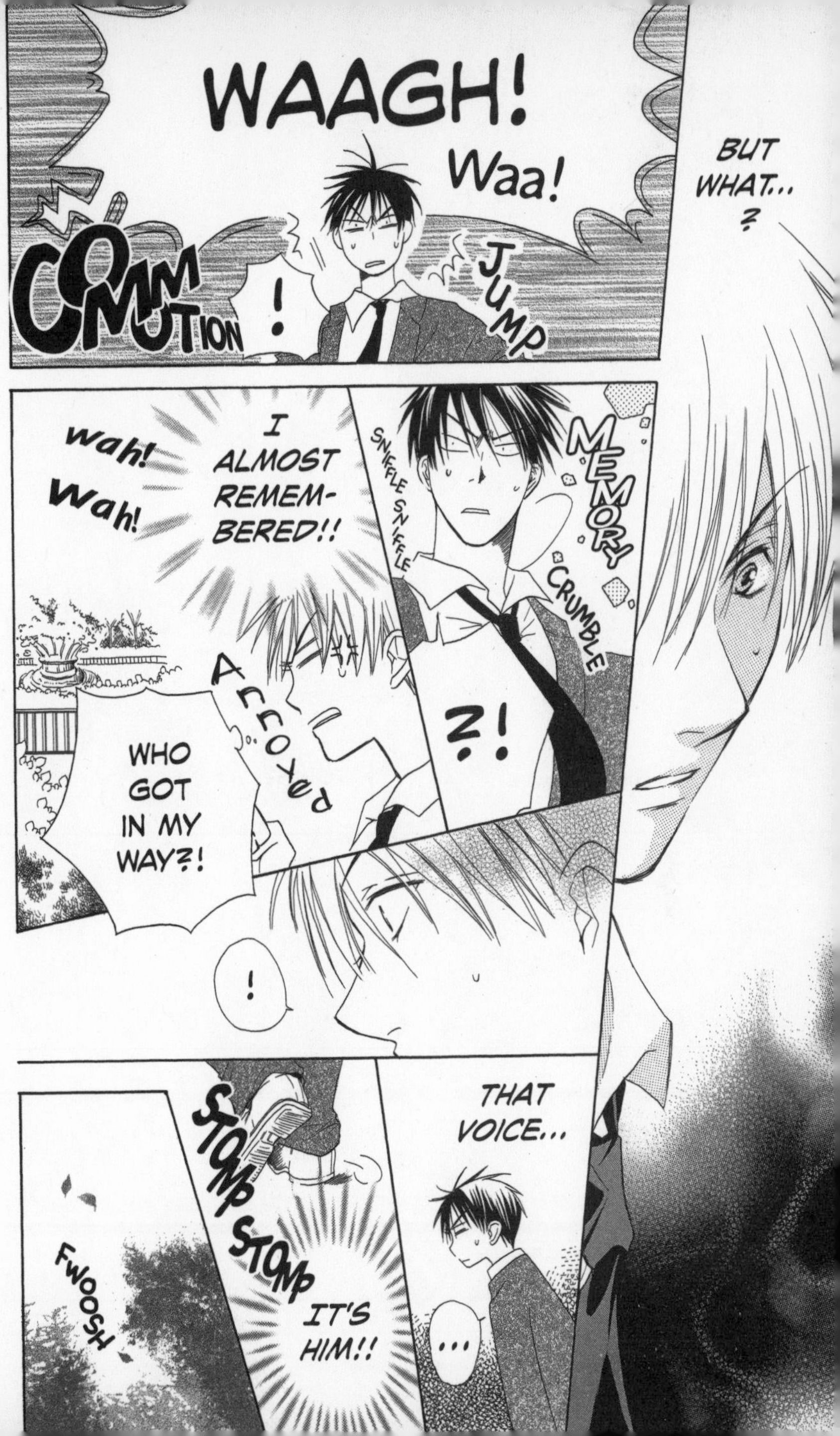
BUT WHAT...?
WAAGH!
Waa!
JUMP
!
COMMOTION
MEMORY CRUMBLE
SNIFFLE SNIFFLE
?!
I ALMOST REMEMBERED!!
wah! wah!
Annoyed
WHO GOT IN MY WAY?!
!
THAT VOICE...
...
STOMP STOMP
IT'S HIM!!
FWOOSH

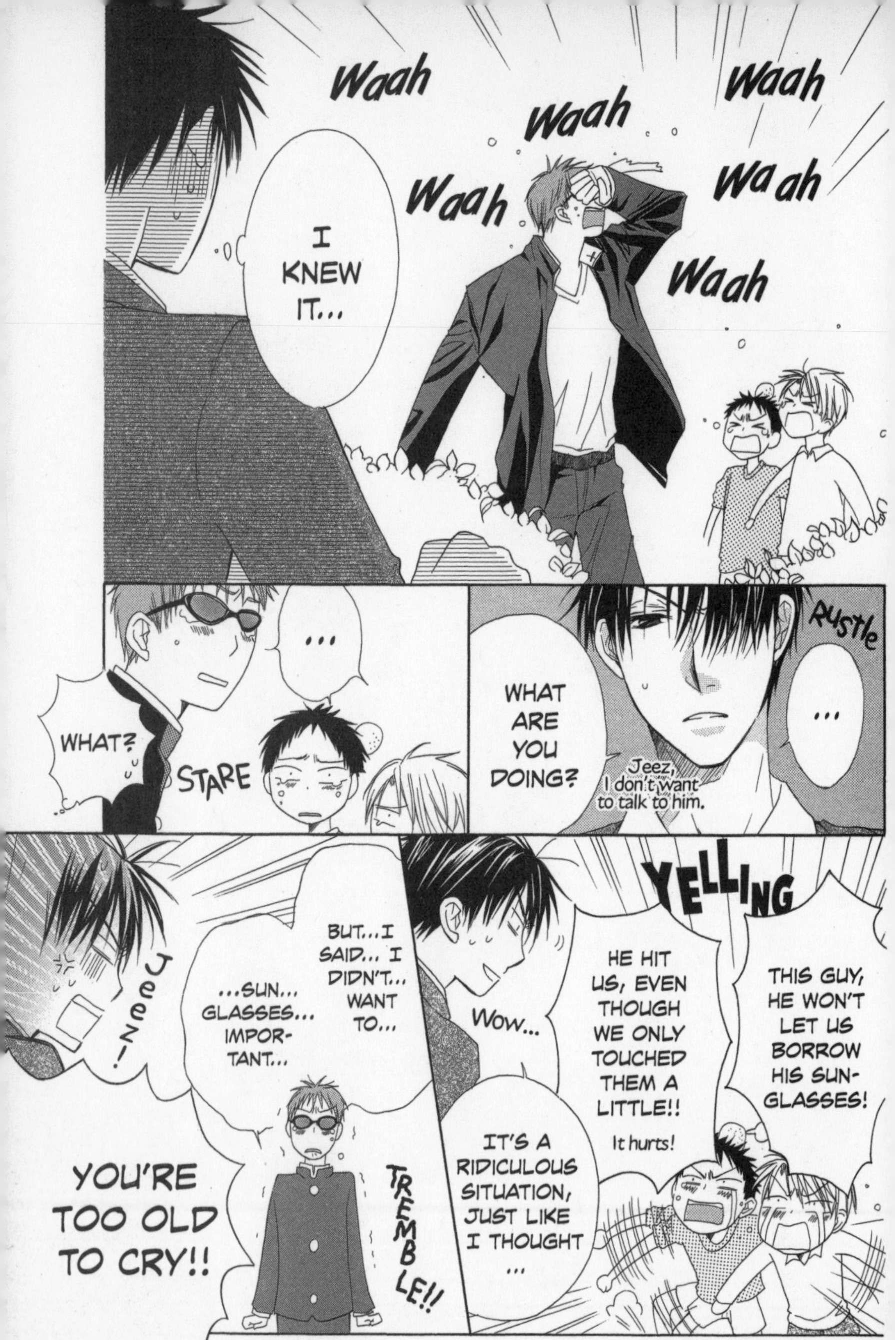
Waah
Waah
Waah
Waah
Waah
Waah
I KNEW IT...
Rustle
...
WHAT ARE YOU DOING?
Jeez, I don't want to talk to him.
...
WHAT?
STARE
YELLING
THIS GUY, HE WON'T LET US BORROW HIS SUN-GLASSES!
HE HIT US, EVEN THOUGH WE ONLY TOUCHED THEM A LITTLE!!
It hurts!
Wow...
IT'S A RIDICULOUS SITUATION, JUST LIKE I THOUGHT ...
BUT...I SAID... I DIDN'T... WANT TO...
...SUN... GLASSES... IMPOR-TANT...
Jeez!
TREMBLE!!
YOU'RE TOO OLD TO CRY!!

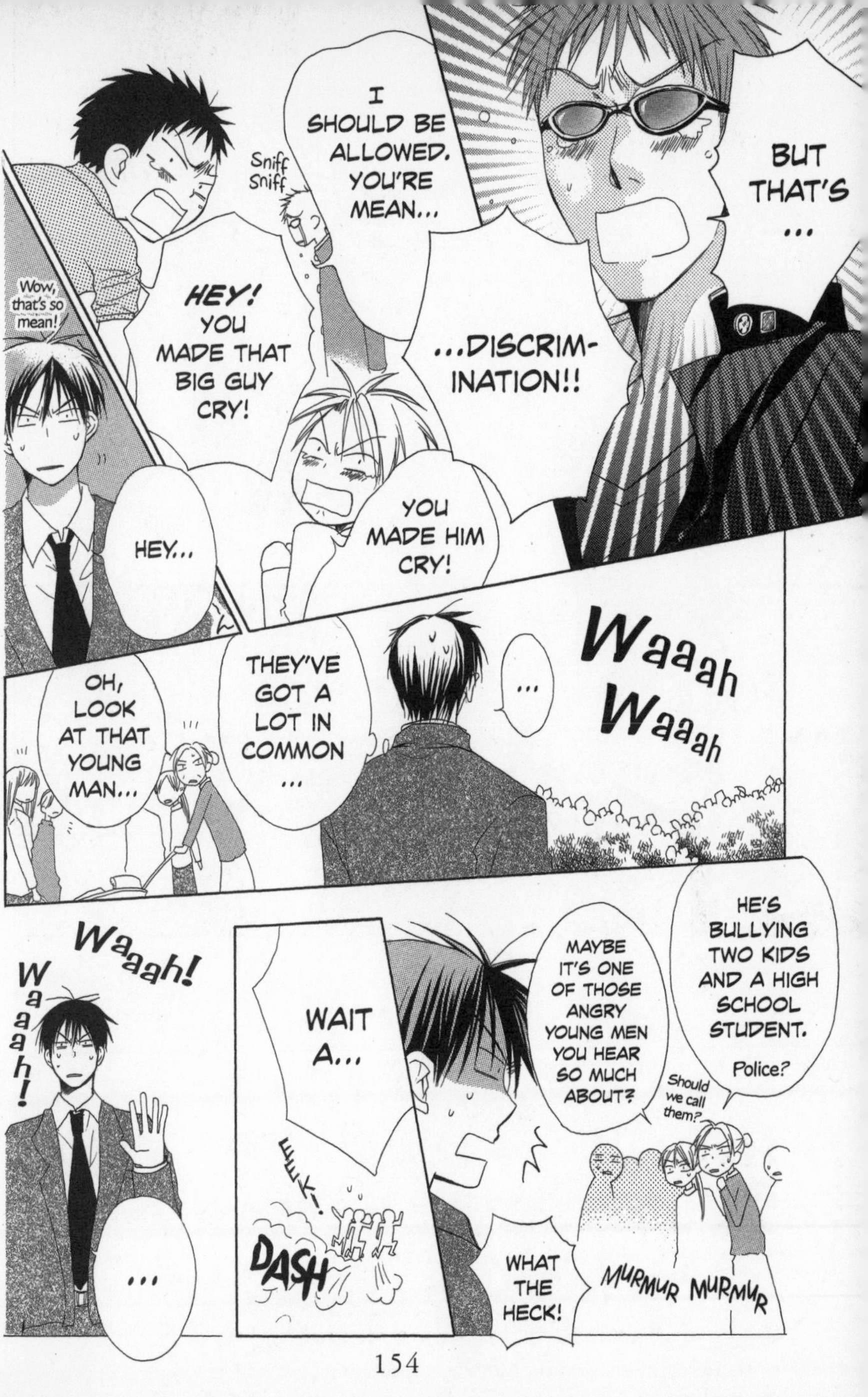
BUT THAT'S ...
...DISCRIMINATION!!
I SHOULD BE ALLOWED. YOU'RE MEAN...
Sniff Sniff
HEY! YOU MADE THAT BIG GUY CRY!
Wow, that's so mean!
YOU MADE HIM CRY!
HEY...
Waaah Waaah
...
THEY'VE GOT A LOT IN COMMON ...
OH, LOOK AT THAT YOUNG MAN...
HE'S BULLYING TWO KIDS AND A HIGH SCHOOL STUDENT.
Police?
Should we call them?
MAYBE IT'S ONE OF THOSE ANGRY YOUNG MEN YOU HEAR SO MUCH ABOUT?
MURMUR MURMUR
WHAT THE HECK!
WAIT A...
DASH
Waaah!
Waaah!
...

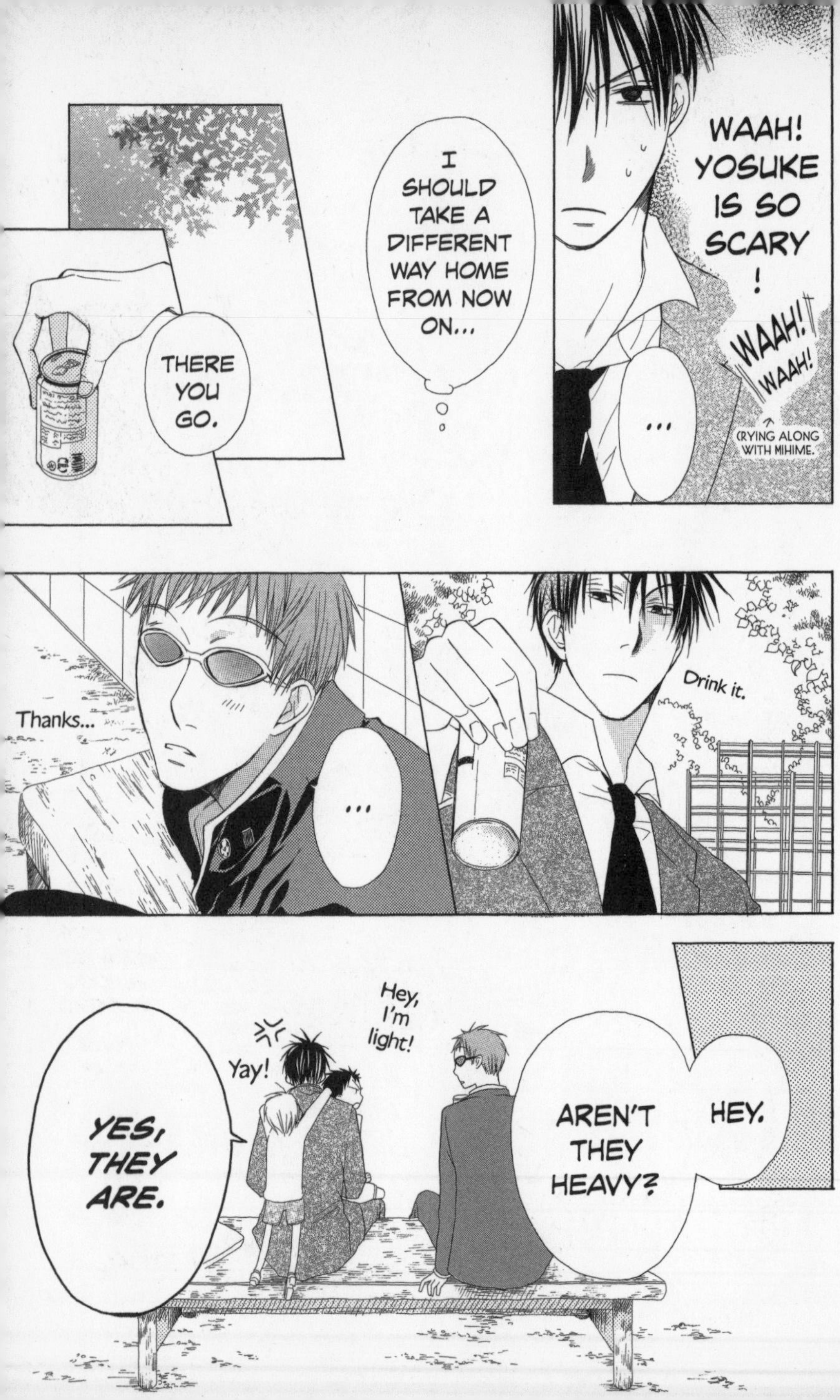

WAAH! YOSUKE IS SO SCARY!
WAAH! WAAH!
CRYING ALONG WITH MIHIME.
...
I SHOULD TAKE A DIFFERENT WAY HOME FROM NOW ON...
THERE YOU GO.
Drink it.
...
Thanks...
HEY.
AREN'T THEY HEAVY?
Hey, I'm light!
Yay!
YES, THEY ARE.

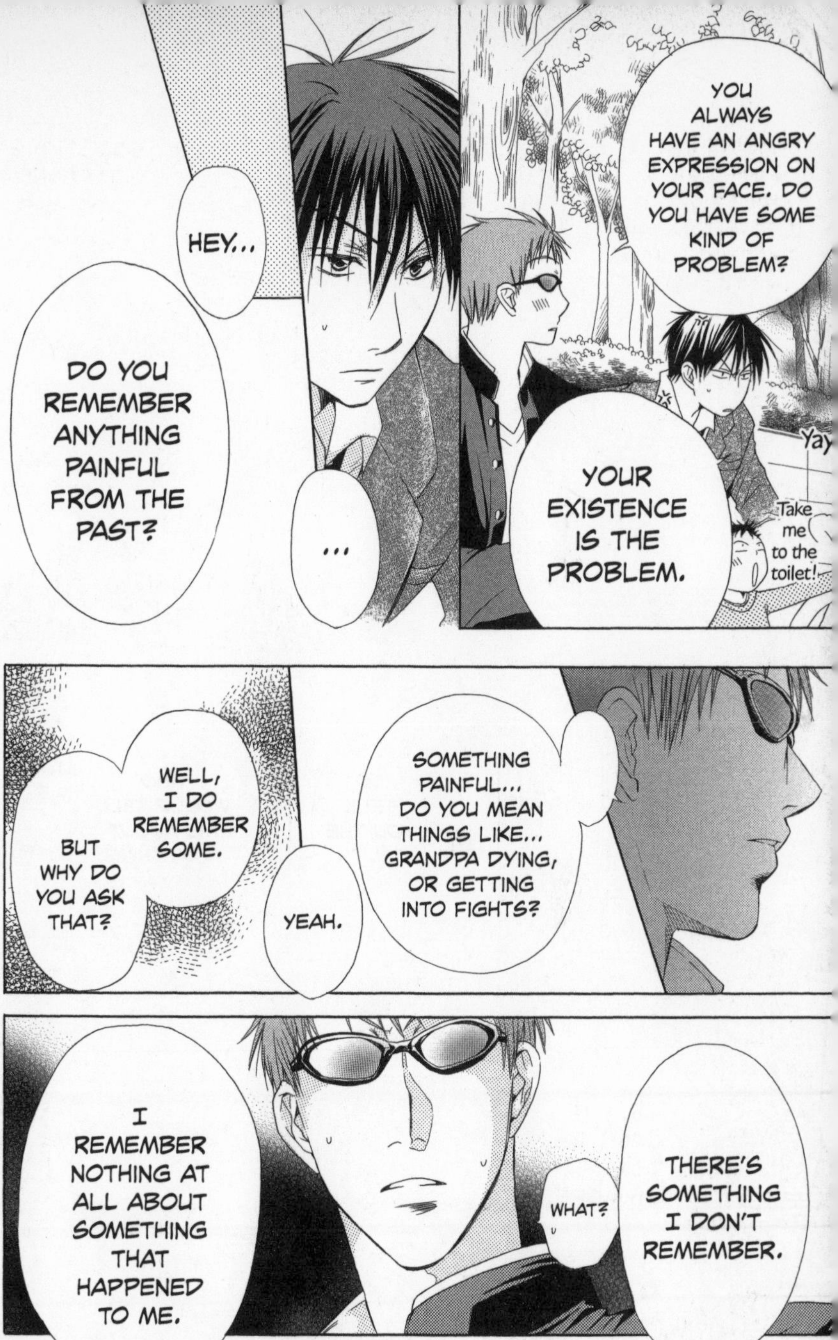
YOU ALWAYS HAVE AN ANGRY EXPRESSION ON YOUR FACE. DO YOU HAVE SOME KIND OF PROBLEM?
Yay
YOUR EXISTENCE IS THE PROBLEM.
Take me to the toilet!
HEY...
...
DO YOU REMEMBER ANYTHING PAINFUL FROM THE PAST?
SOMETHING PAINFUL... DO YOU MEAN THINGS LIKE... GRANDPA DYING, OR GETTING INTO FIGHTS?
YEAH.
WELL, I DO REMEMBER SOME.
BUT WHY DO YOU ASK THAT?
THERE'S SOMETHING I DON'T REMEMBER.
WHAT?
I REMEMBER NOTHING AT ALL ABOUT SOMETHING THAT HAPPENED TO ME.

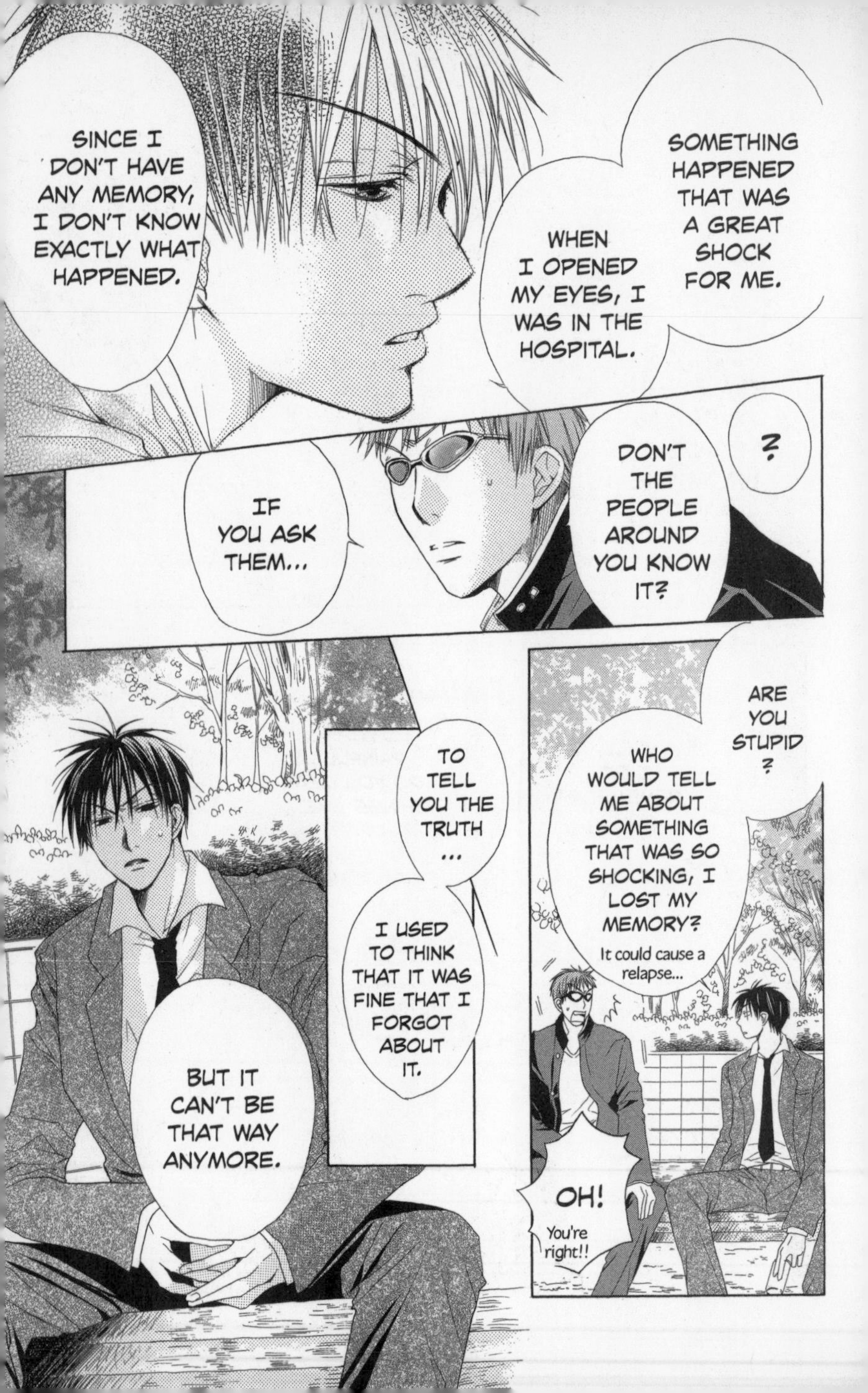
SOMETHING HAPPENED THAT WAS A GREAT SHOCK FOR ME.
WHEN I OPENED MY EYES, I WAS IN THE HOSPITAL.
SINCE I DON'T HAVE ANY MEMORY, I DON'T KNOW EXACTLY WHAT HAPPENED.
?
DON'T THE PEOPLE AROUND YOU KNOW IT?
IF YOU ASK THEM...
ARE YOU STUPID?
WHO WOULD TELL ME ABOUT SOMETHING THAT WAS SO SHOCKING, I LOST MY MEMORY?
It could cause a relapse...
OH!
You're right!!
TO TELL YOU THE TRUTH...
I USED TO THINK THAT IT WAS FINE THAT I FORGOT ABOUT IT.
BUT IT CAN'T BE THAT WAY ANYMORE.

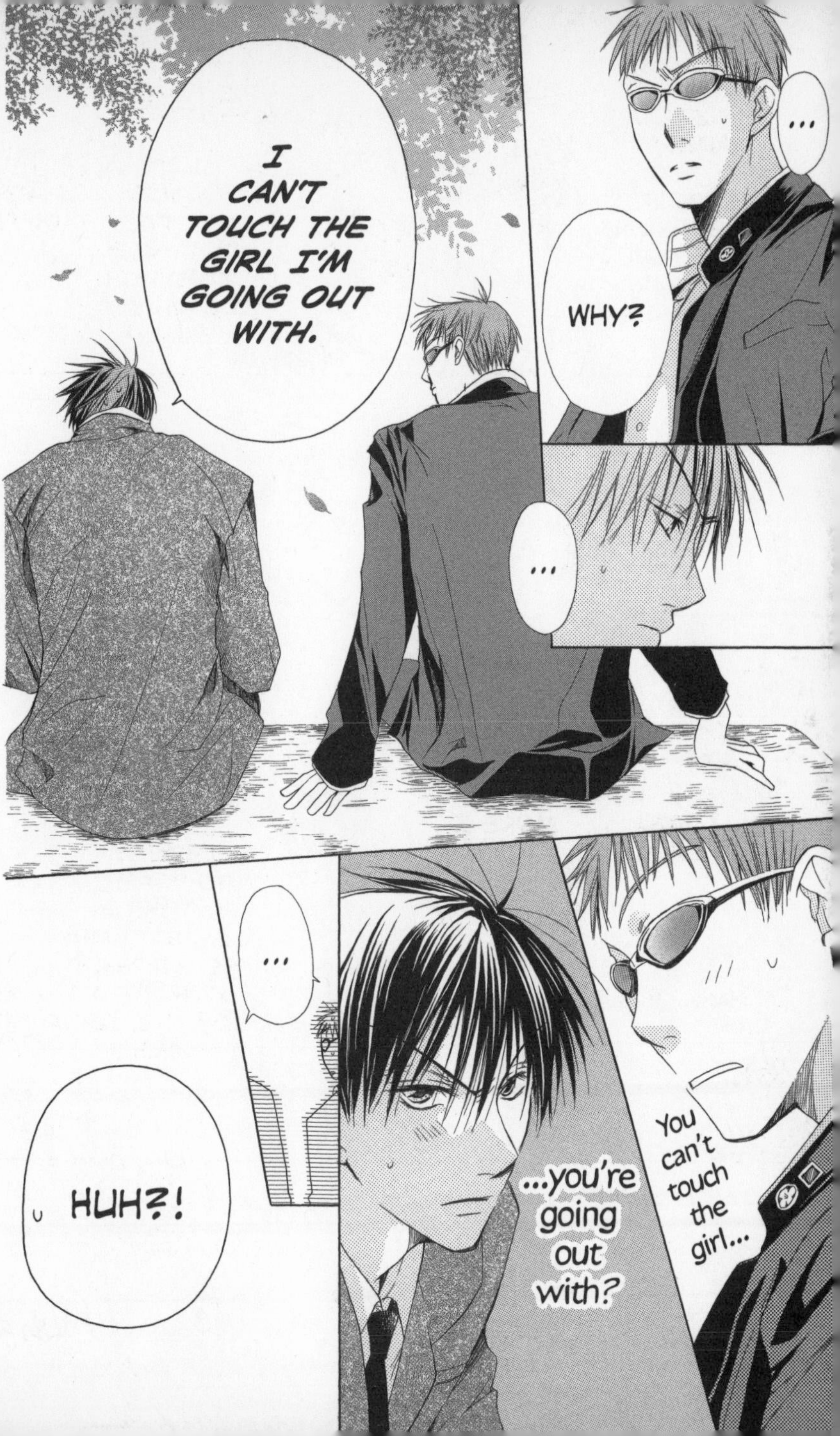
...
WHY?
...
I CAN'T TOUCH THE GIRL I'M GOING OUT WITH.
You can't touch the girl...
...you're going out with?
...
HUH?!

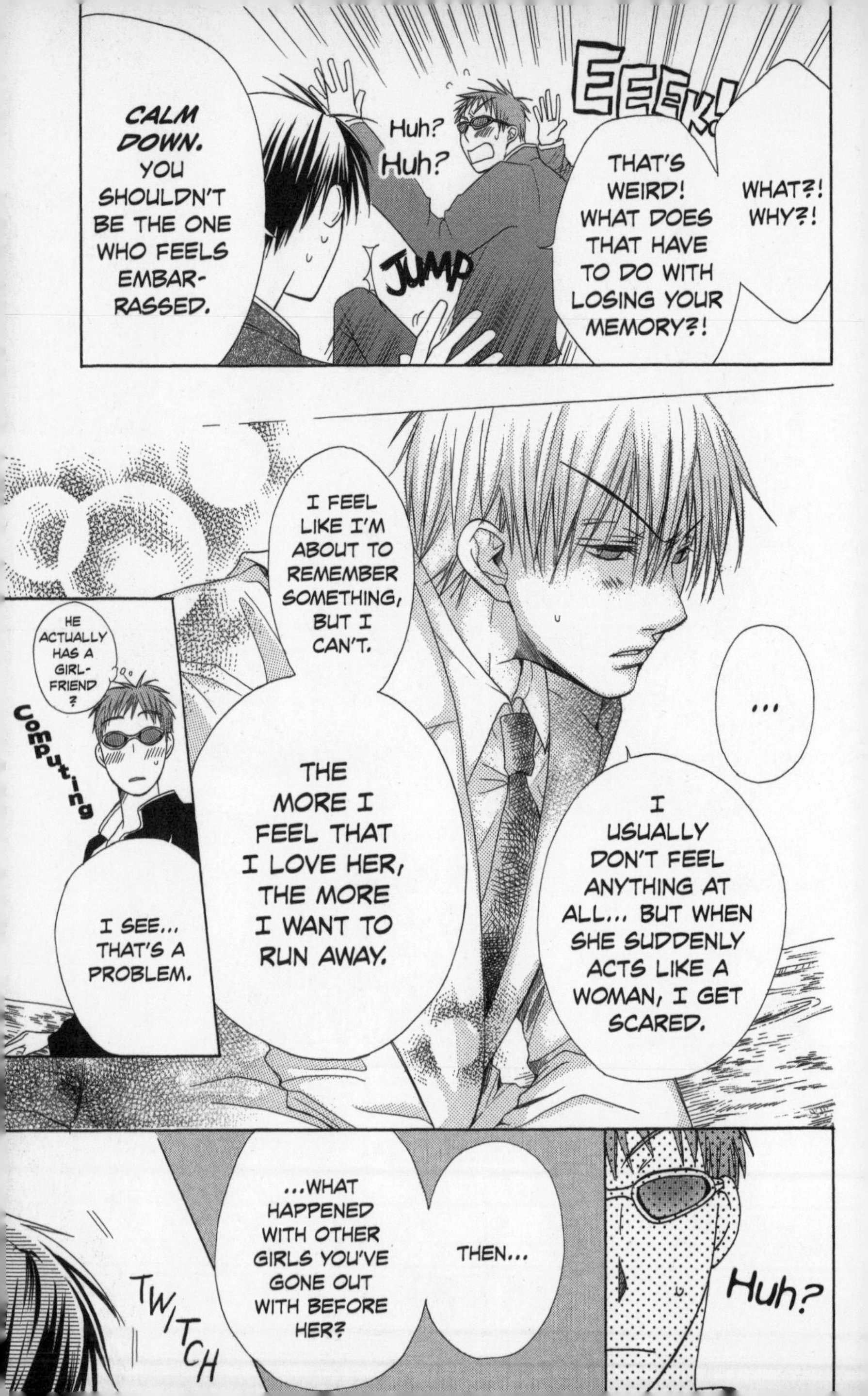
EEEK!
WHAT?! WHY?!
THAT'S WEIRD! WHAT DOES THAT HAVE TO DO WITH LOSING YOUR MEMORY?!
Huh? Huh?
JUMP
CALM DOWN. YOU SHOULDN'T BE THE ONE WHO FEELS EMBARRASSED.
...
I FEEL LIKE I'M ABOUT TO REMEMBER SOMETHING, BUT I CAN'T.
I USUALLY DON'T FEEL ANYTHING AT ALL... BUT WHEN SHE SUDDENLY ACTS LIKE A WOMAN, I GET SCARED.
THE MORE I FEEL THAT I LOVE HER, THE MORE I WANT TO RUN AWAY.
HE ACTUALLY HAS A GIRLFRIEND?
Computing
I SEE... THAT'S A PROBLEM.
Huh?
THEN...
...WHAT HAPPENED WITH OTHER GIRLS YOU'VE GONE OUT WITH BEFORE HER?
TWITCH

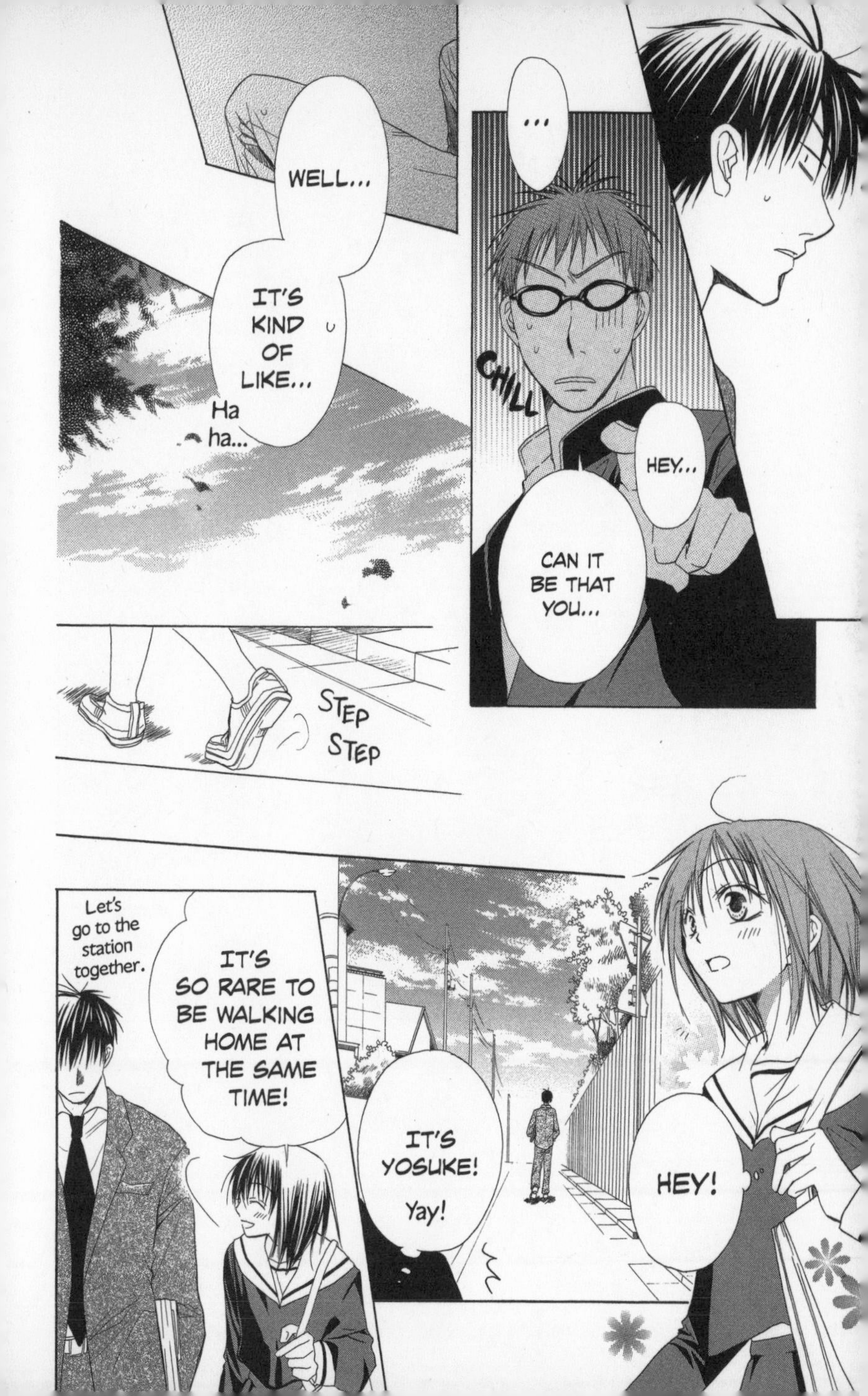
...
CHILL
HEY...
CAN IT BE THAT YOU...
WELL...
IT'S KIND OF LIKE...
Ha ha...
STEP STEP
HEY!
IT'S YOSUKE!
Yay!
IT'S SO RARE TO BE WALKING HOME AT THE SAME TIME!
Let's go to the station together.

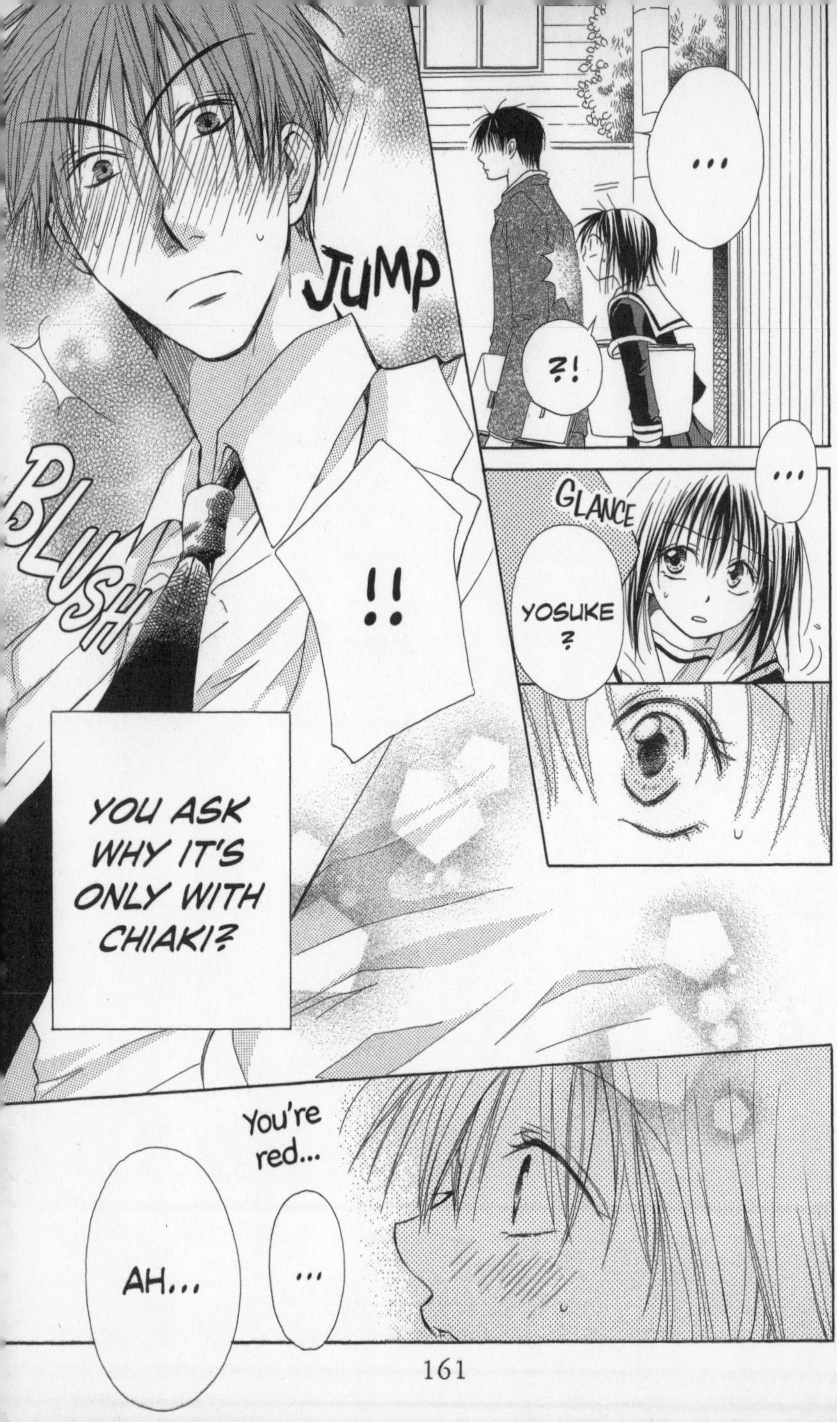

...
?!
...
GLANCE
YOSUKE?
JUMP
!!
BLUSH
YOU ASK WHY IT'S ONLY WITH CHIAKI?
You're red...
...
AH...

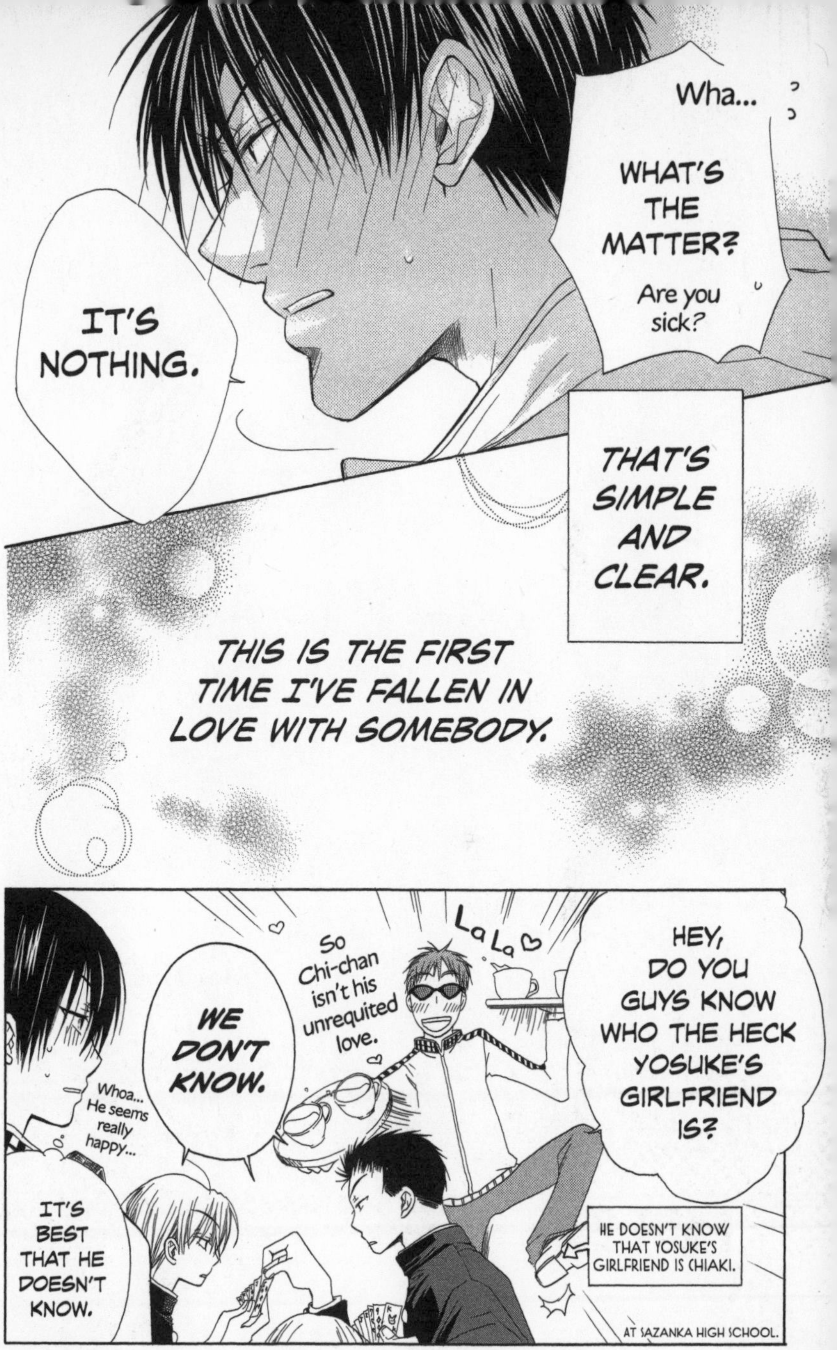
Wha...
WHAT'S THE MATTER? Are you sick?
IT'S NOTHING.
THAT'S SIMPLE AND CLEAR.
THIS IS THE FIRST TIME I'VE FALLEN IN LOVE WITH SOMEBODY.
HEY, DO YOU GUYS KNOW WHO THE HECK YOSUKE'S GIRLFRIEND IS?
La La
So Chi-chan isn't his unrequited love.
WE DON'T KNOW.
Whoa... He seems really happy...
HE DOESN'T KNOW THAT YOSUKE'S GIRLFRIEND IS CHIAKI.
IT'S BEST THAT HE DOESN'T KNOW.
AT SAZANKA HIGH SCHOOL.

The Magic Touch, Part 22/The End

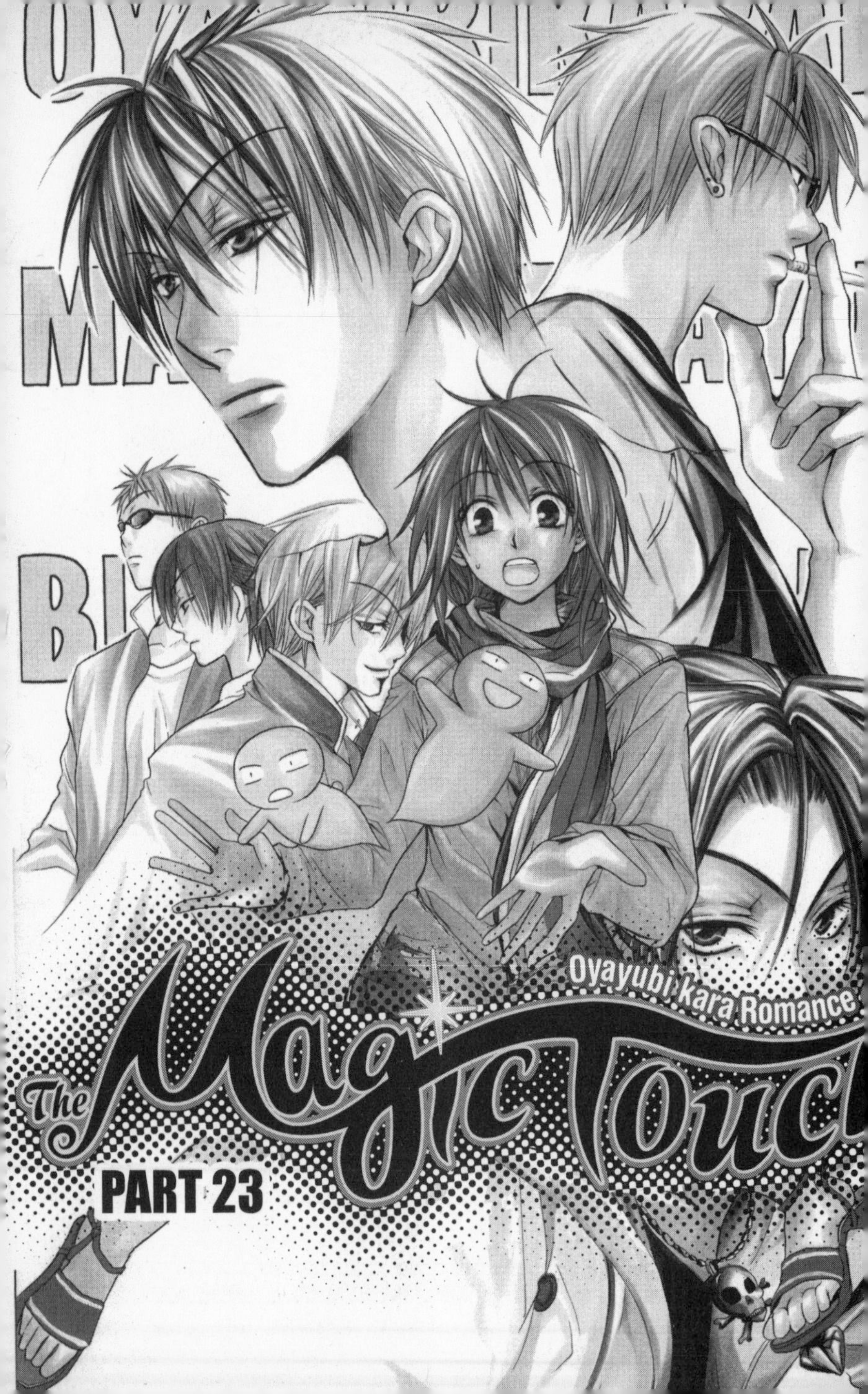
Oyayubi Kara Romance
The Magic Touch
PART 23

SAZANKA HIGH SCHOOL EMERGENCY MEETING ONE

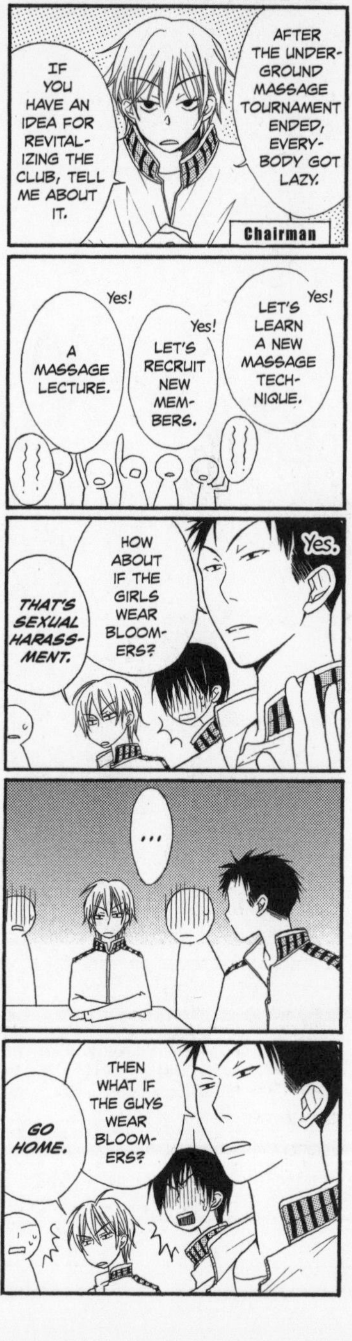
AFTER THE UNDERGROUND MASSAGE TOURNAMENT ENDED, EVERYBODY GOT LAZY.
IF YOU HAVE AN IDEA FOR REVITALIZING THE CLUB, TELL ME ABOUT IT.
Chairman
Yes!
LET'S LEARN A NEW MASSAGE TECHNIQUE.
Yes!
LET'S RECRUIT NEW MEMBERS.
Yes!
A MASSAGE LECTURE.
Yes.
HOW ABOUT IF THE GIRLS WEAR BLOOMERS?
THAT'S SEXUAL HARASSMENT.
...
THEN WHAT IF THE GUYS WEAR BLOOMERS?
GO HOME.

SAZANKA HIGH SCHOOL EMERGENCY MEETING TWO

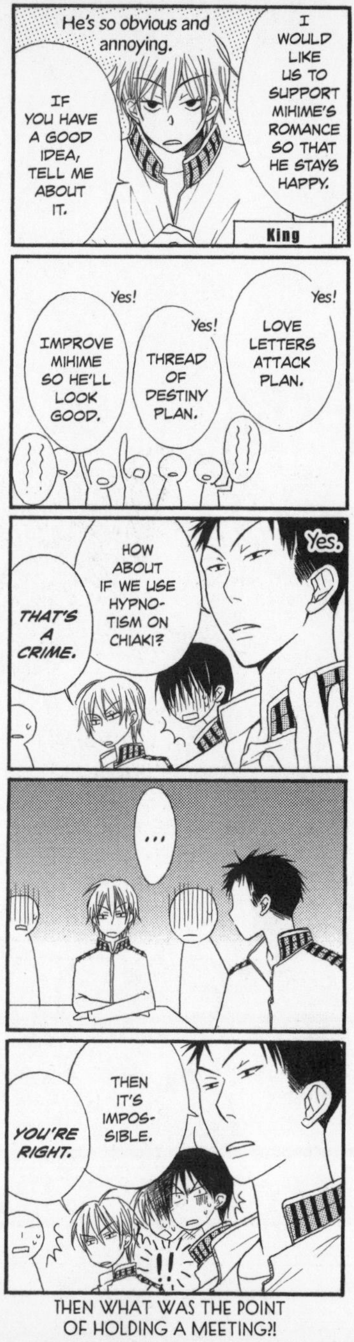
I WOULD LIKE US TO SUPPORT MIHIME'S ROMANCE SO THAT HE STAYS HAPPY.
He's so obvious and annoying.
IF YOU HAVE A GOOD IDEA, TELL ME ABOUT IT.
King
Yes!
LOVE LETTERS ATTACK PLAN.
Yes!
THREAD OF DESTINY PLAN.
Yes!
IMPROVE MIHIME SO HE'LL LOOK GOOD.
Yes.
HOW ABOUT IF WE USE HYPNOTISM ON CHIAKI?
THAT'S A CRIME.
...
THEN IT'S IMPOSSIBLE.
YOU'RE RIGHT.
!!

THEN WHAT WAS THE POINT OF HOLDING A MEETING?!

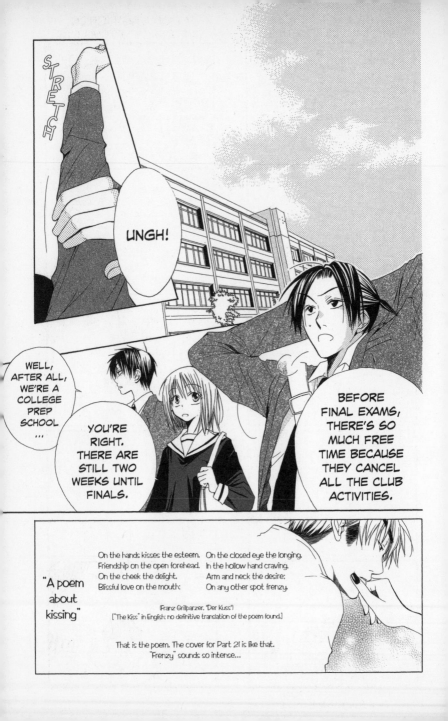

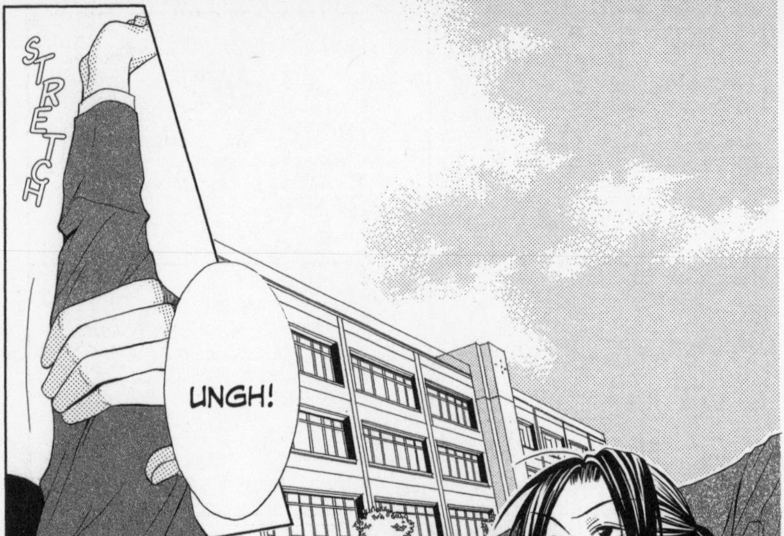
STRETCH
UNGH!
BEFORE FINAL EXAMS, THERE'S SO MUCH FREE TIME BECAUSE THEY CANCEL ALL THE CLUB ACTIVITIES.
YOU'RE RIGHT. THERE ARE STILL TWO WEEKS UNTIL FINALS.
WELL, AFTER ALL, WE'RE A COLLEGE PREP SCHOOL ...

"A poem about kissing"

On the hands kisses the esteem.
Friendship on the open forehead.
On the cheek the delight.
Blissful love on the mouth;
On the closed eye the longing.
In the hollow hand craving.
Arm and neck the desire;
On any other spot frenzy.

(Franz Grillparzer, "Der Kuss")
["The Kiss" in English; no definitive translation of the poem found.]

That is the poem. The cover for Part 21 is like that.
"Frenzy" sounds so intense...

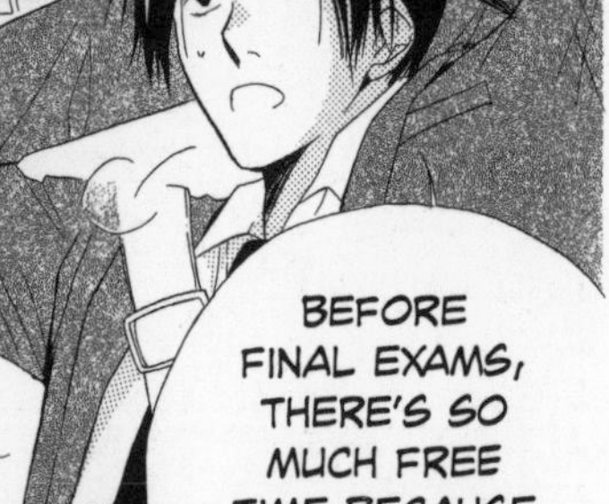

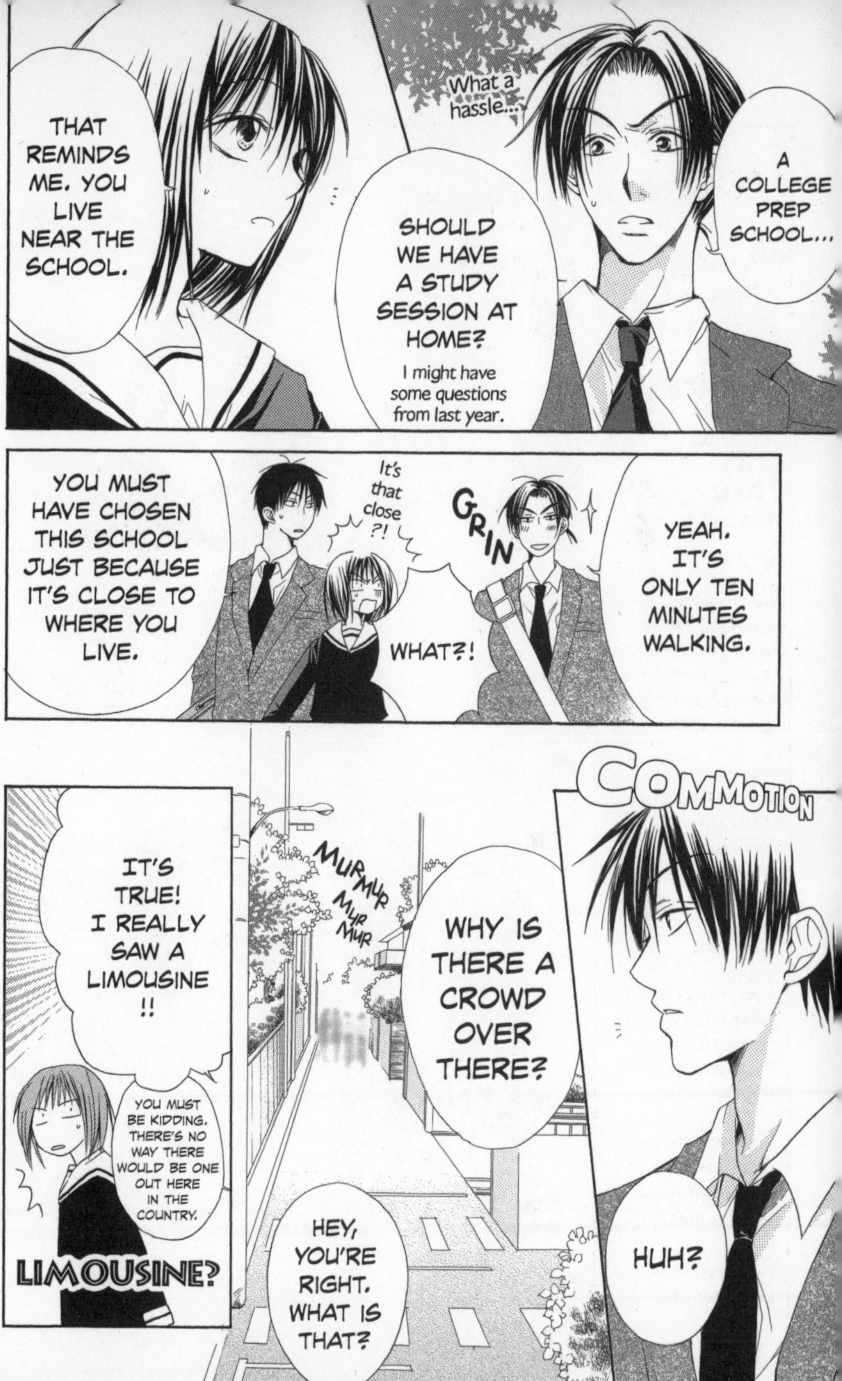
A COLLEGE PREP SCHOOL...
What a hassle...
SHOULD WE HAVE A STUDY SESSION AT HOME?
I might have some questions from last year.
THAT REMINDS ME. YOU LIVE NEAR THE SCHOOL.
YEAH. IT'S ONLY TEN MINUTES WALKING.
GRIN
It's that close?!
WHAT?!
YOU MUST HAVE CHOSEN THIS SCHOOL JUST BECAUSE IT'S CLOSE TO WHERE YOU LIVE.
COMMOTION
WHY IS THERE A CROWD OVER THERE?
HUH?
MURMUR MUR MUR
HEY, YOU'RE RIGHT. WHAT IS THAT?
IT'S TRUE! I REALLY SAW A LIMOUSINE!!
YOU MUST BE KIDDING. THERE'S NO WAY THERE WOULD BE ONE OUT HERE IN THE COUNTRY.
LIMOUSINE?

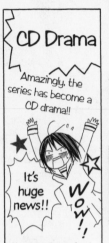

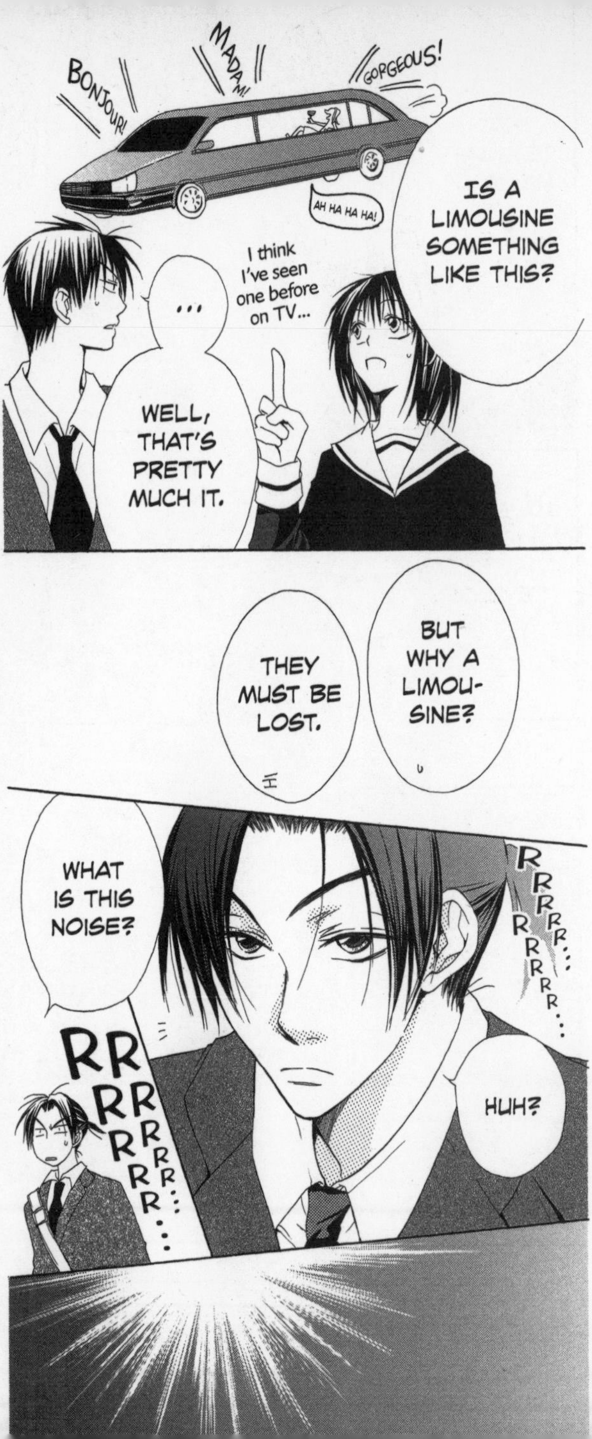
MADAM!
GORGEOUS!
BONJOUR!
AH HA HA HA!
IS A LIMOUSINE SOMETHING LIKE THIS?
I think I've seen one before on TV...
...
WELL, THAT'S PRETTY MUCH IT.
BUT WHY A LIMOU-SINE?
THEY MUST BE LOST.
RRRRRRRRRR...
HUH?
WHAT IS THIS NOISE?
RRRRRRRRR...

CD Drama

Amazingly, the series has become a CD drama!!

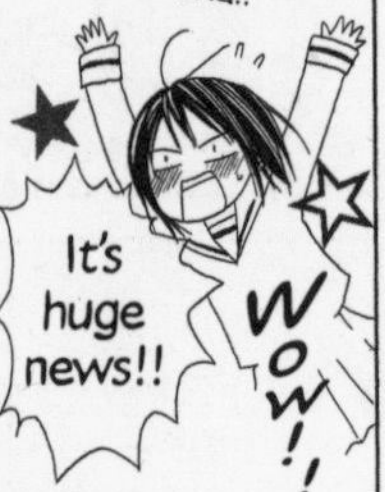
It's huge news!!
WOW!!

I had a really great experience because I was invited to visit the dubbing studio and think about voices for the characters.

Voice actors are so amazing! Wonderful!! Although I was acting weird because I was nervous, at least I understood how amazing the voice actors are.

It was really splendid!! I really felt how different it is when the characters have voices...

It was amazing how Chiaki really seemed like the main character of a girls' manga!!

The details will be in the postscript...

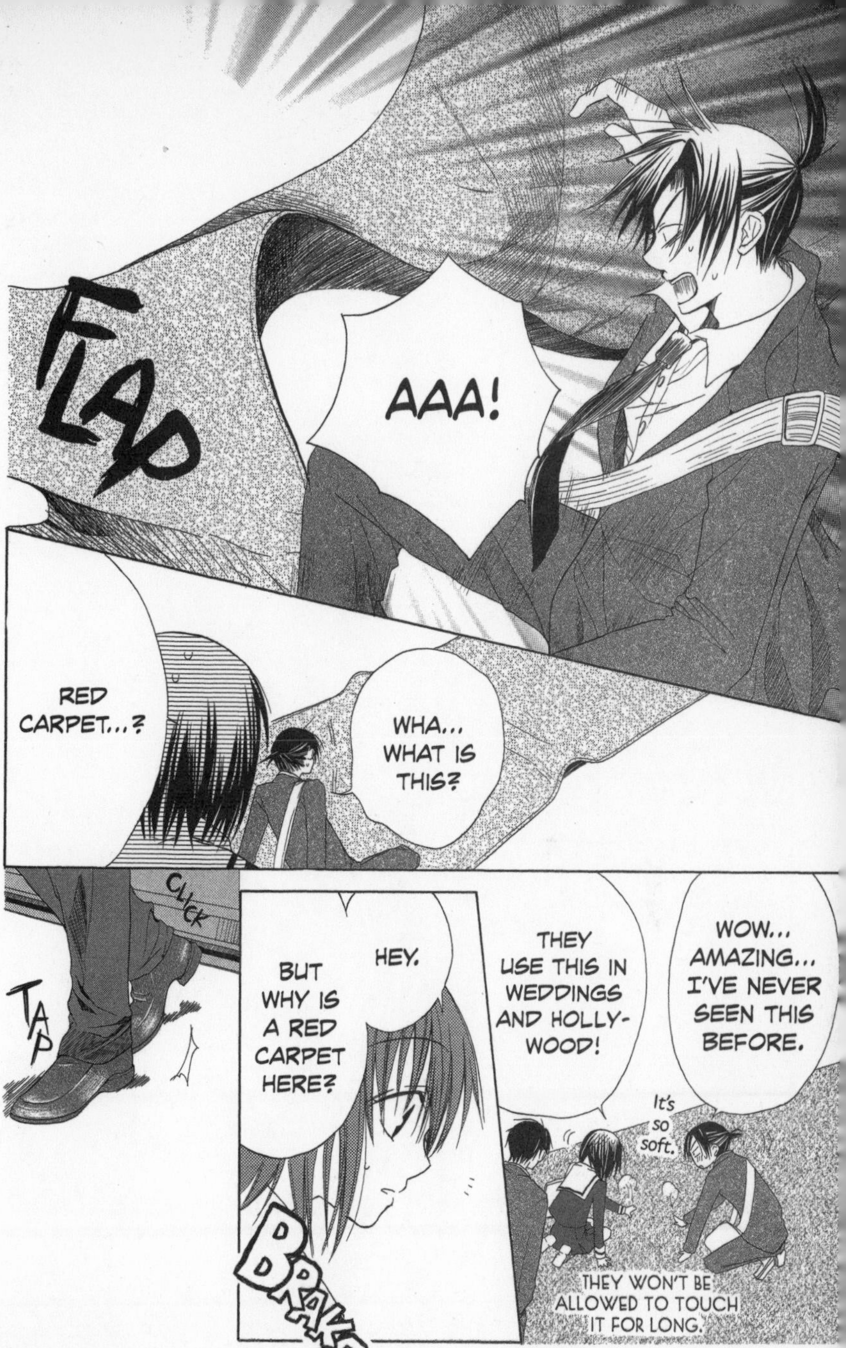

AAA!
FLAP
WHA... WHAT IS THIS?
RED CARPET...?
WOW... AMAZING... I'VE NEVER SEEN THIS BEFORE.
It's so soft.
THEY USE THIS IN WEDDINGS AND HOLLY-WOOD!
THEY WON'T BE ALLOWED TO TOUCH IT FOR LONG.
HEY.
BUT WHY IS A RED CARPET HERE?
BRAKE
CLICK
TAP

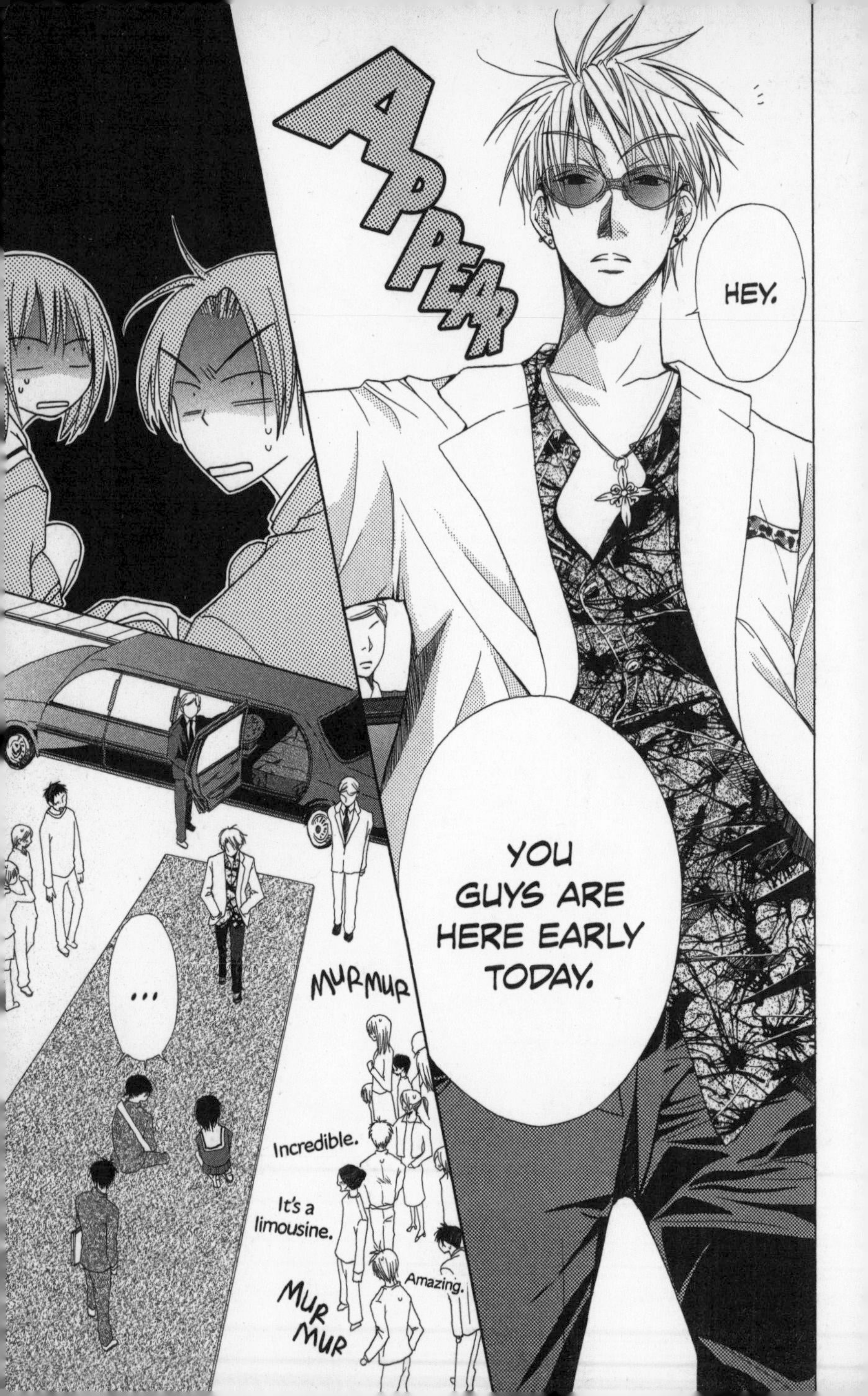
APPEAR
HEY.
YOU GUYS ARE HERE EARLY TODAY.
MURMUR
...
Incredible.
It's a limousine.
Amazing.
MUR MUR

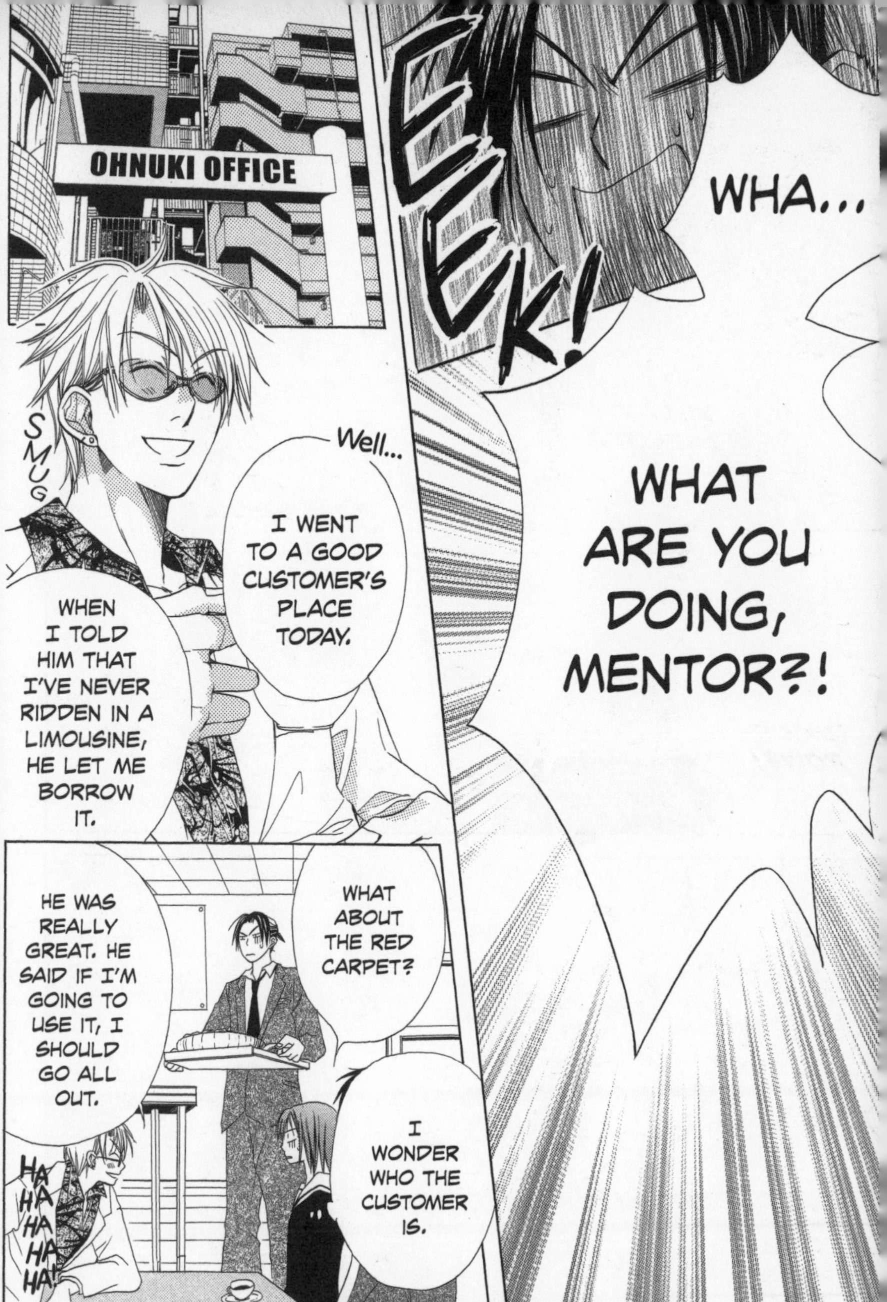
EEEK!
WHA...
WHAT ARE YOU DOING, MENTOR?!
OHNUKI OFFICE
SMUG
Well...
I WENT TO A GOOD CUSTOMER'S PLACE TODAY.
WHEN I TOLD HIM THAT I'VE NEVER RIDDEN IN A LIMOUSINE, HE LET ME BORROW IT.
WHAT ABOUT THE RED CARPET?
HE WAS REALLY GREAT. HE SAID IF I'M GOING TO USE IT, I SHOULD GO ALL OUT.
I WONDER WHO THE CUSTOMER IS.
HA HA HA HA HA!

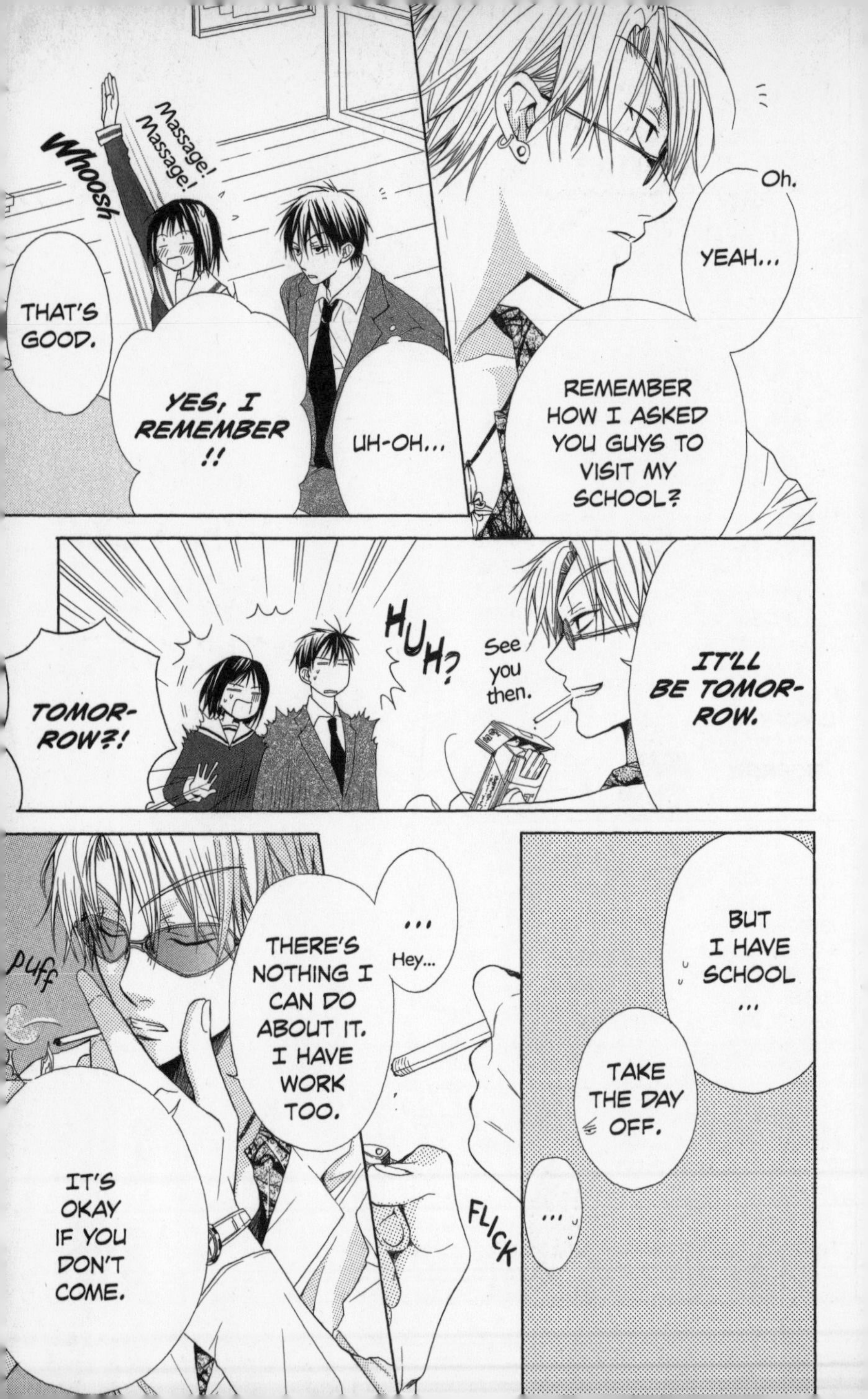
Oh.
YEAH...
REMEMBER HOW I ASKED YOU GUYS TO VISIT MY SCHOOL?
UH-OH...
YES, I REMEMBER!!
Massage! Massage!
Whoosh
THAT'S GOOD.
IT'LL BE TOMORROW.
See you then.
HUH?
TOMORROW?!
BUT I HAVE SCHOOL...
TAKE THE DAY OFF.
...
FLICK
...
Hey...
THERE'S NOTHING I CAN DO ABOUT IT. I HAVE WORK TOO.
puff
IT'S OKAY IF YOU DON'T COME.

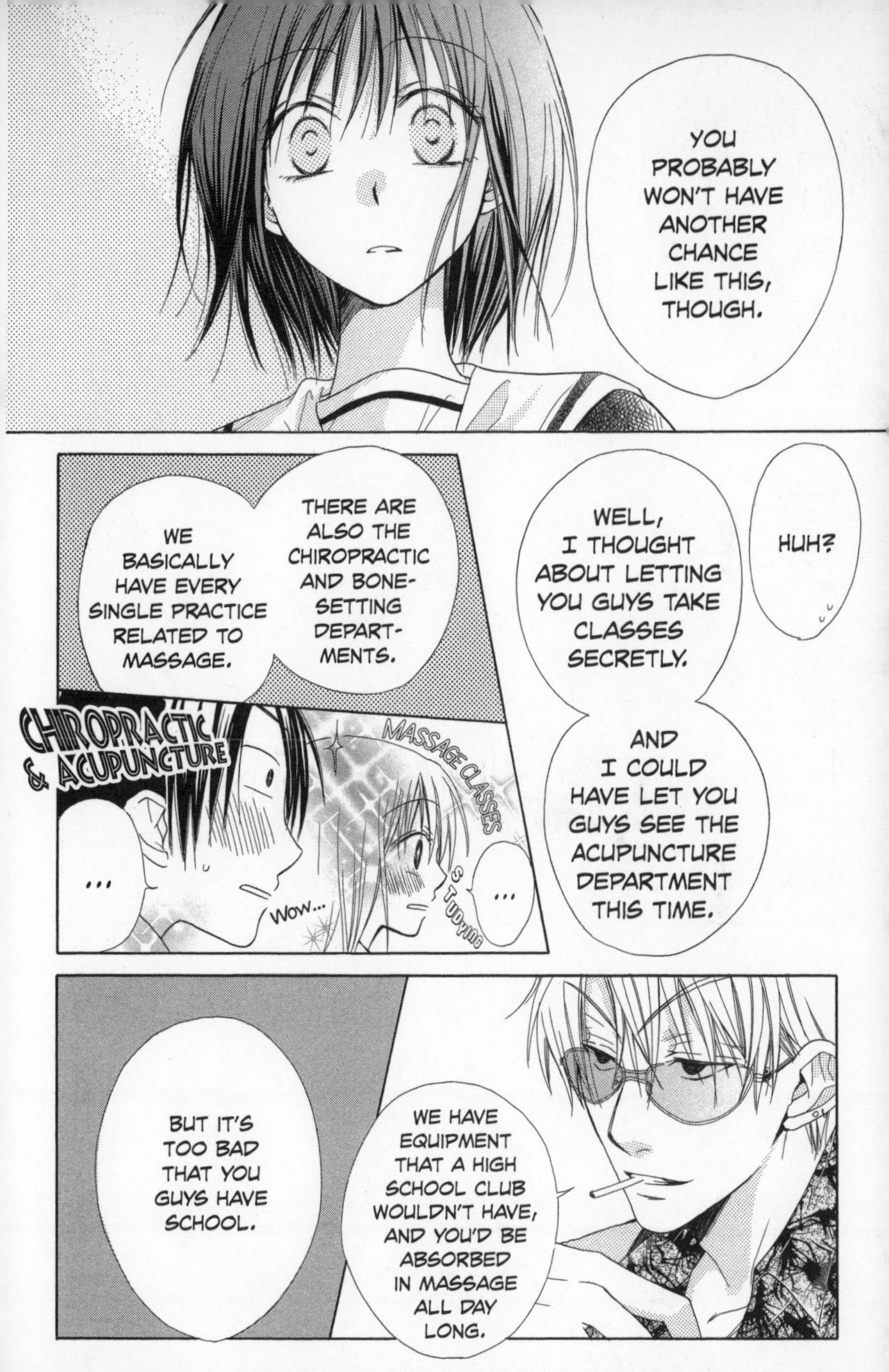
YOU PROBABLY WON'T HAVE ANOTHER CHANCE LIKE THIS, THOUGH.
HUH?
WELL, I THOUGHT ABOUT LETTING YOU GUYS TAKE CLASSES SECRETLY.
AND I COULD HAVE LET YOU GUYS SEE THE ACUPUNCTURE DEPARTMENT THIS TIME.
THERE ARE ALSO THE CHIROPRACTIC AND BONE-SETTING DEPART-MENTS.
WE BASICALLY HAVE EVERY SINGLE PRACTICE RELATED TO MASSAGE.
MASSAGE CLASSES
STUDYING
...
WOW...
CHIROPRACTIC & ACUPUNCTURE
...
WE HAVE EQUIPMENT THAT A HIGH SCHOOL CLUB WOULDN'T HAVE, AND YOU'D BE ABSORBED IN MASSAGE ALL DAY LONG.
BUT IT'S TOO BAD THAT YOU GUYS HAVE SCHOOL.

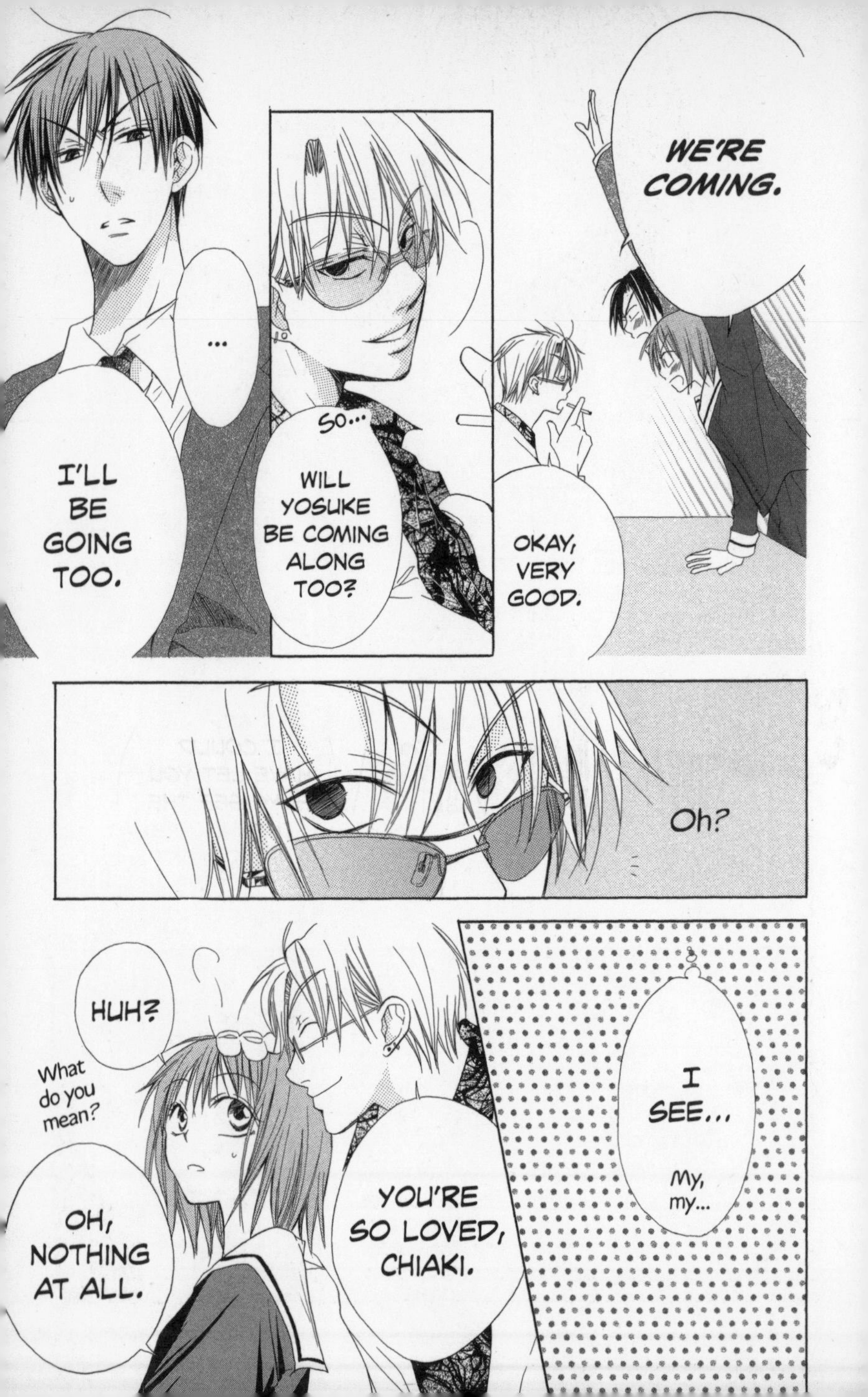
WE'RE COMING.
OKAY, VERY GOOD.
SO...
WILL YOSUKE BE COMING ALONG TOO?
...
I'LL BE GOING TOO.
Oh?
I SEE...
My, my...
YOU'RE SO LOVED, CHIAKI.
HUH?
What do you mean?
OH, NOTHING AT ALL.

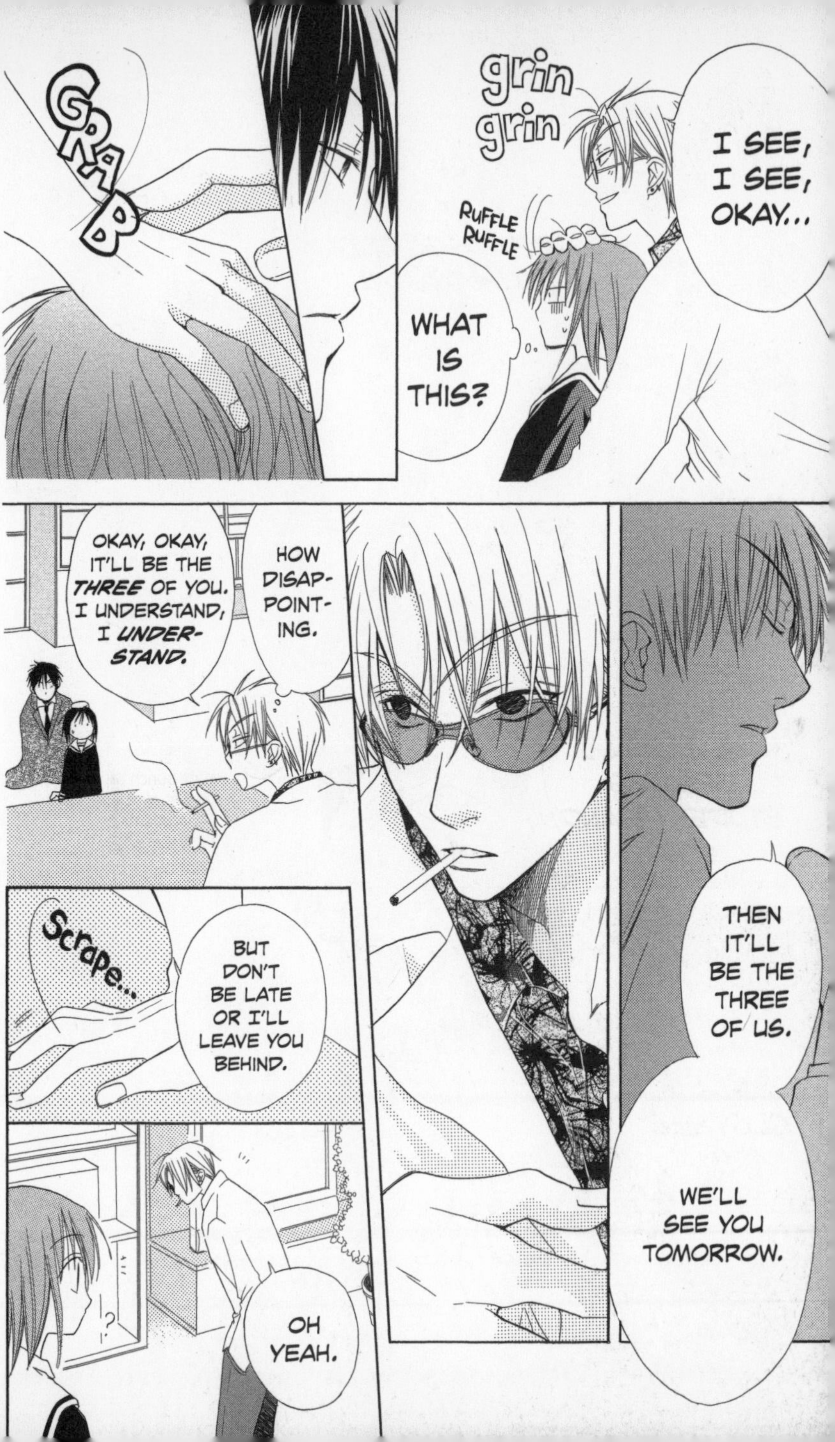
grin grin
I SEE, I SEE, OKAY...
RUFFLE RUFFLE
WHAT IS THIS?
GRAB
THEN IT'LL BE THE THREE OF US.
WE'LL SEE YOU TOMORROW.
HOW DISAPPOINTING.
OKAY, OKAY, IT'LL BE THE *THREE* OF YOU. I UNDERSTAND, I *UNDERSTAND.*
BUT DON'T BE LATE OR I'LL LEAVE YOU BEHIND.
Scrape...
OH YEAH.

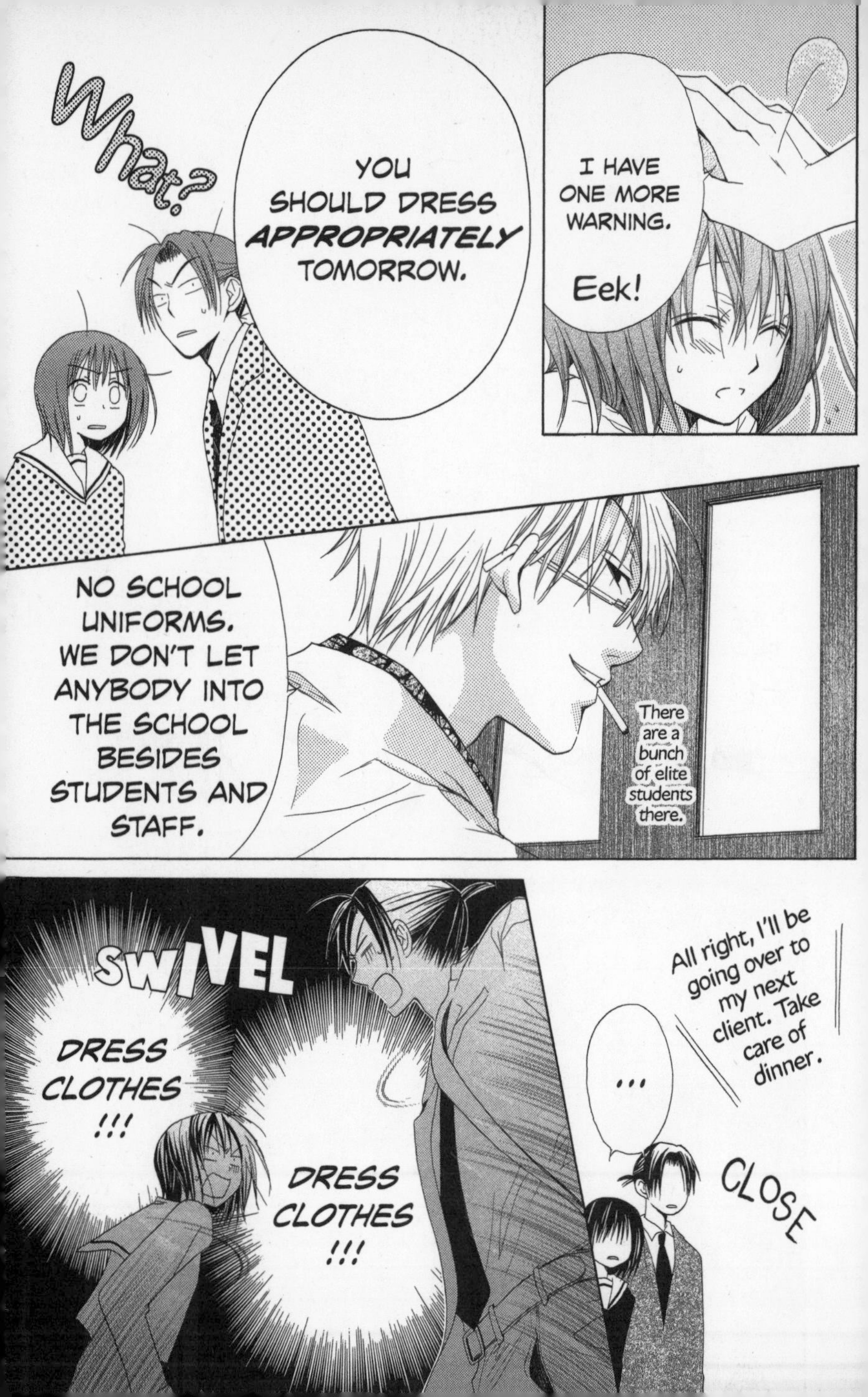
I HAVE ONE MORE WARNING.
Eek!
YOU SHOULD DRESS *APPROPRIATELY* TOMORROW.
What?
NO SCHOOL UNIFORMS. WE DON'T LET ANYBODY INTO THE SCHOOL BESIDES STUDENTS AND STAFF.
There are a bunch of elite students there.
All right, I'll be going over to my next client. Take care of dinner.
CLOSE
...
SWIVEL
DRESS CLOTHES !!!
DRESS CLOTHES !!!

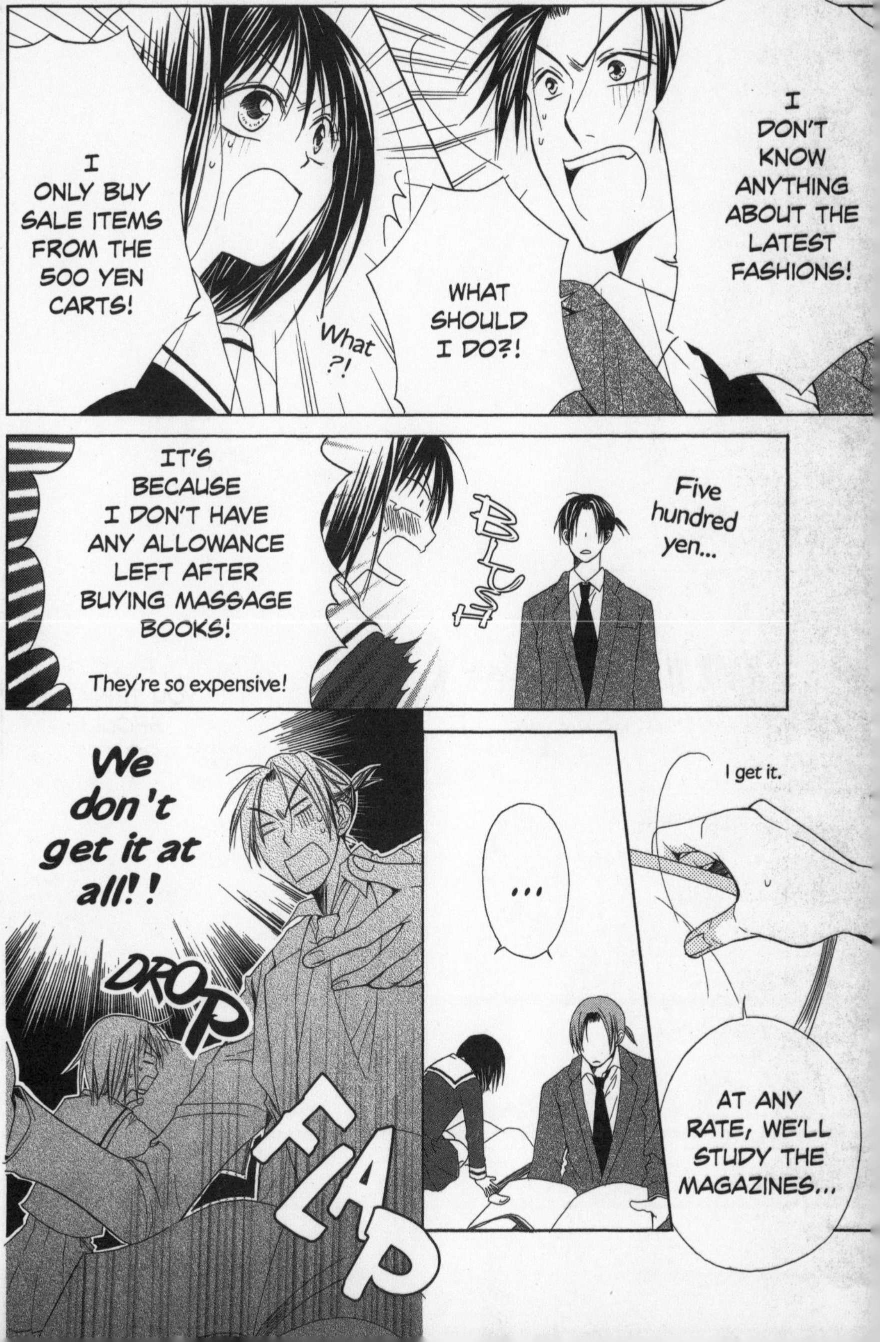
I DON'T KNOW ANYTHING ABOUT THE LATEST FASHIONS!
WHAT SHOULD I DO?!
What ?!
I ONLY BUY SALE ITEMS FROM THE 500 YEN CARTS!
Five hundred yen...
BLUSH
IT'S BECAUSE I DON'T HAVE ANY ALLOWANCE LEFT AFTER BUYING MASSAGE BOOKS!
They're so expensive!
I get it.
...
AT ANY RATE, WE'LL STUDY THE MAGAZINES...
We don't get it at all!!
DROP
FLAP

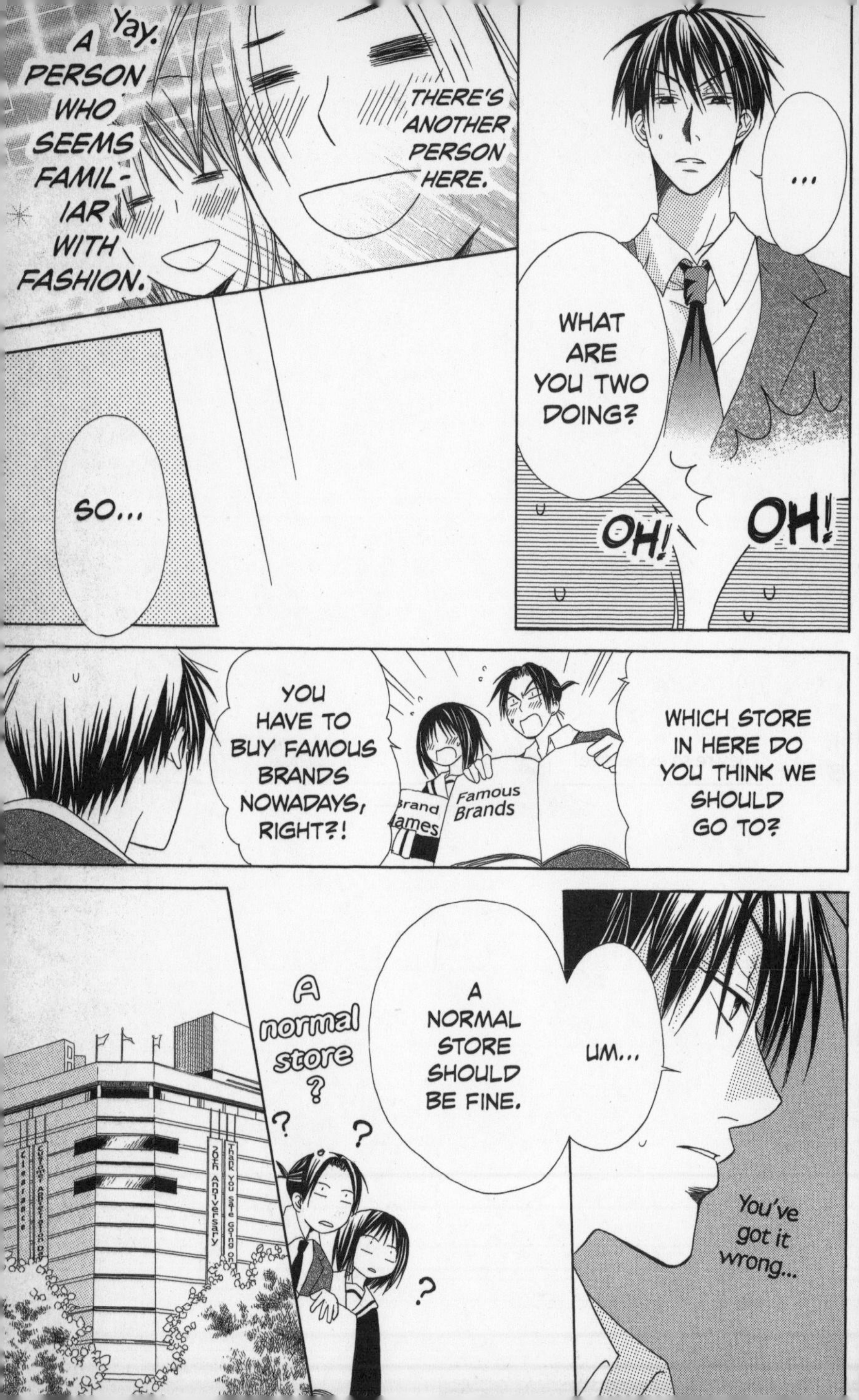
...
WHAT ARE YOU TWO DOING?
OH!
OH!
THERE'S ANOTHER PERSON HERE.
Yay. A PERSON WHO SEEMS FAMILIAR WITH FASHION.
SO...
WHICH STORE IN HERE DO YOU THINK WE SHOULD GO TO?
YOU HAVE TO BUY FAMOUS BRANDS NOWADAYS, RIGHT?!
Famous Brands
UM...
A NORMAL STORE SHOULD BE FINE.
You've got it wrong...
A normal store?
20th Anniversary

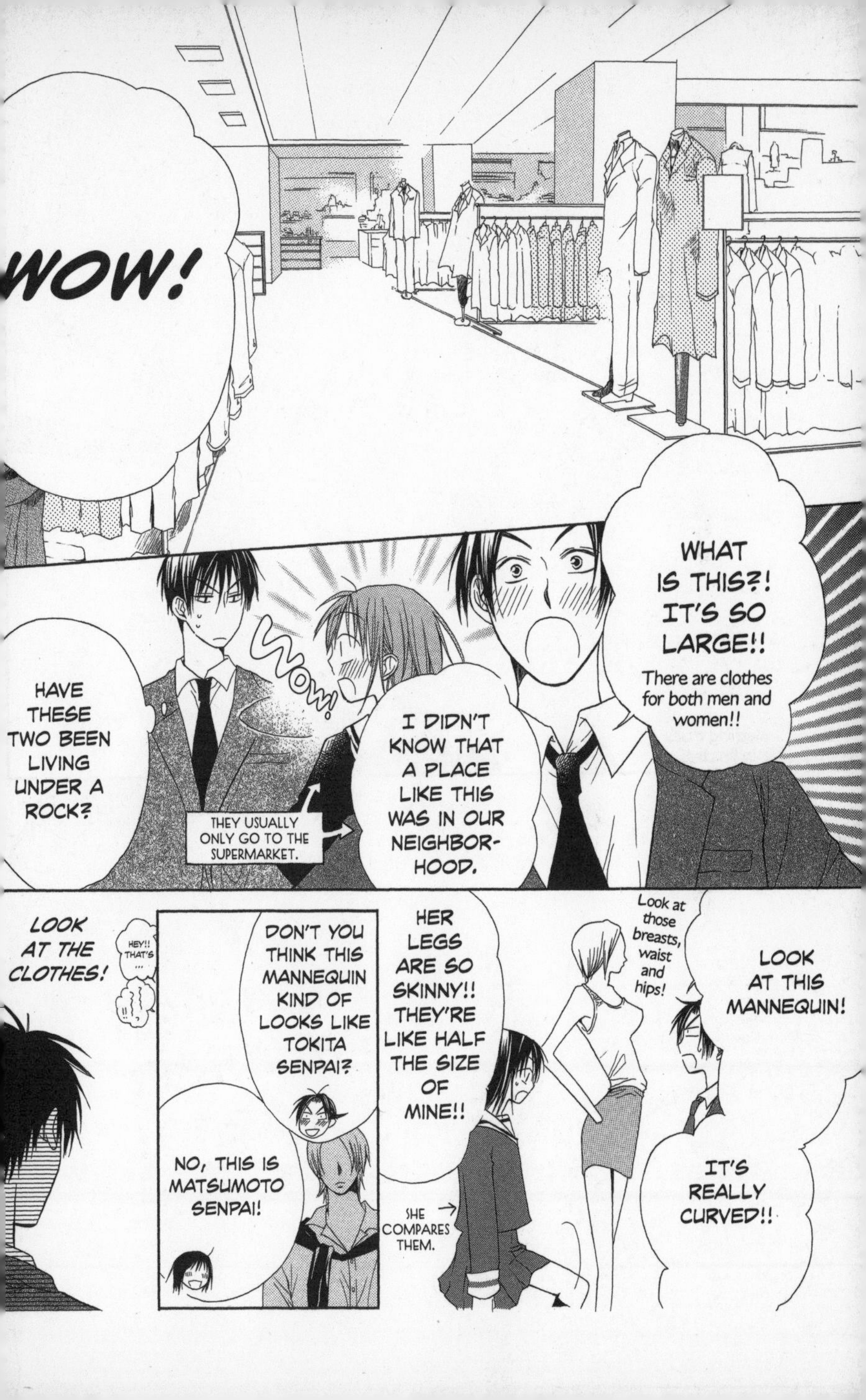
WOW!
WHAT IS THIS?! IT'S SO LARGE!!
There are clothes for both men and women!!
I DIDN'T KNOW THAT A PLACE LIKE THIS WAS IN OUR NEIGHBOR-HOOD.
WOW!
THEY USUALLY ONLY GO TO THE SUPERMARKET.
HAVE THESE TWO BEEN LIVING UNDER A ROCK?
LOOK AT THIS MANNEQUIN!
Look at those breasts, waist and hips!
IT'S REALLY CURVED!!
HER LEGS ARE SO SKINNY!! THEY'RE LIKE HALF THE SIZE OF MINE!!
SHE COMPARES THEM.
DON'T YOU THINK THIS MANNEQUIN KIND OF LOOKS LIKE TOKITA SENPAI?
NO, THIS IS MATSUMOTO SENPAI!
LOOK AT THE CLOTHES!
HEY!! THAT'S ...

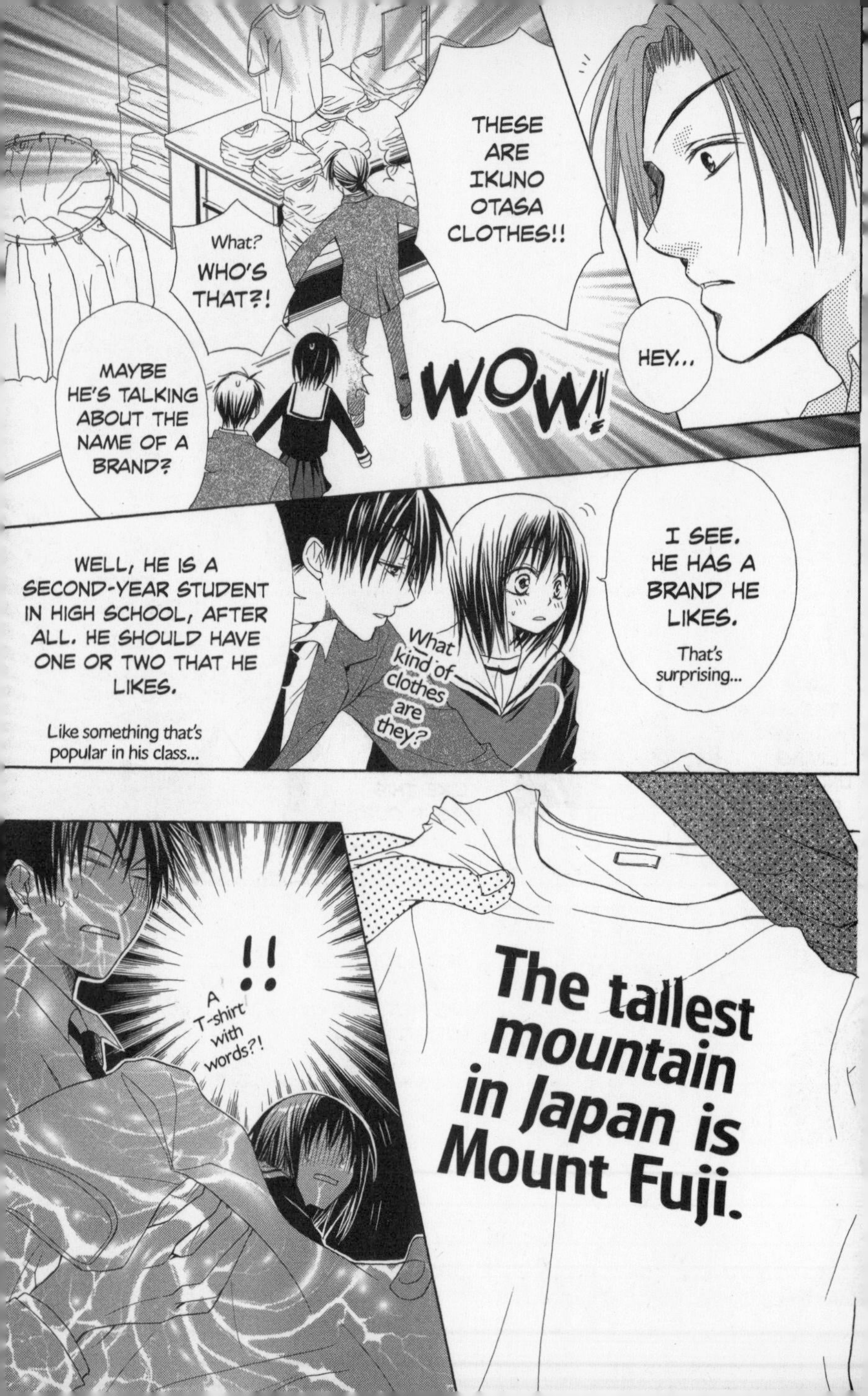
HEY...
THESE ARE IKUNO OTASA CLOTHES!!
WOW!
What? WHO'S THAT?!
MAYBE HE'S TALKING ABOUT THE NAME OF A BRAND?
I SEE. HE HAS A BRAND HE LIKES.
That's surprising...
What kind of clothes are they?
WELL, HE IS A SECOND-YEAR STUDENT IN HIGH SCHOOL, AFTER ALL. HE SHOULD HAVE ONE OR TWO THAT HE LIKES.
Like something that's popular in his class...
The tallest mountain in Japan is Mount Fuji.
!!
A T-shirt with words?!

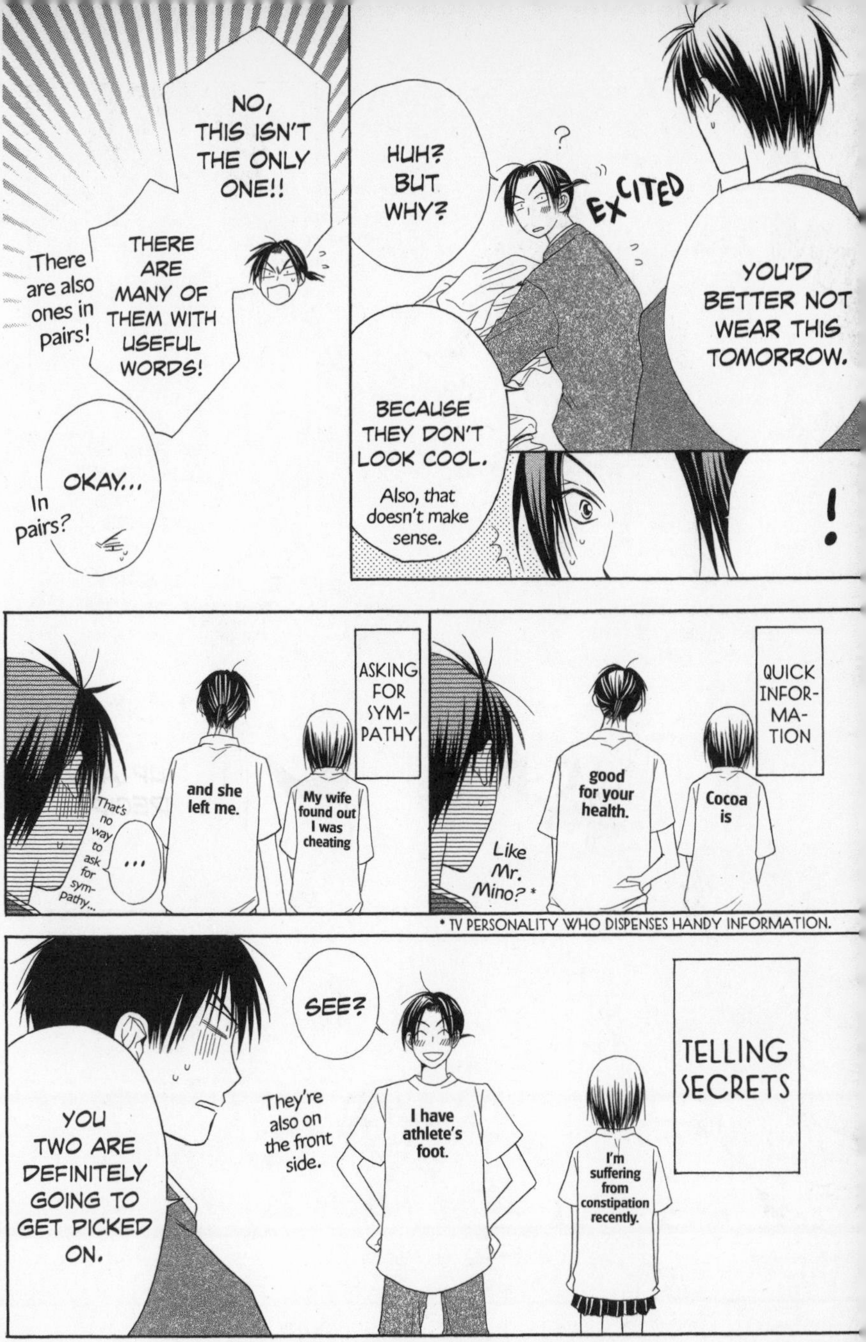
YOU'D BETTER NOT WEAR THIS TOMORROW.
HUH? BUT WHY?
EXCITED
BECAUSE THEY DON'T LOOK COOL.
Also, that doesn't make sense.
!
NO, THIS ISN'T THE ONLY ONE!!
THERE ARE MANY OF THEM WITH USEFUL WORDS!
There are also ones in pairs!
OKAY...
In pairs?
QUICK INFORMATION
Cocoa is
good for your health.
Like Mr. Mino? *
ASKING FOR SYMPATHY
My wife found out I was cheating
and she left me.
...
That's no way to ask for sympathy...
* TV PERSONALITY WHO DISPENSES HANDY INFORMATION.
TELLING SECRETS
I'm suffering from constipation recently.
I have athlete's foot.
SEE?
They're also on the front side.
YOU TWO ARE DEFINITELY GOING TO GET PICKED ON.

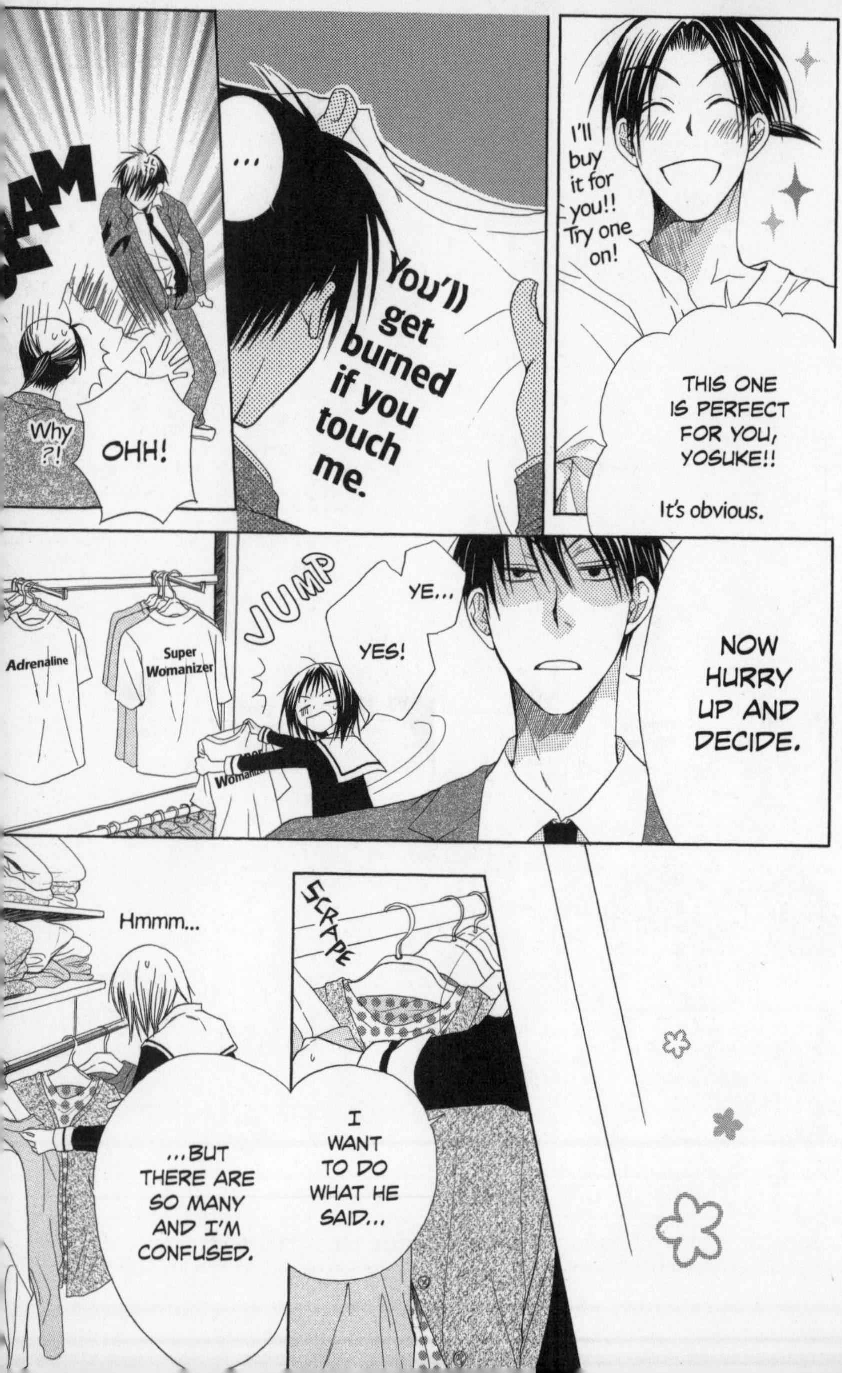
I'll buy it for you!! Try one on!
THIS ONE IS PERFECT FOR YOU, YOSUKE!!
It's obvious.
...
You'll get burned if you touch me.
OHH!
Why?!
NOW HURRY UP AND DECIDE.
YE...
YES!
JUMP
Super Womanizer
Adrenaline
I WANT TO DO WHAT HE SAID...
SCRAPE
...BUT THERE ARE SO MANY AND I'M CONFUSED.
Hmmm...

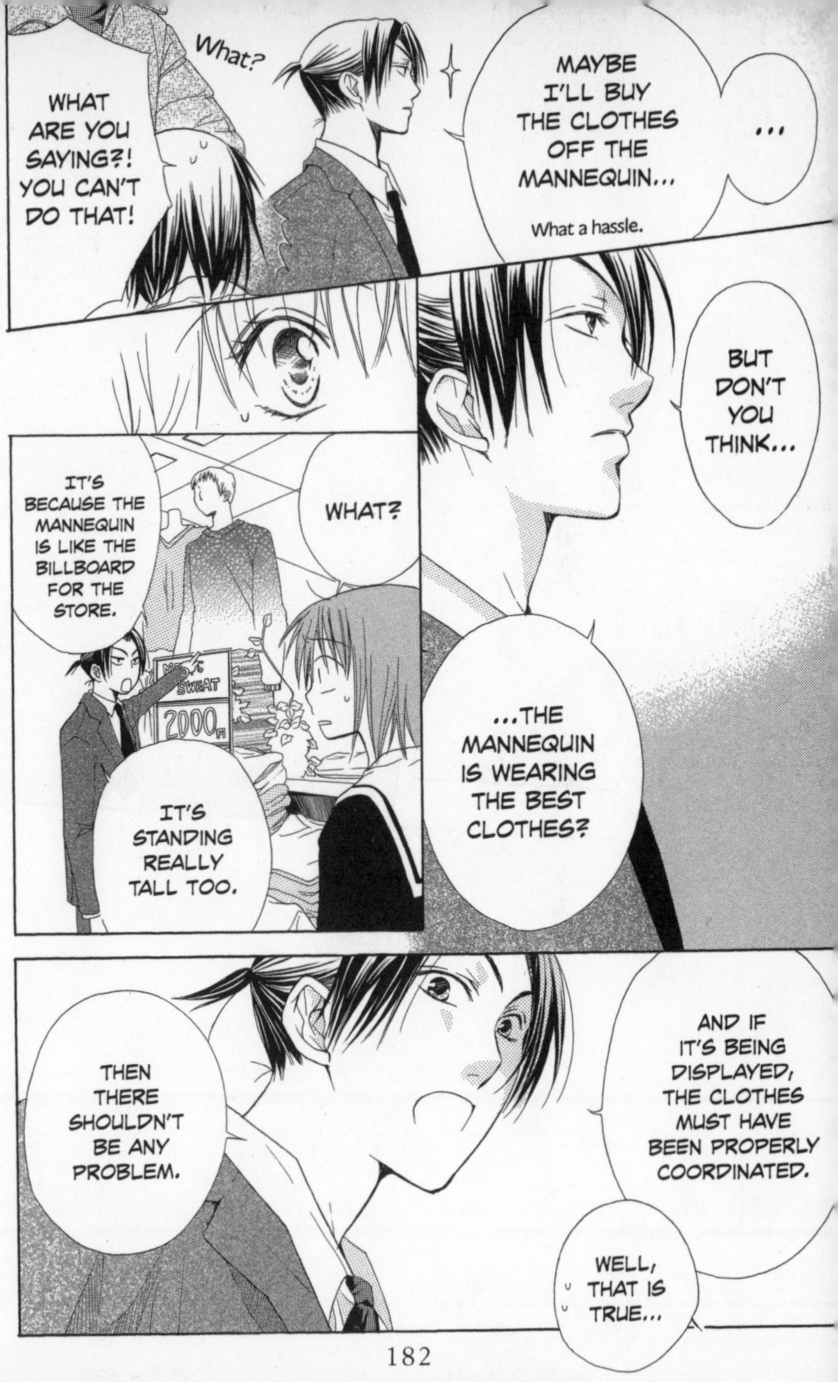
...
MAYBE I'LL BUY THE CLOTHES OFF THE MANNEQUIN...
What a hassle.
What?
WHAT ARE YOU SAYING?! YOU CAN'T DO THAT!
BUT DON'T YOU THINK...
...THE MANNEQUIN IS WEARING THE BEST CLOTHES?
WHAT?
IT'S BECAUSE THE MANNEQUIN IS LIKE THE BILLBOARD FOR THE STORE.
SWEAT
2000円
IT'S STANDING REALLY TALL TOO.
AND IF IT'S BEING DISPLAYED, THE CLOTHES MUST HAVE BEEN PROPERLY COORDINATED.
WELL, THAT IS TRUE...
THEN THERE SHOULDN'T BE ANY PROBLEM.

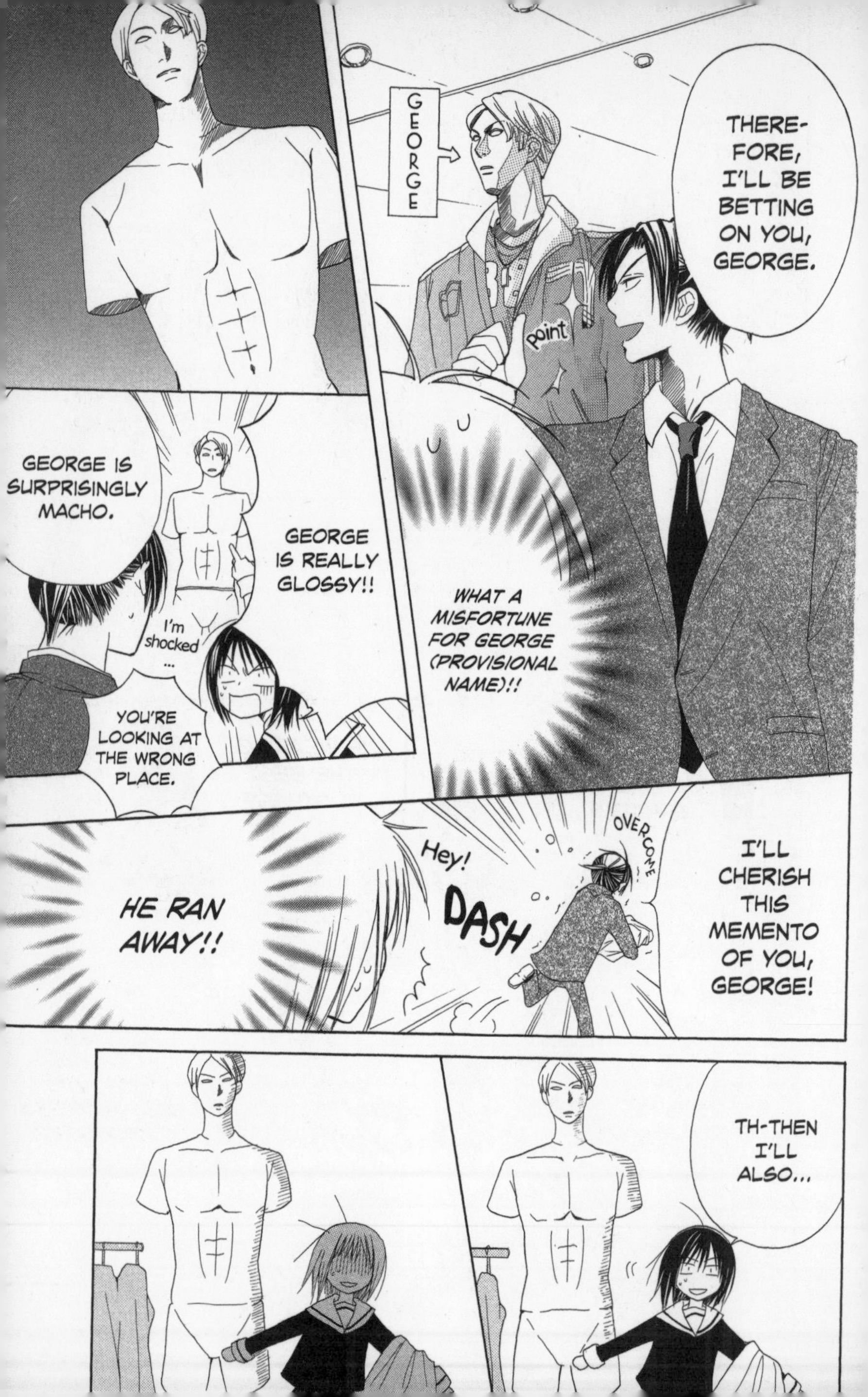
GEORGE
THERE-FORE, I'LL BE BETTING ON YOU, GEORGE.
point
WHAT A MISFORTUNE FOR GEORGE (PROVISIONAL NAME)!!
GEORGE IS REALLY GLOSSY!!
GEORGE IS SURPRISINGLY MACHO.
I'm shocked ...
YOU'RE LOOKING AT THE WRONG PLACE.
I'LL CHERISH THIS MEMENTO OF YOU, GEORGE!
OVERCOME
Hey!
DASH
HE RAN AWAY!!
TH-THEN I'LL ALSO...

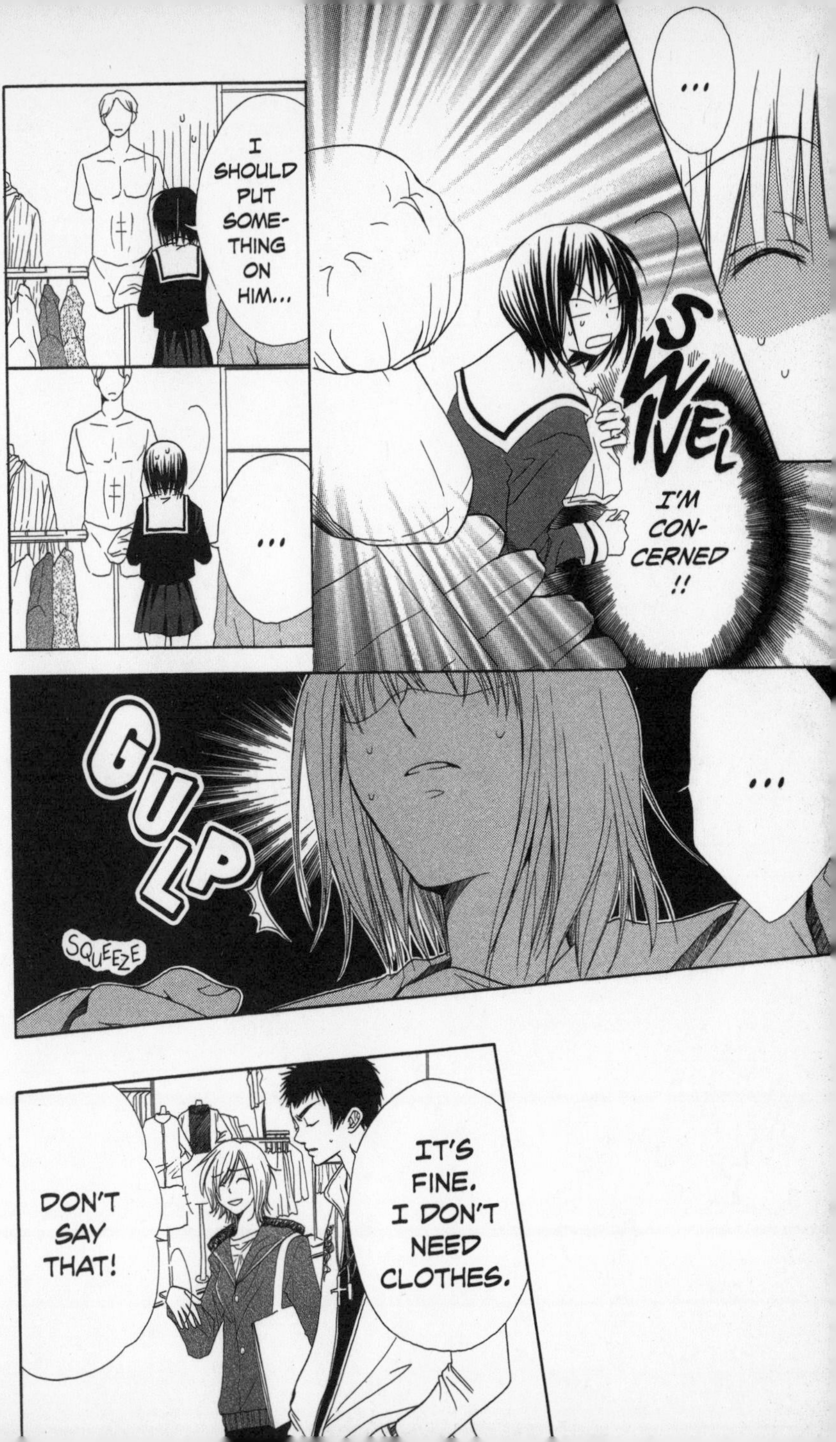
...
SWIVEL
I'M CONCERNED!!
I SHOULD PUT SOMETHING ON HIM...
...
...
GULP
SQUEEZE
IT'S FINE. I DON'T NEED CLOTHES.
DON'T SAY THAT!

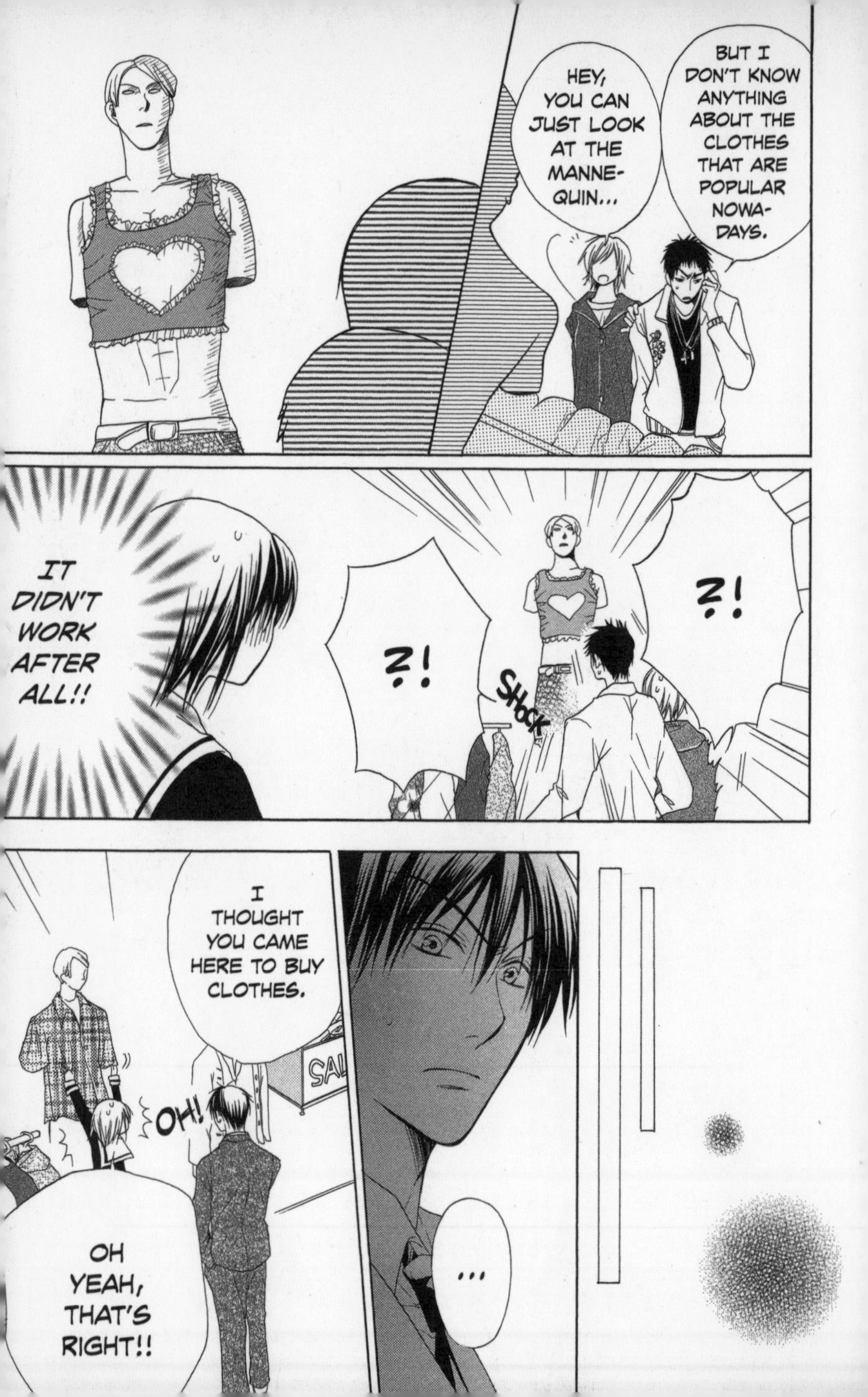

BUT I DON'T KNOW ANYTHING ABOUT THE CLOTHES THAT ARE POPULAR NOWADAYS.
HEY, YOU CAN JUST LOOK AT THE MANNEQUIN...
?!
SHOCK
?!
IT DIDN'T WORK AFTER ALL!!
...
I THOUGHT YOU CAME HERE TO BUY CLOTHES.
OH!
OH YEAH, THAT'S RIGHT!!

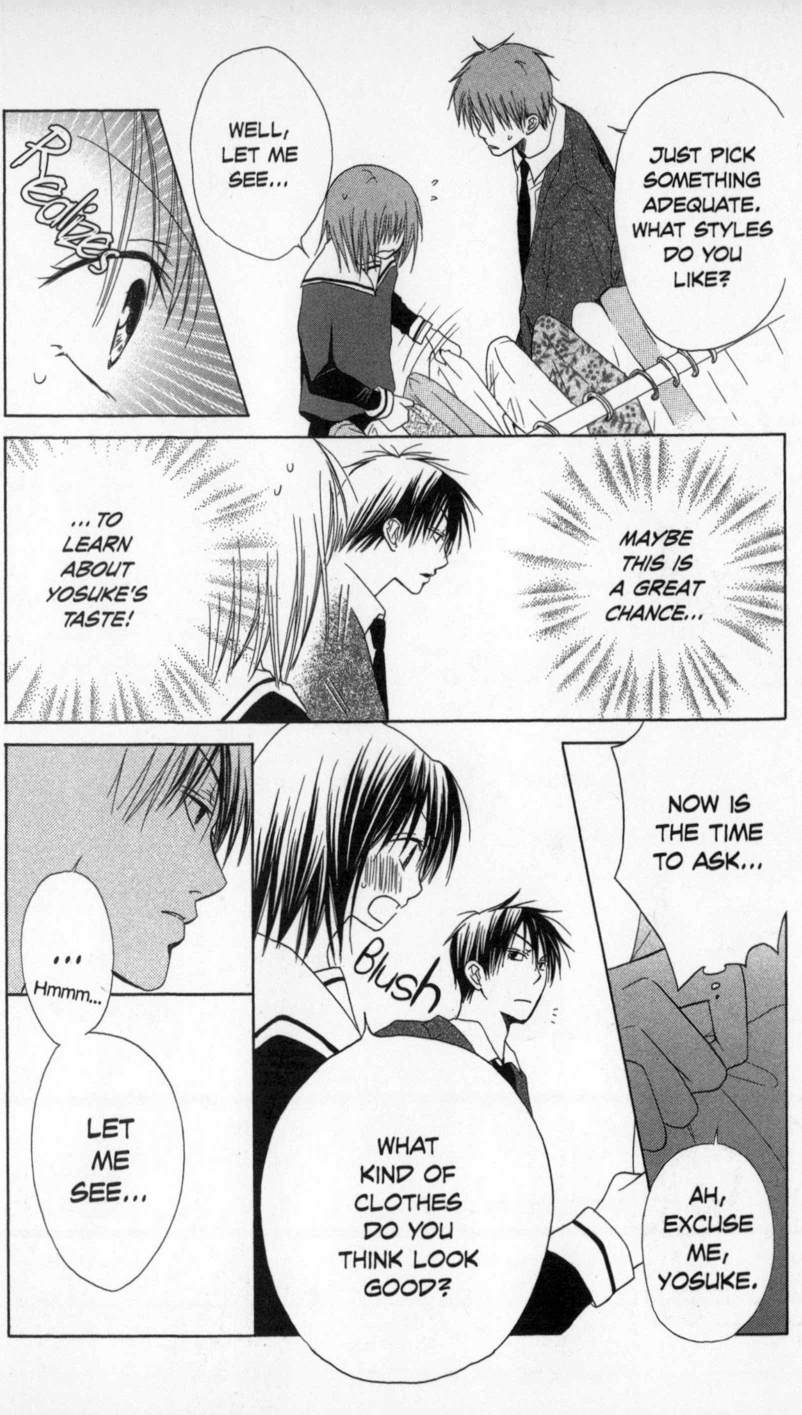
JUST PICK SOMETHING ADEQUATE. WHAT STYLES DO YOU LIKE?
WELL, LET ME SEE...
Realizes
MAYBE THIS IS A GREAT CHANCE...
...TO LEARN ABOUT YOSUKE'S TASTE!
NOW IS THE TIME TO ASK...
AH, EXCUSE ME, YOSUKE.
Blush
WHAT KIND OF CLOTHES DO YOU THINK LOOK GOOD?
...
Hmmm...
LET ME SEE...

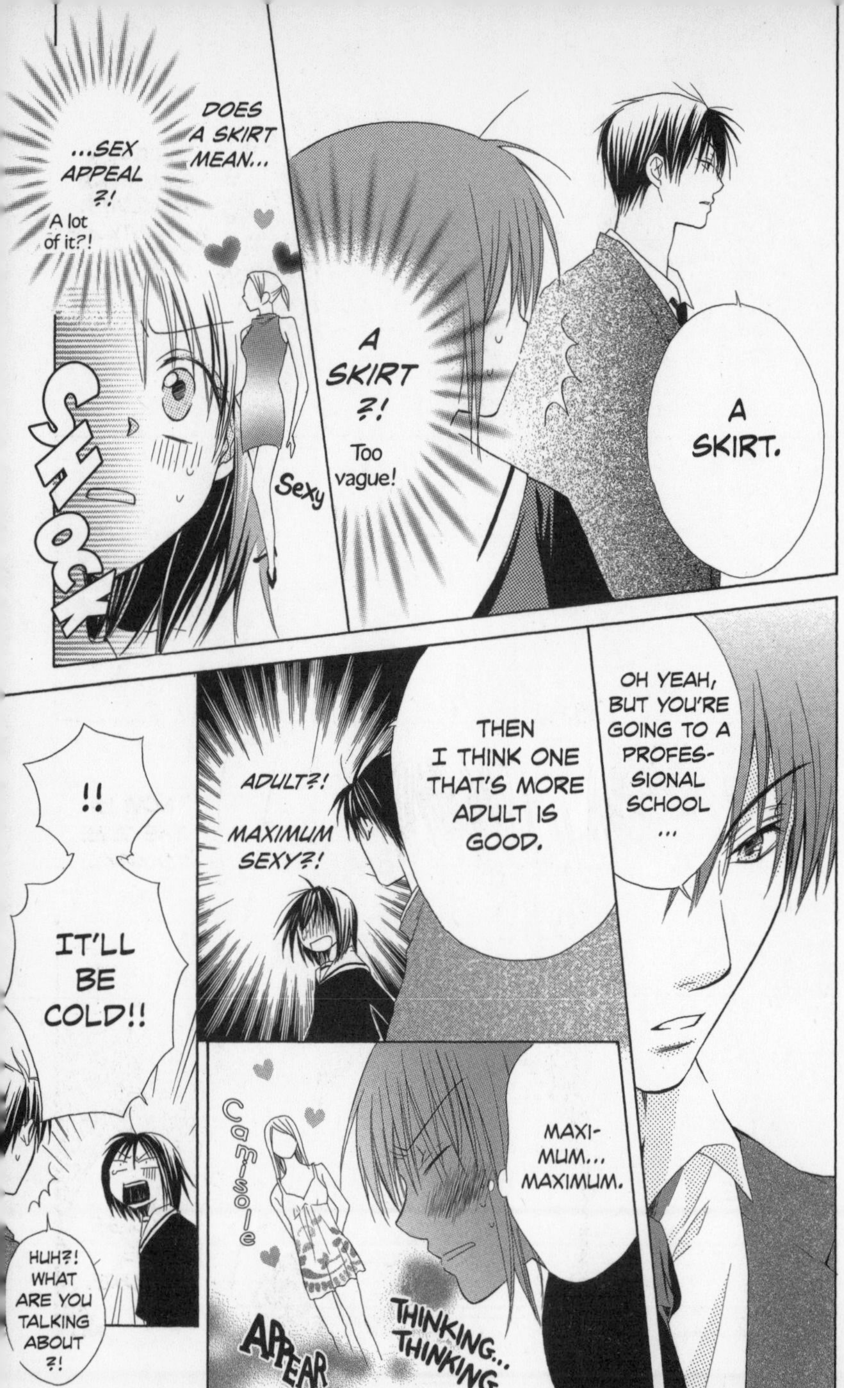
A SKIRT.
A SKIRT ?!
Too vague!
Sexy
SHOCK
DOES A SKIRT MEAN...
...SEX APPEAL ?!
A lot of it?!
OH YEAH, BUT YOU'RE GOING TO A PROFES-SIONAL SCHOOL ...
THEN I THINK ONE THAT'S MORE ADULT IS GOOD.
ADULT?!
MAXIMUM SEXY?!
MAXI-MUM... MAXIMUM.
Camisole
THINKING... THINKING...
APPEAR
!!
IT'LL BE COLD!!
HUH?! WHAT ARE YOU TALKING ABOUT ?!

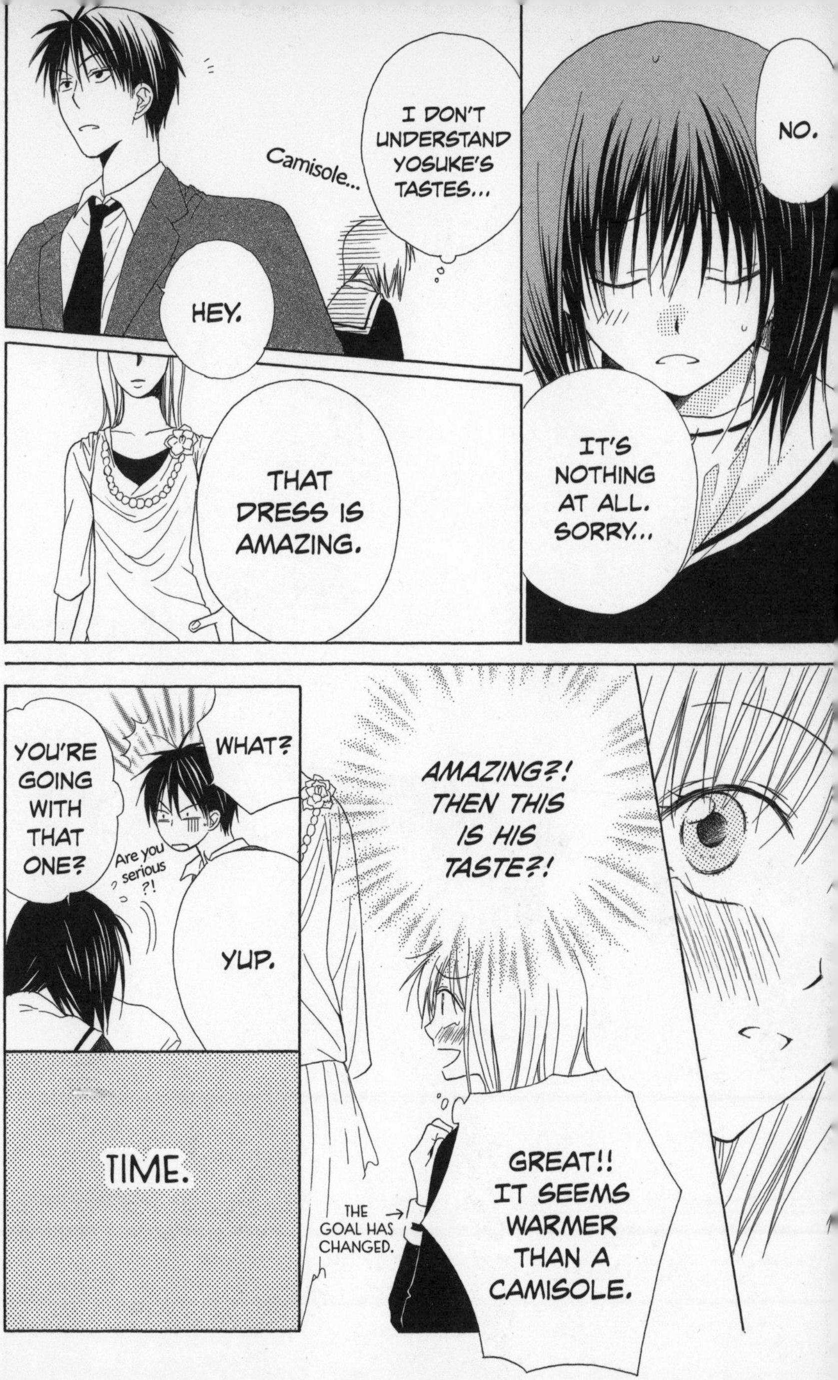
NO.
IT'S NOTHING AT ALL. SORRY...
I DON'T UNDERSTAND YOSUKE'S TASTES...
Camisole...
HEY.
THAT DRESS IS AMAZING.
AMAZING?! THEN THIS IS HIS TASTE?!
GREAT!! IT SEEMS WARMER THAN A CAMISOLE.
THE GOAL HAS CHANGED.
WHAT?
YOU'RE GOING WITH THAT ONE?
Are you serious ?!
YUP.
TIME.

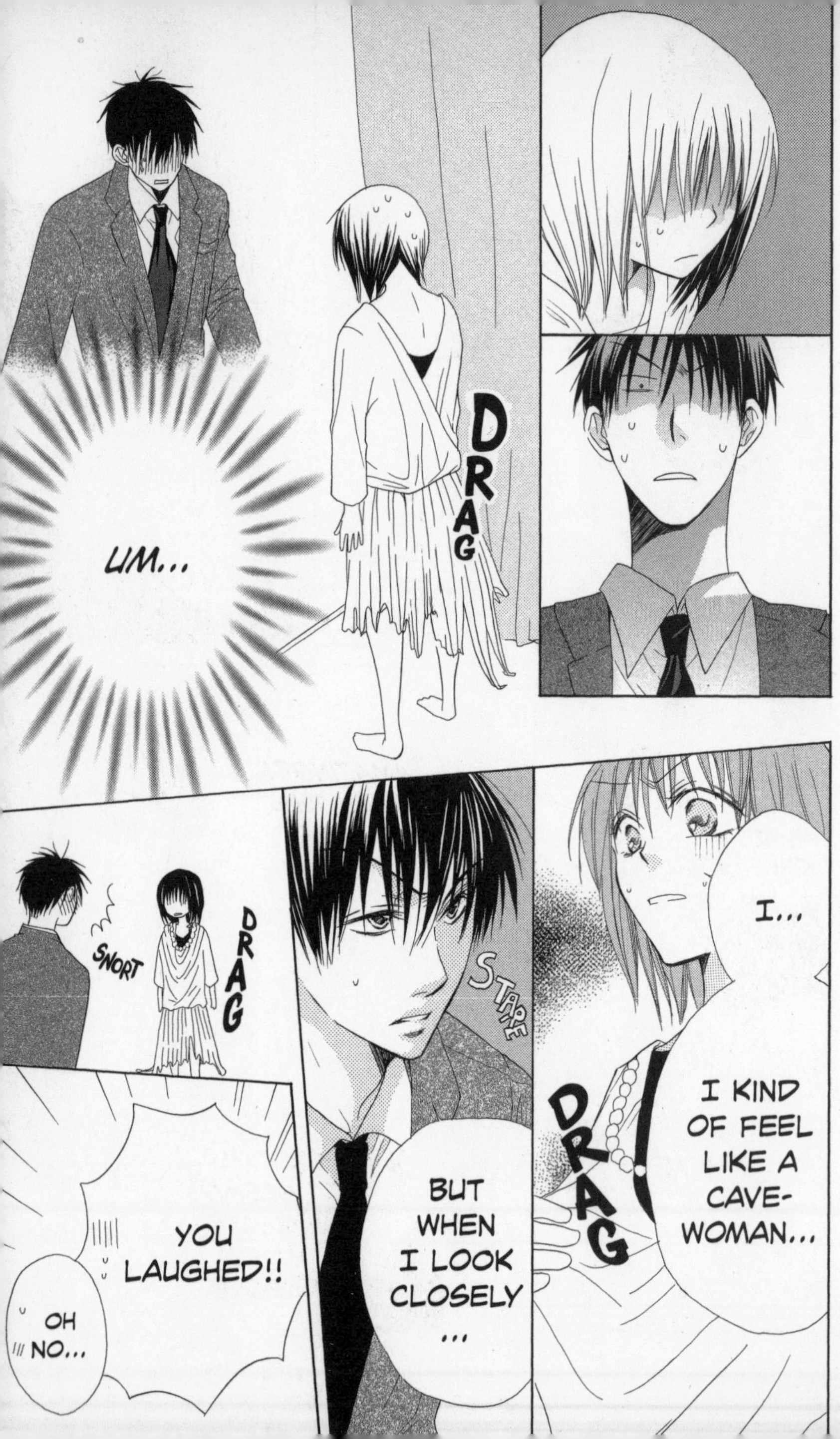
DRAG
UM...
I...
I KIND OF FEEL LIKE A CAVE-WOMAN...
DRAG
STARE
BUT WHEN I LOOK CLOSELY...
SNORT
DRAG
YOU LAUGHED!!
OH NO...

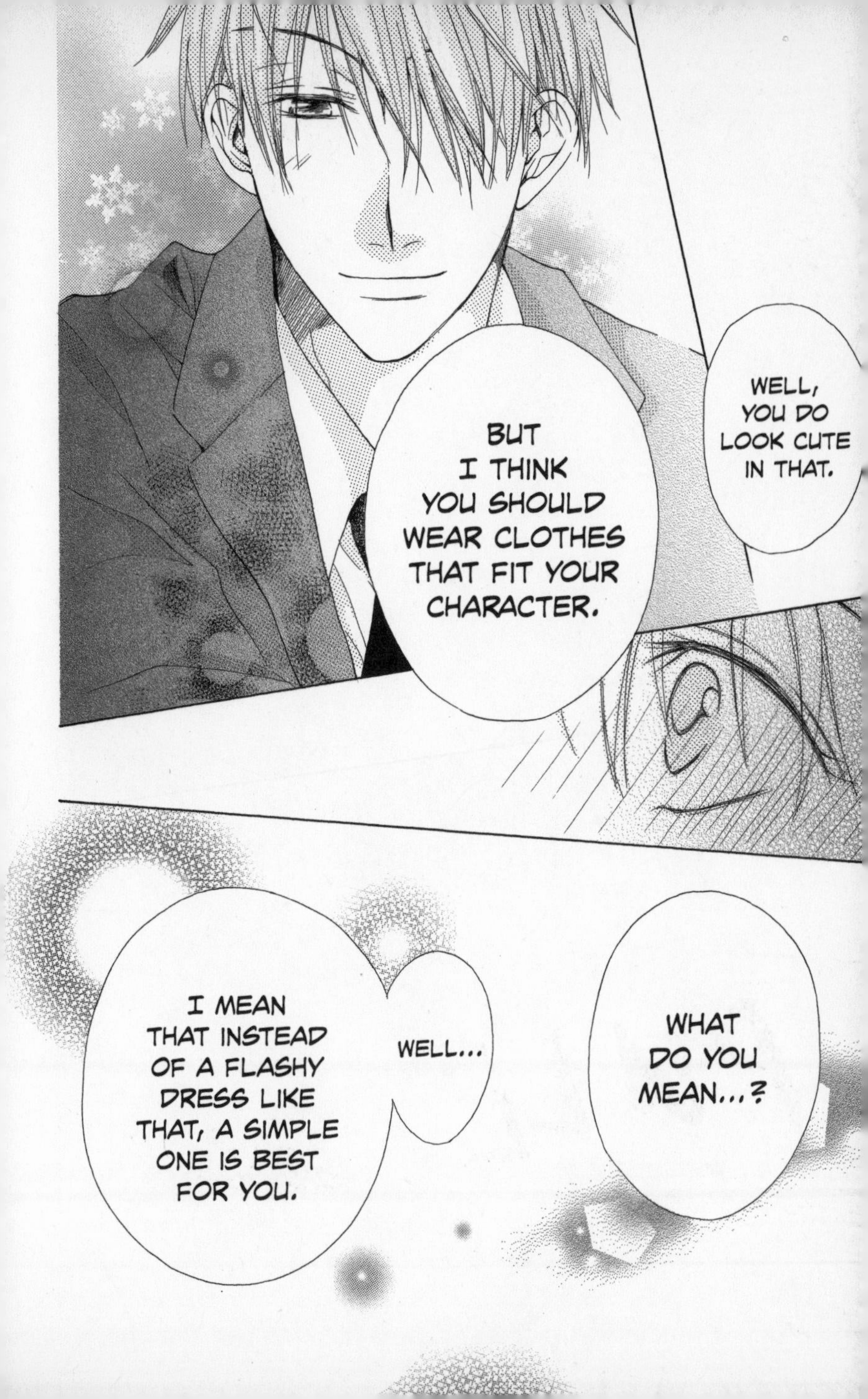
WELL, YOU DO LOOK CUTE IN THAT.
BUT I THINK YOU SHOULD WEAR CLOTHES THAT FIT YOUR CHARACTER.
WHAT DO YOU MEAN...?
WELL...
I MEAN THAT INSTEAD OF A FLASHY DRESS LIKE THAT, A SIMPLE ONE IS BEST FOR YOU.

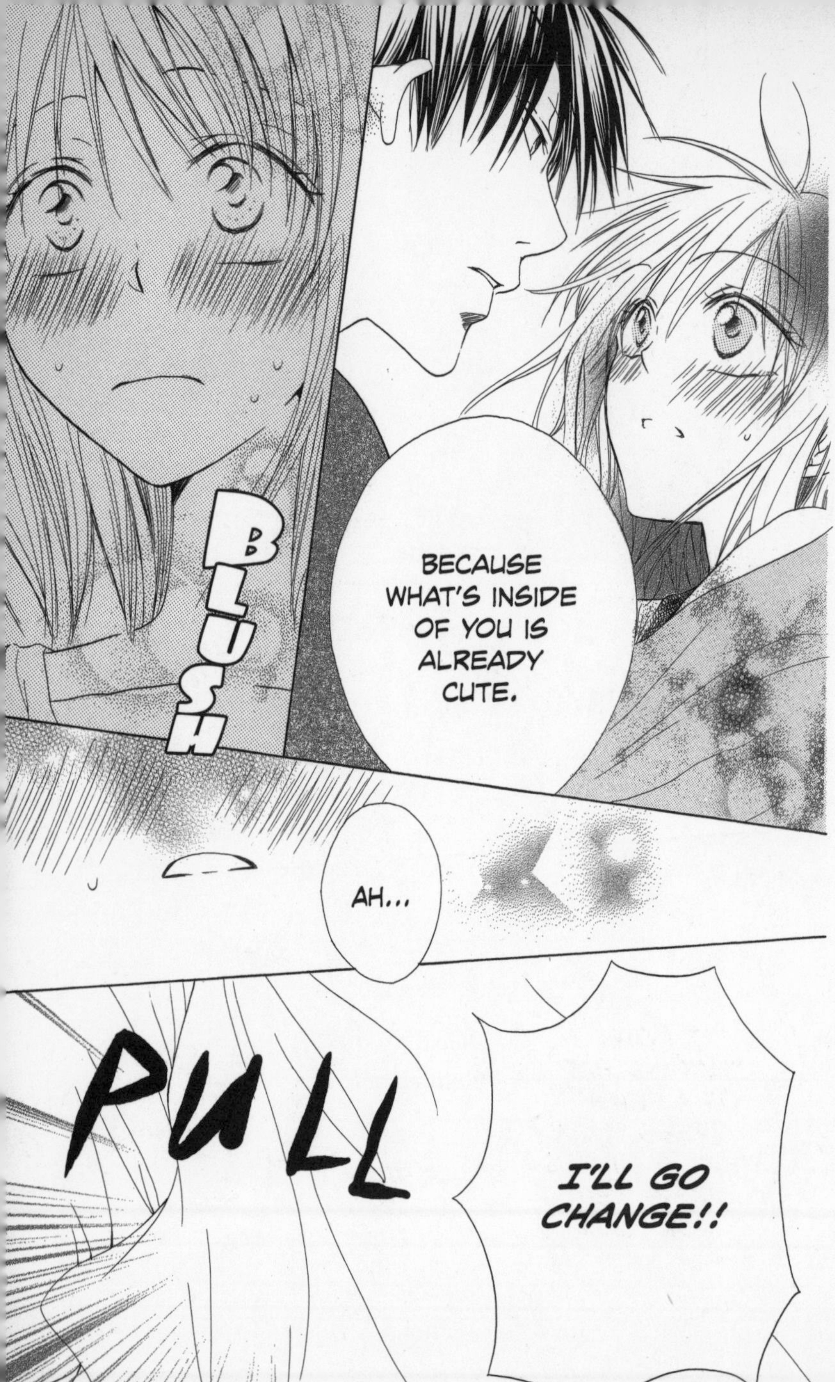
BECAUSE WHAT'S INSIDE OF YOU IS ALREADY CUTE.
BLUSH
AH...
I'LL GO CHANGE!!
PULL

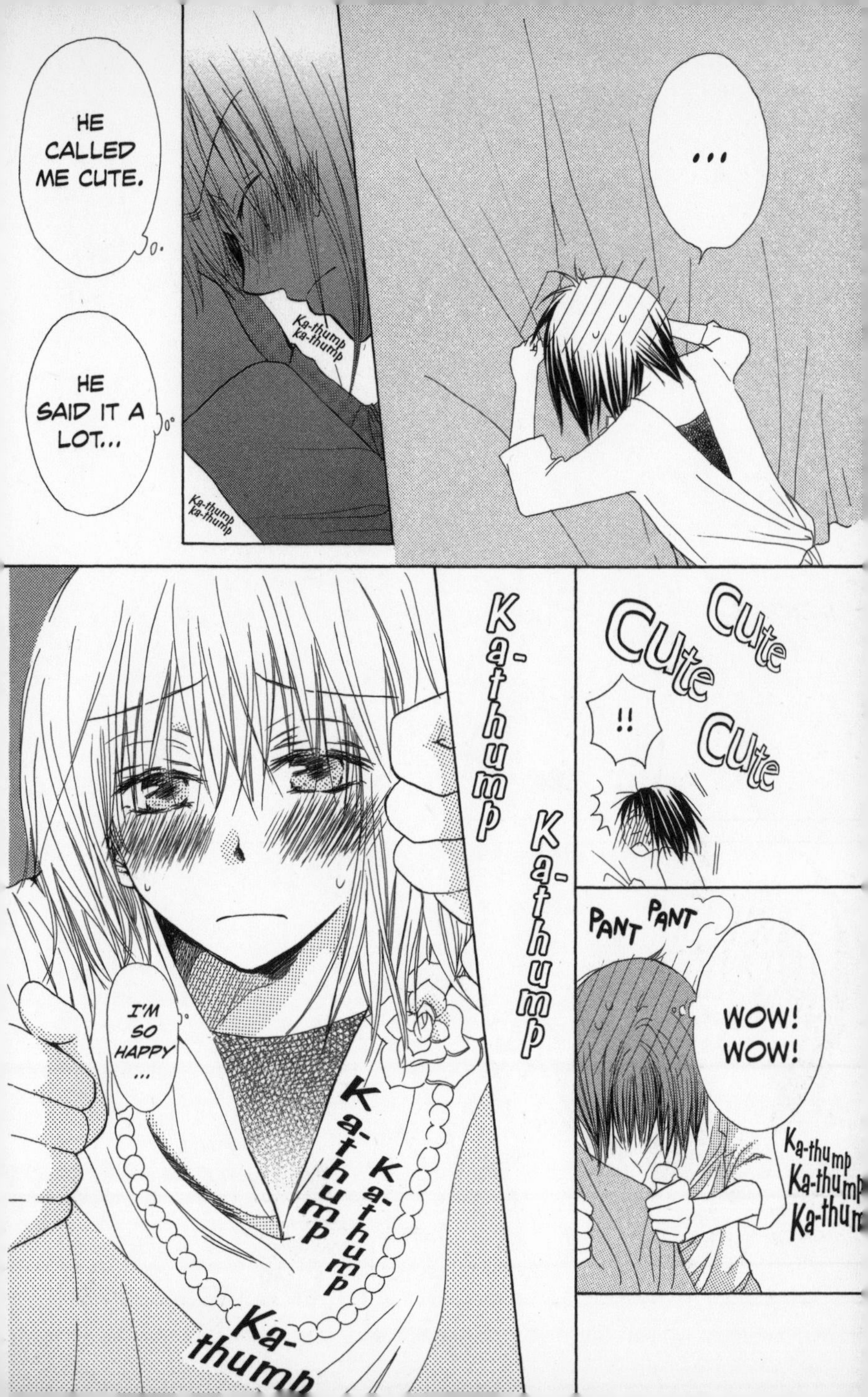
...
Ka-thump ka-thump
Ka-thump ka-thump
HE CALLED ME CUTE.
HE SAID IT A LOT...
Cute Cute Cute
!!
PANT PANT
WOW! WOW!
Ka-thump Ka-thump Ka-thum
Ka-thump Ka-thump
I'M SO HAPPY...
Ka-thump Ka-thump Ka-thump

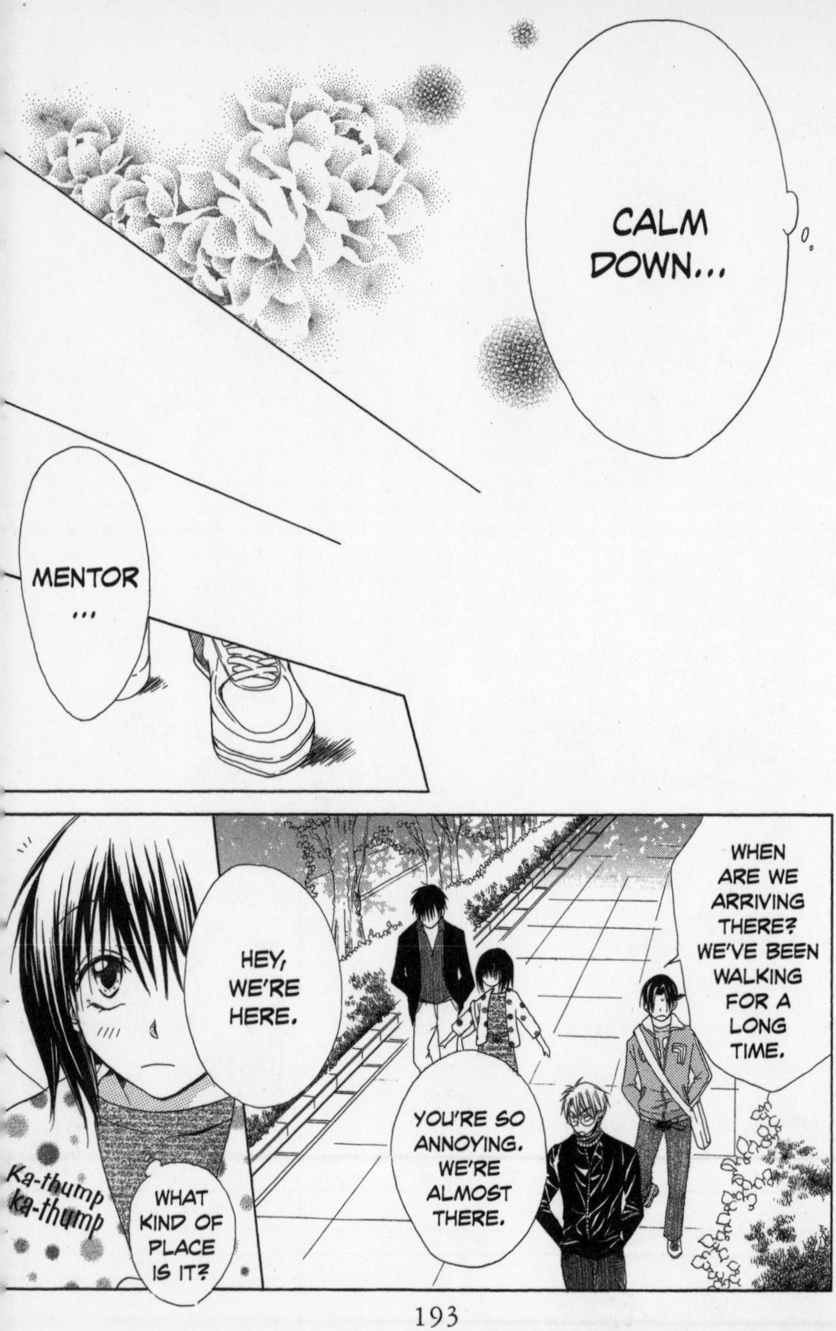
CALM DOWN...
MENTOR...
WHEN ARE WE ARRIVING THERE? WE'VE BEEN WALKING FOR A LONG TIME.
YOU'RE SO ANNOYING. WE'RE ALMOST THERE.
HEY, WE'RE HERE.
WHAT KIND OF PLACE IS IT?
Ka-thump ka-thump

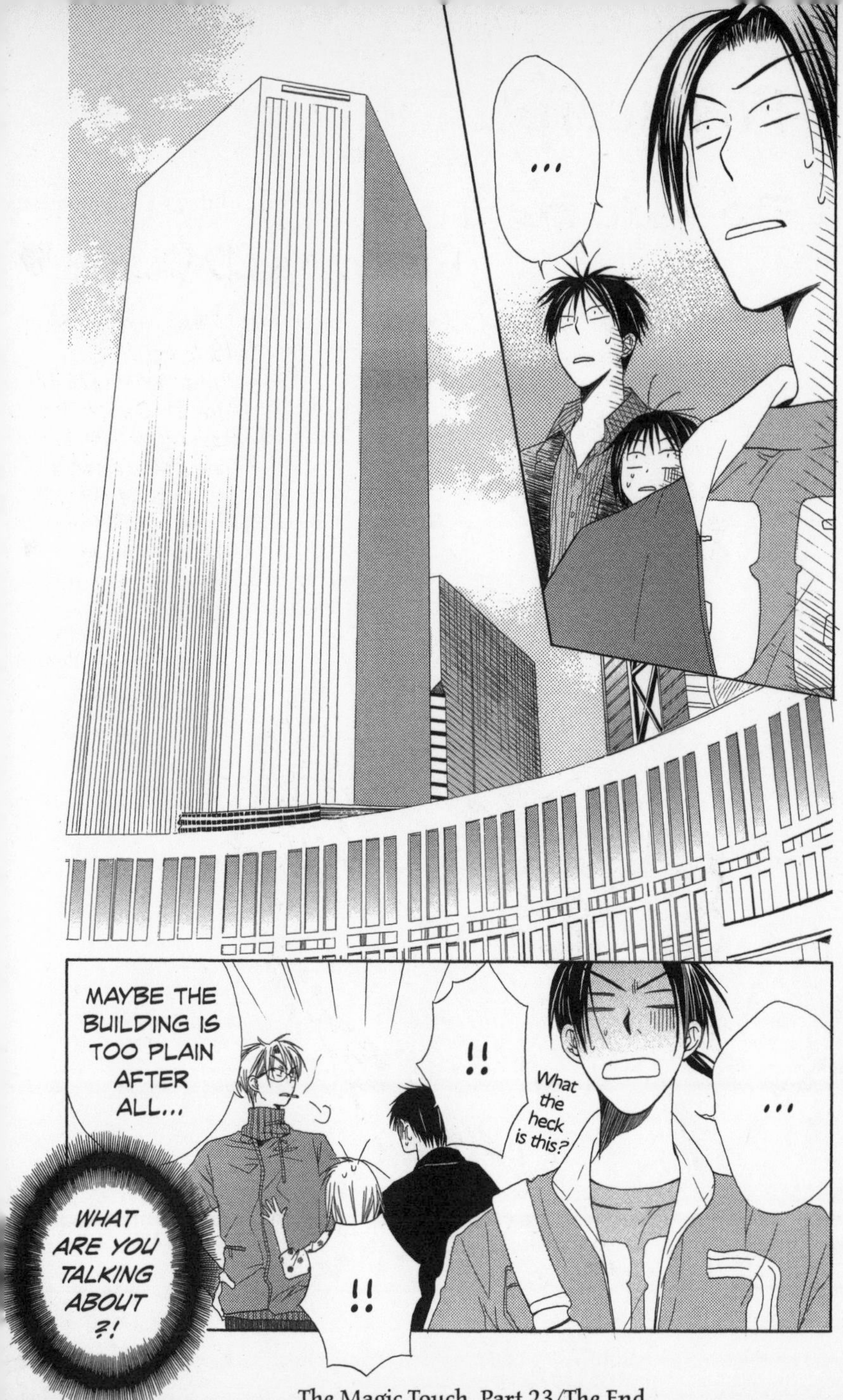
...
...
What the heck is this?
!!
MAYBE THE BUILDING IS TOO PLAIN AFTER ALL...
!!
WHAT ARE YOU TALKING ABOUT ?!

The Magic Touch, Part 23/The End

Postscript

The Magic Touch Has Become a CD Drama! ♥

Price: ¥2,800 (before tax)

★People in the Super Glamorous Cast★

Chiaki Togu: Kanako Tateno
Yosuke Moriizumi: Kenichi Suzumura
Takeshi Togu: Masaya Onosaka
Yuna Aizawa: Rumi Kasahara
Chitose Harumi: Jyunichi Suwabe
Natsue Abe: Masumi Asano

The series' Part 1, "Chiaki and Yosuke Meet" (Comic Book Volume 1) and Part 8, "Yosuke's Massage Prohibition" (Comic Book Volume 2) have become a CD drama. In addition, there are two bonus drama stories! One is about a major uproar over a legendary Secret Tsubo Manuscript, and the other is a Massage Club Tsubo Pressing Lesson.♥ Takeshi and Yuna are fun. I particularly recommend the bonuses.

Thank you for reading this book! It would be great if we could meet again in the next volume! ♡ See you then!

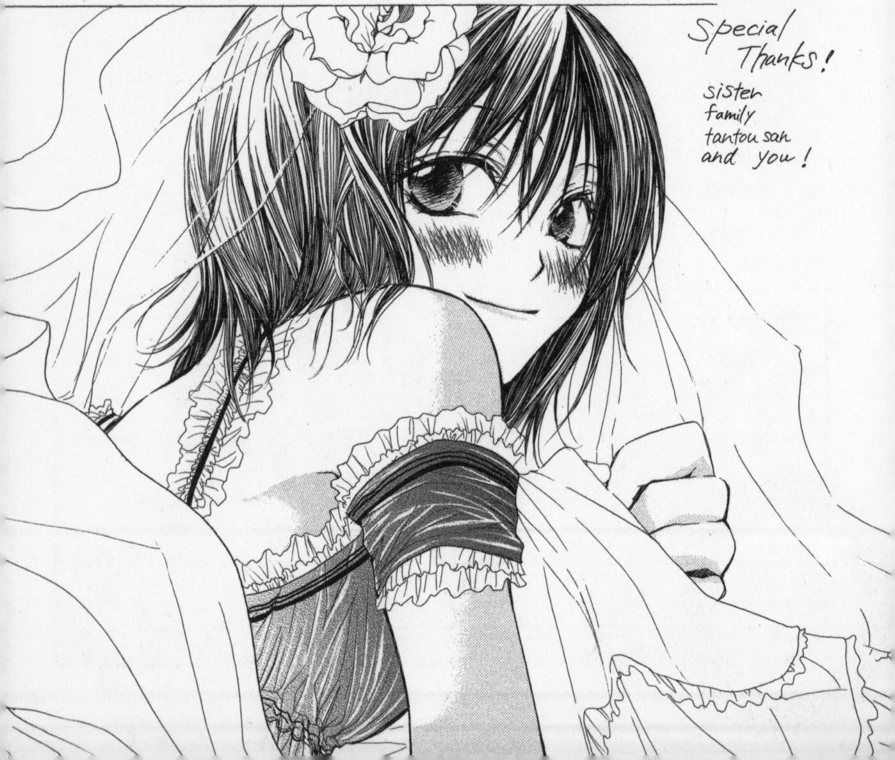
Special Thanks!
sister
family
tantou san
and you!

The Magic Touch
Oyayubi kara Romance

REPORT ON DUBBING THE FIRST ♡ DRAMA CD

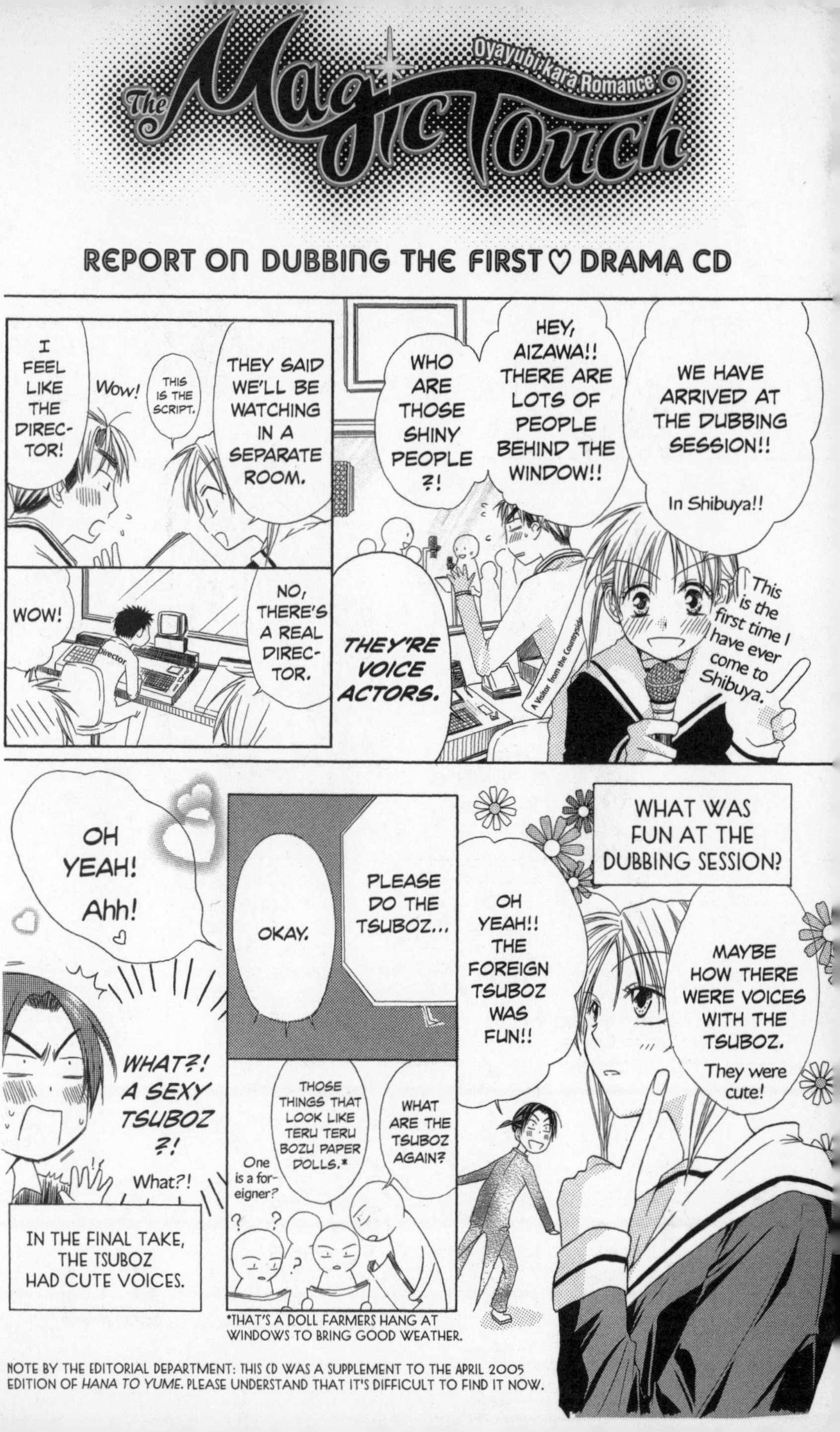
WE HAVE ARRIVED AT THE DUBBING SESSION!!
In Shibuya!!
This is the first time I have ever come to Shibuya.
A Visitor from the Countryside
HEY, AIZAWA!! THERE ARE LOTS OF PEOPLE BEHIND THE WINDOW!!
WHO ARE THOSE SHINY PEOPLE?!
THEY'RE VOICE ACTORS.
THEY SAID WE'LL BE WATCHING IN A SEPARATE ROOM.
THIS IS THE SCRIPT.
Wow!
I FEEL LIKE THE DIRECTOR!
NO, THERE'S A REAL DIRECTOR.
WOW!
Director
WHAT WAS FUN AT THE DUBBING SESSION?
MAYBE HOW THERE WERE VOICES WITH THE TSUBOZ.
They were cute!
OH YEAH!! THE FOREIGN TSUBOZ WAS FUN!!
PLEASE DO THE TSUBOZ...
OKAY.
WHAT ARE THE TSUBOZ AGAIN?
THOSE THINGS THAT LOOK LIKE TERU TERU BOZU PAPER DOLLS.*
One is a foreigner?
OH YEAH!
Ahh!
WHAT?! A SEXY TSUBOZ?!
What?!
IN THE FINAL TAKE, THE TSUBOZ HAD CUTE VOICES.

*THAT'S A DOLL FARMERS HANG AT WINDOWS TO BRING GOOD WEATHER.

NOTE BY THE EDITORIAL DEPARTMENT: THIS CD WAS A SUPPLEMENT TO THE APRIL 2005 EDITION OF *HANA TO YUME*. PLEASE UNDERSTAND THAT IT'S DIFFICULT TO FIND IT NOW.

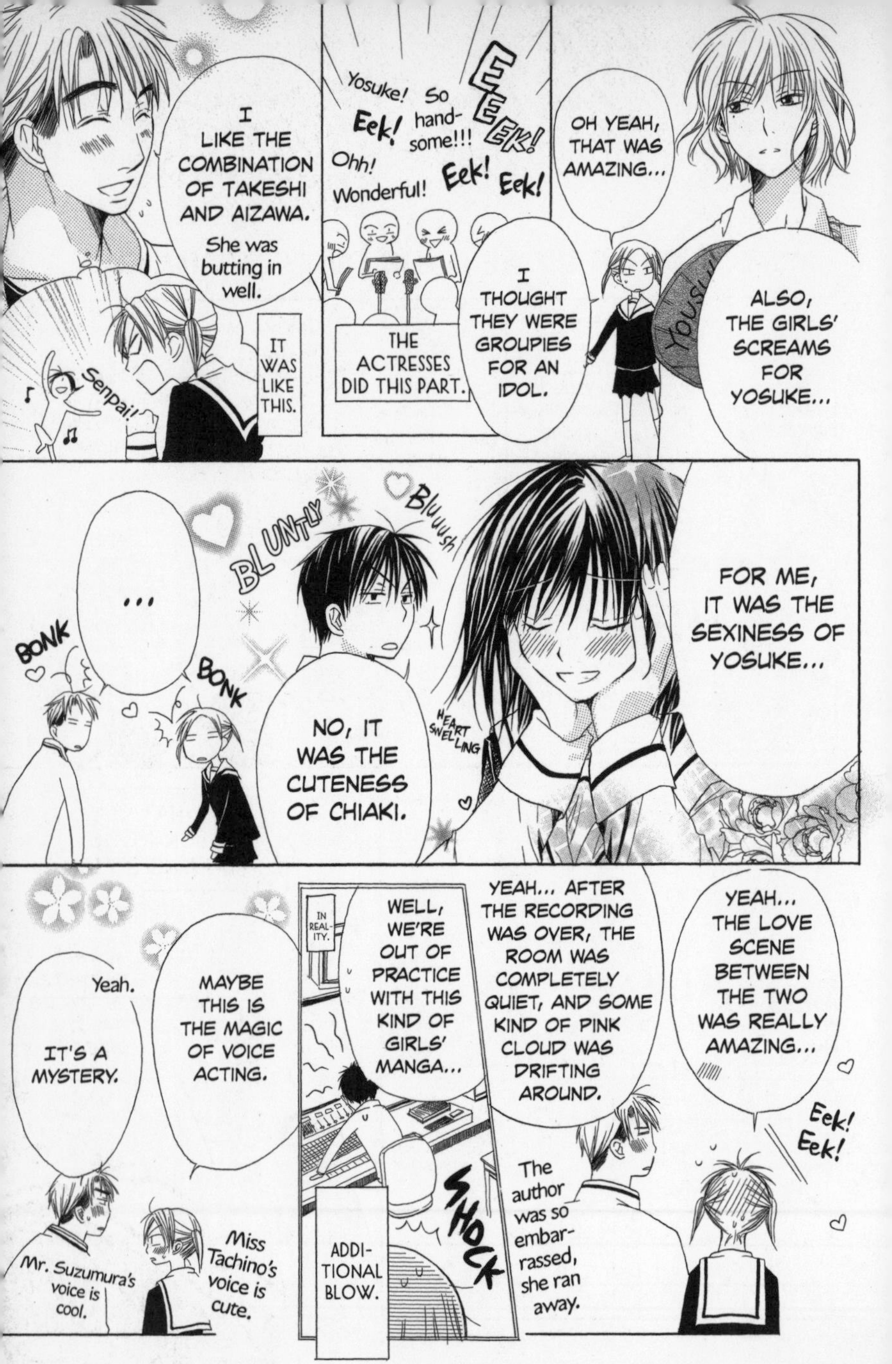
OH YEAH, THAT WAS AMAZING...
ALSO, THE GIRLS' SCREAMS FOR YOSUKE...
Yosuke! So handsome!!!
EEEEK!
Eek!
Ohh! Wonderful!
Eek!
Eek!
I THOUGHT THEY WERE GROUPIES FOR AN IDOL.
THE ACTRESSES DID THIS PART.
I LIKE THE COMBINATION OF TAKESHI AND AIZAWA.
She was butting in well.
IT WAS LIKE THIS.
Senpai!
FOR ME, IT WAS THE SEXINESS OF YOSUKE...
HEART SWELLING
Bluuush
BLUNTLY
NO, IT WAS THE CUTENESS OF CHIAKI.
...
BONK
BONK
YEAH... THE LOVE SCENE BETWEEN THE TWO WAS REALLY AMAZING...
Eek! Eek!
YEAH... AFTER THE RECORDING WAS OVER, THE ROOM WAS COMPLETELY QUIET, AND SOME KIND OF PINK CLOUD WAS DRIFTING AROUND.
The author was so embarrassed, she ran away.
IN REALITY.
WELL, WE'RE OUT OF PRACTICE WITH THIS KIND OF GIRLS' MANGA...
SHOCK
ADDITIONAL BLOW.
MAYBE THIS IS THE MAGIC OF VOICE ACTING.
Miss Tachino's voice is cute.
Yeah.
IT'S A MYSTERY.
Mr. Suzumura's voice is cool.

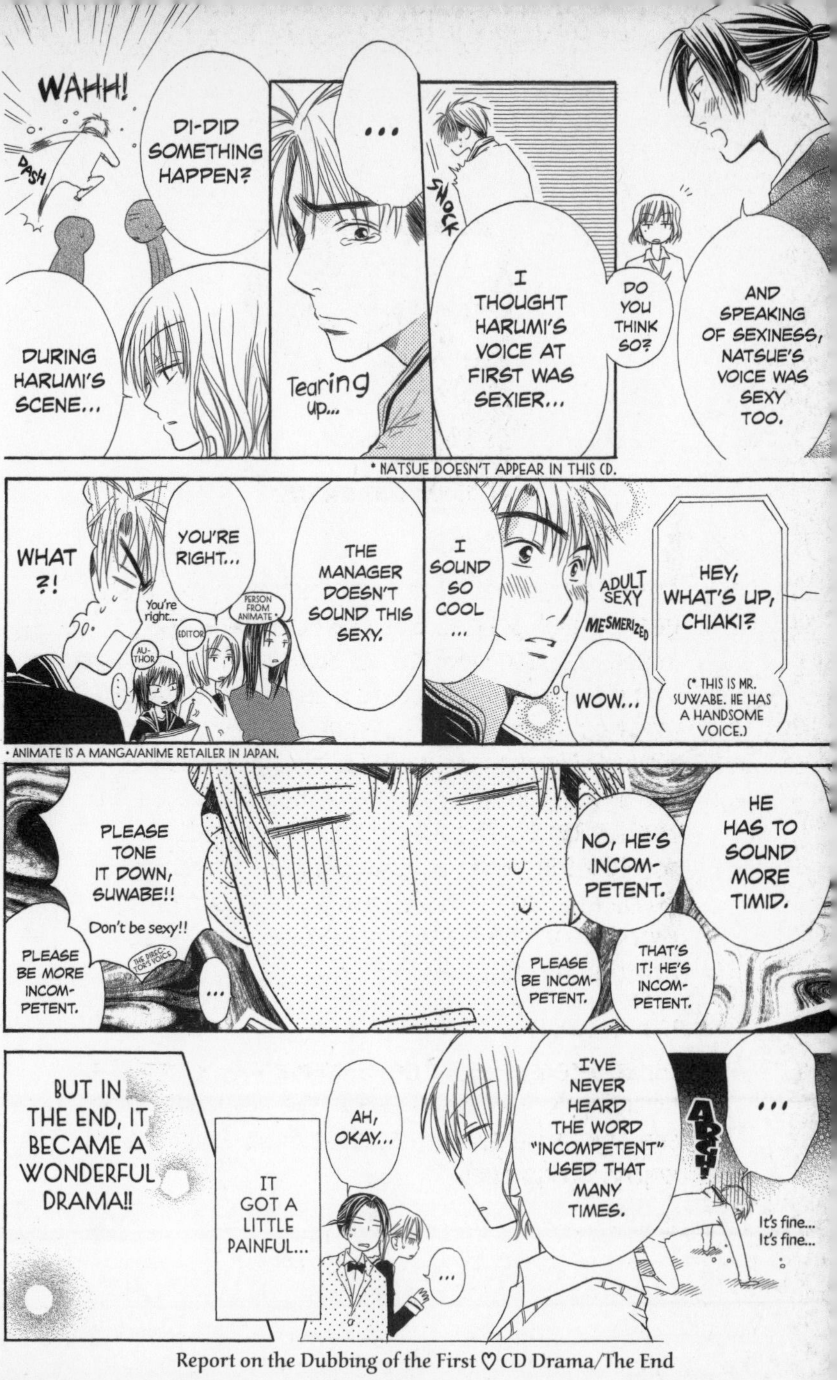
AND SPEAKING OF SEXINESS, NATSUE'S VOICE WAS SEXY TOO.
DO YOU THINK SO?
I THOUGHT HARUMI'S VOICE AT FIRST WAS SEXIER...
SHOCK
...
Tearing up...
DI-DID SOMETHING HAPPEN?
WAHH!
DASH
DURING HARUMI'S SCENE...
* NATSUE DOESN'T APPEAR IN THIS CD.
HEY, WHAT'S UP, CHIAKI?
(* THIS IS MR. SUWABE. HE HAS A HANDSOME VOICE.)
ADULT SEXY
MESMERIZED
I SOUND SO COOL ...
WOW...
THE MANAGER DOESN'T SOUND THIS SEXY.
PERSON FROM ANIMATE
YOU'RE RIGHT...
You're right...
EDITOR
WHAT?!
AUTHOR
...
• ANIMATE IS A MANGA/ANIME RETAILER IN JAPAN.
HE HAS TO SOUND MORE TIMID.
NO, HE'S INCOMPETENT.
THAT'S IT! HE'S INCOMPETENT.
PLEASE BE INCOMPETENT.
...
PLEASE TONE IT DOWN, SUWABE!!
Don't be sexy!!
THE DIRECTOR'S VOICE
PLEASE BE MORE INCOMPETENT.
...
ARGH!
It's fine... It's fine...
I'VE NEVER HEARD THE WORD "INCOMPETENT" USED THAT MANY TIMES.
AH, OKAY...
...
IT GOT A LITTLE PAINFUL...
BUT IN THE END, IT BECAME A WONDERFUL DRAMA!!

Report on the Dubbing of the First ♡ CD Drama/The End

Izumi Tsubaki began drawing manga in her first year of high school. She was soon selected to be in the top ten of *Hana to Yume*'s HMC (Hana to Yume Mangaka Course) and subsequently won *Hana to Yume*'s Big Challenge contest. Her debut title, *Chijimete Distance* (Shrink the Distance), ran in 2002 in *Hana to Yume* magazine, issue 17. In addition to *The Magic Touch* (originally published in Japan as *Oyayubi kara Romance*, or "Romance from the Thumbs"), she is currently working on the manga series *Oresama Teacher* (I'm the Teacher).

Tsubaki-sensei hails from Saitama Prefecture, her birthday is December 11, and she confesses that she enjoys receiving massages more than she enjoys giving them.

THE MAGIC TOUCH
Vol. 4
The Shojo Beat Manga Edition

STORY AND ART BY
IZUMI TSUBAKI

English Adaptation/Lorelei Laird
Translation/Nori Minami
Touch-up Art & Lettering/Ben Costa
Design/Sean Lee
Editor/Eric Searleman

VP, Production/Alvin Lu
VP, Publishing Licensing/Rika Inouye
VP, Sales & Product Marketing/Gonzalo Ferreyra
VP, Creative/Linda Espinosa
Publisher/Hyoe Narita

Published by VIZ Media, LLC
P.O. Box 77010
San Francisco, CA 94107

Shojo Beat Manga Edition
10 9 8 7 6 5 4 3 2 1
First printing, October 2009

www.viz.com

store.viz.com